The Austin Chronicle
MUSIC ANTHOLOGY

NUMBER TWENTY-EIGHT
Jack and Doris Smothers Series in Texas History, Life, and Culture

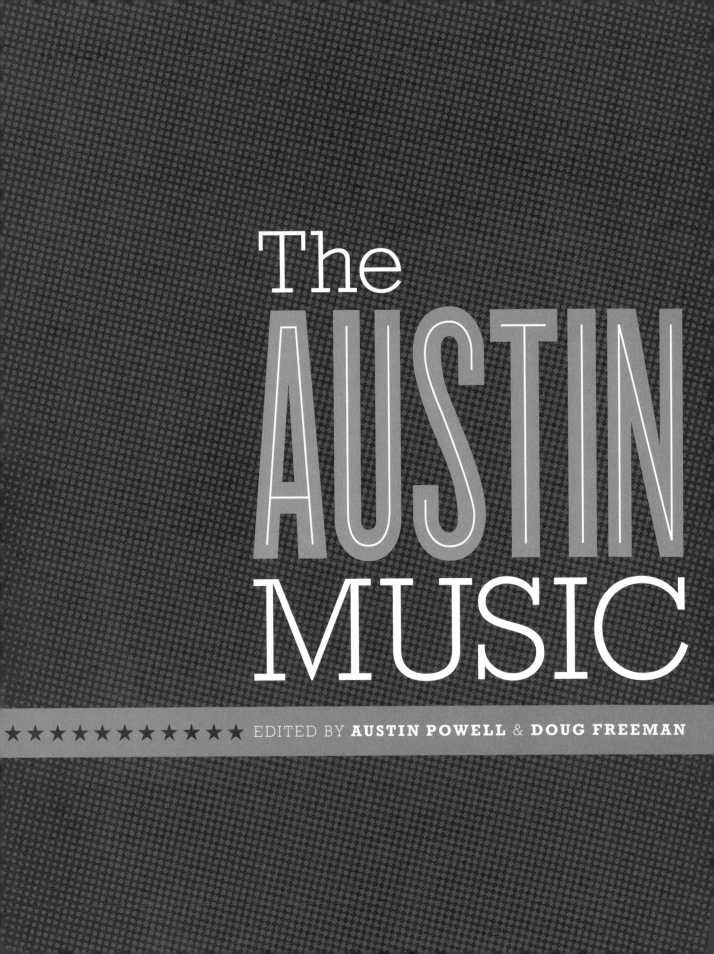

The
AUSTIN
MUSIC

★★★★★★★★★★★★★ EDITED BY **AUSTIN POWELL** & **DOUG FREEMAN**

CHRONICLE
Anthology

FOREWORD BY DANIEL JOHNSTON
INTRODUCTION BY LOUIS BLACK

UNIVERSITY OF TEXAS PRESS ⋎ AUSTIN

Requests for permission to reproduce material
from this work should be sent to:
Permissions
University of Texas Press
P.O. Box 7819
Austin, TX 78713-7819
www.utexas.edu/utpress/about/bpermission.html

The paper used in this book meets the minimum
requirements of ANSI/NISO Z39.48-1992 (R1997)
(Permanence of Paper). ∞

Designed by Lindsay Starr

Library of Congress Cataloging-in-Publication Data

The Austin chronicle music anthology / edited by Austin
Powell and Doug Freeman ; with foreword by Daniel
Johnston and introduction by Louis Black. — 1st ed.
        p.   cm. — (Jack and Doris Smothers series in
Texas history, life, and culture ; no. 28)
    Includes index.
    ISBN 978-0-292-72270-5 (cl. : alk. paper) —
    ISBN 978-0-292-72318-4 (pbk. : alk. paper)
    1. Popular music—Texas—Austin—History and criti-
cism. 2. Musicians—Texas—Austin. I. Powell, Austin,
1975– II. Freeman, Doug, 1978– III. Austin chronicle.
    ML3477.8.A97A97 20100
    781.6409764'31—dc22   2010018574

CONTENTS

THE 1990S

FOREWORD

ACKNOWLEDGMENTS

DOUG FREEMAN AND AUSTIN POWELL

NO SINGLE VOLUME could hope to encapsulate the rich history and vibrant virtuosity of Austin's music scene. Nor can *The Austin Chronicle*'s coverage ever be fully distilled and yet encompass the array of contributors who have passionately documented local music over the past thirty years. While this anthology holds pretensions toward neither, we hope that it may serve as testament to both. Some histories can only be told in the moment: the experiential bloom of the caterwauling riff, the youthful vigor of the band before the break, the weathered drawl of the songwriter scratching at scars. *The Austin Chronicle* is dedicated to capturing those moments, and this collection presents some of the paper's most indelible music writing and photography, attempting to preserve in part the evolving aesthetic of the whole.

In editing this anthology, we could not include numerous articles and artworks for the sake of concision. Likewise, there are local artists worthy of mention who are not found within these pages. As much as possible, we have sought to remain true to the works as originally published, though we have edited everything to some degree and often paired the best photographs of an artist with earlier or later pieces of writing. Some sidebars have been inserted anachronistically as well, coupled thematically with an article rather than appearing chronologically.

This project could not have been realized without the invaluable support and advice of Raoul Hernandez, Louis Black, Nick Barbaro, Margaret Moser, Chris Gray, Audra Schroeder, and countless others. Similarly, Allison Faust, Lindsay Starr, and the University of Texas Press have provided patient and tireless expertise. Many writers and photographers have graciously offered their time, knowledge, and work, especially John Anderson, Todd Wolfson, and John Carrico. This book could not exist without all of them. This anthology is equally dependent upon the entire staff of the paper: the copy editors, production department, office personnel, editorial staff, and sales and classifieds representatives who have made *The Austin Chronicle* a local institution. We are most indebted, however, to the musicians who have enriched this city and our lives beyond measure and to the fans who continue every night to make Austin the Live Music Capital of the World. ◄

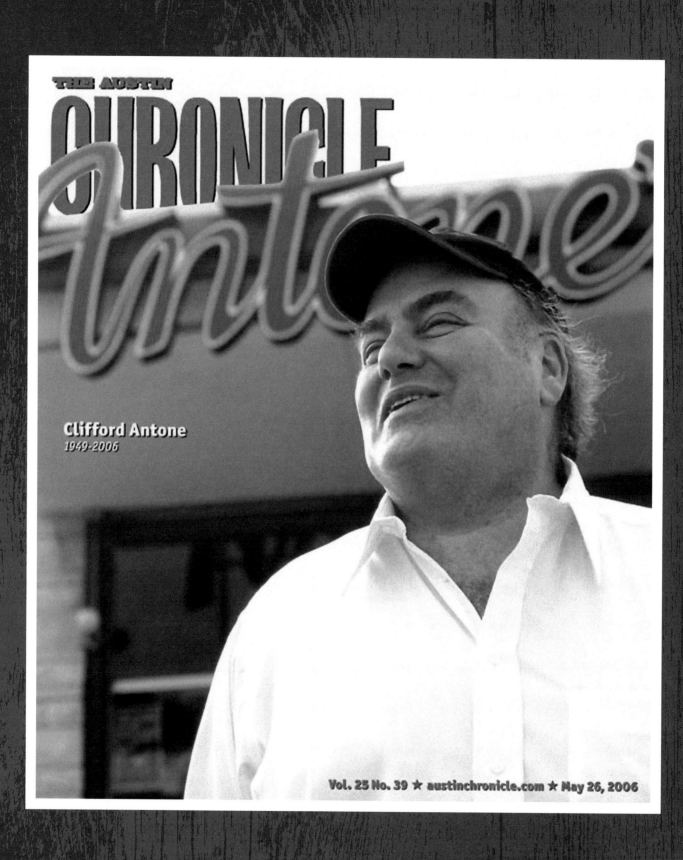

THE AUSTIN
CHRONICLE

Clifford Antone
1949-2006

Vol. 25 No. 39 ★ austinchronicle.com ★ May 26, 2006

INTRODUCTION

LOUIS BLACK
September 2009

AUSTIN, TEXAS, JUNE 19, 2009: Two stories, one concert. Steve Earle is playing the Paramount Theatre solo and acoustic in support of his album of Townes Van Zandt covers, *Townes*. Earle plays a lot of Van Zandt songs and a lot of his own. Earle alone on stage isn't really alone; he's electric, intense, his sound filling the theater. Afterwards I tell him how one of the last times I hung out with Clifford Antone at his club before he died, some band was just cooking on stage. Clifford nudged me, saying "Look up there . . . ," and pointed to the rafters behind and over the stage.

"There's Doug up there just watching the show and grooving."

Townes and Doug Sahm didn't exactly groove in the same ways, but looking up high at the ceiling of the Paramount that night I knew that sure as anything Townes was up there listening. He's digging the music, though if he had talked to Earle afterwards he would have made a few sly jokes at Earle's expense, ribbing him just a bit rather than complimenting him because that was Townes' way.

Backstage, Earle tells a wonderful story about when he was on Letterman recently, performing Townes' "Colorado Girl." The host came up to him afterwards, as he always does, and as the credits rolled, leaned in asking, "Why didn't you do 'Snowing on Raton'?"

Music saturates the city of Austin, always has and likely always will. It's in the air, in the intense unending heat of the summer, in the brief cold of a short winter, and in the constant, sixty-eight-degree waters of Barton Springs. It may be just a slight breeze ruffling the leaves on the trees in the evening or the steam rising from the dry earth in the late afternoon of a too-brutal summer day. It's not that it's so very loud, but that in Austin, Texas, it's always and everywhere.

Cities have often been defined in finite ways. Pittsburgh was a steel town, Chicago the world's hog butcher, and Fort Worth once was the cattle processing capital of Texas. Austin is a city where the common daily background sounds are not just those of jackhammers and railroad cars, where the lifestyle and currency are not just about jobs, families, homes, and money. Awake the city is of music and asleep is dreaming of music.

Music is everywhere and of everyone, coming out of houses, schools, municipal buildings, cars, street corners, clubs, and parks. It's being made by so many people playing every kind of instrument as they perform all different kinds of music—a city of musicians busy practicing, learning, teaching, perfecting, recording, and performing.

Turn, turn, turn to the music everywhere, music being made in the present—but also in the future imagined and a past so honored and relevant it's not really past. The history can go back to traditional

★ THE AUSTIN ★
CHRONICLE

THE AUSTIN CHRONICLE

87-88
MUSIC
AWARD
WINNERS

SXSW

REGIONAL MUS

SURVEY ■ p.

MUSIC FESTIV

SCHEDULE ■ p.

VIDEO SCHEDU
■ p. 58

African-American toasting or Jayne Mansfield performing during the 1950s. It can include the evolution of contemporary gospel by telling the story of the Mighty Clouds of Joy or detail the birth of psychedelic music when the 13th Floor Elevators traveled to San Francisco.

The full history has to touch on yodeling and jamming at Threadgill's and the music that was played—as well as often gestated and matured—at Soap Creek Saloon and the Armadillo World Headquarters. The history spans the down-home rawness of the Split Rail and the literal army of songwriters that sharpened their edges at Castle Creek to the never-ending spawn of Emo's and the other Red River clubs. The story of the great Doug Sahm has to be included, as well as the mythic moment when Willie Nelson moved to Austin after leaving Nashville.

Necessary to the telling of the whole story are so many other stories, in fact far too many other stories. These range from the Big Boys mini-riot and Stevie Ray and Jimmie Vaughan playing together at the Austin Music Awards through the continuing legends of Freda & the Firedogs and Paul Ray & the Cobras. There's the brilliant, brutal cultural counter punch of the Butthole Surfers and Scratch Acid and the contemporary international success of Explosions in the Sky, White Denim, Okkervil River, and Spoon. Currently there is a dazzling number of gifted female singer-songwriters including Shawn Colvin, Eliza Gilkyson, Patty Griffin, and Carrie Rodriguez. Yet, they shine even more in the context of blues legends such as Angela Strehli, Marcia Ball, Lou Ann Barton, Sarah Brown, and Sue Foley. There's almost no way to tell the story without mentioning the Huns, True Believers, Roky Erickson, Townes Van Zandt, the Flatlanders, and Daniel Johnston. This list barely scratches the surface, but in the direction of trying to come close to any comprehensive listing lies madness and near guaranteed institutional commitment.

VOL. 1 NO. 13 ★ MARCH 5, 1982

VOL. 11 NO. 11 ★ NOVEMBER 8, 1991

VOL. 12 NO. 14 ★ DECEMBER 4, 1992

VOL. 24 NO. 31 ★ APRIL 1, 2005

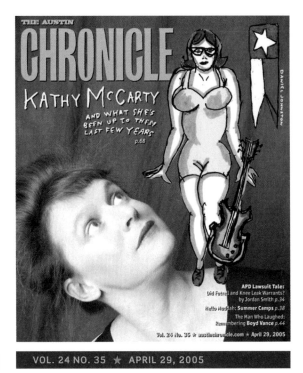

VOL. 24 NO. 35 ★ APRIL 29, 2005

An introduction to Austin music even limited to the past quarter-century and focused by *The Austin Chronicle*'s coverage is necessarily truncated. The Austin scene has never been about only one kind of music or style but rather the full past of music honored with cross-breeding and constant reinvention into innovative explorations that combine music and the slight tastes of remembered music.

Those who end up as music writers and critics usually begin to develop a more intense, co-dependent relationship with music early on in their listening lives. Not just the soundtrack to the lives they are living, music is an integral part of them, expanding possibilities by inflaming dreams and desires. Once the music takes root, it affects and alters life and lifestyle, inspiring imagination and ambition. Music justifies, validates, and helps celebrate. It is for dreamers who imagine that their lives and future can and will be so much richer than the one they are living.

In the spring and summer of 1981, a number of us began to gravitate around Nick Barbaro and Joe Dishner, who had begun talking seriously of starting an alternative paper in Austin. Certainly we were the children of Marx and Coca-Cola but also of politics, film, television, and, most purely and directly, rock & roll. Just as importantly we were the offspring of the *Village Voice*, the *Austin Sun*, the *East Village Other*, the *San Francisco Oracle*, and *Boston After Dark*, sired by *Crawdaddy!*, *Rolling Stone*, *Ramparts*, *I.F. Stone's Weekly*, and Paul Krassner's the *Realist*.

On September 4, 1981, the first issue of the *Austin Chronicle* was published. Produced by our mongrel clan, it was a true hybrid. The conceit of the *Chronicle* from early on was to focus on Austin music. Important national releases were frequently covered, but the emphasis was on the local scene. The *Chronicle* staff

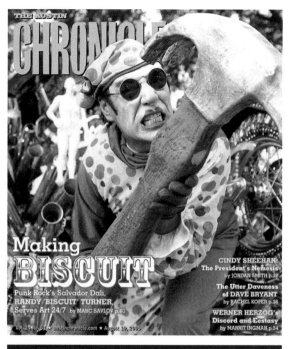

VOL. 24 NO. 51 ★ AUGUST 19, 2005

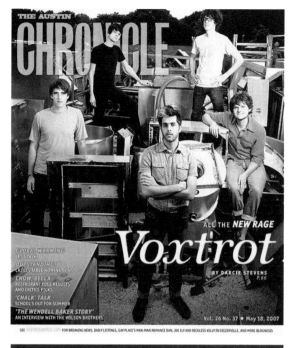

VOL. 26 NO. 37 ★ MAY 18, 2007

decided even before the first issue was published that the paper's primary focus would be on local music, though certainly not to the complete exclusion of covering national and regional acts.

The first breakout content hit at the paper was Margaret Moser's "In One Ear" column. Though it covered road shows coming to Austin and releases by major national acts, its bread, butter, and groupie reporting was mostly focused on what was happening locally. The first major marketing/public relations score by the *Chronicle* was the first *Chronicle* Music Poll results published in 1982. This was followed in 1983 by the Austin Music Awards, honoring the poll winners.

The *Chronicle* covered theater, dance, food, art, politics, film, and comics, among many other things, though from the very beginning what drove the then bi-weekly paper and what brought readers and media

attention to it was music. Moser's "In One Ear" column was followed by Michael Corcoran's "Don't You Start Me Talking," which became the bi-weekly must-read of the entire music community. The column was about music but also about Michael; the column was about Michael but also about music.

Around Thanksgiving 1986, *Austin Chronicle* publisher Nick Barbaro and I, at the urging of Roland Swenson and Louis Meyers, decided to start an annual regional music business meeting in Austin. Swenson had worked many different music business–related jobs but was then working for the *Chronicle;* club booker and band manager Meyers had offices in the same building as ours.

The first South by Southwest Music Conference and Festival took place March 1987. It was relatively successful from the start. In the decade and a half after that first event, similar events were tried in

VOL. 26 NO. 49 ★ AUGUST 10, 2007

VOL. 27 NO. 21 ★ JANUARY 25, 2008

VOL. 27 NO. 45 ★ JULY 11, 2008

literally hundreds of cities. None really worked. We were intimately aware of this as SXSW Inc. tried to launch a few other events of its own.

The secret ingredient that made it work, we discovered, was Austin—not only the culture of the city, as well as its respect and understanding of that culture, but the very music scene. No other city was as hospitable as Austin. Even more important, no other cities had as many well-known journeyman and/or cult, regional acts as Austin, acts with many loyal fans that were into them and followed their music but were not hordes in the millions.

All of it finally came together to create an alchemical transcendence, a multidimensional, completely unique world lacking in traditional restrictions, populated by great musicians, endless music enablers, passionate fans, all kinds of artists, and brilliant writers, passionate about music.

There have always been a lot of good music writers in Austin and not just at *The Austin Chronicle*. Other established publications' attention to music, however, ebbed and flowed. Other music publications came and went. Over its twenty-eight-year history (as of September 2009) the *Chronicle* has been dogged and steadfast in its devotion to all kinds of music coverage. Reviews of records, tapes, CDs, online music, and live shows are crucial to this coverage. These are coupled with show recommendations by both national and Austin acts and profiles of local talent. Included as well are thought pieces, overviews of the local music business, pieces following certain bands on tour, and detailed histories of bands, clubs, scenes, and musicians—those still thriving and the ones now gone. On an ongoing basis the writing has been accompanied by some of the best available music photos and art, outstanding photo features on musicians, dozens of memorable covers, and over twenty-five years of memorable AMA posters.

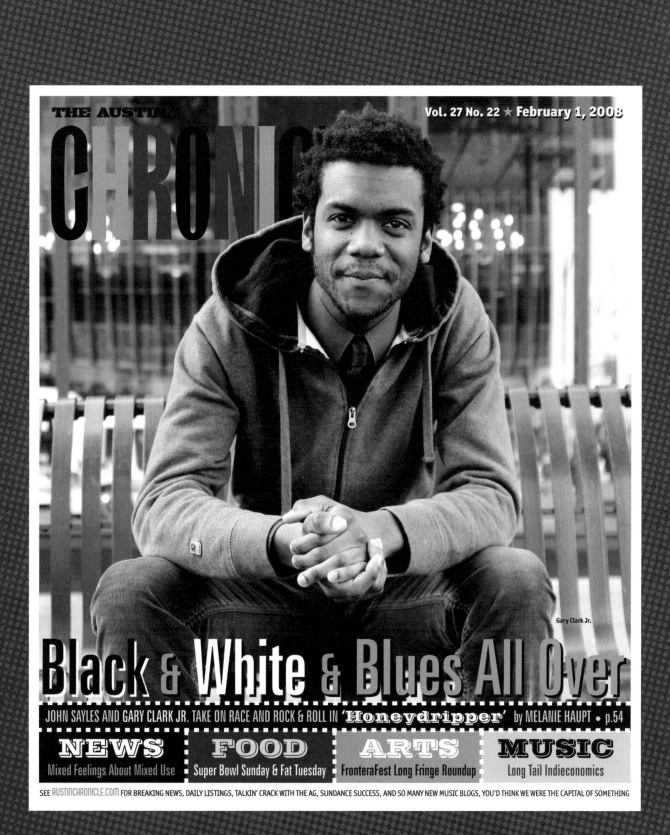

THE AUSTIN **CHRONICLE**

Vol. 27 No. 22 ★ **February 1, 2008**

Gary Clark Jr.

Black & White & Blues All Over

JOHN SAYLES AND GARY CLARK JR. TAKE ON RACE AND ROCK & ROLL IN 'Honeydripper' by MELANIE HAUPT • p.54

NEWS
Mixed Feelings About Mixed Use

FOOD
Super Bowl Sunday & Fat Tuesday

ARTS
FronteraFest Long Fringe Roundup

MUSIC
Long Tail Indieconomics

SEE AUSTINCHRONICLE.COM FOR BREAKING NEWS, DAILY LISTINGS, TALKIN' CRACK WITH THE AG, SUNDANCE SUCCESS, AND SO MANY NEW MUSIC BLOGS, YOU'D THINK WE WERE THE CAPITAL OF SOMETHING

There are those who will argue that this introduction should have provided an historical overview that included hundreds of names of acts, solo artists, clubs, and memorable shows—or at the very least offered some of the many stories that have passed into local legend. An attempt at such coverage by necessity would have been painfully incomplete, leaving out so much more than could be included in this space. Instead, this introduction is an eclectic overview, one I hope that is in tune with this extraordinary anthology that attempts to cover all the varied elements, stories, and sounds that have birthed Austin music and have continued to keep it vital, ambitious, and relevant.

This anthology offers years of immediate coverage of the music and the scene. There are the city, the music, musicians, clubs, and concerts. There are the history, the national renown, the festivals, and the amazing amassed collection of music released from here. There are also the expansive lifestyle and rich culture of a music city.

Finally, there is the media coverage: the critiquing, celebrating, recommending, and criticizing of the music and those who make it, the story told as it was happening, the contemporaneous shaping of the myth. The *Chronicle*, though by no means alone in that pursuit, has been the most steadfast. It seems unlikely that any of the other media covering the scene have enjoyed the ongoing adventures nor have had nearly the ridiculous amount of fun as have the contributors at the *Chronicle*. This is not in spite of but because of all the hard work, intensity, last-minute reporting, all-night writing, passion, pain, and pleasure that comes with the job. At the end of the day, when an issue is out and the *Chronicle* building empty, there is only one thing of which you can be sure, only one thing that keeps the writing as fresh, impassioned, electric, and imaginative as the scene: whether at home, in the car, at the clubs, or in concerts, much of the staff is listening to or playing music. It has always been that way and still is, as it is of Austin.

Music is of the *Chronicle* and the people who put it out.

This one is for Doug Sahm, as they all are, who until the day he died made more music than all those grooving Nashville cats did taken together. ◀

The Austin Chronicle
MUSIC ANTHOLOGY

The 1980s: An Introduction

MARGARET MOSER
Austin Chronicle Senior Music Writer, 1981–Present

WITH ONE EYE on the future and the other looking over its shoulder, 1981 opened with a thunderous door-slamming at the Armadillo World Headquarters after a decade of redefining Texas music. A scant four months later, the punk palace Raul's shuttered, and, for a few months, times felt appropriately grim in that Reagan era. Yet, one door never closes without another opening.

The great trifecta that defines Austin is politics, the University of Texas, and the arts, especially music. Those elements fused in the 1960s and were set into motion by the social change that settled during the 1970s, while the 1980s reaped the benefits of those decades, as translated by music and media.

And what a decade it was! Post-Armadillo Austin music swaggered forth, its thriving punk scene at Club Foot finding curious camaraderie with another marginalized sound, the blues, at Antone's. Both would come into their own within five years of the *Chronicle*'s maiden publication. Country at the Broken Spoke and folk at the Cactus Cafe grew strong, evolving the Lone Star imprint on roots-rock. Jazz lurked in the shadows while rock & roll blushed with New Sincerity at Liberty Lunch. Sixth Street still echoed empty at night in 1981. By 1989, it throbbed at the heart of a revitalized community. Nothing fueled the city's sense of its place in musical history more than MTV filming *The Cutting Edge* in 1986. The name said it all. Or so we thought.

It's difficult to describe just how free we felt back then, our passions liberating us to the beat of Talking Heads and Ramones. Many a cool fall night in late 1981, editor Louis Black, publisher Nick Barbaro, and I crawled out a window to sit on the gravel-laden asphalt roof of our shabby West 16th offices, looking out over the shifting downtown skyline. The notions that ran through our heads were inconceivable, unrealistic, and utterly euphoric to imagine.

It should be noted that the *Chronicle*'s original musical sensibility belonged to Jeff Whittington. He was the original music editor, an arbiter of taste, list freak, and Lester Bangs fan. His column at UT's *Daily Texan* had been the source for punk and new music, and he brought that cool with him to the paper. Whittington, who died in 2001, created the *Chronicle*'s Music Poll in 1982, which begat the Austin Music Awards in 1983, and he edited the Music section through 1984.

In 1987, the annual Thursday night AMA ceremony became a convenient way to introduce an entirely new kind of musical presence to Austin, South by Southwest. Suddenly, *Chronicle* music wasn't just covering the beat and reviewing records, we had world-class acts handed to us and the chance to posit local talent beside the majors the way we'd always dreamed. And although it was two more calendar years before the decade changed, in many ways the creation of SXSW signaled the beginning of the 1990s and the end of the 1980s.

Without question, it heralded the beginning of a new era of music coverage in *The Austin Chronicle*. ◄

HE COMES FROM
LUBBOCK, THE FABLED
TEXAS FLATLANDS, AS
INHERENT IN HIS MUSIC
AS THE WINDS THERE
THAT BLOW INFINITELY
ON THE PLAINS.

On the Road with Joe Ely

VOL. 1 NO. 16 ★ APRIL 2, 1982

MARGARET MOSER

1981 WAS A GOOD YEAR for Joe Ely. It was right on the heels of the Clash's 1980 American tour, the one that kicked Ely into the national spotlight. The group of four upstart musicians from England, who were spearheading the new musical forces, came face to face with the same dervish energy, the same emotion they'd been screaming about, all wrapped up in this one-man whirlwind.

Ely is the quintessential Texas musician. The *Live Shots* and *Musta Notta Gotta Lotta* LPs provided some of the best music of this or any other year. Most of his songs are original material, written by himself or compadre Butch Hancock, but even his cover songs bear Ely's distinctive style.

He comes from Lubbock, the fabled Texas flatlands, as inherent in his music as the winds there that blow infinitely on the plains. His songs drive the band onto a breakneck course from honky-tonks, hard living, and the high plains to rowdy, reckless rock & roll and some of the loveliest ballads you'll ever hear. What makes Ely great is his uncompromising performances. When he's onstage he never quits, never stops, he just thunders along.

His songs are ripe with imagery, the tangible kind that touches us all, but Ely has cultivated his music into a fierce and passionate sound that works both live and on recordings. In a way, Ely carries on the Buddy Holly tradition, an obvious comparison but valid all the same. It's a sound that transcends categorization, but defines Texas music.

NEW ORLEANS, LOUISIANA—Out on the road, even a short stint like this one, everything is different. When you're on the road, there are no rules. That's why you hear stories of bands ripping up hotels and tearing up bars while they're out on tour. Tossing a TV through a window into a swimming pool isn't as destructive an action as it sounds when you've spent more than two or three nights in the sterile confines of hotels and motels. It's sort of a natural reaction against the antiseptic surroundings. A way to release aggression when you just tore the umpteenth "Sanitized For Your Health and Protection" banner off your toilet seat so you can use it without some nurse smiling at you. That's why I wasn't surprised to hear Joe Ely had swiped a wheelbarrow from the construction site by the pool at the Fountain Bay Hotel, trundled it into the elevator, up to the sixth floor, and wheeled it out onto the balcony where they heaved it down into the tennis courts, six stories below. No one complained to the desk.

Or that guitarist Jesse "Jake" Taylor, while on the balcony that night, flipped over the railing and clung for dear life as the rest of the band hauled him back up.

The Louisiana version of honky-tonking is going down Bourbon Street and going into every bar. That's exactly what Smokey Joe Miller, the band's ace sax player, and Ely did the night before the New Orleans show, except that Smokey Joe, with sax in hand, walked in and played with every band playing, welcome or not. Ely would wait patiently and when Smokey Joe would take his leave, Ely would drape Miller's coat majestically about his shoulders as they walked out, followed to the next bar by a crowd that once swelled to about thirty people, all cheering him right into the next club.

Tupelo's is a little tavern north of the neighborhood I grew up in. The club holds about half as many people as the Continental and has somewhat the same atmosphere: a curious mixture of punks, a couple new romantics, a few older hippie types, and lots of danc-ers, with the heart of the club being the stage.

A full house greeted the band enthusiastically and the band acknowledged it by turning the evening into a full-blown, rip-it-up Joe Ely night. Onstage Ely is in his element. He turns a sly grin to the audience, the kind of lovable bad boy smile that could hustle you into a pool game, take you for all your money, steal your woman without even trying, then buy you a drink to help you ease your troubles.

As the band works through Ely's repertoire, "Musta Notta Gotta Lotta" nearly works the crowd into a frenzy. "Crazy Lemon," "Boxcars," "Not Fade Away," and "Road Hawg" keep the beat going. Keyboard player Mike Kindred is hammering out some crazed piano as drummer Robert Marquam lays down the bottom. Michael Robberson's bass thunders through and Smokey Joe plays a slurring sax against Ponty Bone's sassy accordion.

This band is Ely's backbone, some of the finest musicians ever assembled in Texas. Ely's done his time as a solo and acoustic musician, but the limit-less possibilities of a band was Ely's best move. They ease down to just the right level and tempos for the ballads such as "Honky Tonk Masquerade," the wistful "Wishin' for You," and Butch Hancock's exquisite "She Never Spoke Spanish To Me." Jimmie Gilmore's paean to "Dallas" is the band at its best. The steady rhythms and the infectious lyrics make it one of the most popular of their numbers.

BATON ROUGE, LOUISIANA—Baton Rouge is more the real Louisiana; New Orleans is like the kid on the block who always had better toys than you did. The azaleas are pastel clouds of white, pinks, and purples all over town. The club where the band is playing tonight is called Faces, once well known as the King-fish. It's quite a switch from Tupelo's, but the plusher

seating and spacious layout is a welcome contrast to the New Orleans show, and gives you a better idea of the unpredictable situations bands face while touring. Kind of a rock & roll feast or famine situation.

The Baton Rouge audience loves Ely as much as the New Orleans crowd, only there's twice as many people here. The crowd seems to be more familiar with him as requests are hollered from all over in between numbers. Launching into Hank Williams' "Honky Tonkin'," the band fires up the audience once more. Later in the show as he's taking a break during "Fools Fall In Love," he grabs a bottle of Dixie beer with his free hand, niftily pries it open with a couple of quick bites with his teeth, spits out the cap, and turns back to the microphone. As the song finishes, he turns and leaves the stage for a few songs while Ponty Bone knocks 'em out on accordion and sings "Don't You Lie to Me," fingers flying up and down the keys. Jesse Taylor picks it up a couple of songs later, doing "Gangster of Love," and Ely comes swaggering back after the song finishes.

"Have you heard the news?
There's good rockin' tonight!"

Ely should know; he writes that kind of news.

AUSTIN, TEXAS—The road that took Joe Ely out of the flat, dusty terrain of Lubbock to one-man gigs with a guitar at the One Knite to opening for the Rolling Stones in Phoenix, Arizona, has taken some rocky turns. But there's no stopping Ely: this road is his life, and the offers just keep coming. And Ely's music just keeps coming, having successfully bridged whatever gap remained between country music in its truest sense and rock & roll in its purest form. It's safe to say that he's on the verge of becoming one of the great ones.

"And I wish hard livin' didn't come so easy to me." ⬅

Joe Ely and Jesse Taylor at Gruene Hall, March 1982. Photograph by Martha Grenon.

JOE ELY BAND WITH LITTLE CHARLIE [SEXTON]

CLUB FOOT

While Jesse Taylor's hand is healing, Little Charlie is standing in on lead guitar with the Joe Ely Band. Charlie is cocksure. Charlie is megafun. Charlie is 14 years old. No shit. He's got it all: dazzling craftsmanship coupled with gaunt good looks, underscored by the slicked-back black hair, rolled-up shirt sleeves, and black jeans tucked into high cowboy boots. Charlie is obviously being initiated into Elyism by a pro. The pro! By turns Charlie and Joe give vent to snarled grins and pointed moans. Charlie also knows what we ladies love to take home as souvenirs—guitar picks! I think everyone on the dance floor got one. I know *I* did, and I fought like a mean bitch to get it. I'm sorry gang, punk is dead, Ely lives, and Charlie is waiting in the wings to take the torch whenever Joe passes it. Long live the ongoing Texas honky-tonk music revolution! Have you heard the news? BABS MODERN

VOL. 1 NO. 22 ★ JUNE 25, 1982

Joe Ely and Little Charlie [Sexton] at Club Foot, June 1982. Photograph by Martha Grenon.

LOU ANN BARTON
OLD ENOUGH
WARNERS

On her debut album, Lou Ann Barton glides through torchy ballads and liberating shuffles with the grace of a seasoned professional and the innocence of an ingenue. Barton quivers with rhythm and shakes with the blues on *Old Enough*; the lady could squeeze tears from a stone with just a twitch of her gifted vocal cords.

Though Barton first made her mark in the bars of Ft. Worth, *Old Enough* doesn't opt for the noble savagery of a honky-tonk meltdown. Instead, co-producers Jerry Wexler and Glenn Frey have enlisted the Muscle Shoals studio crew to provide a polished backing that avoids sterility and brings Barton's vocal prowess to the surface. The band burns at the right times and turns the flame down low when need be.

By deftly balancing compositions by contemporary songwriters (Frankie Miller, Marshall Crenshaw) with older covers (Walter Jacobs, Hank Ballard) Barton acknowledges her roots while her vision remains focused firmly on the future. She employs a guttural growl to propel rocking numbers like "I'm Old Enough" and "Finger Poppin' Time," while on ballads such as "It's Raining" and the stunning "Maybe," Barton caress-es the lyrics with full-bodied tones, elongating or truncating syllables to reveal hidden nuances.

Old Enough should satisfy blues purists as well as radio programmers with its emotional intensity and accessible production. Lou Ann Barton sings sugar-coated blues with a 100 proof core—sweet and intoxi-cating. **JODY DENBERG**

VOL. 1 NO. 17 ★ APRIL 16, 1982

BIG BOYS
FUN FUN FUN
MOMENT EP

This is one of the best records of 1982, and I don't just mean one of the best local records. From the 100-mph hardcore of "Apolitical" to the party-down funk of "Hollywood Swinging," this record is a crowd-pleaser and a rabble-rouser. But Texans already know how great the Big Boys are; this EP may be just the thing to clue in the rest of the world. They're already start-ing to take note of the Big Boys on the West Coast, where just a couple of months ago X asked them to open one of their biggest shows; it shouldn't take too many spins of "Fun Fun Fun" on KROZ to make the rest of California pay attention. The title track of this EP is one of the best slices of pure rock & roll I've heard this year or any other. **JEFF WHITTINGTON**

VOL. 2 NO. 1 ★ SEPTEMBER 3, 1982

Big Boys' first show at Raul's, November 27, 1979. Photograph by Ken Hoge.

In One Ear

VOL. 2 NO. 2 ★ SEPTEMBER 17, 1982

MARGARET MOSER

WANDERING AROUND SOAP CREEK on opening night a couple of weeks back, there seemed to be a missing element. I couldn't put my finger on. It wasn't the salsa; George Majewski's famous hot sauce was there. The old Wurlitzer was in place, even Billy Bob was at the door. Hmmm. Oh yes!! WHERE WAS DOUG SAHM???!? Soap Creek is simply not Soap Creek without the Texas Tornado and just in time to allay my fears, around the corner came Doug Sahm, the man to whom Texas owes much for his contributions to country, Tex-Mex, and R&B, not to mention New Wave and punk.

My respect and love for Doug Sahm's music goes back to my junior high days when the only consolation I had from the move from New Orleans to San Antonio was that the Sir Douglas Quintet lived there. As a seventh grader, I regarded "She's About a Mover" as the greatest song—only to be replaced the next year by "96 Tears" (talk about great regional music). The SDQ was the first major (and they *were* major) group I ever saw perform live. That was sixteen years ago. Doug Sahm has never lost the whirlwind intensity with which he plays, and I've seen him go through many styles over the years. I've witnessed Sahm play nights of country music in all its blue-collar, crotch-warmed beer glory, and come in the next night with five Chicano horn players from San Antonio's Westside and blow a hole in your soul. Prolific isn't the word, neither is multitalented, though they come close. Whatever it is, Sahm makes his debut at the new Soap Creek the 22nd and 23rd. Don't wear socks—Doug'll rock 'em off.

Doug Sahm holding court at Soap Creek Saloon, 1973. Photograph by Burton Wilson.

Between Rock and a Hard Place

VOL. 2 NO. 3 ★ OCTOBER 1, 1982

MARGARET MOSER

IT'S NEARLY IMPOSSIBLE to remember Austin back in the mid-1970s when there was no punk or New Wave. Their effect on the music scene here is still being reckoned with as a force. Just as Raul's can be pinpointed as the beginning of new music in Austin, so can the Skunks be recognized as the most durable of the bands that started out there. Survival of the fittest you might say.

Even their debut was auspicious. They were literally the first band on the stage at Raul's, though founding member Jesse Sublett asserts, "We never should have had spiked hair and stuff. We weren't that kind of band." Still the band did fit into the general look and sound of Raul's.

"We were the first guys on the block, but we were the underdog," Sublett comments. "To the hardcore punks we were hippies, and to hippies we were punks."

The Skunks' quicksilver adaptability wasn't as readily apparent in their early days. Much of the attention paid to the band focused on guitarist Eddie Munoz, a chipmunk-cheeked, spike-haired refugee from a rock band called Jellyroll, whose good looks often surpassed his guitar expertise. Jesse Sublett, another Jellyroll alumnus, looked like the same kind of spike-haired cute boy with more on the ball as a bass player and less of an obnoxious foul mouth than Munoz. Billy Blackmon gave the band its steady bottom on drum, his quiet personality a vivid contrast to the more colorful Sublett and Munoz.

The band's first real change was evidenced when Munoz departed to roadie for Elvis Costello. He was replaced by Jon Dee Graham. The band shifted from their "angry young men" to a more casual, but still intense, sound. With Graham in tow and Sublett at the helm, the Skunks began a determined effort to rise above the rut so many local bands were beginning to fall into. Instead of the six-night-a-week routine some groups use to build up a following, the Skunks immediately launched a touring campaign that took them to New York in August 1979 to play CBGB's, the godfather of American punk clubs. Gigs like that made them more determined to pursue touring as a way of building their following. It was during this time that "Push Me Around" (*Live at Raul's Club*) was the most requested song on KLBJ for two weeks running.

1980 had more changes in store for the Skunks as Graham departed the band and was replaced by Doug Murray. Several months later Doug's twin brother Greg replaced Billy Blackmon on drums. The significance of this isn't readily apparent: you have to remember that at one time the Skunks were probably the most actively disliked band in the Raul's scene. The twins had been two-thirds of Terminal Mind, a group that essentially represented everything the Skunks didn't, but their quality was more intangible and aesthetic, rather than concrete and linear. Basically, the addition of the Terminal Twins to the Skunks threw a monkeywrench into a whole line of New Wave and punk elitism. Did the Murrays make the Skunks more valid? Did the Murrays "sell out" by crossing to a somewhat more marketable sound? Was Sublett now acceptable?

One can quibble about the aesthetics and basics of rock, but certain facts are undeniable. The Skunks have emerged as the foremost rock band in Austin: a tasteful mix of traditional hard rock shot with the freshness of New Wave. The result is a powerful dose of electrifying rock, very hard and very Eighties.

The road ahead may not always be the smoothest, but you won't have the Skunks to push around anymore. ◀

> **"TO THE HARDCORE PUNKS WE WERE HIPPIES, AND TO HIPPIES WE WERE PUNKS.**"
>
> JESSE SUBLETT

The Skunks tour Washington, D.C., 1982. Photograph by David Fox.

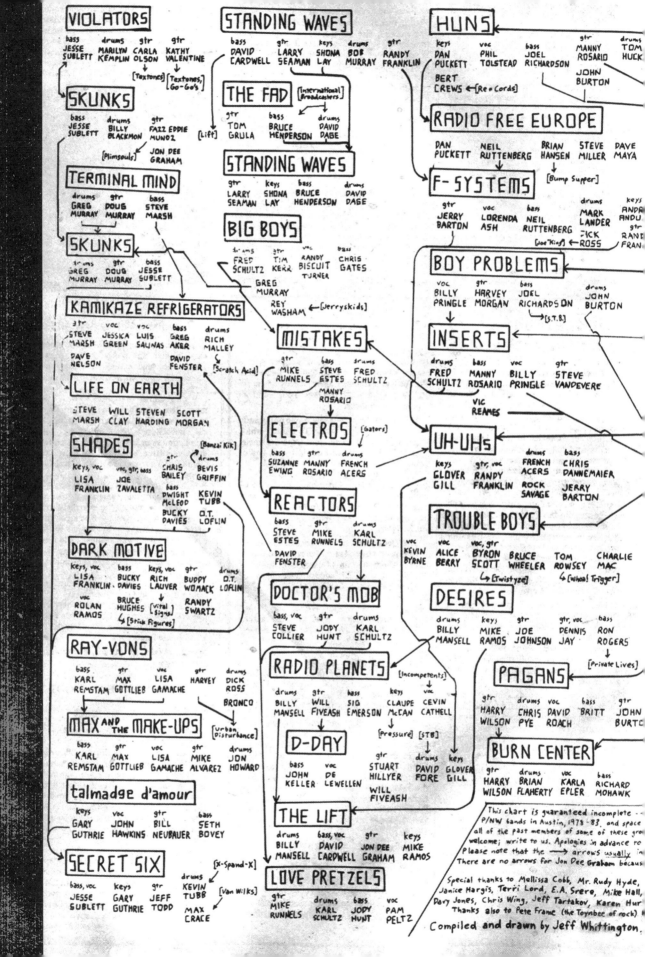

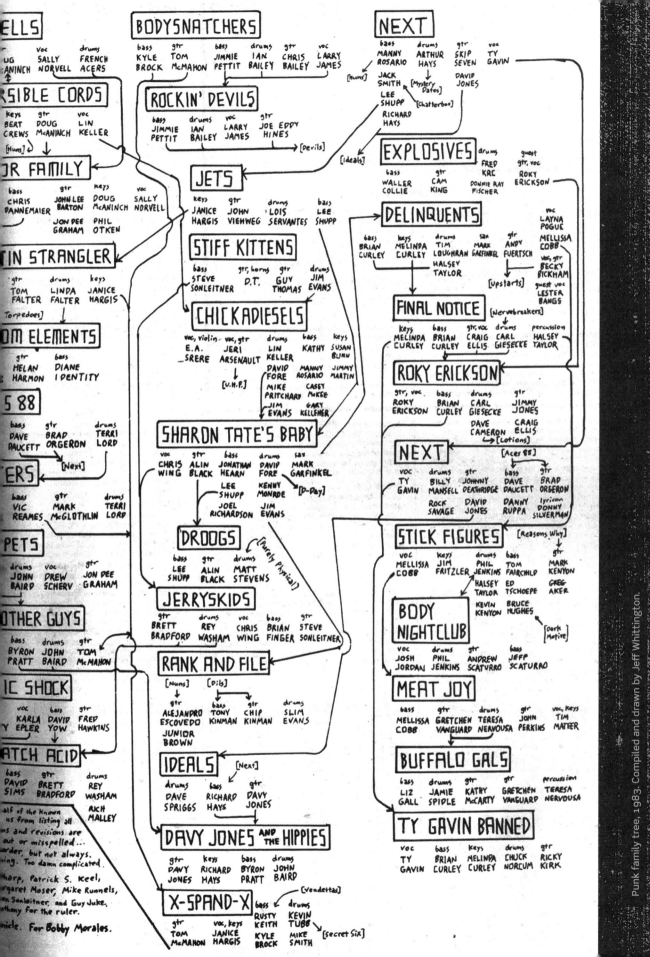

Punk family tree, 1983. Compiled and drawn by Jeff Whittington.

RAUL'S
A VERY SELECT DISCOGRAPHY

45s:

➡ Big Boys: "Frat Cars" b/w "Reaction"
➡ Joe "King" Carrasco: "Buena" b/w "Tuff Enuff"
➡ D-Day: "Too Young to Date" b/w "Every Time I Ask You Out"; "Right to Know" b/w "Metroplex"
➡ The Dicks: "Dicks Hate the Police" b/w "Lifetime Problems"
➡ F-Systems: "People" b/w "Naked Kiss"
➡ The Huns: "Busy Kids" b/w "Glad He's Dead"
➡ The Next: "Little Girls" b/w "Women Should Be Wilder"
➡ Reactors: "It's Not Important" b/w "Cold Eyes"
➡ Mike Runnels: "Only with You" b/w "Channel 19"
➡ The Skunks: "Earthquake Shake" b/w "Can't Get Loose"; "What Do You Want" b/w "The Racket"
➡ Standing Waves: "Don't Worry" b/w "Integrated Circuits"

EPs:

➡ The Bodysnatchers: *I Want That Girl*
➡ Joe "King" Carrasco: *Bad Rap*
➡ The Next: *Make It Quick*
➡ Reversible Chords (the Re*Cords): *Guyana Holiday*
➡ Rockin' Devils: *In the Red*
➡ The Skunks: *Cheap Girl*
➡ Standing Waves: *No Judy; Vertigo*
➡ Terminal Mind: *I Want to Die Young*

ALBUMs:

➡ Lester Bangs & the Delinquents: *Jook Savages on the Brazos*
➡ Big Boys/The Dicks: *Live at Raul's*
➡ The Delinquents: *The Delinquents*
➡ The Dicks: *Kill From the Heart*
➡ Jerryskids: *What Do They Want and How Will They Take It?*
➡ The Judy's: *Washarama*
➡ The Skunks: *For Your Love*

MARGARET MOSER

VOL. 14 NO. 9 ★ OCTOBER 28, 1994

Mama, What's a Cowpunk?
On the Lone Prairie with Rank and File

VOL. 2 NO. 4 ★ OCTOBER 15, 1982

DENNIS NOWLIN

RANK AND FILE is playing the Buddy Holly Birthday Celebration in Lubbock at a remodeled horse race-track. From the audience, a pair gets up to dance in the dirt. The male wants to two-step. He grabs her about the waist and starts to shuffle. She sways, bobbing cork-like in his arms and shaking her fist to the beat of the drums. They laugh. She starts to two-step, and he breaks away to bob. This pleasant confusion illustrates the manifold richness of Rank and File's music.

The band combines elements of reggae, country, and rock (punk and regular) into a heterogeneous mixture that brims with well-spaced rhythm, melodic guitar, and vocal work that can be as harmonious as the Everly Brothers or as distinct and unfettered as Johnny Cash. With their debut on Slash Records, *Sundown*, soon to be shipped, Rank and File forge a new, strong link between innovation and tradition, Waylon Jennings & the Waylors and Bob Marley & the Wailers, the subtle and the overwhelming, creating a sound that doesn't fit anyone but them.

As a whole the tunes that Chip Kinman, Tony Kinman, Alejandro Escovedo, and Slim Evans put forth have a feel that fits into any above category without crass mimicry. They are creatures of no particular genre. They were all members of early American punk bands and, at the same time, huge fans of country,

Rank and File, 1982. Photograph by David Fox.

> ## "IN THIS DAY AND AGE THERE AREN'T TOO MANY BANDS THAT CHALLENGE THE SENSIBILITIES OF COUNTRY MUSIC.
> ### ALEJANDRO ESCOVEDO "

reggae, and rock & roll. Chip, who collaborates on most of the songs with brother Tony, helps explain the situation merely by listing his favorite albums.

"There are two albums I admire a lot: *Mean as Hell* by Johnny Cash and *Black-heart Man* by Bunny Wailer. Those albums I can listen to and just get so inspired by the beauty of it. I think those albums are perfect." Both albums are folkloric and essentially the work of broad inspiration. Wailer even covers the Woody Guthrie song "Bound for Glory," making for a cultural cross-reference that Rank and File surely appreciate and actuate themselves.

Bassist Tony Kinman owes a lot to Johnny Cash vocally and lyrically. His baritone works in similar ways to Cash and the words are as straightforward and earnest as the Man in Black. For instance, in "Conductor Wears Black," a turnaround on "Bound for Glory" ("This train carries liars, this train carries thieves"), the sentiments are out front, plain, stark, and marvelously delivered.

The music is on a par with Tony's singing. Chip's leads usually fit inside the frame of the song, working in and around the scratchy rhythm guitar of Escovedo. Evans continually augments a solid backbeat, but the music wasn't always this tight. When Rank and File first came to town gigs were hard to find. A few dates here and there, but nothing promising. It's no easy row to hoe when you play "cowpunk."

After playing a few acoustic gigs at the Alamo Lounge, the band started to perk some ears and subsequently pack the intimate-when-empty Alamo.

"The acoustic dates helped turn a lot of people on to our songs," says Chip. "There was a lot less technology between us and the audience. Two mics, if I remember correctly." Escovedo agrees: "Those were key gigs for us. It helped us break out of what we were doing at the time."

A few years back Waylon Jennings had a hit entitled "Are You Sure Hank Done It This Way." The song ripped at a certain conservatism in country and questioned the madness to the method of Nashville. Rank and File are the lineal descendants of this song. "Yeah, I wish we had wrote that," Chip says. "That expresses our sentiments in a lot of ways. Get it away from the accountants and back to the pickers."

"In this day and age there aren't too many bands that challenge the sensibilities of country music," says Escovedo, the son of a singer in Mexican bands and brother to some of the forerunners of Latin jazz. "There's a lot of people who carry on the tradition, but not the tradition of change. One aspect of country music that people rarely put their finger on is how diverse country really is."

Tony adds: "I think it is a change, that there is a lot of honesty in what we are doing. If we were a certain type of present-day country band, we'd try to boogie it up and grow our hair long. If we wanted to appeal to a more New Wave audience, we'd be more jokey about it. We'd be arch-country. We're trying to do it the hard way, which is putting some of ourselves on the line within this musical form. I think what we're doing is a change . . . at least for us.

"When we started performing we started in punk rock because that's what we were. It afforded the opportunity to get up and be ourselves. When we changed musically, we kept our punk rock outlook. That's where we came from. But you can read interviews with Hank Williams where he says 'Don't confuse it with any more than three or four chords. Keep it simple.' That's punk rock."

Williams' credo for country breaches societal gaps. Rank and File follows that line, too. They have found a new approach to the same old tune, which is the best way to go about it. ◂

THE FABULOUS THUNDERBIRDS
T-BIRD RHYTHM
CHRYSALIS

It took the pop touch of producer Nick Lowe to set the Fabulous Thunderbirds on the right track. That the Thunderbirds are making the transition from being a blues bar band to being the pre-eminent sound of Texas rhythm and blues is evident, but Lowe's deft touch and ear for crack rhythms combines the best of both styles. While the T-Birds' first three albums were recorded with a more traditional blues approach, Lowe gives their sometimes dry style a fuller and predictably more rock & roll sound. Frontman Kim Wilson shines in the album, alternately blowing hot and cold blues harp, contributing most of the originals mixed with classics and giving his sly vocals a work-out on Dave Bartholemew's "The Monkey (Speaks His Mind)," "Poor Boy," and "Can't Tear It Up Enuff." Jimmie Vaughan milks some of the sweetest guitar this side of B.B. out of Huey Meaux's "Neighbor, Tend To Your Business" and "How Do You Spell Love?," and blisters others like "My Babe." Keith Ferguson's bass and Fran Christina's drumming may be the most solid working rhythm section around. *T-Bird Rhythm* drives right to the heart, with love and soul. **MARGARET MOSER**

VOL. 2 NO. 6 ★ NOVEMBER 12, 1982

GENE RAMEY BAND
PIGGY'S, MARCH 12

"I've been waiting 40 years to hear Gene Ramey," said a man who lives next to Ramey on Robertson Hill. "I've got all these 78s from way back in the '30s and '40s, but I'd never heard him 'til tonight." He looked very happy; so did the couple who said they knew Mr. Ramey through the Lions Club. That was the funny thing about this special night—to many people in the standing-room-only audience, Ramey was a legend and a neighbor at the same time.

The musicians Ramey played bass with on those 78s were gods in the jazz pantheon: Charlie "Bird" Parker and Jay McShann. Saturday night he was just having fun in his second Austin performance since being coaxed out of retirement. The supporting cast couldn't have been much better: Rick Lawn, director of the UT Jazz Ensemble, on sax; Steve Schwelling of Fala Fala on drums; and guitarist Richard Spencer.

During the second set, Lawn motioned to Rich Harney halfway through "A Night in Tunisia" and Harney slid right into the groove on Piggy's baby grand. Ramey looked over in surprise, shouting "Go ahead." And he did. With Harney contributing his remarkable talents on the ivories, the performance really took off. "We were just waiting for you," a pleased Ramey told Harney during the break. "Now we're really going to give you a workout."

Ramey's method takes a little adjustment for ears accustomed to the grandstanding of modern bass-ists. At times his bass sounds like a pacemaker—a steady quiet pulse that feels almost feeble until you catch the persistent energy in those lines walking straight from the heart. **GREG STEPHENS**

VOL. 2 NO. 15 ★ MARCH 18, 1983

BIG BOYS, REALLY RED, CROTCH ROT

CLUB FOOT, MAY 13

Tonight everyone was a hero. After an eternity's freeze, the punks—John Bird's vandals and water-drinkers—brought their music back to Club Foot. And did furniture fly against the walls? Did security kick ass? Did the young tennis ball heads charge the stage and mangle the microphones, prompting club management to expel them and their kind, once and for all, from Club Foot's hallowed confines?

Maybe in someone's fantasy, boss, but not on Friday the 13th. On this night of hardcore heaven, 650 strong (including minors) had a cock-knocking good time at the expense of nothing except a few tired myths that warranted mercy killing. Crotch Rot led off with a brand of sound that put to rest any curiosity I'd had about what noise a sea cow would make if it nose-dove into a paper shredder—harmless and worth a few snickers, especially the subterranean lead vocalist and the blazing drummer who couldn't be a day over 14. Then came Houston's old troopers Really Red, fronted by the thoroughly uninteresting U-Ron Bondage but much-improved in spite of him, uncorking a well-rehearsed set while the slam-dancers executed lemming-lunges from the edge of the stage.

The Big Boys owned the evening, of course—not just the headline spot and the audience's energy, but also the spirit of the entire extravaganza. Graciously thanking Club Foot for giving hardcore another shot, the BB's then gave the club every reason to ask for more. On another day I would call them to task for their overzealous Gang of Four allegiance, but in Austin there's nothing like the Big Boys, nothing so frenetic and unrelenting while at the same time personifying celebration. Tonight everyone was a hero, but the Big Boys were mine. **ROBERT DRAPER**

VOL. 2 NO. 20 ★ MAY 27, 1983

LYLE LOVETT

EMMAJOE'S, MAY 18

He said it was his first twilight. It certainly shouldn't be his last. Lyle Lovett hails from East Texas but emmajoe's convinced him to wander west. His voice, reminiscent of David Halley, has a cutting edge which serves to plant his songs even deeper. With those songs, laden to the breaking point with experience and emotion, and his simple show, just himself on guitar and Roland Denney on a suitably restrained stand-up bass, Lyle is a troubadour in the most original sense of the term. Most of his tunes were simple country songs (that's country in the general sense, not as in C&W), but he handles an occasional blues number quite well also. It was interesting to note that his show attracted such local luminaries as Butch Hancock and Nanci Griffith (she even got up to sing a few). The name Lyle Lovett may be new around here now, but I'd say his star is one to watch.

ELAINE BLODGETT

VOL. 2 NO. 21 ★ JUNE 10, 1983

Lyle Lovett and Walter Hyatt. Illustration by Nathan Jensen.

Texas Flood
Stevie Rising

VOL. 2 NO. 23 ★ JULY 8, 1983

MICHAEL HALL

"GREAT DAY," GRINS STEVIE Ray Vaughan, pulling out a cigarette. "I'm *happy*." He's ambling among the frantic last-minute tour preparations being made by his road manager Cutter Brandenburg, chattering animatedly like a boy scout going away to camp for the first time. Every few seconds, it seems, he pauses just long enough to grin wide again, as if he's in possession of the world's craziest secret.

Stevie's not grinning merely to stretch his cheeks. After years of bars and clubs and rumored-legend status, his name has broken big recently, in connection first with the Rolling Stones, then David Bowie, and now his first album, *Texas Flood*, and its executive producer John Hammond. The record is selling like a cult favorite, while critics are falling all over themselves with praise. Vaughan even has a video on MTV, "Love Struck Baby," one of the few blues videos on the station. And in an hour he will be leaving Austin for a month-long trek (maybe more—"we keep adding dates because we can't fulfill what all these promoters want," says Cutter). "I'm so happy," he laughs as he lights his cigarette, "I could just shit."

Wait a minute. This is a blues artist we're talking about. Unless there is some kind of revival going on,

Double Trouble: (l–r) Tommy Shannon, Stevie Ray Vaughan, and Chris Layton at the Austin Opera House, 1982. Photograph by Martha Grenon.

blues barely pays the bills, much less guides one to any kind of fame or fortune. Blues musicians, black and white, travel the chitlin circuits, occasionally put out virtually ignored records, and generally keep a coterie of fans happy.

Stevie Ray Vaughan is a different kind of blues artist. Unlike other white blues guitarists—Eric Clapton, Michael Bloomfield, Keith Richards—who came to blues as intrepid but naive tourists in a dangerous, unknown land, Vaughan has been living and soaking up blues his entire life. He grew up in one of the most fecund blues environments in the country, Texas, home of cryptic late-night radio and T-Bone Walker, Bobby "Blue" Bland, Junior Parker, Gatemouth Brown, etc. At age eight he was playing along with R&B and blues records his older brother Jimmie brought home.

"Watching Jimmie learn to play was ridiculous," says Stevie of the Fabulous Thunderbirds' guitarist, "'cause he didn't really start. He picked up the guitar and he already played. I wanted to do it too." He did, in a succession of bands that has filled 21 of his 28 years.

Vaughan plays what he knows, what he grew up with, and like his brother, what some would say he was born with. That style, of course, has influences, and Vaughan credits his brother, Jimi Hendrix, Hubert Sumlin (Howlin' Wolf's guitarist), Albert King, Freddie King, B.B. King, Albert Collins, and Django Reinhardt. If any one strain jumps out—on *Texas Flood* you can hear every branch of his bloodline—it quickly falls back into the mix, and except for the paeans to Hendrix in his live shows, none dominate. The influences have stewed for so long, and in so many juices, that the blend is Vaughan's own.

This is no longer sorrowful music, or the music of the oppressed, or the music of the past—Vaughan makes you forget you are listening to the blues. He blows at you like an unnameable tempest, his guitar screaming and shuddering and soughing and pulling you across grates of full-chorded fury, a sound that never stops for reference points or homages to the

This is no longer sorrowful music, or the music of the oppressed, or the music of the past—Vaughan makes you forget you are listening to the blues.

long ago. At 28, Vaughan is not yet a blues master; there are many who play faster and slower, subtler and more thoroughly. He's no blues purist, and he's no blues evangelist. He's a young white kid cocky enough to keep his lodestar under his hat, tough enough to wear black, and cool enough to dismiss David Bowie.

Ah, David Bowie. Stevie gave *Let's Dance* much of its roots punch; he was supposed to do the same for Bowie's six-month world tour, the tour of the year by all accounts. Luckily he has his own band and his own record to promote. "I'm much happier about playing with Double Trouble," he insists. "This band means a lot more to me than that one ever could. It's just not as real to me." Unfortunately the fracas between the two parties has up until now given Vaughan most of his publicity.

Texas Flood is changing that. Maybe the best thing about the album is that it doesn't sound like a modern studio blues record. Play it loud and there are three musicians in the room, with no strings or horns or dubs to muck up the rug. Stevie would be the last to treat his power blues as a parlor game.

"We just set up and played," he says. "That's all you've got to do. That's all you're supposed to do. Why go in there and doctor everything? Why not sound like you sound?" It took eight days to complete *Texas Flood*—two days to record the music, two for vocals, two to mix, and two to master. "There were only two overdubs, 'cause I broke a string twice."

If you've seen him play live, the only real surprise is how faithful *Texas Flood* is. The songs are vigorous

Stevie Ray Vaughan preps for his first national tour, 1983. Photograph by Susan Grady.

yet concise, flooding the room with sound but letting you up for air, until the next wave roars past. There are no prolix journeys into guitar excess. There is only one extended solo, on Vaughan's trademark "Texas Flood," and the three instrumentals are varied enough to maintain interest even for those unenamored of a fervid guitar.

Vaughan's voice lurks throughout, as distinctive as his guitar playing. Some discount it as an unnotable tenor, but they're either expecting another black imitator or they're not looking deep enough. It is a backhanded, lowdown drawl, sometimes sensuous and sometimes gnarled, that never waxes ethereal (subtlety is not Vaughan's strong suit) but always complements and reinforces—listen to the fearsome lilt in "Pride and Joy": "You mess with her you see a man get mean." Vaughan's never had any vocal coaching, learning instead by observation. "Kim Wilson taught me a whole bunch, just by watching him. Johnny Copeland too. George Jones is the greatest singer in the world," declares Stevie. "But for the stuff I usually listen to, O. V. Wright and Copeland are the best."

What if, contrary to everyone's fearless predictions, he doesn't get famous? Vaughan paraphrases friend and fellow bluesman Johnny Copeland: "'The people that are in the Top 40 make all that money because they've got to. Their expenses are so high that they have to make that much money to survive. If they go broke, they don't know what to do.' But Johnny's never been rich," says Stevie. "He's never made all that much money. He puts it like this—'If I have money and I get hungry, I eat. If I don't have money, I don't get hungry.'

"Think about it," he continues. "If the guy loses everything, it doesn't bother him. 'Cause he never started off with any kind of attitude about being a star or rich guy. If I get fame and fortune, I probably won't know what to do with it. I'll probably ignore it and try to continue doing what I do." ◄

STANDING WAVES
THE NIGHTLIFE, SEPTEMBER 17

The last time I wrote about the Standing Waves was in the fall of 1978. We were all different back then: it was their first press, my first attempt to chronicle the "punk scene"; they couldn't play too many chords and I couldn't spell their names right. They got their first gig playing for the Huns' post-arrest benefit, then built a clan of devotees at the Ark Co-op. Maybe ten bands back then dared align themselves with the New Wave movement.

Since then, the Raul's generation has turned on, tuned in, and burnt out, and the Austin rock & roll scene finds itself with few survivors. Those who left found God, real estate, mass media, and inertia. Two of those who survived—Joe "King" Carrasco and D-Day—have something to show for it.

I was once among you—you, the Standing Cynics. But the Waves are now a band which, more often than is customary, betters its predecessors; they don't sound like Tom Verlaine or XTC or Talking Heads any longer; they fill a void I never knew existed, which means emphatically: they have come into their own.

Who are Larry Seaman and Bruce Henderson if not the U.S.'s budding, brooding answer to Squeeze's Tilbrook & Difford, or at least a more harmonious counterpart to XTC's Partridge & Moulding? Have you seen them lately? I hadn't, not since around the release of *Vertigo*, which did little to quell my doddering nostalgia for the old Waves—a band of so many faces, and so many colorful egos to match, that it was destined to dazzle and fizzle out for good. Two years ago? Has it been that long? I digress.

Have you seen the Standing Waves in the last few months? At absolute worst, there's nothing wrong with them that a top-notch producer couldn't brush aside in a day's work. At best, the Waves epitomize the unforgettable pop band: unpretentious but intelligent, irresistible but enigmatic, and retaining both the respectful hint of familiarity and the brash ring of innovation.

Standing Waves, 1982. Photograph by David Fox.

Sure I'm cheerleading, but I have a drool war rant that gives me the right. Besides: Have you seen Seaman play guitar recently? Or the way Henderson has assumed an alluring personality that at the same time enhances Seaman's? Have you heard their Simon & Garfunkel crooning on "Only Memories" or the brittle gloom of "No Conviction"? Have you noticed Shona Lay's ability to make her obsolete Yamaha organ sound like an ensemble of synthesizers, all the while looking as if she's painting her nails? Or drummer David Dage's indispensable contribution to the band's unfailing harmonies? My hat's off to the Standing Waves; from here on up, I check the chip on my shoulder at the door. **ROBERT DRAPER**

VOL. 3 NO. 3 ★ SEPTEMBER 30, 1983

BUTTHOLE SURFERS
BUTTHOLE SURFERS
ALTERNATIVE TENTACLES

It doesn't really say what speed this should be played at (though 69 rpm is suggested), so I tried both 45 and 33. Go with the 45, but save the 33 experience for slow nights. Not monolithic speed-bangers, the B. Surfers (from S.A.) are clever and decent musicians, great arrangers, and best of all, deliciously profane— "Bar-B-Q Pope," "The Shah Sleeps in Lee Harvey's Grave" ("There's a time for drugs and a time to be safe / But Jimi Hendrix makes love to Marilyn's remains"). A surprise hit. **MICHAEL HALL**

VOL. 3 NO. 9 ★ DECEMBER 23, 1983

BLAZE FOLEY

AUSTIN OUTHOUSE, JANUARY 15

The Austin Outhouse, definitely a time warp in its own right, deserves high praise for having the continuing courage to book "unknowns." The club itself maintains an ambience somewhere between the now defunct Spellman's and Taco Flats. This class establishment, which welcomes dogs, provides set-ups, and tolerates South-of-the-River dress codes, presented on this cold January evening one of the area's best kept secrets: songwriter Blaze Foley, whose presence, wardrobe, and songwriting abilities further define the word "original." One of the last performers to wear ties and duct-taped sports jackets, his repertoire includes songs about Girl Scout Cookies, bouffant matrons, a Reaganesque "Oval Room," and some of the most sensitive love songs heard in some time.

Blaze managed to outshine his lap-steel backup Bob Gay (fretting with a half-full tabasco bottle) and guest artist Rick Cardwell, no slouch in the songwriting department himself. Blaze outblazed everyone, combining a basso profundo voice, fine finger-style guitar playing, and the strongest stage presence since Jerry Jeff took the pledge. So let's hear it, folks, for the Austin Outhouse for being its own anachronism seven nights a week, and for Blaze for being himself. **ROB KLEIN**

VOL. 3 NO. 11 ★ JANUARY 27, 1984

Marcia Ball, 1984. Photograph by Ellen Wallenstein.

Marcia Ball's Evolution from Country Kicker to Blues Singer

VOL. 3 NO. 12 ★ FEBRUARY 10, 1984

JODY DENBERG

MARCIA BALL makes great gumbo that is beaucoups yumbo. Chicken and oysters are some of her favorite ingredients to mix in with the okra pods and other edibles in this Creole concoction, but on this particular sunny day in South Austin, as the carpenters and painters shuffle through her kitchen with hammers and brushes in tow to give her new home a facelift, Marcia Ball is peeling shrimp. The variations on the gumbo theme are seemingly endless.

Of course, not all of Marcia's creative juices are spent over a hot stove. Most of her cooking goes down on nightclub stages along the crawfish circuit that winds through Texas and Louisiana, where, along with her four-piece band, Ms. Ball brews another heady blend.

Although her reputation was earned primarily as a country and western singer, since 1980, Marcia has been wowing audiences and inspiring happy feet with a spicy stew of blues, R&B, soul, and rock & roll that is drawn from the American heartland. The musical heritages of cities like Chicago, New Orleans, Detroit, Memphis, and Austin have all found a home in her emotionally expressive vocal timbre and the long, slender fingers of hands that both caress and pound 88 keys of ivory. Marcia Ball has found that, as with gumbo, the variations on the blues theme are also endless. And sometimes it seems as if she and her band won't rest until they've whipped up at least 57 varieties.

As longtime Austinites are well aware, rhythm and blues is just the latest musical vein Marcia has mined in a performing career that began in the early Seventies and is ascending into the Eighties with the release of her new album on Rounder, *Soulful Dress*. During the early 1970s, at now defunct spots like the Split Rail and the original Soap Creek, Ball was the cowboy sweetheart who rode bareback along Austin's progressive country trail until it proved to be somewhat of an artistic dead-end.

"I discovered that I really didn't want to play country music for rednecks," Ball recalls without a hint of bitterness. "That's what happened to me and country music. When we played country music then, we played for hippies. We played at the Broken Spoke, and it was fun. At the Silver Dollar and places like that you kind of get treated like a jukebox 'cause people don't clap. You had to play current Top 40 country music, and that was not the country music that I liked and wanted to do."

Despite her initial fame, playing country music wasn't as natural for Marcia Ball as the soulful rhythm and blues she grew up listening to and now performs. Which is not to say that her fondness for R&B is a direct correlation of being raised in Vinton, Louisiana, a town just across the Sabine River from Texas.

At 17, Ball struck out for Baton Rouge and Louisiana State University. After dropping out, Marcia, who had been playing a little folk music around the house on her guitar, met a bunch of musicians who invited her to audition for a rock & roll band. Her tryout was a tie-dyed triumph, and it landed her with Gum, a band she laughingly recalls as "real psychedelic." About a year later, Marcia Mouton married, became Marcia Ball, and did what every paisley-blooded young American did back in those days. She headed for San Francisco.

But Marcia and her husband never wound up in the land of love and Haight. The Balls' car broke down in Austin, and as fate will have it, they never left.

In the winter of 1972, bassist Bobby Earl Smith needed a band (his had just broken up) and he

> ## "I DISCOVERED THAT I REALLY DIDN'T WANT TO PLAY COUNTRY MUSIC FOR REDNECKS.
>
> **MARCIA BALL** "

approached Ball, who had sat in with his previous aggregation. Along with guitarist John Reed, drummer Steve McDaniels, and steel guitarist David Cook, Ball and Smith became Freda & the Firedogs, a combo which lasted over two years and played a large role in Austin's progressive country hay-daze.

"Bobby Earl pretty much taught me country music, and I really got into it. We all did. Nashville was fun then. And besides that, we had godfathers. We were in a national movement at the time. *Sweetheart of the Rodeo* had preceeded us, Commander Cody were doing their thing, and Asleep at the Wheel were out in California. We had Willie looking over our shoulder and Jerry Jeff coming 'round the bend. It was all happening at the same time. It was a great time to be getting into country music—Nashville was hot, and Willie was just about to take over. So for us it was like, carte blanche, y'know?"

Freda & the Firedogs never recorded an official record, although Smith did later release a reunion LP, which Ball says "wasn't a particularly good musical night and wasn't a particularly well-recorded tape. It wasn't a good indication of what the Firedogs were about."

After her incarnation as Freda, with a succession of bands that began with Marcia Ball & the Misery Brothers, the tall, wide-eyed vocalist began to explore a wider selection of material. Though country and swing were still a part of her repertoire, Smokey Robinson and Marvin Gaye were also heard through Marcia's musical grapevine. And at the end of 1978, Marcia made it to Nashville to record *Circuit Queen*

for Capitol Records, with a stellar lineup consisting primarily of Emmylou Harris' band: Rodney Crowell, Albert Lee, Bee Spears, and Mickey Raphael.

Marcia's initial vinyl foray is now out of print, and its author doesn't even own a copy. "I think they've been melted down for Wings albums," she jokes in retrospect. "Without sounding sour grapes or even rude about it, I don't think I had any high hopes for what was actually going to come of it. Maybe that's just a self-protective sort of thing where you don't get your hopes up too high. I enjoyed the process of doing it, but I didn't really expect to become an overnight sensation as a result of it—and as a matter of fact, I didn't!"

Until two years ago, Marcia's band was a clearinghouse for some of Austin's finest blues players; her current band, though, is her tightest yet. Each member has a background in a different shade of the blues, and together they have created a fine record. Listening to *Soulful Dress*, you can almost picture Marcia at her Yamaha electric piano, a long slit-skirt hugging her svelte figure, a broad smile on her face, and one high-heeled shoe keeping the beat while poised on her other ankle. The album runs through a gamut of styles, from a humorous version of Dave Bartholomew's "Jailbird" and Slim Harpo's "That's Why I Love You" to a gender-bending of Bobby Bland's "Don't Want No Man" and some superb Ball originals like the elegantly phrased "My Mind's Made Up" and the swingin' "A Thousand Times."

With her family life settling down, a studio being built behind her house, and her roadwork extremely successful, it appears that the years Marcia Ball spent paying dues are now paying off. *Soulful Dress* is the icing on Marcia's cake. And since it is only her first album for the Rounder label, she may be back in the kitchen again soon—juggling gumbo, the rhythm and blues. ◀

FREDA & THE FIREDOGS
FREDA & THE FIREDOGS
PLUG

SUPERNATURAL FAMILY BAND
LUBBOCK LIGHTS
AKASHIC

THE CONTENDERS
THE CONTENDERS
GADFLY

GREEZY WHEELS
"FINDING HAPPINESS"
"MONKEY IN THE CHURCH"
TANA

Freda & the Firedogs, 1972. Photograph by Burton Wilson.

Four recent local reissues here, each one a milestone of Austin's progressive country era in its own inimitable way. Freda & the Firedogs is the legendary lost recording from Atlantic Records, capturing the beloved local band at its 1972 zenith. In addition to Jerry Wexler's expert production and remastering by local country radio pioneer Joe Gracey, Freda pushes the boundaries of country, from Loretta Lynn ("Fist City") and Hank Williams ("Jambalaya") to blues (Taj Mahal's "EZ Rider") and folk traditionals ("Make Me a Pallet"), with Marcia Ball's youthful, distinctive vocals. After the enormously popular Uncle Walt's Band disbanded locally, the power duo of Champ Hood and Walter Hyatt teamed up in Nashville with Steve Runkle, Jimbeau Walsh, and Tommy Goldsmith to form the Contenders, from 1976 to 1978. This self-titled CD is the reissue of their one and only vinyl album, plus the requisite extra tracks. The band's considerable experience resulted in an astonishingly eclectic sound that was adept at rock & roll ("Talk"), ballads (the gospel-inflected "Lack of Love"), country ("Walking Angel"), and blues ("Chain of Emotion"). The multitalented, multigenerational Hancock family performed as the Supernatural Family Band in the Seventies and early Eighties before relocating to

Austin, and *Lubbock Lights* captures their essence. Recorded live for vinyl at Lubbock's Texas Spoon Cafe & Bar in 1986, the CD offers three Tom X bonus tracks ("The Desert Blues," "The Marfa Lights," "Lubbock Lights"). The album has a wistful, nostalgic feel as it hearkens as much to Texas classics ("Faded Love," "San Antonio Rose") as it does patriarch Tommy Hancock's days with the Roadside Playboys and the family band magic. Freda & the Firedogs were hot stuff when Greezy Wheels first roared onto the scene in the mid-Seventies. Their album *Radio Radials* was as hugely popular as they were, another family affair with Cleve Hattersley, his fiddle-playing wife Sweet Mary, sister Lissa Hattersley, and an extended family of talents. After 20-odd years of dormancy, the band revved up and put out 2000's *Millennium Greezy* and last spring began a creative campaign to its fan club called "Song of the Month." With the recent release of the CD single "Finding Happiness" and "Monkey in the Church," the Wheels roll more than halfway toward the finished product. This is not Nashville-defined country; Greezy Wheels' whimsical pop influences are ever present in the charmingly folky, if slightly irreverent, quirky little songs. MARGARET MOSER

THE DICKS, JEFFERSONS, HICKOIDS, FUDGE TUNNELS

VOLTAIRE'S BASEMENT, APRIL 21

History was made, rather remade, Saturday night when all four members of the original Dicks reunited onstage to insult, shock, challenge, preach at, and otherwise entertain one of the largest audiences yet to descend the stairs to Voltaire's Basement. Their reunion was the high point of an exhilarating evening that had every band on the bill putting on performances that surely ranked as some of their finest.

The Fudge Tunnels opened, followed by the Hickoids (which is when I arrived). They took the stage, tossed corn at the crowd, and lurched into one thrashed-out country tune after another. Despite their ultra-casual performance and seemingly amateurish sound, they've obviously worked hard on their songs and presentation, successfully mating hardcore to country and coming up with a hybrid that simultaneously embraces and mocks both musics. With the mixed feelings of love and disgust only a Texan could know, the Hickoids take both genres' sharp edges, file 'em to a point, and keep the result from getting too nasty by tempering everything with abundant humor. Lead singer Jeff Smith adopts a nasal twang to sing a frenzied version of Hank Williams' "Cold Cold Heart," not so much because he's ashamed of the material, but because he's sophisticated enough to know that singing it straight would be more dishonest than his camped-up way. A mask is used, partly to hide behind, but mostly so more truth can be revealed.

The Jeffersons, next up, also used humor to conceal/reveal what they think and care about. Lead singer Buxf Parrot was particularly inspired this night, partly because all of his former bandmates were there and he didn't want to disappoint (or be upstaged). He needn't have worried. His forceful,

theatrical stage presence had everyone paying attention as he baited them with remarks like "at least I didn't pay four bucks to see YOU assholes!"

The "new Dicks," as they're referred to in Austin, took the stage well past midnight. Looking like a sweating Buddah perched on the edge of the stage, his rich, powerful voice filling the smoky little room, Gary Floyd showed what has made him one of the most popular performers on the punk circuit. Regaling the crowd with harsh leftist political rhetoric, taunting and teasing his detractors, only a critic could find fault with his gutsy approach. I found the way he got much of the audience to ape his every move, echo his every thought, a little frightening. He comes off a bit paternal and his dogmatic approach reeked of authoritarianism: even when the sentiment is "we don't need no fuckin' war" a group chant always sounds a little like a Nazi youth rally.

The "new Dicks" are rather faceless save for Gary, but the original Dicks, who closed out this remarkable night, well . . . let's just say that there's never been another group like them. And let's mean it, too, because they topped everything else on this hard-to-top

Saturday night at the bookstore: the Dicks' Gary Floyd. Photograph by Ken Hoge.

THE DICKS
DICKS 1980–1986

ALTERNATIVE TENTACLES

For musicians, anger was not in short supply in 1980. It was requisite for punk, the flamethrower for hardcore, and it came in all shapes and sizes. In Austin, the arc between punk anger and nascent hardcore were the Dicks, the queerest of the queer. The Big Boys may have been bigger but the Dicks were harder. The Big Boys screamed but the Dicks seethed. The Big Boys were politically aware but the Dicks were political. And now the CD cornerstone of Texas punk can be laid with the release of *Dicks 1980–1986*. Twenty-one tracks were culled for this take-no-prisoners collection, which covers both the Austin- and San Francisco-based versions of the band, allowing even the most casual listener an unusually cohesive journey of the band from its first EP *Dicks Hate the Police* to their swansong track on the Texas punk compilation *Cottage Cheese from the Lips of Death,* "Guilbeau," a moody, Morrison-esque harbinger of lead singer Gary Floyd's next band, Sister Double Happiness. In between is an unholy union of raving anti-homophobia, anti-war, and anti-hate anthems laid out on the skeleton of classic garage-punk, and raising itself like Mr. Bones from the vinyl graveyard to do a tap-dance back into our skulls, if only to remind us just what punk at its best could be. The original Dicks—Gary Floyd, Buxf Parrot, Pat Deason, and the late Glen Taylor—open the album irresistibly off-beat and blindly off-key on the meandering fury of "Dicks Hate the Police," "Lifetime Problems," and the trite sentiment of "Fake Bands," then systemically reconstruct the politics of punk in "Saturday Night at the Bookstore": *"You . . . and your fat fucking wife coming out of Safeway on a Sunday afternoon and see me standing there and don't even speak to me . . . 'cause I sucked your cock through a gloryhole. . . ."* The Dicks stomp this turf just as the Velvet Underground did with "Sister Ray," continuing with the utterly brilliant "Wheelchair Epidemic," and thrashers "Shit on Me," "Rich Daddy," and "Kill from the Heart." The band morphs on track 13, with Floyd back in San Francisco, recruiting Tim Carroll, Lynn Perko, and Sebastian Fuchs, and marking distinctly more melodic social awareness though no less compromising. By the time the Dicks zipped it closed forever in 1986, they did so with such savage grace no one who'd heard them walked away innocent. MARGARET MOSER

bill, and had nearly everyone in the place swinging and swaying along with them. It sounded like they'd never been apart. The show-ending encore was even—gasp—a love ballad. Gary couldn't let himself stand completely naked—he snarled the last "Baby I love you"—but the meaning was clear enough anyway. Is THAT what this punk stuff is all about?

BRENT GRULKE

VOL. 3 NO. 18 ★ MAY 4, 1984

RAY WYLIE HUBBARD
DIXIE'S BAR & BUS STOP, APRIL 26

From time to time, references appear in the local press rehashing the obituary notices of Austin's early '70s Progressive Country movement, perhaps mentioning a few dinosaurs spotted grazing with their guitars in some pasture near Luckenbach. Fortunately, Ray Wylie Hubbard doesn't spend much time in the past tense. His eclectic, electric blend of boogified country is as compelling now as his lower-keyed redneck mothering was a decade ago. Hubbard performed two sets of new and old material that proved his lyric creativity is not shackled to either one style or a bygone epoch. Hubbard sang about shifting sands, promised lands, Billy the Kid, women on the skids, gamblers whose luck won't hold, nice girls whose resistance won't fold, and what it feels like to be sitting on top of the world driving a '69 Chevy with those Deep River blues, wishing hard living didn't come so easy in Dallas after midnight. Ray Wylie has confounded the ambulance chasers with his ability to write songs that grab you in lots of places and turn you any which way but off. If in the next few years another Austin-based songwriting genre of national aspect arises, he will certainly be in its forefront.

L. E. MCCULLOUGH

VOL. 3 NO. 19 ★ MAY 4, 1984

SONGWRITERS RECOGNITION SERIES
BUTCH HANCOCK

He writes songs as Balzac wrote novels; often and well, and often long as well. He interprets them with a phlegmatic rasp recalling Bob Dylan's before the conscience of a generation wrecked his motorcycle and discarded his cigarettes, a similarity which has distracted many fans from realizing that Hancock is really the Southwest's answer to Neil Young: always interesting, sometimes flaky, often brilliant, and blessed with apparently endless fecundity.

Any serious consideration of Butch Hancock makes labels drop like drunks at a frat brawl. Is he a rural mystic or a cold-eyed ironist? Romantic tune-smith or myth-hungry poet? Drawing on the weird inner life that is the birthright of creatively inclined Lubbockians, Hancock has been all of those things at one time or another, in the course of one song or another. He is especially adept at coaxing metaphors from imagery—nature elements in many songs, artifacts or technology in others, like the tracks where "the lonesome boxcars roll"—and though many of his lyrics are carried on familiar folk and country progressions, he also has some exquisitely crafted melodies to his credit.

Coming off a long spell in a studio recording himself and others for television, Hancock should have at least 40 or 50 freshly incubated songs to pick from, as well as his usual enormous back catalog. The *Austin Chronicle* is pleased to present a Texas songwriter—not produced by Sidney Pollack. CHRIS WALTERS

VOL. 3 NO. 11 ★ JANUARY 27, 1984

Why I Worry About Joe "King" Carrasco

VOL. 3 NO. 21 ★ JUNE 15, 1984

MICHAEL CORCORAN

THEY LET JOE "King" Carrasco off the leash again. It was at the Auditorium Shores free Wednesday concert and everyone in our "When will Joe King injure himself seriously" pool was present. I have two dollars on Sept. 13, a bet that was in jeopardy many times this evening as the metabolistic maniac did full flips into the crowd from the top of P.A. speakers, among other follicle-erecting stunts.

Maybe he has cancer. That's it—six months to live so why not? Perhaps he's realized that he'll never really be Mexican, no matter how many over-the-border transfusion trips he makes, so he wants to end it all in a blaze of Hispanic-styled glory. I wouldn't automatically discard that theory. We're talking about the guy that never went back to mass after they changed it from Latin to English. And this was a religious guy. Joe "King" Carrasco, we're worried about you. You can't keep doing this to yourself—twenty-foot leaps, guitar solos in traffic, somersaults—remember, Gale Sayers only had four full years, and he wore pads.

But how can Joe be stopped and helped when audiences continually allow themselves to be cut into confetti by his antics and bouncy party music. Carrasco & the Crowns are the musical equivalent of Gene Kelly's puddle-stomping choreography in *Singing in the Rain*: exuberant, carefree, sloppy, and lifting. "96 Tears," "One More Time," "Party Weekend," "Wooly Bully," one right after the other. Too many encores, but that's like going to a good restaurant and getting too much food. ◂

Joe "King" Carrasco's Texas two-step at Raul's, 1979. Photograph by Ken Hoge.

URANIUM SAVAGES' 10TH ANNIVERSARY CELEBRATION

SOAP CREEK SALOON, JULY 28

The Uranium Savages have had ten full years to perfect their lunatic-fringe musical satire, and their sardine-squished fans got exactly what they came for: mayhem, music, and madness that didn't quit 'til way past closing time. Irreverent and totally irrepressible, Kerry Awn and his back-up "Shrovinover Unit #709" with Artley Snuff and James Hamlin created pure havoc begging for acid flashbacks, singing "I Snort the Line" repressive country-style, hurling themselves into the delighted audience, and simulating all manner of kinky sexual experiences. They opened with their "Sweat Theme" and deadpanned Jerry Jeff Walker in a hilarious "Home to Minnesota." David Arnsberger was slimily superb as Sweathog Burrell. Kent Temple on guitar completed the quartet of original Savages, but newer additions to the band carried their own weight: David Perkoff and Tom Colwell on horn and sax, David Duffy on drums, Tom Clarkson on bass, and guitarist Charles Ray. It was all the old favorites done with gusto: "Idi Amin Is My Yardman," "Taco," "Girl Crazy," "Back in the MHMR." **MARYBETH GRADZIEL**

VOL. 3 NO. 26 ★ AUGUST 24, 1984

GLASS EYE

THE BEACH, AUGUST 28

Like blue roses, flying fish, and Christmas in July, some things are best left unexplained, and in turn, benefit from it. Case in point is Austin's Glass Eye, who's been popping up on some unexpected bills (with the Butthole Surfers at Uncle Sue-Sue's recently) as well as holding forth for God-knows-how-many Wednesdays at the Beach. With a minimum of fanfare and to-do, this combo has successfully used these midweek sets to begin building a solid local following.

Musically, Glass Eye flirts with a variety of forms, from industrial bang-bang to a perverse sort of funk. The group really hits the mark, however, somewhere in between. The truth must be told: this *is* pop, dear friends, and pop is the better for it. The components are identifiable, but the formula is elusive. Only the chemists know for sure, and I suppose they're not talking just yet. Right up front is the big barking bass guitar of Brian Beattie (also seen with Franklin, Marsh, and Beattie). Where he leads, all ears follow and it's a genuine musical thrill to see him work. The prime attraction here, though, is the songs. Kathy McCarty (ex–Buffalo Gals) is shaping up as one of this town's more adventurous tunesmiths, and when she and Beattie both lean into one of those patented vocal choruses, the goosebump index shoots through the roof. This is Austin's Crown of Creation, but these kids have got somewhere to go.

The band has its faults to be sure. Their stage presence is so low-key as to be almost nonexistent, and their "just folks" approach will keep them off the larger stages for awhile. Still, what we are seeing here is the fermentation of some pretty compelling stuff. **DAVID DAGE**

VOL. 3 NO. 26 ★ AUGUST 24, 1984

DINO LEE

VOL. 4 NO. 1 ★ SEPTEMBER 7, 1984

MICHAEL CORCORAN

IF YOU HAVEN'T SEEN Dino Lee & the White Trash Revue, words will not help you. The thesaurus goes only as far as Arizona and Dino is legging up Hollywood Boulevard in reaper robe, purple metallic wig, white-framed cheaters, and pink bathroom slippers.

Calling him "tacky" is like labeling David Berkowitz "disturbed." The word just doesn't go far enough. Tacky is wearing a Davy Crockett hat, but what do you call a guy who wears one under sheik headware? "Squeeze my lemon and let the juice run down my legs" is suggestive lyricizing, yet put it next to Dino's words to "Wayne Newton is a Dyke" and you've got Debby Boone's next single. Dino Lee is Austin's answer to a rhetorical question. He's a sorority sister's blind date nightmare. The opposite of hot is cold. The opposite of your parents is Dino Lee.

Dino Lee & the White Trash Revue, winner of the Best & Worst Thing to Happen to Austin Music at the 1986 AMAs. Photograph by Martha Grenon.

Wild get-ups, trashy themes, musical hodgepodge, porno lyrics, buxomy tarts—it all sounds like one hell of a novelty act, but you'd better use a better choice of words, Mister, or you'll be asked to leave. "Novelty" is an ugly word, best known as part of the cliche, "The novelty is starting to wear thin." With a crack band like the White Trash Revue the only things that start to wear thin are the soles of your shoes. Featuring a veritable all-star at every position, including accordionist Ponty Bone who takes over the vocals during Dino's costume changes, these montanas can really kick the goat's head around a bit. Next time diversity and music both come up in the same paragraph, think of the band that can cover George Jones and the Holy Modal Rounders, dabble in Latino roof-raising, put ladles of James Brown on the show-stopping "Everybody Get Some (But Don't Get Any On Ya)" and in between all that can spit out fast beat rock so steamy it'll take the wrinkles out of your clothes.

In a town nicknamed "The Backlash Capitol of Texas," success is almost always followed by seasons of snideness. Dino Lee's quick rise as the High Priest of the Bi-Weekly Extravaganza is not of the proportion of Ely or T-Birds, but he *has* outgrown the Continental Club for its roomier sister, Liberty Lunch, which would usually cause a little bit of dirt to fly; but you'd have an easier time of finding someone to badmouth Bear Bryant in Alabama than to utter a negative comment about Dino Lee. At a White Trash outing you'll see the old blues hacker next to the kid with hair the color of school lunch spaghetti sauce, a Sixth Street club owner sharing the restroom trough with the guy who sleeps on the floor at his friend's house, athletes next to drug addicts: all tossed together like the homemade salad when the boss comes to dinner. Everybody doesn't like something, but nobody doesn't like Dino Lee. ◄

BLAZE FOLEY

BLAZE FOLEY

VITAL RECORDS

It's a Saturday morning, and I'm lying on the living room couch listening to Blaze Foley's new album. The people downstairs seem to be smoking a lot of pot or else there's a brushfire of the stuff somewhere in the neighborhood; the unexpected cool of the day is welcome and Foley's voice and lyrics put it all into focus, recalling different mornings in different places, good times and bad times.

Every time I listen to Foley, I try to figure out how he gets so much mileage out of so little. His songs are far from word-heavy and most of the lyrics wouldn't translate well onto the printed page, but when you hear him sing, he tells you where he's been and what it's like to be there. Since I've been in some of those places, listening to him has as much to do with memory as it does with exploration.

The album was produced at Muscle Shoals, and though at times it reminds me of some of my favorite records produced there, at other times the production gets in the way—a little too elaborate for some songs, a little too slow for others, maybe a little too repetitious overall. Still, Foley's biggest problem with this record is going to be that it's so hard to categorize. The songs combine elements of R&B, country, and folk in such extraordinary ways that it becomes difficult to label this album as any one type of music. Except fine music, which is what it is.

I'm remembering mornings spent on floors, on beds, on couches. I'm thinking of going downstairs and meeting the neighbors. I'm about to make one of those calls that never work out—that just end up with too many different kinds of goodbyes and no hellos. I'm feeling hung over even though I didn't drink anything the night before, and I keep listening to this album over and over. **LOUIS BLACK**

VOL. 4 NO. 1 ★ SEPTEMBER 7, 1984

DAN DEL SANTO
WORLD BEAT
PLEASURE

Africa and South America dominate the world map projection printed on this record's label. The Caribbean is in there too, but North America and Europe barely poke through the margins. It's an accurate index to Dan Del Santo's aesthetic. Unlike those counterculturists who dabble in ethno-pop to offset their discomfort with current Western pop, Del Santo is a certifiable maniac for the stuff. He has sampled vast amounts of Hi-life, Soukous, Salsa, Ska, Reggae, Juju, etc., thoroughly digested all the interrelated rhythmic and melodic styles, and added it to a comprehensive knowledge of blues, country, jazz, and rock & roll. The result is what newspaper headline writers like to call a "rich potpourri" of international pop.

A typical Del Santo tune piles terse horn charts onto a dense rhythm track—dense, but accessible. There are many exciting unison passages, and the musicians trade phrases in the manner of traditional jazz groups as well. Because Del Santo's songs are relatively brief and carefully shaped, he is able to elicit crisp performances from Tomas Ramirez, Paul Ostermayer, Robert "Beto" Skiles, et al., performances blessed on the whole with a good deal more punch than those given in the context of Jazzmanian Devil or the Fairlanes. Skiles' percussive piano effects on the title track are especially exciting, and the horn players are consistently excellent. Rock Savage continues his reign as a drummer of matchless skill and flair. Del Santo himself plays a howling good guitar, as always.

For all the solid entertainment value he delivers, there is surprising divergence of opinion whenever Del Santo's name comes up in mixed company. This is due as much to the eccentric grain of Del Santo's voice as it is to strangeness of musical terrain. Gifted with an odd vocal instrument, he strives for unusual effects with it, rumbling, growling, stretching syllables in unexpected places, or crooning like some kind of atavistic Bing Crosby. As vocal styles go, it takes some getting used to, but is by no means uninteresting. Perhaps it is the didactic tone of the lyrics he's singing that tends to grate. He might consider working with other lyricists, or at least shifting his emphasis toward songs like "Love So Sweet," which works because the lyrics give Del Santo and Carmen Bradford an easy emotional framework they use to develop a relaxed, satisfying rapport.

World Beat is one step closer to the international pop synthesis Del Santo's been distilling these past few years. He has already moved beyond the point where many ethno-pluralist musicians get stuck, in that his quotations from a particular genre sound less like quotations than fully integrated facets of a coherent style. Provided the wherewithal to make more records, he should be able to take it even farther.

CHRIS WALTERS

VOL. 4 NO. 2 ★ SEPTEMBER 21, 1984

POISON 13
POISON 13
WRESTLER RECORDS

Finding their point of reference in 1960s garage rock, filtered through 1970s punk (both filtering earlier strains of American blues, rhythm and blues, and country), Poison 13 are well-versed in their musical history and very aware of their past. Theirs is a garage rock aesthetic, based on a thorough knowledge and respect for the trashy hybrids that American music has produced, as well as a love/hate relationship with the culture that produced it. They play Willie Dixon songs not like they wished they were Howlin' Wolf, but instead like they wished they were a band innocent enough to sing black blues without guilt or pretension, in short, like a 1960s garage band could. And that's where they find their niche, and a strange state of grace, 1980s sophistication being a move towards raw, earnest simplicity that acknowledges, mocks even, its own inability to find its way back home—and thereby moves ahead.

With the Big Boys currently in a funk, Poison 13 is the musical outlet for two of the chunky children, bassman Chris Gates and guitar twister Tim Kerr. Along with singer Mike Carroll, drummer Jim Kanan, axe-wielding Bill Anderson, and producer Spot, they've created the aural equivalent of a chainsaw massacre. Make that *The Texas Chainsaw Massacre,* because it has a somewhat detached (though hardly dispassionate) feel to it, like a movie, the work more of devotees of the deranged than the deranged themselves. And slow that film down to 16 frames a second, because the music isn't thrashy and superfast; it's metalloid—heavy, chunky. It doesn't shred, it gnaws.

True to their plastic-pop-culture roots in garage rock, they mix their songs with those of their mentors. "Spoonful" doesn't really need to be covered by anybody, but they do it, and not badly, with Kerr's bent-guitar sustain adding an appropriate tension to the song. Likewise, "Codeine," the Buffy St. Marie tune, is rendered with a paste-on sneer that even the Barracuda can't top. Their own songs aren't belittled in this classic company either, with their dark humor and cartoon playfulness reaching a pinnacle in "One Step Closer," a revision and upshot of "Don't Fear the Reaper." This music lets you take it or leave it each time. Poison 13 takes it: call 'em punk traditionalists and learn to live with the contradiction.

BRENT GRULKE

VOL. 4 NO. 9 ★ DECEMBER 21, 1984

POISON 13, ZEITGEIST, TRUE BELIEVERS
CONTINENTAL CLUB, DECEMBER 29

When this show was first advertised several scenemakers wrote it in as Best Local Show in the *Chronicle* Music Poll in anticipation. It was a dream line-up of three of the most exciting new bands in town. After an exhilarating set by True Believers, there followed standard brilliance from Zeitgeist, everybody's favorite band, and then capping the chordfest was the musical relative of a saloon brawl delivered with excess but without excuse by Poison 13, "the boys of boister." This is why we live in Austin, for nights like these.

True Believers feature Javier and Alejandro Escovedo, former members of West Coast pioneer punk bands the Zeros (Javier) and the Nuns (Alejandro). Alejandro was also a charter Rank and Filer. The Escovedos' true belief in the power of music was forged by a covey of older brothers that includes vintage Santanans Coke Escovedo and Pete Escovedo, who taught his daughter Sheila to thump the skins. You know Sheila Escovedo as Sheila E, and she knows True Believers as her uncles' band. Need more credentials?

Bassist Denny DeGorio backed Jorma Kaukonen for a spell and also played for the Offs, a great punk reggae band from S.F. Guitarist Jon Dee Graham's past contains the Skunks and the Lift, and on drummer Rey Washam's resume you'll find Jerryskids, Scratch Acid, and the Big Boys. Put these players together with tough songs like Alejandro's "Hard Road" and the Velvets' "Foggy Notion," and it's like unleashing a pack of hungry bull terriers in a butcher shop. They really tear the flesh off the bone. Tell you what, go and see True Believers and if you don't like them come see me and I'll refund your cover charge. Polygraph required.

More nice people who caused whitebread youngsters to behave in a way that betrays their inheritance is Zeitgeist, an outfit with personality, pop sense, girls, boys, and smarts. If it was possible to

Zeitgeist, 1985. Photograph by Andrew Long.

buy stock in musical groups, E. F. Hutton would tell you to buy Zeitgeist, NOW! Those who doubt Zeitgeist's national threat haven't seen what they've done to the poor Dream Tractor, Rain Syndicate, and the Love Parade, who were all foolish enough to let Zeitgeist open for them.

The elements of their style: John Croslin—guitarist, singer, great songwriter, who'd be even greater if there wasn't already a Lou Reed. Kim Longacre—guitarist, singer, songwriter, the natural talent responsible for more crushes than a trash compactor. Cindy—a good bass player considering she has long bangs, wears her hat cocked back, and has no last name. And, of course, there's Garrett Williams, the soul of the group on drums who's got a set of masochistic Ludwigs and knows most of the words to "Sweet Jane," which is fast becoming the "Louie, Louie" of the Mousse set.

It's enough that Zeitgeist puts the "rev" in revive with great covers like the Charlie Brown theme and a version of "Blue Eyes Crying in the Rain," in which the tongue never once comes in contact with the cheek, but it's the origs that put them a few paces ahead of the rest of the Beach-niks. "Legendary Man," "Freight Train Rain," and "Without My Sight" are so good I wondered who did them originally.

The hushed tones started during Zeitgeist's set and spread through the Continental like an oil spill. "Poison 13 has a bar tab!" Gasp! That's a nightmare of the magnitude of finding out that your pilot is Roky Erickson or that someone gave David MacDonald a Mr. Microphone for Christmas. But Poison 13 is a band that handles adversity well—especially when they're drunk. True Believers set the pace, Zeitgeist kept it bouncing, and Poison 13 made perfectly sure that God had been wakened from his nap. Now what were you saying about Raul's? **MICHAEL CORCORAN**

VOL. 4 NO. 11 ★ JANUARY 11, 1985

OMAR AND THE HOWLERS
I TOLD YOU SO
AUSTIN RECORDS

In a town full of reverent white blues purists, Kent "Omar" Dykes is truest of all to his roots. Elements of Memphis, Chicago, and other urban blues centers turn up in his sound, but unlike his other Austin peers, his sound owes more to the Mississippi Delta than the city, a crude, over-amped roar that calls forth images of ancient 1940s and 1950s R&B, fresh from the country, scared and defiant.

Following personnel changes since the release of 1980's *Big Leg Beat*, the band's sound has become even more lean and unpolished: no-frills drumming; inventive but uncluttering bass playing; and terse, economical guitar riffs and leads. As on the debut though, the instrument of distinction is Omar's gruff, no-nonsense voice, closer to Howlin' Wolf than anyone this side of Captain Beefheart. Even when the lyrics are trite and cliched, Omar's vocals demand that you take them seriously.

Anytime you put a bar band on vinyl you lose much of the energy, spontaneity, and spirit that they have live, and this is one band where that loss is a substantial one. Fortunately the recording was obviously done mostly live in the studio with only vocals overdubbed, and the result is a clean, well-recorded testament to their onstage onslaught. At times it's a bit sterile, but barring a live recording, it's probably the best one could hope for. The songs, all originals, are uniformly solid, with the last three cuts of the second side, "Ice Cold Woman," a stormy shuffle, "I'm Wise to You Baby," a Chuck Berryan rocker, and "East Side Blues," an Albert King/Stevie Ray Vaughan–styled slow blues that features some of Omar's most inspired guitar work, being standouts. **BRENT GRULKE**

VOL. 4 NO. 10 ★ JANUARY 11, 1985

BUTTHOLE SURFERS
PSYCHIC . . . POWERLESS . . . ANOTHER MAN'S SAC
TOUCH AND GO

I was going to use this space to review the new Swans LP when I received a rather sobering letter that caused me to rethink my role as a critic. Since I've always felt that the exchange of conflicting ideas is what makes rock journalism most exciting, I've decided to forgo reviewing a record and publish the response I got from one of Austin's junior high school librarians regarding some recordings I sent her for the school. Her name has been withheld for what should be obvious reasons. **BRENT GRULKE**

Dear Mr. Grulke,

I have always assumed that, as a respected critic for what you call "an arts and entertainment publication," you have had only the best of intentions by mailing me copies of records by some of (your words) Austin's premier recording artists. However, after previewing the latest, one by the (expletive deleted) Surfers, I am no longer certain that this is the case. I am not a prude, sir, but this recording is blatantly obscene and has, to the best of my knowledge, no redeeming social value. I understand the necessity of young people being exposed to varying points of view, and I also am aware that sometimes these views will not be the same as mine, but tell me, what possible good can a lyric like: "Pass me some of that dumbass (their word, here only as example) over there, hey boy, I tell you"—followed by grotesque laughing, belching, spitting and retching—do anyone, particularly an impressionable seventh grader? I only wished that I had paid attention to the earlier records you sent me, two apparently by these same anal retentive degenerates, especially since you tell me that this is their best record to date. What, pray tell, could be their worst? Fortunately those records were quickly removed from circulation when a teacher heard them and told me that they had apparently been damaged by a faulty stylus.

If you think that sentiments like "negro observers are counting heads in single bars" are funny, I'd like you to speak to some of my negro friends—there are limits in this world, and this "musical" group surpasses all of them. Humor is one thing, Mr. Grulke, racism is quite another. If you feel it necessary to send me any more records, please be certain that they are in good taste. If it is true, as you say, that all the critics enjoy this band, I can only wonder about the current state of criticism in this country. I will return your record as soon as I find out what my daughter did with it. And, no, I don't think I will be able to attend your staff party.

Sincerely,
(name withheld)

VOL. 4 NO. 11 ★ JANUARY 25, 1985

B.W. STEVENSON
CACTUS CAFE, DECEMBER 14

There are undoubtedly a fair number of Austin music aficionados from the early 1970s who have wondered these past years whatever became of singer/song-writer/guitar picker B.W. Stevenson, the artist cited in Jan Reid's *The Improbable Rise of Redneck Rock* as the Most Likely of all his mid-1970s progressive country peers to succeed big time in the music biz. As a recent appearance revealed, there's good news and then there's good news. The good news is that B.W. is back actively performing in Texas and record-ing an album in L.A.; the good news is that the lengthy period of exile has not diminished his formidable vocal prowess nor diluted the subtle magnetic grip of his lovelorn, lovebred lyrics.

B.W. possesses a voice that can float like a feather, howl like a blue norther, lull you gently to sleep, or blast you out of your chair. It's a voice that once heard is not easily forgotten or confused with another, achieving in its uppermost falsetto regions a soul-baring intensity aptly counterpointed by a rolling, droning, six-string chordscape of simple yet support-ive figures on old hits like "Say What I Feel," "Peaceful, Easy Feeling," "Shambala," and "My Maria," as well as newer material destined for his upcoming LP. Judging from the enraptured expressions and enthusiastic response of the 100-plus audience members, it is a voice that still finds plenty of kindred echoes wher-ever it travels. **L. E. MCCULLOUGH**

VOL. 4 NO. 12 ★ FEBRUARY 8, 1985

True Believers. Photograph by Martha Grenon.

Obviously True Believers

VOL. 4 NO. 14 ★ APRIL 5, 1985

CHRIS WALTERS

We live in a two-room flat
and barely make the rent
Before the checks are cashed,
the money is all spent
Some folks are born to walk,
while others get to ride
It sure looks easier on life's other side
I just want to run with the rebel kind

BUCK CHERRY (as sung by the True Believers)

THE TRUE BELIEVERS ARE BACK from two-and-a-half weeks in the west. Everyone involved describes as a dream tour: great moments piling up like the loaves and the fishes, the crowds big and uproariously enthusiastic, the members of Los Lobos, for whom they were opening, treating them like favored kid brothers, and the cognoscenti of Los Angeles agog ("Sometimes they sound like one big guitar," wrote Don Waller of the *L.A. Times*). Understandably, they're walking on air.

Since a round of superlatives, however justified, would strain the credulity of readers who haven't heard the True Believers tear into "The Rebel Kind," "All Mixed Up Again," "Home," or "Hard Road," guitars cracking like steel whips, here's a useful analogy: the True Believers are a real-life version of *The Seven Samurai*. If the notion seems nutty, recall how Kurosawa's warriors, widely disparate in temperament and approach, complemented each other's strengths and cancelled out each other's weaknesses. It was more than merely Toshiro Mifune looning it up. Sagacity,

stoicism, practicality, and naive enthusiasm were also personified, creating a balance at first tenuous, and finally awesome, as the force of personality and experience came to bear on a desperate situation.

A tour through the individual biographies of the True Believers would yield many good stories, mainly having to do with the events of Year Zero (1977) and its aftermath.

But rock & roll is not war. Years practicing and playing are compressed into an hour or two of uncomplicated excitement. That's what happens on a tape that was made of the March 11 show in Vancouver, as the band charges up against their limits so hard they seem to be playing the electricity culminating in the last climax of *Hard Road*.

As the rushing chords cool off just slightly and Alejandro Escovedo, sounding as though he's just seen a pack of wolves at the front door, sings "The load is heavy, times are tough, I've seen plenty, that don't have enough," then all five of them come down as hard as they can on a riff that describes every vicious cycle the world has to offer. Every time I've seen them recently, they grin wildly at this moment; maybe it's because they know they're countering the world's offer with the best parts of themselves.

A TOUR THROUGH the individual biographies of the True Believers would yield many good stories, mainly having to do with the events of Year Zero (1977) and its aftermath, as all of them cut their teeth in bands designated as punk. Javier Escovedo (Alejandro's younger brother) took his inspiration from Johnny Thunders' playing with the New York Dolls, and went on to play with the Mainstreet Brats and the Zeros.

Alejandro didn't pick up an instrument until he was 23 or so, when he joined the Nuns in San Francisco; he went to the Judy Nylon Band and Rank and File, the latter a band he started.

Bassist Denny DeGorio played with the Offs, another of that city's punk groups, and he put in time with Jorma Kaukonen, weird former guitarist with the Jefferson Airplane. Jon Dee Graham played with Moon in Eagle Pass, where he was raised, and the Whippets, the Skunks, the Gators, Five-Spot, and the Lift in Austin, first as a moonlighting UT student, later as a fulltime musician. Rey Washam had drummed all over the hardcore map: Jerryskids, the Big Boys, and Scratch Acid, the latter still an active project for him (he hasn't quit the Big Boys either).

Those credits take in about every hyphenated subset of post-punk music, from neo-country to art-punk to power-pop. This tour of the trends tells you a lot about what the True Believers have learned and what they are distilling. But it doesn't tell much about them that really counts. It doesn't give away the secret of Alejandro Escovedo's knack for terse, vivid lyrics; it doesn't tell how Washam manages to beat hell out of his drums and still keep awesome time, or how DeGorio plays bass like a herd of elephants dancing on air. It doesn't explain Javier Escovedo's talent for tuneful pop bashing, or the guitar riffs and songwriting craft that apparently flow through Jon Dee Graham's veins instead of blood. All of that cannot be explained and wouldn't be such an earthly delight if it were.

As for the history of the band per se, there isn't all that much to tell. After Alejandro left the ranks of Rank and File, he called up his brother Javier in Los Angeles. Javier had been largely inactive since the breakup of the Zeros and was ready for action. With Keith Carnes playing drums, the True Believers debuted with Los Lobos at Club Foot and worked all over the city, playing lofts, parties, and beer joints. A group of intensely loyal fans coalesced within a few months.

Though a West Coast tour went well enough, recording sessions with David Kahne (producer of the first Rank and File album) proved abortive. Carnes left under circumstances described as more or less amicable, though obviously painful for all. Rey Washam's drumming provided an immediate lift, and with the recruiting of Jon Dee Graham, the stakes were raised to dizzying heights. Most people who follow Austin music know Graham as the best hard rock guitarist in town; a much smaller number were aware that he wrote many of his various bands' best songs; and almost nobody knew he has a decent singing voice that has the possibility of becoming terrific. Since joining the Believers, he's been learning lap steel guitar and using it on two songs onstage. He plays piano and wants to work that into the band as well. But most important, his songwriting matches Escovedo's for emotional and melodic power and deals the band a fabulous wild card.

In sum, the True Believers can hold their own with any young band in America right now and, as Yeats would have it, the best is yet to be. As good samurai, they need each other, and we need them. Want them, too. ◀

ZEITGEIST
TRANSLATE SLOWLY
DB RECORDS

The way anyone that's heard Zeitgeist has come to know them is as a garage band. A melodic, well-rehearsed, dynamic, professional garage band, but a garage band nonetheless. On this LP they've gone for a fully produced, carefully arranged sound that highlights the nuances and subtlety of their sound. Instead of a chiming cataclysmic roar, where the parts only serve to create the whole, they've tailored a rich tapestry of interwoven parts.

It isn't a flawless job; I detect a few flubbed notes here and there, I think that enclosing a lyric sheet was a mistake (discourages translating slowly), and a couple of the tunes just don't kick the way I imagine they might, but all told I still can't think of a more impressive debut LP by a local band in the last several years.

You've already heard too much about the thoughtful southern pop music dominating college radio now, mostly because of R.E.M.'s success. But their sound is definitely more southwest than south, and they're less self-conscious than most of their literate, college educated peers, largely due to the plaintive, folksy vocal style of Kim Longacre and lyrics that generally tend to stay away from the pained and poetic mode that so many intelligent young songwriters fall into in the belief that it imbues their work with greater seriousness.

One of the best songs on the record (along with "Legendary Man," the re-mixed "Freight Train Rain," "Sound and the Fury," and "Without My Sight") is called "Things Don't Change." That is something of a lie, particularly in Zeitgeist's case. They change as fast as the Texas weather. Every time I think I've got a bead on who and what they are, they move again, just like magicians. **BRENT GRULKE**

VOL. 4 NO. 20 ★ MAY 31, 1985

DOCTORS' MOB
HEADACHE MACHINE
WRESTLER RECORDS

Back just a couple of years ago it was considered the worst sort of faux pas to admit to enjoying pop music. It might have been okay to like "pure pop" or "power pop"—Nick Lowe, Buzzcocks, Shoes, dBs, and the like—but only because their lyrics frequently presented them as intelligent ironists who knew the joke their music was. Pop that was actually popular was supposed to have been forever defiled by punk, music that meant to destroy rock and its history.

As we all know, punk choked on its own contradictions and fragmented into ever smaller subgenres. Any ideals that the initial thrust may have carried were quickly subsumed by a murky veil of defeat and nihilism, and the ability to directly influence the mainstream culture while standing apart from it was lost. Punk's political power was gone.

Doctors' Mob fits well into this context. The group sprung from the ashes of punk (in their original incarnation they were a mod band) with one ear to the street and one to the radio. A year ago it was hard to tell what the Doctors' Mob was trying to do; they were unfocused, noisy, and more often than not, drunk. They recorded tracks with Patrick Keel that never saw release, and their sound changed as often as a debutante's clothing. Clubowners weren't happy with their loud stage volume and penchant for unprofessional sets, as likely to consist of Seventies arena rock standards as their own material. It seemed more than likely that the band would never be known outside of Austin.

Still, their following steadily grew, particularly after the Replacements gained recognition (not that the Mob aped the Minneapolis guys, just that now their sort of punk-pop music had a place). Even when loud, drunk, and sloppy, no, especially when loud, drunk, and sloppy, their attitude saved the

43

show. Self-effacing and funny, the Mob knew how to charm a crowd. And they kept playing wherever and whenever they could. Somehow the sound came into focus and the apparent madness behind their method started to make sense. It was a smokescreen. Lead singer, songwriter, and rhythm guitarist Steve Collier was burying lovelorn sentiment, myths, and dreams beneath walls of guitar, melodic hooks, alcohol, and humor, too wordly wise to expose himself clearly, but too knowing not to try.

So finally we get an LP from them, and guess what? No covers. No junk. And quite a few nods to classic pop formula: love songs, pretty melodies, anthemic lyrics, hooks. The noisy, abrasive side doesn't get subverted either, largely due to Chris Gates' production, with the guitars way up in the mix and the vocals mashed into it. It's flat but well-recorded, John Viehweg's studio-honed engineer's ear making certain the sounds go on the tape right and Gates making sure it doesn't get antiseptically clean. The result is the proper presentation for a band that straddles the line between noise and melody, inspiration and craft. Doctors' Mob could have gone the straight pop route (where are those Keel tapes anyway?) or they could have gone the straight punk route (except listen to "Hangers On"), but instead they're neither and both. One of the best cuts on the record (along with a gorgeous ballad called "The Difference") is called "Why Should You Care Now?" The song and the band answer the question. **BRENT GRULKE**

VOL. 4 NO. 24 ★ JULY 26, 1985

Don't You Start Me Talking
The Cutting Edge

VOL. 5 NO. 1 ★ SEPTEMBER 6, 1985

MICHAEL CORCORAN

LOCAL PROPERTY VALUES have not noticeably risen since the Austin segment of *The Cutting Edge* finally aired on MTV Aug. 25. The show was great fun to watch, especially the segments on show-stealer Daniel Johnston, Toshio Hirano, Dino Lee, and Timbuk 3, and Poison 13's ten seconds, but I don't think too many outside our small but growing circle will be coaxed into a condition resembling elation over our consensus weak vocals, strong hairstyles, and come-as-you-are wardrobing. The "New Sincerity" bands—True Believers, Wild Seeds, Dharma Bums, Zeitgeist, and Doctors' Mob—have got the best scene in town but they failed to project why to the rest of the country. They're all better bands than what *The Cutting Edge* eye caught, as is Glass Eye. Biscuit's poetry was cute and well-delivered, but Austin without poetry is like a day without sunstroke, and three selections from the Bisk were a tad much. Also, the Joe "King" Carrasco acoustic thing at Red River Motors deserved more barbaric attention in the editing room. And didn't the band introductions with the hand-held camera get old after about the third act? Let us be thankful for the experience this whole *Cutting Edge* business brought to our hip little cul-de-sac and let us feel relief that we can all go back to acting somewhat normal again. "Somewhat" being the key word. ◀

DANIEL JOHNSTON

VOL. 5 NO. 3 ★ OCTOBER 4, 1985

LOUIS BLACK

THE LAST BAND finished playing about fifteen minutes ago, and Glass Eye should be up soon. It's break time at the Beach, which all too frequently betrays its convenience store origins; the noise inside has reached saturation level, and though most everyone is outside enjoying some fresh air and pleasant scene making, it's still more than crowded. I'm leaned against the wall right by the corridor to the bathrooms, listening to the hubbub—watching the swirl, waiting. Standing around the room are an impressive number of local musicians and writers, also waiting.

Without fanfare or introduction, a slight, obviously nervous singer holding an acoustic guitar steps up to the mike and starts playing and singing. His playing is awkward, his singing shaky. The musicians and writers are leaned forward. This is who they've been waiting for. At first the talk seems to continue unabated, this singer swimming against a hard upstream current, a voice packed with passions and innocence near-quavering:

> Down from the depths of nowhere
> You know you'll hear them coming
> And no one can stop them
> The Marching Guitars.

The guitar-playing inexperienced but deliberate, the guitar used for emphasis, a chord struck, a pause, another chord. The talk starts fading, dies down to just the all-the-time scene-makers and romantic flirters around the bar who would talk through a Bob Dylan/

Elvis Costello duet. Most of the club is poised, watching, captivated; someone asks "Who is this?" They're shushed. Some aren't sure if this is a joke or not.

> And no one knows who they are
> They come from afar
> They do what they have to do
> And turn into big stars/And no one can stop them
> The Marching Guitars.

A song haunted by itself. Nightmare into pop observation, abstract into cultural admonishment. The singer finishes his song, the room bursts into applause.

The performer seems both pleased and terrified, as though this, his Austin performance debut and its warmly enthusiastic reception, is a moment he has always dreamed about, clearly imagined, but is in no way ready to deal with. He does two more songs and heads off stage to a corner booth where he holes up, waiting for things to calm down enough, the crowd to lose themselves in Glass Eye, so that he can safely make a break. Daniel Johnston, former carny worker, onetime art student, would-be comic artist, transplanted West Virginian, and extraordinary songwriter, has arrived.

Since that debut a few months back, Johnston has played his trademark short two or three song sets before any number of Glass Eye gigs, opening for a variety of other bands, at Woodshock and at *The Cutting Edge* taping where as a last minute guest he captivated the audience and ended up being featured prominently in the finished show. The recent *Rolling Stone* piece on Austin music referred to the "frayed nerve acoustic songs of Daniel Johnston." And bands have started covering his material, lots of them.

And as Johnston has performed more, the controversy has begun to rage. This awkward innocent whose songs drip an uncanny spiritualism, a naive

cynicism, an inability to distinguish between despair and hope, seeing in each the other. Powerful incantations of a forever-pilgrim, a stranger in many strange lands whose access to community is through the language of rock. A songwriter and performer whose most public voice speaks the yearnings, dreams, and experience of a terrible private heart through a vocabulary learned from recordings and radio. A writer both hopelessly original and obviously not mature, shoving cliches between phrases stolen from the most personal of visions.

Some find him an exciting, refreshingly creative talent. Others can't believe this, think his fans deranged or determinedly perverse. This emperor not only has no clothes on but barely understands the concept of wardrobe. Small debates range. Corcoran tells me of sitting at a table with several women who think Johnston's fans are cruelly leading him on, consciously declaring the freak as art, exploiting a naive talent to create a short entertainment for jaded sensibilities.

Right. And bands keep covering his material. More and more people go see him live. Everyone argues about him. I find myself playing his three tapes (*Yip! Jump Music*; *Hi, How Are You*; *Retired Boxer*) over and over. Find myself haunted by one of his public performances, left cold by another. Fascinated. To me there is little question about his talent. In fact, almost none at all.

> When I was out in San Marcos
> A year ago today
> They probably would have put me in a Home
> But I threw all my belongings
> Into a garbage bag
> And out into the wilderness I did roam.

I talk to Daniel about Daniel. Born in Sacramento in 1961, he and his family (youngest of five children)

A song haunted by itself. Nightmare into pop observation, abstract into cultural admonishment.

soon ended up living in New Cumberland, West Virginia. Here his father, a member of the famed Flying Tigers during World War II, an engineer who once worked on Minutemen missiles, has a job with Quaker State Oil.

"It was really wild in West Virginia because all we had was records." Records and radios. Songs to be listened to, again and again. "When I was 19, I wanted to be the Beatles, was disappointed when I found out I couldn't sing." But there he was and anyway he tried. Johnston and his friends listened to lots of music; when asked to name influences he poured out names: Lennon, Dylan, "Yoko Ono as much an influence as John Lennon," Neil Young, David Bromberg, Sex Pistols. But then he stops, thinks, and answers about influences, "Beatles, just the Beatles, you know the Beatles, Beatles, Beatles, yes the Beatles."

After high school he went to a branch of Kent State near his family's home. Lasted two-and-a-half years in the art program and loved it. In fact moved to Texas on the advice of a guy from Marvel Comics, moved here because he wanted to be an artist— wanted to be an artist and anyway, in 1983 there weren't any jobs to be found in West Virginia.

First he went to Houston, lived with his brother, and worked at Astroworld. Then to San Marcos, where he joined the carnival. Stayed with it for five-six months, met Arnie the Carny who supplied him with the song title "I'll Do Anything But Breakdance for Ya Darling." Made corn dogs and during "the wildest summer of my

Daniel Johnston clocks in at McDonald's, 1989.
Photograph by David Fox.

47

life" traveled through Colorado, Wyoming, New Mexico, Arizona. It was a great experience: "Danger and wild times, I really enjoyed myself . . . the Carnival really got me writing again." And it ended in Austin, which was where he had wanted to go all along.

> Listen folks I gotta tell you now
> I've been singing the blues and walking the cow.

In Austin, Johnston found work at a fast food restaurant and began to hand out tapes to everyone he met. Everyone, everywhere. Handed out tapes and wrote songs. Handed out tapes that many listened to and wanted to hear more. Which is why the audience was waiting that first night at the Beach.

Handed out tapes to musicians and soon groups were covering his songs. Doctors' Mob, Glass Eye, the Rhythm Rats, Black Spring, and so on. Suddenly,

though he protests that he hasn't really paid dues, that maybe he's not ready, Daniel Johnston's becoming a star on the scene.

Johnston is playing around a lot these days, has a song on *The Cutting Edge* show, bootleg tapes of which are probably the number one video item in town these days, and has three cassette tapes out. If you run into him he'll give you one if he has any with him. Otherwise, *Retired Boxer* is available at Record Exchange, Waterloo, and Inner Sanctum now, and *Hi, How Are You* should be soon.

> Now here I am
> And here I stand
> With a Sweet Angel
> Holding my hand
> I live my broken dreams. ◄

DANIEL JOHNSTON
Hi, How Are You

Daniel Johnston, what is he?

Is he a despoiled tooth fairy, cast out of Mount Olympus by checkered demons? A stone naif, touched by God? *Hi, How Are You* is on sale at local record shops. It's short, and it sounds like it was recorded in somebody's living room on a ghetto-blaster. (It was.) It's intense, hilarious, embarrassing. There are at least two classic tunes on it: "Walking the Cow" and "Desperate Man Blues," the latter an amazing piece of musical schizophrenia. Using found music, in this case a schlocky big-band "jazz" recording by Johnny Dankworth, Johnston has produced a truly harrowing blues, funny and existential at the same time. But maybe it's not right to read too much into this music. Daniel Johnston is a normal guy, troubled by what he sees around him, and he writes songs about it. It's as simple as that. Or is it? Johnston's art is simple, but not easy. I don't think he's being consciously weird, either. Some say he isn't playing with a full deck. I think he just assigns different values to the cards. RICHARD DORSETT

VOL. 5 NO. 8 ★ DECEMBER 13, 1985

Artist Guy Juke and Daniel Johnston at *The Chronicle*, 1986. Photograph by Martha Grenon.

NOT DANIEL JOHNSTON
How, Hi Are You:
The Unfurnished Album

KRIPPLED KOW

This is a great tape. The guy who did it is a brilliant satirist. I listened to it about fifteen times. Some of the songs on it are better than my own. I'm going to try and get this guy a gig and suggest that he bill his band as "Back by Popular Demand." Then the bill would read: "Not Daniel Johnston, Back by Popular Demand." This is a thoroughly entertaining tape. Actually it's a bit spooky for me to listen to it. But it's a great tape. You've got to listen to it. It's really funny.

DANIEL JOHNSTON

ED. NOTE: This parody tape of Johnston features such songs as "Milking The Dog," "Lipless Love," "I Wanna Be Psychedelic," "She Stopped in the Middle of the Highway," "Two Jennifers," "Bob Dylan," and "Nervous Schizoid Love Breakdown In Hell."

VOL. 5 NO. 18 ★ MAY 9, 1986

I Walked with a Zombie: Roky Erickson and R.E.M.'s Peter Buck, 1985. Photograph by David Fox.

"

I SCARE EVERYBODY BECAUSE I'M SO HORRIFYING, Y'KNOW? I LIKE GORE ALL THE TIME. I CAN STAND DEATH OR KILLING ALL THE TIME, TOO.

ROKY ERICKSON

Fables of the Undead Roky Erickson Meets R.E.M.

VOL. 5 NO. 3 ★ OCTOBER 4, 1985

THOMAS ANDERSON

PETER BUCK IS ONE COOL GUY. Not only is he the guitarist for R.E.M., one of the coolest bands in the world these days, he's also one of the friendliest, most unaffected people I've come across in the music world. The legendary Roky Erickson is another. So upon finding out that Peter is an ardent admirer of Roky's work, your reporter brought Roky and his mom Evelyn out to the City Coliseum to meet him when R.E.M. were in town. What was originally intended as a brief chat stretched into a fascinating afternoon-long affair, covering topics ranging from cannibalism to fraternity parties, from Ivan Pavlov to Doug Sahm. The first half of the interview takes place on one of R.E.M.'s tour buses parked inside the Coliseum while the band waited to begin their sound check. The rest of it out on U.S. 290, heading south, for dinner in Oak Hill (Roky's idea).

ON THE BUS

AUSTIN CHRONICLE: *I know you like horror movies a lot.*

ROKY ERICKSON: Yeah, *Friday the 13th*; I like *Halloween* a lot, "the night he came home." I like the way it ends; it was the boogie-man after all. The story says Jason went swimming one night, late one night about midnight, and the camp counselors heard him and they were playin' cards or relaxin', y'know, watching TV or playin' guitar; so they heard him out there screamin' and drownin' and they just sat there and kept talkin'; they could've gone out and saved his life; he could've been alive today.

PETER BUCK: Do you ever watch old horror movies that are less splatter movies but are still real scary, like *Psycho*?

RE: Yeah. Oh yeah. Now I love *Psycho*. *Psycho* is real good.

PB: I think it's great that they never show anything really violent, but it's the scariest movie ever made.

RE: Yeah, see, Alfred Hitchcock is real scary because sometimes he'll walk on the set, y'know? You'll just see him walk by, and he's real scary like that.

PB: Is "The Creature with the Atom Brain" a real movie?

RE: Oh yeah, it's real scary.

PB: What's the dialogue in that song? I can never figure it out.

RE: Well he says, "I told you I'd come back. You sent me away to prison many years ago. When I was in prison I swore I'd come back. And now I have come back. I told you I'd come back. I'm from Buchanan. Remember Buchanan? I don't look like him, but I am him. Don't you recognize the voice, Jim? I promised to see you die. And I will."

PB: Those last few lines are the only ones I could figure out. Is that you doing that or is that from the movie?

RE: Yeah, that's me doing it, but the movie is really scary. You sit down in one of those films all alone and you say, "Well, here I am. In about ten minutes it's gonna get so scary, I mean that overpowering darkness is gonna be everywhere . . ."

ROKY'S MOM: Tell him about the *Gore Gazette.*

RE: Oh yeah, the *Gore Gazette*'s a neat little thing. That's Rick Barrett, Rick Sloane or Rick Barrett, anyway he's from New York and he sends me the *Gore Gazette*, and he's got all the goriest films in it.

THOMAS ANDERSON: Was "Two-Headed Dog" inspired by any movie in particular?

RE: Y'know, I'm a Communist, and Pavlov is this scientist in Russia, and he made this two-headed dog. He did experiments. He just put a head on another dog to see if it'd live. Some kind of Russian experiment. But I don't think he really did that. Russians are just that way, y'know?

(Michael Stipe enters)

TA: We're talking about horror movies; you want to get in on this?

MICHAEL STIPE: I'm not real up to date on horror movies. I went to see *Night of the Living Dead* once at a drive-in with a bunch of friends of mine and I was real excited by it because it was a real old print of the movie, and all the white was fading into the black, and all the black was fading into the white. And I was real excited by this and so I was telling all my friends, and I was pointing out these things to them, and they were all agreeing with me and really getting into it, "Yes! Yes! I can see that!" Then I found out the next day that they were all out of their minds on drugs.

RE: Who was this?

MS: Just some friends. Just some people I used to hang out with.

RE: Watchin' horror movies.

MS: Yeah, and I was makin' all of these really great observations, and they were agreeing with me for the first time ever. It was kind of depressing the next morning . . .

RE: You're the singer, right?

MS: Yeah.

RE: Maybe you can help me with my throat problems.

MS: You have throat problems?

RE: Yeah, I have these things, adenoids or something.

MS: I eat really good. I don't know how much that helps because I smoke a pack a day. I've never lost my voice except once. I lose it in my dreams, but I've been doing this since I was 3 years old.

RE: Smoking since you were three?

MS: No, just losing my voice in my dreams. You know, when you're in your dreams and a big hairy monster comes and you try to scream and nobody can hear you *(gasps)*, like that.

RE: "In space, no one can hear you scream."

MS: That's right. The sound of one tree clapping into a forest, or something . . .

(Michael Stipe exits)

TA: Do you think you scare people?

RE: Oh yeah, for sure. I scare everybody because I'm so horrifying, y'know? I like gore all the time. I can stand death or killing all the time, too.

(somewhere on 290 South)

PB: There was a real marked change when you went out on your own (from the Elevators), you went straight into horror. Were you interested in that kind of stuff when you were in the Elevators?

RE: In the Elevators I was a lot into horror but, y'know, like Tommy Hall, when he'll have a kilo of weed sittin' out in the garage . . . So when they busted us, with that big mouth of his, it was a bad scene. There's no way the police could be nice to us, not with his talkin' all the time. Y'know, because they thought some guy was into stills and everything, not really drugs.

TA: What's your book [*Openers*] like? I haven't had a chance to look through it.

RE: It's a book of religious poems and everything. I wish you all could see *The Hearse*; we're gonna have to get that movie and watch it. It's been out a while, but it's a real scary one. Those films, y'know, they really touch you. You really wouldn't want to miss 'em.

MOM: Roky had another arrest in '68. They put him in a mental hospital.

PB: So how did you finally get out of there?

MOM: His brother had some good lawyers.

RE: Yeah, it's real sad, but then it isn't sad.

MOM: The whole place was murderers.

TA: How long were you in there?

MOM: Three years.

RE: Probably about that long.

MOM: That's when he wrote this book. So something good came out of the ashes.

PB: Did you do a lot of writing when you were in there?

RE: I did a whole lot of writing there. I've got all that stuff back at the house.

PB: When you got out, didn't you start working with Doug Sahm?

RE: I guess in a way, I did this one called "Two-Headed Dog" and "Starry Eyes."

PB: I've got that, that's great! I've got a live record of yours; it's a bootleg I think. And you tell a lot of these ghost stories between songs.

RE: Which one is that? A live bootleg, huh?

PB: Yeah, it's called . . . it's got white vinyl and a real crazy colored cover. I can't remember what it's called.

RE: It's something like *Weird Tales*.

PB: Yeah, *Weird Tales*, that's it! You seem like a really friendly person. It's kind of surprising you're into such scary stuff.

RE: Well thank you. Yeah, some of those ghost stories I read are real good. ◀

BUTTHOLE SURFERS

RITZ THEATRE, NOVEMBER 14

~~Dear Mr. President,~~
~~Dear Congressman,~~
Dear Mom . . .

STUART GILBERT

VOL. 7 NO. 6 ★ NOVEMBER 27, 1987

BUTTHOLE SURFERS

RITZ THEATRE, APRIL 28

. . . But even though I haven't actually visited the abyss, I've definitely been out playing in the footholes.
   Love, Junior

STUART GILBERT

VOL. 7 NO. 18 ★ MAY 6, 1988

Butthole Surfers headline Woodshock, July 1986.
Photograph by Jerry Milton.

BUTTHOLE SURFERS, CARGO CULT

FIFTH STREET THEATRE, SEPTEMBER 20

The throng, which surprisingly wasn't the usual mass of jaded sophisticates and scene burnouts, was young, refreshingly ill-mannered, and very short. Magenta mohawks abounded on the sidewalk outside the club, as punks and their elders mixed in cheery tribal communion. Inside, the view through the plate glass windows was great. You could sit at the bar, have a smoke, and watch the action as startled passersby warily crossed the pavement on their way to Sixth Street and beyond.

Cargo Cult came on, and they were a solid, bopping gas from the first song to the last, a breakneck, heart-bursting rendition of Freddie King's "Goin' Down." Mr. Biscuit, clad in white Man-From-Glad rags with bologna sandwiches taped to his ample frame, is obviously the star of this band. The other members seemed a bit too serious, but they turned in a tasty set. My only problem with Cargo Cult is their lack of more good original tunes; the cover songs they played were more memorable than their own. Still, they haven't been around that long and given time they could be special.

It had been nine months since the Butthole Surfers last played here, and well over a year since I had seen them. The second they slammed into their first number I realized just how much I had missed them. The singer, dressed and cross-dressed in various outfits, had what looked like yellow trade beads braided into his long, stringy hair, which only once in the entire set was pulled back out of his face. He didn't look human. The rest of the band was like a nightmare straight out of Krafft-Ebing.

With their two drummers flailing away like dervishes and the guitarist (also wearing a dress) pulling unbelievable sounds out of the ether, the Surfers worked their way through most of the songs from their three records, plus some new ones. They turned in amazing cover versions of the Beatles' "Come Together" and Donovan's "Hurdy Gurdy Man." With the monolithic sound they achieved, I was reminded of the John Coltrane Quartet of the early 1960s. They've stretched the boundaries so far you really can't call it rock & roll anymore. **RICHARD DORSETT**

VOL. 5 NO.3 ★ OCTOBER 4, 1985

CHARLIE SEXTON
PICTURES FOR PLEASURE
MCA

Charlie Sexton is going to be bigger than Corey Hart and John Parr put together. This is not a compliment.

Longtime Austinites will remember Sexton as Joe Ely's wunderkind protege, the kid called "Little Charlie" who was playing top-notch blues, rock, and rockabilly on some of Austin's best stages at an age when most of his contemporaries were in elementary school. Even before Charlie ceased being little and began fronting his own bands, it became obvious that he was going places: he had the sound, the look, and the talent, talent nurtured for most of his life.

Well, he went places all right—L.A., where, after a team-up with Billy Idol's producer and a reported $400,000 worth of overproduction by eight engineers, he has emerged with an album virtually indistinguishable from the pack of interchangeable "artists" cluttering up FM radio and MTV. Of course, Sexton will now be cluttering 'em up too; he'll have hits, become famous, get rich, be on the cover of *Tiger Beat*, and play the Erwin Center. Goody for him; poverty's "out" nowadays. Besides, maybe all the time he was playing those blazing blues riffs and gritty rockabilly runs he was really yearning to be Aldo Nova.

All this isn't to imply that the album doesn't sound good. The sound is great, so clean you could sterilize surgical instruments in it. It also has a big, E Street fullness to it that'll have fans boogieing politely in their seats all the way from the Garden to the Forum. All the cliches are in exactly the right places that Dr. Pavlov calculated will have the maximum punch with all the targeted demographic groups.

Yep, the record has almost everything, and it's nit-picky to quibble about the few things it doesn't have, but I can't help but miss such things as "heart" and "soul." Sexton knows about these things, or he never would have been able to play the way he did for so many years; even producer Keith Forsey knows something about them, having done some gripping work with Idol and Donna Summer. So why'd he leave them out on this record? And where's the guitar, Keith? Not much lead here, and what there is tends to be buried among the rhythm tracks and drum machines.

The line "Charlie Sexton sold out" isn't valid criticism because we don't know what's going on in his head. Maybe he always wanted to be an MTV-clone hitmaker, in which case he never had much to sell in the first place. Maybe he got caught in the same kind of trap John Mellencamp was in ten years ago, when he looked up and found that his record company was calling him "Johnny Cougar" and dressing him like the Fonz.

So maybe it's not Big Charlie's fault. Maybe it's even part of a canny plot on his part to get all America listening to him and then move on to making music that's a bit more original and a bit more substantial than this. For the time being, we're left with this album, the latest sad example of the more-is-better school of record-making or, more precisely, the more-expensive-is-better school, which seems to believe that zillions of dollars' worth of 64-track excess can cover up a basic paucity of ideas in the music and passion in the performance. Considering that Roky Erickson's "Don't Slander Me," a single with far more primordial rock & roll power than Sexton's entire album, was recorded for $700 makes the rumored expenditure of nearly half-a-million on this mess all the more inexcusable.

But then, there's almost never an excuse for spending that kind of money on an album—unless it is approached as a major investment. (Background vocals here are credited to "Merchant Bankers"—honest!) In order for the money to be recovered, Sexton must become a major star. That doesn't leave much room for taking chances. And the kind of money that could give a dozen groups a chance at developing an audience is all bet on one horse that must come in. It's a shame.

But, hell, do your part. Buy the Charlie Sexton album out of Austin patriotism (you don't have to listen to it). Help MCA get over their cold sweat as they wait out the first sales reports. Then hope that for the next album they'll give him $10,000 and Dave Edmunds, and then maybe we'll get an album worth playing more than once. **JEFF WHITTINGTON**

VOL. 5 NO. 8 ★ DECEMBER 13, 1985

Rolling With the T-Bird Rhythm

VOL. 5 NO. 13 ★ FEBRUARY 28, 1986

CHRIS WALTERS

THE NAME FITS. It suggests a mingling of the glamorous and the tacky, a smooth seduction cloaked in the garb of an outrageous come-on. It's a double entendre implying sleek automobiles useful for impressing young girls as a preamble to stealing their virtue and horrible wine of the sort a man might drink during the night following the day when his wealthy fiancé fails to show up for the wedding. And, as countless pundits enthralled by their ability to see the obvious have pointed out, the Fabulous Thunderbirds play out the metaphor to near perfection.

At this late date in our wild century, a vehicle powered by internal combustion is an ordinary thing. So is a blues band. A blues change is a blues change. There are a finite number of them, they are relatively easy even for a beginner musician to learn, and they have become tired beyond measure with repetition over the years. Yes, boredom and monotony are locked into the very bone structure of the blues. Only skilled practitioners of alchemy can transform the trough water of generic blues into the quicksilver of bright, passionate blues (or dark, passionate blues, for that matter), while deviating hardly at all from the notes and chords passed down from Mississippi plantations through Chicago and Memphis streets and New York, Los Angeles, and Houston recording studios, and smoke-filled nightclubs everywhere.

Alchemy, ineffable and inspired, determines the difference between a hunk of scrap metal on wheels and a Thunderbird, the difference between a blues bar band and a group of musicians who can make you forget that you've heard a million times over the notes they are playing, make you forget the sweat pouring down your body and ruining your clothes.

Facts are simple and facts are straight, so here are a few. Raised in California, singer and harp player Kim Wilson played with innumerable blues bands there (including one with Lowell Fulson), sometimes sneaking his original songs into the sets by passing them off as bona fide obscurities by Little Milton or whomever. As far as anybody knows, none of those combos left behind any artifacts. No matter. By the time Wilson made his way to Austin, he was good, real good, his playing and singing rich and full, his style expansive and hearty, a perfect vehicle for party hollers and sexual innuendo.

Wilson could be made of circles; Vaughan is all angles. He has the lean, hard, dour look of a man whose bad side you would strain your resources staying off of.

There (here, but it was a different town then, if you follow my drift), he connected with Jimmie Vaughan, a friend from previous tour stops in Austin, finally starting the Fabulous Thunderbirds in 1975. Vaughan, as everybody except a few tribesmen in the Sulu Archipelago knows by now, is the older brother of Stevie Ray Vaughan, who can be seen on television warning us not to mess with Texas. A disciple of Freddy King, Vaughan knocked around his native Dallas during the '60s, spent some time in California, returned to Dallas, married, hauled garbage for a bit, then moved to Austin, where he played behind Angela Strehli and Lewis Cowdrey in Storm. Storm crashed and blew through 1973, leaving no significant artifacts either.

What a pair these two make! Wilson luxuriates in his beefy body, thinning hair, sideburns and mustache, all of which contribute to a refined patina of sleaze, an air of bemused hedonism. He could be the unflappable maitre d' of a Chicago speakeasy in the 1920s,

a used car salesman of thirty years ago surrounded by gleaming fins, or the ringleader at an orgy. Seen at a certain angle, his face bears a telling resemblance to Groucho Marx.

Wilson could be made of circles; Vaughan is all angles. He has the lean, hard, dour look of a man whose bad side you would strain your resources staying off of, and once on it spend years working back into his good graces, perhaps never quite succeeding. The isolation and melancholy of the Southwest are written all over that face. So it is not surprising when his guitar playing turns out to be as tough and hard-edged as Wilson's style is rounded and earthy. They are an ideal team, seemingly impervious to bad luck.

After years working the unholy grind of the club circuit—imagine endless hours in vans on the freeway, a new music business weasel in every town, enough booze to float the *Queen Mary,* and inexpensive women—the Fabulous Thunderbirds had a keen interest in acquiring some Pink Cadillacs. Who could blame them for wanting to grapple with the bitch goddess variously known as the big time, success, comfortably well off, sitting pretty, "just like ZZ Top."

Trouble was, weasels in human form kept throwing up roadblocks. The first three Fabulous Thunderbirds albums, well, dog shows are usually better promoted than the first three Fabulous Thunderbirds albums, though the pill may have been easier to swallow in light of the records not being all that great. The fourth Fabulous Thunderbirds album, a Nick Lowe production crackling with humor and zest called *T-Bird Rhythm*, was recognized by everyone as great. As luck would have it, the revolving door spun around at the record company just as *T-Bird Rhythm* started to hit its stride in the marketplace. The new weasel team had no stake in making it a hit and so let it die.

The Thunderbirds played a few dates with the Rolling Stones in 1981, and Stevie Ray Vaughan's career

fell into the hands of professionals who made of him a large star, which helped a bunch. The Fabulous Thunderbirds entered the studio with Nick Lowe's old partner Dave Edmunds to make *Tuff Enuff,* an album of scintillating rock and jump blues, for Wilson and Vaughan had long since extended the reach of their alchemy to include many variants of blues and rhythm and blues dance music, especially and delightfully bringing elements of Louisiana rock & roll. Like Indians on the horizon in a cheap western, weasels came out of the woodwork, for the group's new record label bet the farm on the new Gino Vanelli product. That label no longer exists, and *Tuff Enuff* did not appear at your favorite record store in late July of 1985, as planned.

The group is now contracted to the largest record company in the world, CBS. A man named Charles Comer, who came to this country with the Beatles and talks in long, perfectly composed press releases, sits in his Manhattan office telephoning upwards of a dozen countries a day on behalf of his clients, an impressive roster now including guess who. Comer is an independent publicist of legendary repute, and anyone who doesn't recognize that in these times publicists hold the keys to the palace, why, that person is a fool.

Tours are being booked, some with Jimmie Vaughan's younger brother headlining, some without. "Tuff Enuff" will be heard in the next Ron Howard film, there is talk of it showing up on *Miami Vice*, an admittedly perfect place for its socky opening with tremelo. The record, both single and album, has entered the *Billboard* charts in high position. Reviewers are madly thumbing through their thesauruses for new, more grandiloquent adjectives.

What could go wrong? Plenty, but things have never looked so good for a band whose lead singer had the nerve to tell an interviewer "mainstream is kind of like a piss puddle comin' out of a wino on Sixth Street." For that alone he deserves to make it. ◄

Don't You Start Me Talking

VOL. 5 NO. 17 ★ APRIL 26, 1986

MICHAEL CORCORAN

AUSTIN MUSIC SUCKS

Musicians. What a bunch of crybabies. It's my fault nobody shows up at their gigs. How dare I favor an inferior band to theirs! Who do I think I am? I must be stupid if I can't recognize their greatness. All they do is play goddamn music. In junior high, kids would be called sissies and beat up for such an activity. Nowadays we worship our instrument-players. And it really

THAT'S IT! NO MORE MR. NOT A BAD GUY ONCE YOU GET TO KNOW HIM!

takes the carpool lane to their heads. Ever have a pretty good friend and then they joined a band? After that they've only got one topic of conversation, and it's not world hunger. They've all got Marshall egos, turned up to ten. And I'm not just talking about the Vaughans, Elys, Nelsons, or Carrascos; this bug is city-wide. I recently sponsored a talent show of twenty-one new bands at the Continental, and some of them were pulling shit you'd expect from premenstrual Streisand. And every damn one of them thought they should have won.

Don't you start me talking about these goddamn ingrates! Their voting me as Worst Thing to Happen to Austin Music is like calling Mother Teresa a child molester. After all I've done for Austin. Then the Beach holds its "Not Cool Enough for the *Chronicle*" Awards and I win "Most Hated Critic." The trophy was a toilet seat on which was written "Dump Corky." That's it! No more Mr. Not A Bad Guy Once You Get To Know Him! I can put girls' names **in bold print** so they'll like me. **Lisa Gamache**. See? This is my column, and they'll take it from me when they pry it from my cold, dead hands.

Let's get it all out in the open. Let's let it fly. Daniel Johnston: It's just a cruel joke we've played on you. We really don't think you're brilliant; we think you're a squirrel. How did you like my Kim Fowley impression? . . . Will Sexton: Need a title for your upcoming LP for MCA? How about *Magic Coattail Ride*? When the press starts interviewing you, don't forget to tell them about the book which inspired you most, the Jerry Van Dyke autobiography . . . Still Will: Why did you make cutthroat motions when I started telling Alex about seeing you and two guys in suits and Allan Cox, the under-30 bassist, out to lunch together? . . . How To Kiss: as your music progresses so should your name. Maybe on the sixth or seventh date you should call yourselves Forms Of Contraception . . . Miles and Lucinda: C'mon, we won't think any less of you. Drop the phony accents.

Stevie Ray Vaughan: I think you need to change haircutters. The place you go to now is not so great. You should've been tipped off when you saw that all the barbers wear black hoods with holes cut for the eyes . . . LeRoi Brothers: How does it feel when you make #8 on the Scandinavian charts and then see that Omar & the Howlers are #4? Hollow? I thought so . . . Lou Ann Barton: Don't feel bad just because one person calls your new record "wimpy." And what does Richard Carpenter know? . . . Jon Dee Graham: After listening to your guitar solo on Glass Eye's "I Don't Need Drugs," I'm puzzled as to why you played the guitar behind the back in a studio where no one could see it . . . The Hardcore Scene: Hello. Hell-oh-oh. Anybody home? You know the punk scene is really radical when the main local punk record label backs down against the Tolkien estate.

Zeitgeist: Refresh my memory. Aren't you the band with Jennifer Cook? No wait, I remember now. You used to play the clubs, right, wearing straw hats and Mardi Gras beads? I haven't seen you folks in a long time. Kinda hard getting gigs these days, huh? Stick with it. This is just a tough town to make it in. Listen, I could probably get you a gig opening for the Cavemen. It doesn't pay, but the exposure is good . . . Asleep at the Wheel: Hang in there. This urban country thing's about to get big all over again. I say it's gonna happen right after the Christopher Cross revival peaks . . . Hickoids: Your drum problems have been solved by the invention of a drum machine that gets drunk and messes up . . . Butthole Surfers: Malcolm McLaren's been trying to get hold of you. He wants you to star in his sequel to *The Great Rock 'n' Roll Swindle*. He says all you gotta do is play yourselves . . . Dino Lee: I found a daily schedule sheet that looks like it belongs to you. It reads: 7–8am: Bullshit girlfriend on why-I'm-home-so-late. 8am–2pm: sleep. 2–5pm: fix hair. 5–5:30pm: show hair to girlfriend. 5:30–7pm: Re-do hair. 7–7:03pm: Work on new material. 7:03–10pm: Make sure hair is OK after working on new material. 10pm–1am: Listen to all Dino Lee records while reading clippings. 1–2am: Visit as many nightclubs as possible looking for girls whose self-respect account is overdrawn. 2–7am: Research upcoming *Lolita* theme show. ⬅

ED. NOTE: Due to the unusual nature of Corcoran's column in this issue, there was considerable doubt around the office as to whether it should be run at all. One staffer even suggested that publishing it might place Corky in imminent danger of serious bodily harm. It was at that point that we decided to run it.

ANGELA STREHLI
STRANGER BLUES
ANTONE'S RECORDS

It can be downright frustrating listening to Angela Strehli sometimes. It's hard for me to find fault with a voice like hers—stiletto-sharp at one turn, magnolia sweet the next—a voice that for the fourth time has earned Ms. Strehli "Best Female Vocalist" recognition in the *Chronicle* Music Poll. Likewise her crack band, blasting out the blues every week at Antone's, is one of the best in a city known for its blues giants. It's not the quality of Angela Strehli's music that frustrates me; it's the paucity of her recording output that leaves me thirsting for more. Only a few 45s sprinkled out over the years, but my feeling of desperation has been temporarily alleviated with the release of her new three-song EP, *Stranger Blues*.

Of the three rockers included here, the title track is a real gem, destined to be remembered. Angela has never sounded better as she rip-roars her way through this Elmore James chestnut. Guitarist Denny Freeman, one of Austin's most underrated musicians, has at last left his mark for posterity, passionately tearing into a screaming slide solo that would have made Elmore sit up and smile. In fact, this EP is as much a Denny Freeman vehicle as it is a showcase for Angela. After all, the pair has been musically inseparable for years now, complementing the fire in each other.

"Voodoo" again finds Ms. Strehli blowin' smoke with Freeman giving his whammy bar a run for its money. "Wang Dang Doodle" is the weak link here. While not a bad performance, the effort just doesn't click as well as it should. The song is well-suited for bringing out the growl in Angela's voice, but there is also a vulnerable side to this woman that deserves to be heard. She's got several slow-burners that come to mind. Well, maybe next time. And maybe next time will mean a full-length album's worth of music from Austin's reigning Blues Queen. **JAY TRACHTENBERG**

VOL. 5 NO. 18 ★ MAY 9, 1986

DARDEN SMITH
NATIVE SOIL
READIMIX

There's no way this album could have been anything other than good. Even if Darden weren't a great song-writer and a great arranger, which he is, the record is filled with enough talented musicians to carry it. Try Ponty Bone on accordion, Riley Osborne on piano, Dan Huckabee on dobro, David Halley and John Inmon on guitar, and Lyle Lovett and Nanci Griffith on backing vocals. In addition, the album features Gene Elders doing fine on fiddle, Paul Glasse on mandolin, James Fenner on percussion, and regular band members Roland Denney (bass) and Paul Pearcy (drums). The full band only adds to the beauty of Darden's tunes, as he continues his move from folk to honky-tonk. His voice falters a little on "Veteran's Day," but for the most part is as strong and vibrant as his song-portraits. He has a unique perspective on life that combines talent, soul, and wit, all to a rare degree. "Keep an Open Mind" is special because the boogie/bluesy feel of it reveals yet another side of Darden. This young man has tremendous potential. **ELAINE BLODGETT**

VOL. 5 NO. 22 ★ JULY 4, 1986

Don't You Start Me Talking
Woodshock, 7/26

VOL. 5 NO. 24 ★ AUGUST 1, 1986

MICHAEL CORCORAN

WOODSHOCK WAS SPECIAL. Is special. Ugly sounds in a beautiful setting. Kids in mohawks and combat boots sloshing in streams. The universality of nature. Coming on to mushrooms as Guardez Lou throws layers of sonic fixins on Col. Kurtz to show the fine line between Cambodia and Xanadu. Acid vendors in the crowd. The threat of a fight that never breaks out. The feeling that everything is under control finally overtaking the knowledge that it can all fall apart at any moment. Security guards without faces. Like they never left: Poison 13 with Tim Kerr, the Offenders, Butthole Surfers unleashing the brain rodents who sniff around on a full stomach. Oboyo upping the energy ante. Strappados making four in the morning feel like half past midnight. Scratch Acid being Scratch Acid. Every band reaching inside and pulling it out. U-Men, Texas Instruments, the Screws. Bing Bang Bong. Fresh kegs arriving like buses, and then the traditional Hickoids sunrise set with more people on stage than in the audience. You can never have enough of a good thing. ◀

Timbuk 3 The Family That Plays Together Stays Together

VOL. 5 NO. 25 ★ AUGUST 15, 1986

SARAH WIMER

AT THEIR LAST Hole in the Wall gig before leaving to tour England, the club was even more packed than it typically is when Timbuk 3 is playing. There is no dance floor, only tables jammed together. Nevertheless, seven couples were dancing. A heady exultation crackled through the air at being among the cognoscenti who were enjoying this band before the rest of the world discovered them, while their gems of songs could be savored one last time in close proximity.

Fans wondered whether Timbuk 3 would ever play the Hole again, with an EP, *Airwave Jungles*, already out in England and their album, *Greetings from*

Barbara and Pat MacDonald of Timbuk 3, 1986. Photograph by Martha Grenon.

Timbuk 3, being released domestically. Like the tales of gorgeous girls being stopped on the street by a photographer who makes them famous, Timbuk 3 was signed by I.R.S. Records, America's premier independent label, early this year.

Up on stage, a low-key couple sings and plays on, consumed by their music. Pat MacDonald is wiry, with dark tousled hair. He seems like he might have grown up in a rough neighborhood where he had to fight to survive; a hungry look still gleams in his eyes. His rangy wife Barbara's manner is more relaxed. With long flaxen hair, she's not beautiful by conventional standards, yet seems to glow as they perform, her beatific expression almost saintly—some Midwestern madonna who seems like she should be carrying sheaves of grain. As their song "I Love You in the Strangest Way" proclaims, "In a world of black and white, we meet halftone gray. We're different as day and night."

> **"RIGHT NOW I DON'T WANT TO PLAY WITH ANYBODY I CAN'T SLEEP WITH."**
>
> **PAT MACDONALD**

Pat MacDonald writes the songs, plays electric guitar, and has a whole slew of harmonicas beside him. Barbara plays a hollow-bodied electric, and sometimes violin and harmonica. They trade leads. The third member of the band is the most controversial. The funky, rhythmic bottom of Timbuk 3's music, the bass and drums, emits from the jambox sometimes known as T-3PO, positioned passively behind the couple. The rhythm tracks are played and recorded by Pat.

Timbuk 3's music is impossible to categorize, either musically or topically. The songs vary incredibly from tender love songs such as "I Need You" to sarcastic, incisive political commentary in "Just Another Movie" to dissonant psychedelia in "In a Jambox," spanning the gamut from folk to funk to futuristic, with little tastes of other styles tossed in. The lyrics are consistently clever, but substantive and layered with meaning, wryly commenting on life. A section of "Life is Hard" goes:

> *After he stiffed a waitress, ran out on his tab*
> *Big Mac had a heart attack in the back of a*
> *   yellow cab.*
> *By the time the sound of sirens of the ambulance*
> *   was coming*
> *His heart had stopped beating, but the meter*
> *   was still running.*

> *Life is hard*
> *You can't buy happiness no matter what you do,*
> *Can't get to heaven on roller skates*
> *Can't take a taxicab to Timbuktu.*

Their harmonies are intimate and tight; the melodies so hook-laden that they invite singing along and linger in the mind. Pat and Barbara's intertwining guitar styles are different; his is spare and chunky, largely rhythm, while she improvises, embellishing and ornamenting in a filigree mode.

Whether they were daring fate or laughing at it, when the MacDonalds knew that I.R.S. honchos were coming to town to scout out bands for the Austin segment of *The Cutting Edge*, they made posters for their gig at the Mid-City Roadhouse with the slogan, "As seen on MTV." Label VP Carl Grasso's first stop was to hear Timbuk 3, whose tape had already impressed him, and ask them to be on the show.

At that point, Timbuk 3 had been gigging in Austin less than a year, having moved here from Madison, Wisconsin. "We got personally involved because of the music," Barbara says. They were classic dark horses, largely unknown in local scene-making circles. Timbuk 3 opened the first of three nights of taping for the show; then I.R.S. invited them, along with Zeitgeist and the Dharma Bums, out to Los Angeles to perform for *The Cutting Edge* preview. When they finished their set, I.R.S. president Miles Copeland invited them to his office the next day to discuss a record deal.

The concept of employing an untempermental jambox evolved partially from frustration, partially from necessity. As Barbara explains, "We had all these great songs that were written with a band in mind." Yet Barbara admits that when Pat first came up with the solution of his taping the drum and bass parts, she thought it was a "terrible idea." She came around when she realized that having a jambox as the third member of their band would enable them to play anywhere, even on the streets for spare change if need be.

The drum machine has certainly worked for Timbuk 3, and they know it won't quit, leading Pat to assert that drum machines are "the greatest invention since the electric guitar." I.R.S. likes their concept too.

"I think they really like our autonomy," Pat expounds, "the fact that we can call our own shots. They know what we're about, and they know that they like us. They don't want the energy to be dissipated. I think they just kind of feel real comfortable with not having to deal with more people."

The MacDonalds credit their love of three-year-old son Devin, who's in England with a nanny while they tour, as a major force in keeping their relationship together. Barbara calls Devin the "crazy glue," also the name of another song.

"It's just that we love our kid so much and part of that has to do with loving each other," Pat reflects. "It seems to me that one thing that helps is that the stability of our relationship was established before we got into this musical thing together, so it didn't all come at once . . . Right now I don't want to play with anybody I can't sleep with. I like the intimate thing; I like the tight relationship Barbara and I have, and I want to pursue that musically.

"I don't want to water it down. It's gotta be love in a way." ◄

JERRY JEFF WALKER, NANCI GRIFFITH
PARAMOUNT THEATRE, SEPTEMBER 9

There's something beautifully incongruous about Jerry Jeff Walker standing, guitar in hand, in the middle of the venerable Paramount Theatre before 1200 upwardly mobile Austinites, singing "Pissin' in the Wind."

It just goes to show that you can take Nashville refugees like Walker out of the smoke-filled honky-tonks and put 'em in plush settings like the Paramount or Dallas' Venetian Room, but the rebellious artist within can't always be tamed. At 44, Walker has seen more ups and downs than a state fair roller-coaster in his private life, as well as his public career that spans two decades. But after battles with the bottle and the IRS that earned him a national reputation as a rowdy "gypsy songman" (the title of his latest work), Walker has cleaned up his act and launched, with wife Susan, his own record company, Tried & True Music, Inc.

At the Paramount, Walker showed why, despite everything, his music career has endured. From classics written in the 1960s such as "Mr. Bojangles" and "Little Bird" to newer songs like "Layin' My Life on the Line," he had the audience eating out of his hand. The crowd included the likes of the Governor, who presented the native New Yorker with his official Texas citizenship papers, Connie Nelson (Willie's better half), and author Bud Shrake. The audience stomped, hooted, and sang along to tunes like "Redneck Mother" and listened in rapt attention to Walker's newer, mellower songs such as "She Knows Her Daddy Sings," a paean to his 8-year-old daughter, Jessie. It would be all too easy for a talent like Jerry Jeff Walker to slip into the commercial mediocrity, but his music and songwriting retains a rough-hewn integrity and endearing folksy quality unparalleled in today's homogenized music industry.

Opening for one of Austin's remaining musical legends was up-and-coming songwriter/recording artist Nanci Griffith, another homegrown product who has taken her considerable charm and talent to Nashville but remained true to her musical roots. Alone with her guitar in the Paramount's spotlight, Griffith, in her 30s and a veteran of barrooms and festivals for ten years, looks to be but a vulnerable youth. In looks and sound, the striking Texan reminds one of Emmylou Harris ten or fifteen years ago. But musically, Griffith's lilting voice is more reminiscent of her childhood idol, folksinger Carolyn Hester. However, like Harris, she can growl out some hot-rockin' tunes such as "Red Brick Floor" or Richard Dobson's "Ballad of Robin Wintersmith."

Griffith's forte, though, remains her own ballads, poems set to music about the people, places, and books that have influenced her life. She mesmerized the audience with title songs like "Once in a Very Blue Moon" and "Last of the True Believers," from her two latest albums on Rounder/Philo. And from snatches of strangers' conversations heard between sets, Austin's newest Nashville sweetheart has won some new converts. **ROB MCCORKLE**

VOL. 6 NO. 3 ★ OCTOBER 10, 1986

THE LAST DAYS OF THE BEACH

THE BEACH, SEPTEMBER 26-27

The Beach, after more than two years of faithful service to the, uh, seedier aspects of the Austin music scene, took its last bow fittingly, with two nights of shows in which about a dozen bands participated. For some of them it was a dubious homecoming. The cast Friday featured Beach originals Zeitgeist, Texas Instruments, and Guardez Lou, who worked over the dancing feet and memory cells of all of us who watched them there so many times before.

Singer Paul Horsey of Guardez Lou kept the crowd amused, as he always does, with various stunts—most involving unnatural acts with a porcelain Mardi Gras mask and Vampire Blood—and, this time, with Silly String as well. Well done, Horsey, but the band was also right on cue as it always is, despite guitar problems. Zeitgeist really tore that night, with a fine combination of melodies such as "Freight Train Rain" and "Things Don't Change" that helped take them from the Beach to bigger and better things two summers ago. By the time they played around 2am, the crowd had largely evaporated, leaving behind a small but highly dedicated core of rapt fans, reminiscent of days of yore.

The last band to grace the stage of the Beach Saturday was the Hickoids, as obscene, manic, and uncontrolled a group of mutants as ever whopped a geetar. They played on and on and on until finally leaving, by ones and twos, trailing epithets, probably to puke, at 4am. Well, almost. But that's not the point. Neither is it the point to balance the "bad" of the Beach with the "good," but rather to consider something else. That is, where will the next shows be?

Think back. Who ever went looking for the Beach in the first place? I didn't. One day I just ended up there, maybe it was to read a book or to brood. But I went back another night. And another. Hell, I was frequenting the Beach before the fountain was hooked up, and when there was sand on the deck outside. I remember when they put up the Carta Blanca card tables out there, and I remember times there weren't half enough people there to even need them. I saw Zeitgeist, Texas Instruments, Glass Eye, and scores of other, no-longer-existent bands play there for their first time.

The Beach was, in the memories of a lot of people, one of the best. But it's worth no more than the people, the music, and, most importantly, the spirit that was there—things, fortunately, that can be packed up and shipped out to any place at all that can hold the folks to make it happen. **STEVE JOHNSON**

VOL. 6 NO. 3 ★ OCTOBER 9, 1986

Stevie Ray Vaughan
Straight from the Heart

VOL. 6 NO. 18 ★ MAY 15, 1987

MICHAEL CORCORAN

IT WAS A MUGGY AUSTIN NIGHT in the summer of '86 and Stevie Ray Vaughan looked bad. Without acknowledging the applause of the sunburned multitudes pressed up against a chain-link fence, Stevie emerged gingerly from a big black limo and used a silver-tipped cane to pick his way to the side of the River Fest stage. His 31 years had been multiplied like dog years and almost suddenly he was old, frail, and out of breath. His skin was gray and one size too big. You didn't need a doctor to diagnose the obvious: Stevie Ray Vaughan was dying.

Exene Cervenka of X has the word "Temptation" tattooed on the back of her hand, so she can see it every time she reaches. Vaughan had it written all over his body as he took the stage to join his brother Jimmie's band, the Fabulous Thunderbirds. Stevie's hands, which had reached for so many bottles and joints in 15 years of hardcore roadhousing, fumbled with the cord as if controlled by an apprentice marionetteer. The eyes were slits, the nose almost boneless, and the legs as rubbery as Gumby's just out of the microwave.

Someone in the band counted off—one, two, three, four—a blues shuffle kicked in, and suddenly, almost miraculously, Stevie Vaughan came back to life. The electricity from his white Stratocaster seemed to flow through him. His fingers tapdanced all over the fretboard, finding notes that go right for the knees and bend up the spine. He plays guitar like Keith Moon played drums; nothing in moderation.

"He gets plugged into his soul's emotions. He wails and he's mellow all at the same time" is the way brother Jimmie describes Stevie's playing. Of Jimmie, Stevie says, "I guess he's more of a reserved player than I am. He plays about this much (holds up both index fingers about an inch apart) of what he knows."

Together on the River Fest stage, the brothers Vaughan were the musical counterpart of a couple of monkeys going berserk in a hardware store, with Stevie airplaning down the aisles unshelving fixtures

YOU DIDN'T NEED A DOCTOR TO DIAGNOSE THE OBVIOUS: STEVIE RAY VAUGHAN WAS DYING.

and gadgetry, while Jimmie sprayed the area with nuts and bolts. T-Bird singer Kim Wilson, fueled by Stevie's regenesis and the relentless guitar slinging, leapt into the fray with a meaty harmonica solo. When he finished blowing, he stepped back, looked over at the Vaughans digging in for the pounce, and said, "OK, whicha you boys wants to go first?"

It took the promoter's frantic cutthroat motions to finally end the jam at 11:59. Wilson walked off muttering that they were just getting warmed up, while the Vaughans tucked their Strats into bed for the night. When Stevie reached the wings, a roadie handed him his cane, then led interference to the trailer that served as the dressing room. It would be hours before the black limo backed as close to the trailer door as possible and took Stevie Ray Vaughan home.

Four months later, it was an ambulance that was taking Stevie Ray Vaughan, and it wasn't rushing to his house. After a show in Switzerland, Stevie had collapsed. Drifting in and out of consciousness on the way to the hospital—they say that this is when your whole life flashes before your eyes. If that was

Stevie Ray Vaughan and Little Charlie [Sexton], 1981. Photograph by Ellen Wallenstein.

the case with Stevie, he probably saw himself as a little boy, listening to the blues records that Jimmie brought home. He saw an eight-year-old kid taking three strings off his first guitar so he could play bass for his brother, who was already a hotshot at 12. He heard the music of Albert King, Howlin' Wolf, and Chuck Berry, while he sat in his old room back in Dallas trying to bring order to the shapely peninsula of wires and wood that sat in his lap. Stevie Ray Vaughan took a long look at his life and told himself, "This has got to come to a screeching halt."

"This" was drugs and alcohol. When asked what he was addicted to, Vaughan says, "everything." The rest of the European shows were cancelled and Vaughan, along with Double Trouble bass player Tommy Shannon, checked himself into a clinic in Marietta, Georgia, which specializes in drug and alcohol dependency. 1986 had been a rough year for Vaughan. His father, Big Jim, had died and the band's equipment had been stolen when he went to Dallas for the funeral. But Vaughan was determined that '86 would not be his last year. It wasn't.

Stevie Ray Vaughan and Double Trouble's new album is called *Live Alive*, which seems to signal that they've finally run out of cool names for live double LPs. The "Alive" in the title is cumbersome. It makes it hard to mention the record without getting mixed up. But "Alive" is the most important word to Vaughan right now. Though the tracks were recorded when it appeared that the product might be released posthumously (Stevie's final homage to Hendrix) it hit the stores when Vaughan was in full rebound from his substance addiction.

As the album entered the charts and headed for the Top 40, Vaughan was prouder of numbers which became progressively higher: 26, 48, 79, 84. On Jan. 21 he was ecstatic, not because his "Superstitious" video (with a cameo by the song's writer Stevie Wonder) had been added to MTV's heavy rotation, but

because that date marked the 100th consecutive day he had been totally clean. He told one Houston reporter, "I have no reason or desire to use (drugs or alcohol) because I have so much to look forward to. And I'm the healthiest I've ever been in my life."

Though Vaughan's substance abuse was well-known among his longtime friends and followers, it just never seemed so serious because he was always in such control when he played guitar. He hadn't always been great, but you'd have to find someone who knew him as young as nine to testify to that.

Now that Vaughan has shrugged a big chunk of his personal woes, can he continue to sing and play the blues with conviction? This isn't such a stupid question when you consider Warren Zevon's output since cleaning up, but it was one which was quickly answered when Stevie and Double Trouble played Austin for the first time since the new lease on life was notarized. Many longtime Vaughan-o-philes said it was the best of all the times they had ever seen him (and of course they told how many times that had been). He played longer than usual and some fans gushed that they could actually make out a few of the lyrics. He still dresses like a colorblind Rhoda Morganstern, and there's not a clinic in the world that can cure him of the *Fistful of Dollars* hat, but Stevie Ray Vaughan is rockin' harder and better than ever.

John Lennon said that "the blues is a chair, not a design for a chair or a better chair . . . it is the first chair. It is a chair for sitting on, not for looking at. You sit on that music." For the first time in almost 20 years, Stevie Ray Vaughan stands straight, in the middle of the stage. When he gets tired of standing straight he doesn't look for something to lean on. He just plugs in and falls into that big easy chair. And when he walks off, nobody hands him a silver-tipped cane. It wasn't really silver anyway. The guy who sold it to him just told him it was. ◀

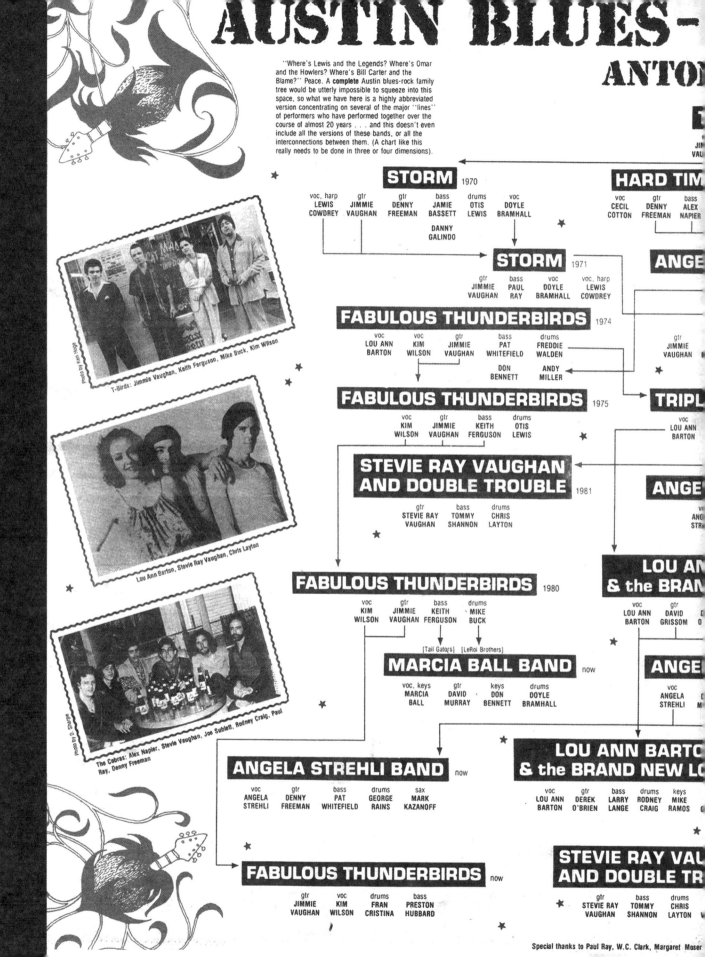

AUSTIN BLUES—

ANTON

"Where's Lewis and the Legends? Where's Omar and the Howlers? Where's Bill Carter and the Blame?" Peace. A **complete** Austin blues-rock family tree would be utterly impossible to squeeze into this space, so what we have here is a highly abbreviated version concentrating on several of the major "lines" of performers who have performed together over the course of almost 20 years . . . and this doesn't even include all the versions of these bands, or all the interconnections between them. (A chart like this really needs to be done in three or four dimensions).

T

JIMMIE
VAUGHAN

STORM 1970

voc, harp	gtr	gtr	bass	drums	voc
LEWIS COWDREY	JIMMIE VAUGHAN	DENNY FREEMAN	JAMIE BASSETT	OTIS LEWIS	DOYLE BRAMHALL
			DANNY GALINDO		

HARD TIM

voc	gtr	bass
CECIL COTTON	DENNY FREEMAN	ALEX NAPIER

STORM 1971

gtr	bass	voc	voc, harp
JIMMIE VAUGHAN	PAUL RAY	DOYLE BRAMHALL	LEWIS COWDREY

ANGE

FABULOUS THUNDERBIRDS 1974

voc	voc	gtr	bass	drums
LOU ANN BARTON	KIM WILSON	JIMMIE VAUGHAN	PAT WHITEFIELD	FREDDIE WALDEN
			DON BENNETT	ANDY MILLER

gtr
JIMMIE VAUGHAN

FABULOUS THUNDERBIRDS 1975

voc	gtr	bass	drums
KIM WILSON	JIMMIE VAUGHAN	KEITH FERGUSON	OTIS LEWIS

TRIPL

voc
LOU ANN BARTON

STEVIE RAY VAUGHAN AND DOUBLE TROUBLE 1981

gtr	bass	drums
STEVIE RAY VAUGHAN	TOMMY SHANNON	CHRIS LAYTON

ANGE

v
ANG STR

FABULOUS THUNDERBIRDS 1980

voc	gtr	bass	drums
KIM WILSON	JIMMIE VAUGHAN	KEITH FERGUSON	MIKE BUCK

LOU AN & the BRAM

voc	gtr	
LOU ANN BARTON	DAVID GRISSOM	O

[Tail Gators] [LeRoi Brothers]

MARCIA BALL BAND now

voc, keys	gtr	keys	drums
MARCIA BALL	DAVID MURRAY	DON BENNETT	DOYLE BRAMHALL

ANGE

voc	
ANGELA STREHLI	M

ANGELA STREHLI BAND now

voc	gtr	bass	drums	sax
ANGELA STREHLI	DENNY FREEMAN	PAT WHITEFIELD	GEORGE RAINS	MARK KAZANOFF

LOU ANN BARTO & the BRAND NEW LO

voc	gtr	bass	drums	keys
LOU ANN BARTON	DEREK O'BRIEN	LARRY LANGE	RODNEY CRAIG	MIKE RAMOS

STEVIE RAY VAU AND DOUBLE TR

gtr	bass	drums
STEVIE RAY VAUGHAN	TOMMY SHANNON	CHRIS LAYTON

FABULOUS THUNDERBIRDS now

gtr	voc	drums	bass
JIMMIE VAUGHAN	KIM WILSON	FRAN CRISTINA	PRESTON HUBBARD

Photo by Ken Hoge

T-Birds: Jimmie Vaughan, Keith Ferguson, Mike Buck, Kim Wilson

Lou Ann Barton, Stevie Ray Vaughan, Chris Layton

Photo by D. Osborne

The Cobras: Alex Napier, Stevie Vaughan, Joe Sublett, Rodney Craig, Paul Ray, Denny Freeman

Special thanks to Paul Ray, W.C. Clark, Margaret Moser

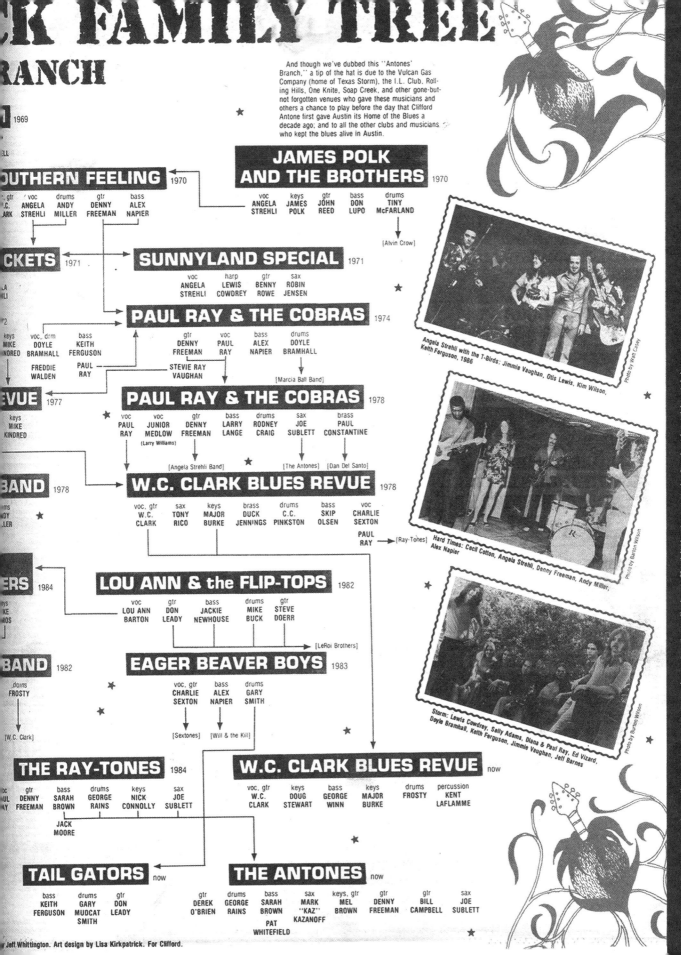

K FAMILY TREE

RANCH

1969

And though we've dubbed this "Antones' Branch," a tip of the hat is due to the Vulcan Gas Company (home of Texas Storm), the I.L. Club, Rolling Hills, One Knite, Soap Creek, and other gone-but-not forgotten venues who gave these musicians and others a chance to play before the day that Clifford Antone first gave Austin its Home of the Blues a decade ago; and to all the other clubs and musicians who kept the blues alive in Austin.

★

JAMES POLK AND THE BROTHERS 1970

voc	keys	gtr	bass	drums
ANGELA STREHLI	JAMES POLK	JOHN REED	DON LUPO	TINY McFARLAND

[Alvin Crow]

OUTHERN FEELING 1970

voc	drums	gtr	bass
ANGELA STREHLI	ANDY MILLER	DENNY FREEMAN	ALEX NAPIER

★

SUNNYLAND SPECIAL 1971

voc	harp	gtr	sax
ANGELA STREHLI	LEWIS COWDREY	BENNY ROWE	ROBIN JENSEN

CKETS 1971

PAUL RAY & THE COBRAS 1974

gtr	voc	bass	drums
DENNY FREEMAN	PAUL RAY	ALEX NAPIER	DOYLE BRAMHALL

keys	voc, drm	bass
MIKE NDRED	DOYLE BRAMHALL	KEITH FERGUSON

FREDDIE WALDEN   PAUL RAY

STEVIE RAY VAUGHAN

[Marcia Ball Band]

VUE 1977

keys
MIKE KINDRED

PAUL RAY & THE COBRAS 1978

voc	voc	gtr	bass	drums	sax	brass
PAUL RAY	JUNIOR MEDLOW	DENNY FREEMAN	LARRY LANGE	RODNEY CRAIG	JOE SUBLETT	PAUL CONSTANTINE

(Larry Williams)

[Angela Strehli Band]   [The Antones]   [Dan Del Santo]

★

BAND 1978

drums
NDY LLER

★

W.C. CLARK BLUES REVUE 1978

voc, gtr	sax	keys	brass	drums	bass	voc
W.C. CLARK	TONY RICO	MAJOR BURKE	DUCK JENNINGS	C.C. PINKSTON	SKIP OLSEN	CHARLIE SEXTON

PAUL RAY → [Ray-Tones]

LOU ANN & the FLIP-TOPS 1982

voc	gtr	bass	drums	gtr
LOU ANN BARTON	DON LEADY	JACKIE NEWHOUSE	MIKE BUCK	STEVE DOERR

→ [LeRoi Brothers]

RS 1984

keys
KE MOS

BAND 1982

drums
FROSTY

[W.C. Clark]

EAGER BEAVER BOYS 1983

voc, gtr	bass	drums
CHARLIE SEXTON	ALEX NAPIER	GARY SMITH

[Sextones]   [Will & the Kill]

THE RAY-TONES 1984

gtr	bass	drums	keys	sax
DENNY FREEMAN	SARAH BROWN	GEORGE RAINS	NICK CONNOLLY	JOE SUBLETT

JACK MOORE

W.C. CLARK BLUES REVUE now

voc, gtr	keys	bass	keys	drums	percussion
W.C. CLARK	DOUG STEWART	GEORGE WINN	MAJOR BURKE	FROSTY	KENT LAFLAMME

★

TAIL GATORS now

bass	drums	gtr
KEITH FERGUSON	GARY MUDCAT SMITH	DON LEADY

THE ANTONES now

gtr	drums	bass	sax	keys, gtr	gtr	gtr	sax
DEREK O'BRIEN	GEORGE RAINS	SARAH BROWN	MARK "KAZ" KAZANOFF	MEL BROWN	DENNY FREEMAN	BILL CAMPBELL	JOE SUBLETT
		PAT WHITEFIELD					

Angela Strehli with the T-Birds: Jimmie Vaughan, Otis Lewis, Kim Wilson, Keith Ferguson, 1986
Photo by Watt Casey

Hard Times: Cecil Cotton, Angela Strehli, Denny Freeman, Andy Miller, Alex Napier
Photo by Burton Wilson

Storm: Lewis Cowdrey, Sally Adams, Diana & Paul Ray, Ed Vizard, Doyle Bramhall, Keith Ferguson, Jimmie Vaughan, Jeff Barnes
Photo by Burton Wilson

Austin Blues–Rock Family Tree: Antones Branch, 1985. Compile by Jeff Whittington. Art design by Lisa Kirkpatrick.

y Jeff Whittington. Art design by Lisa Kirkpatrick. For Clifford.

We Got Some Stuff in Store

The Blues Reunion Concert of T. D. Bell & the Cadillacs

VOL. 6 NO. 20 ★ JUNE 12, 1987

MARTHA HARTZOG

IT'S A SULTRY SUNDAY afternoon in May at the Victory Grill on E. 11th Street. The reunion concert of a classic Austin blues band, T. D. Bell & the Cadillacs, is scheduled for Juneteenth, and the rehearsals are beginning. This is the first time the band has played together in twenty years. The sounds they are making echo with the rich memories of all the good times they had from the early Fifties to the late Sixties as they toured throughout Texas, always returning here to the Grill.

Up on the bandstand, Erbie Bowser lifts his hands off Robert Shaw's old piano and spins around on the bright red and chrome art deco stool he carries around with him wherever he goes to play. "Hey, Ghost, come on up here!" he calls to the tall, raw-boned man in a straw hat, sitting down below. "He's my nach'ral partner and we got some stuff in store," he tells us with a grin.

"Ghost" is Grey Ghost, R. T. Williams, now 83 years old. He's got some twenty years on Erbie. Ghost began his blues career in the 1920s playing piano and singing for minstrel shows. His repertoire encompasses every form of blues imaginable, from country to barrelhouse to show tunes that Bobby Short and Mabel Mercer would sing. When Ghost gives you "Nobody Knows You When You're Down and Out" or "One Room Country Shack," the power of his voice and the phrasing in his hands are those of a blues master.

Next to Erbie Bowser stands Tyler D. Bell, the band's leader, powerful and dignified, who has built a successful trucking business over the last twenty years since the band was active. Bell, Bowser, and Williams are the core of the band. Together they span five generations of Texas blues and their influence on younger musicians has assured that their musical heritage is passed along. W.C. Clark got his start playing with T. D. Bell & the Cadillacs and will join them on bass for the concert.

THE MUSICIANS BEGIN with a warm-up shuffle in G, oblivious to the chaos of paint cans, tools, and rolled-up carpeting around them. This part of the Victory Grill has been closed for some years now, and owner Johnny Holmes is refurbishing it especially for the reunion concert. The roof's been mostly fixed, though part of the ceiling fell in due to the heavy May rains, narrowly missing Shaw's piano, a precious heirloom.

The concert is the brainchild of Tary Owens, a man with a perpetual smile on his face these days. During the 1960s Owens went out and made field recordings of Texas blues giants like Lightnin' Hopkins, Mance Lipscomb, and Ghost. Owens was instrumental in organizing concerts to bring these relatively undiscovered bluesmen to Austin to perform before student audiences. Now he wants to see that the importance of musicians like T. D. Bell and others is documented and recognized. "You diggin' down to the roots of the people," Erbie Bowser tells him.

Blues in Austin began like blues everywhere—on the front porches, on the backroads, and in the juke joints—wherever black people congregated to have fun and make a little music. It began in the cotton fields and sugarcane fields in the late 19th century, and by the 1920s, when Grey Ghost began playing in

Taylor, Texas, it had made its way to Houston's Fourth Ward, Dallas' Deep Ellum, and Austin's East Side.

If you were a young man who stayed up all night to practice the guitar or begged and borrowed practice time on a neighbor's piano, and you were from Taylor, or Rockdale, or Smithville, you might end up in Austin on 11th Street and from there travel all over Texas playing the blues circuit. When asked how he learned to play the piano, Grey Ghost always says, "I guess I just have a big ear."

NOW THE WARM-UP SHUFFLE in G is over and without missing a beat, T. D. Bell moves to center stage. The famous T-Bone Walker riffs that made club owner Johnny Holmes ask T. D. to leave Rockdale in 1949 and come to the big city of Austin to play in his club, resound through the room. T. D. begins with "Bobby Sox Baby," the only song Johnny Holmes would let him

Blues in Austin began like blues everywhere—on the front porches, on the backroads, and in the juke joints—wherever black people congregated to have fun and make a little music.

play at first, a tactic aimed at building up a following for T. D. He then segues into "The Things I Used To Do." As we clap and smile and say "alright!" T. D. beams and says, "Abba dabba dabba. It's copacetic."

On V-E Day, the day the European war ended in 1945, Johnny Holmes opened the Victory Grill, serving lunches and short orders. After a few years, he added on a two-level nightclub in back and began to book blues acts from all over the U.S. B.B. King, in a recent interview, remembered Johnny Holmes and the Victory Grill with fondness and respect.

Blues Reunion: (l–r) Blues Boy Hubbard, James Kuykendall, T.D. Bell, "Little Herman" Reese, William Fegan, William Lewis, Wilbert Brown, Johnny Holmes, and R.T. "Grey Ghost" Williams. Kneeling: (l–r) Ewell DeWitty and Erbie Bowser. Photograph by Martha Hartzog.

Roosevelt "Grey Ghost" Williams. Photograph by Martha Grenon.

HOLMES CONTINUED AS a promoter, booking acts all over Texas for the next twenty years. In the early Fifties he put together T. D. Bell & the Cadillacs as a house band and opening act for the likes of King, Big Mama Thornton, and Bobby Blue Bland. Stationed at Fort Hood in the Fifties, Bland got his start at the Victory Grill by winning talent contests Holmes held there, and recently told Holmes, "You are one of the first promoters we remember. You're number one in my book."

In the early Sixties, at the beginning of the integration movement, some of the black clubs on E. 11th, notably the IL Club and Charlie's Playhouse, began to accept the presence of white students from UT. Kids like Tary Owens, Bob Simmons, Gilbert J Shelton, myself, and others of the "Old Austin Syndrome" that John Kelso writes about but never knew then, would go to these clubs to listen to the blues and dance.

Many of Austin's better known white blues practitioners learned to play by playing on the East Side with black bands—Angela Strehli, Bill Campbell, and the Vaughan brothers come to mind. James Polk & the Brothers was the first integrated band, featuring white musicians Angela Strehli and John Reed.

THE FANS WHIR ON, stirring up the damp air mixed with dust. People drop in and out of the Grill to see what's going on. A policeman peers in, surprised to see activity in the usually locked-up ballroom, and leaves happy to hear about the concert plans. When the T. D. Bell band decides to take a break, Blues Boy Hubbard & the Jets take the stage. Like W.C. Clark, Blues Boy also started out with T. D. Bell. As the band tunes up, the irrepressible Bowser stays on at the piano, saying, "If I see I'm too wrong, I'll step down. I am where I once was. It's no big deal, but I enjoy it." ◄

Don't You Start Me Talking
An Open Letter to Michael MacCambridge

VOL. 7 NO. 9 ★ JANUARY 1, 1988

MICHAEL CORCORAN

CONGRATULATIONS on your appointment as the *Statesman*'s new pop music columnist. As you will soon find out, this is a great music town; "boffo," you'd call it if you were still writing for *Variety*. Though you were selected over several pretty good local writers, you'll be starting off at a disadvantage because Austin is a mistress you'll have to get to know before you can go all the way. We're a big city full of small towns, with more cliques than a Russian Roulette tournament. You're moving to an overly sensitive town where saying the wrong thing, asking the wrong question can sometimes cause irreparable rifts. Here are some examples of bad things to ask certain people:

True Believers: "When's the new record coming out?"

Eric Johnson: "What's your favorite Jeff Beck record besides *Tones*?"

Lou Ann Barton: "Does the Betty Ford Center have cable?"

Roky Erickson: "Who's this 'they' you keep talking about and how do you know they're on their way here with bloody axes?"

Gibby Haynes: "So, what video are you going to play first?"

Joe Ely: "Don't you play guitar for Bobby Keys?"

Clifford Antone: "Isn't it great when these old black guys do Rolling Stones' songs?"

Keith Ferguson: "How did you get the nickname 'Pinky'?"

Jerry Jeff Walker: "Is it true that your real name is Ron Crosbie, you're from upstate New York, you used to be a drunken asshole, and you named your son Django?" ←

DONGFEST
DONG HUONG, DECEMBER 12

I have seen the future, and it is Dong Huong. It is coarse. It is anarchic. It is beautiful.

Dong Huong is a tiny club north of Hyde Park. They once sold Vietnamese food; since early summer, however, they have sold underground music, often to pitifully small audiences. Things may be changing though, if Saturday was any indication of things to come. The Dongfest was an incredible event, characterized by ear-splitting guitar jams, drunken violence, and frenzied abandon. Sex, Satan, and rock & roll permeated the heavy December air.

Dong Huong was well prepared for the show. Tie-dyed sheets provided a stage backdrop. American flags were hung upside down. An active keg stood in the corner. Video cameras recorded the spectacle. Seven bands played, many had played Noisefest. Mind Splinters, Thanatopsis Throne, Pocket FishRmen, DJ Horowitz, ST-37, Qween Penis, Ed Hall, and EKU squeezed sound out of a sound system which at times was adequate, but was often strained. It began early with Mind Splinters' short set. Thanatopsis Throne played next, a force field of confrontational noise.

By the end of the Throne set a strange mood had pervaded the club. Members of the audience called for "Satan," and warned of his inevitable arrival. Pocket FishRmen motored without stop through a torn, bluesy set. They had come to rock. A short interlude of chaos ensued at the close of their show as DJ Horowitz tried to perform some of his solo numbers but was prevented from doing so by Nazi Satanists, bent on guitar noise. ST-37 played next with lights flashing and the overwhelming sound burning holes in audience ears.

Satan finally arrived in the form of Qween Penis. The beer had run out but the audience refused to quit early. The Penis ripped through a tough, blue set proving themselves anything but average. They are undoubtedly a major hardcore spectacle, a band impossible to ignore. One of Dong Huong's oldest bands, Ed Hall, performed next. This is an intelligent outfit, with carefully constructed sets and songs that are as tough as seeds. Finally, as audience members drifted home to sleep, EKU finished off the show with several songs played in a jerky, explosive way.

The whole thing was over somewhere after three in the morning. Those left were exhausted. I woke up thinking about it this morning and the whole thing was so strange that it's like a well-remembered dream. **ERIC LORD**

VOL. 7 NO. 10 ★ JANUARY 15, 1988

WILD SEEDS
MUD, LIES & SHAME
PASSPORT

This is a statement. It's a statement that Mike Hall and his various collaborators are damned good at writing songs that, at their best, strike a wonderful balance between humor and the kind of insight that hurts but has to come out anyway. It's a statement that you can be smart and still be unpretentious, and combine that mind-set into rock & roll that utterly resists any impulse towards pomposity.

Mud, Lies & Shame (hate the title) is a really remarkable record, consisting of eleven very good songs, including a couple that may just be great. It sings, and it swings: nearly every song is blessed with an instantly memorable melody and at least a couple of turns of phrase skillful enough to provoke admiration. Some of this stuff even sounds like folk music: songs such as "You Will Be Married to a Jealous Man" and "Virginia" (written by the departed guitarist Bo Solomon) sound familiar enough that you're sure you've heard them somewhere else. But then you bump up against "If I Were a Storm," and you know that this is classic, not familiar, that its capability to stick in your memory is due entirely to skill, not repetition of a formula.

Where the Seeds' skill really shows is in the songs where they don't seem to be serious. "I'm Sorry, I Can't Rock You All Night Long" is (a) a hilarious semi-novelty that (b) stands up over repeated listenings because there's some musical interest there and (c) a song that actually has, under its humor, some intelligent comments about sex and rock & roll. "Debi Came Back" could have easily been a Dylanesque jape, a skillful combination of words over a nice melody, but there's more of a story there than it seems at first.

No, this is a deceptive album. Other bands, particularly in the college radio ghetto, are content to write clever pop songs and let it go at that. Mike Hall and the Wild Seeds have put together a showcase for their talents that makes you aware that there's much more where this came from. Although Kris McKay is a semi-regular part of the band, they don't push her up front except for the glorious album closer, "All This Time." They don't push anything up front: the way this band shows off is by laying back, and that's real smart. It makes you wonder what you're not seeing.

ED WARD

VOL. 7 NO. 13 ★ FEBRUARY 26, 1988

Ray Benson
at the Wheel

VOL. 8 NO. 2 ★ SEPTEMBER 9, 1988

JOHN T. DAVIS

"HUEY LEWIS HAD the best line on these things," Ray Benson was explaining. "He said, 'You know why they call 'em fairs? Because they're not great, and they're not bad.'"

You could almost hear the rimshot over the long distance miles as Benson delivered his punchline. No doubt about it, he knew whereof he spoke. Fairs—state, county, and local—are one half of the duality of a country musician's life: in the spring, country bands hit the rodeo circuit; in the fall, it's out to the fairgrounds, land of the corn dog and the Tilt-A-Whirl. Benson and his band, Asleep At the Wheel, have been playing fairs for, Jesus, just about all of their nineteen years.

It's not a bad life, as gigs go. The shows are usually short, and early in the afternoon or evening. The crowds are uniformly adoring. The high exposure gives Benson ample opportunity to schmooze with fans, ply country radio disc jockeys with beer, sell a couple of records, and continue his quest for the Grail of fairs, the Perfect Pecan Sweet Roll . . .

All that and get in a round of golf every day, too.

The Wheel was up in Minneapolis last week, grinding out the days at the Minnesota edition of the state fair. They were sandwiched in between Restless Heart and, as Benson charitably put it, "a lot of other fair-type acts." It was an ideal opportunity for the band to tout their 11th album, *Western Standard Time*.

If the ritual seemed routine, the album was anything but. It may be that *Western Standard Time* embodies more of an emotional commitment on Benson's part than any other Asleep At the Wheel album.

Ray Benson of Asleep At the Wheel, 1998.
Photograph by John Carrico.

RAY BENSON'S
FAVORITE SONGS ABOUT TEXAS

1. "Miles and Miles of Texas"
2. "I Got Texas in My Soul"
3. "Beautiful Texas"
4. "San Antonio Rose"
5. "Remember the Alamo"
6. "Texas Me and You"
7. "Screw You, We're from Texas"
8. "Texas Blues"
9. "You're From Texas"
10. "There's a Little Bit of Everything in Texas"

VOL. 23 NO. 13 ★ NOVEMBER 28, 2003

Brother Ray is the musical incarnation that Ray Benson has conjured up in his own fractured image.

As the title implies, the record is a reprise of classics and older songs that are near and dear to the band's heart.

Or, to be more precise, to Benson's heart. He is the ongoing constant, the hub, if you will, of the Wheel. He assembles the tracks, writes a good deal of the original material, produces the albums, and, when it suits him, drives the tour bus. Over the years, more than 70 musicians have played in Asleep At the Wheel, but it is Benson who has always set the band's agenda and articulated its vision. So when he gets his pronouns confused, speaking of the band as "I" instead of "we," it's not arrogance talking, it's just a fact of life.

Western Standard Time is a sort of palimpsest of Benson's personality. His musical persona has been colored by sources as diverse as Glenn Miller, and Commander Cody & His Lost Planet Airmen. Ray Charles is in there, too, as is Ernest Tubb and even, God help him, Leroy Van Dyke. And looming over it all, of course, is the towering shadow of Bob Wills, whose Texas Playboys popularized Western Swing, the shotgun marriage of jazz, country, blues, big band pop, and minstrel show standards that inspired Benson to step onstage as a bandleader.

"Cody gave us our start in every way, shape, and form," said Benson, recalling the band's genesis in West Virginia in 1970. Later, the two groups bounced around the same Left Coast honky-tonk circuit, centered around joints such as the Longbranch Saloon, in Berkeley. In '73, after the Wheel moved to Austin, they often shared a bill with Cody at the Armadillo World Headquarters.

So Benson resurrected Cody's biggest hit, "Hot Rod Lincoln," for the first single from the album. "He's not actively touring now," he explained, "and I didn't want everybody to forget him. Plus, it gave me a chance to do the song, which I'd always wanted to do. I hope it's a hit, though, because I don't want to stand up and growl that thing every night if it's not."

Well, maybe he can delegate it to Brother Ray, the fellow who looms over his compatriots onstage, swinging a microphone cord like a demented Stardust Wrangler. Brother Ray is the guy who Just Says Thanks, beseeching the audience to look into his red-rimmed eyes and answer for him the musical question, "Am I High?" Brother Ray is the only conceivable country singer who could be the illegitimate offspring of Ernest Tubb and Larry Bird.

Brother Ray is the musical incarnation that Ray Benson has conjured up in his own fractured image. Like Asleep At the Wheel itself, Brother Ray was created out of whole cloth. Hell, somebody had to do it.

"What we do is very contrived and conceptualized," Benson explained. "Nobody was born to be Asleep At the Wheel. This Jewish kid from Philadelphia had to decide that he wanted to do this stuff. As opposed to, this is a product of my environment. . ." he sputtered with laughter at the thought, ". . . I know nothing else. I could have easily formed a dozen different kinds of bands, but I didn't want to. I wanted to do this.

"And so far, we've gotten away with it." ◄

BAD MUTHA GOOSE & THE BROTHERS GRIMM

REV IT UP—JUMP THE FUNK

FABLE

This EP is the sort of record that I always knew Bad Mutha Goose could make. They not only accomplish on record what they do live, they take their material into new places. This is a far better record than their first EP, which, shall we say, was a learning experience.

There are two versions of "Rev It Up" here, a song about driving a fast car that becomes possessed once it gets on the highway. The song lifts guitar riffs from Hendrix's "Voodoo Chile" and Sam & Dave's "Soul Man." The "Purple Voodoo Mix" version layers different parts of the regular song over each other, creating an incoherent but unified whole. Everything at once, it's total confusion.

"Jump The Funk" is the crowning glory of the EP. The chiming guitar of Tim Kerr opens the song, which eases into an unshakable groove and totally cuts loose. Denia Ridley's smooth and exceptional vocals are out front with able backing. Ryan Walker lays down a well-controlled popping, slapping bass groove and meaty, soulful accents are contributed by the horn section. This unburdened and inspired performance shows the unmistakable influence of 1970s funk (particularly Parliament) and 1980s go-go.

"Texas" is bound to offend some people with its excessive vulgarities (eight "shits," twenty-four "fucks, fucked-ups, fuckings," seven "motherfuckers" and three belches). It's a stark look at the ugly side of Texas—violent encounters with police, drunken excess: "We scrapin' the bottom of the barrel/Goin' all the way tonight/Party with the devil." A side of Bad Mutha Goose not really seen in performance, this down-and-out song has some subtle, splendid bass playing and a funk rhythm guitar that evokes a bluesy feel.

GEORGE LEAKE

VOL. 8 NO. 11 ★ NOVEMBER 11, 1988

ALVIN CROW & THE PLEASANT VALLEY BOYS

BROKEN SPOKE, DECEMBER 20

When I arrived at the Broken Spoke, Alvin Crow & the Pleasant Valley Boys were backing up an energetic Doug Sahm on some Texas favorites, including "Is Anybody Goin' to San Antone" and "Worry, Worry, Worry." The sound system sounded cleaner than I'd ever heard it at the Spoke and the relaxed atmosphere made for a fun set for all the musicians. Roger Crabtree was flawless on the harmonica; Rick Crow played some of the best licks I've heard from a country guitarist in a long time; Scott Walls' steel guitar cried, screamed, and soothed; and Crow demonstrated once again that he is one of the best fiddlers around. D. K. Little, after a bit of coaxing, took his place at the mike for a few numbers ("Four, Five Times," "There's Still a Lot of Love in San Antone") and even showed his tattoo. No, not that one.

While Crow took a break, Jimmy Ray Harrell, Todd Jagger, and Drew Casteneda joined Crow's rhythm section, T. J. McFarland and Don Bacoch, for an eclectic set ranging from rhythm and blues to swing to bluegrass. I dare say it was the first time a Jimmy Cliff tune had been performed with bluegrass instrumentation at the Broken Spoke. Crow joined Casteneda for "In the Night" and then picked up his electric guitar for several rockabilly songs, including "Blue Christmas." About that time Kimmie Rhodes and her husband, Joe Gracey, along with their little angel Jole, took the stage for some of the best music of the evening ("Jole Blon," "Texas Blues"). By the time Eric Hokkanen plugged in his fiddle it was a full boat, the ghosts of Bob Wills and his large band filling the timeless dance hall with timeless music.

"The good news," says James White, owner of the Broken Spoke, "is that we're not gonna change a thing." It's good to know that country music, the real deal, lives on in Alvin Crow, the Pleasant Valley Boys, and the Broken Spoke. **TODD JAGGER**

VOL. 8 NO. 19 ★ JANUARY 13, 1989

ROBERT EARL KEEN, JR.
THE LIVE ALBUM
SUGAR HILL

Two kinds of composers exist in the popular music world: those who write songs and *songwriters*. While the former simply have vocals as another aspect of their music, the latter use lyrics to create vivid, engrossing images that lock themselves into your mind.

Robert Earl Keen, Jr. is a songwriter. And appropriately, on the opening cut from his new *The Live Album*, he sings "Words can paint a picture sharper than a photograph." In the manner of other master folk artists such as Jerry Jeff Walker and Guy Clark, Keen's words do just that—one can clearly envision what he's singing about, and easily feel the emotions he's trying to express.

It's fitting that Keen would do a live recording, because an audience draws out his best qualities. His love songs, especially "I Would Change My Life" and "Who'll Be Lookin' Out for Me," grip the Dallas Sons of Herman Hall crowd with melancholy; his rocking numbers, like "Going Down in Style," work them into a fever.

His best quality is his sharp sense of humor. In "The Front Porch Song," Keen's hilarious monologue about himself and friend/co-author Lyle Lovett gives the tune a dimension far above Lovett's version. And "Copenhagen" brings screaming laughter from the crowd.

Like Lovett, Keen gives the country/folk fan more than music; he brings an originality and wit that other performers simply don't have. If you've never seen him perform, one listen to *The Live Album* will have you running to the Cactus Cafe for his next show.

LEE NICHOLS

VOL. 8 NO. 21 ★ JANUARY 27, 1989

It Does Make You Want to Dance

VOL. 8 NO. 27 ★ MARCH 10, 1989

JOHN T. DAVIS

IT WOULD BE INSUFFICIENT to refer to Rusty Wier as anything other than an institution. Since beginning his professional career in the early 1960s, the Manchaca-born singer-songwriter has outlasted city managers, any number of the gin mills that used to employ him, and damn near every savings and loan in town. Only the South Texas Nuclear Project seems destined for a longer tenure in the popular imagination.

Wier is the quintessential Austin musician, at least in his predilection for mixing rock and country with a smattering of folk and blues, and letting the stylist chips fall where they may.

"I do other people's songs, but people don't always recognize them by the time I get through with them," he observed one day as he guided a crumbling VW van across town in a quest for pancakes and coffee. It was about one in the afternoon. "Rusty-fication, I guess you'd have to call it," he added. A passenger in the van suggested that Wier's ability to make material conform to his style might be regarded as a blessing in disguise.

A blessing, that is, if one craves long absences from employee rolls, time clocks, or profit-sharing plans. Despite a career uncluttered by hit records, Wier has always worked, following his muse from one beer joint to the next. He has to think back to his teenage years to recall his last day job. His fans wouldn't have it any other way. Wier's gigs have been a component of life in Austin for more than twenty years.

Rusty Wier at the Rome Inn, 1977. Photograph by Ken Hoge.

Still, as many have observed, it is not a life to get old in. Wier is a literal greybeard of the city's musical community. In his mid-40s, he has children playing in their own bands. He's a lifer.

And a craftsman. If nothing else, Rusty Wier has refined playing in a joint down to its essence. With an economy that seems almost Zen-like, Wier defines his art: "I like gigs where I can talk to folks and entertain 'em. There's nothing in the world I'd rather do. The first time anybody ever applauded for me, I was screwed for life."

There were years of bands—the Spades, the Centennials, the Deeds—in which Wier labored as a drummer. It wasn't until after a tour of duty in the Lavender Hill Express, an early 1970s vintage country-rock group, that he got out front on guitar. "Gary Nunn (another Lavender Hill member) would get on me," he recalled. "I was more a showman than a drummer, and I had a hard time with the meter. Gary was the only

Wier is the quintessential Austin musician, at least in his predilection for mixing rock and country with a smattering of folk and blues, and letting the stylist chips fall where they may.

one with balls enough to call me on it. So I guessed I'd better learn to play guitar."

Then the songs began to come, and the familiar persona began to emerge—the lanky figure crowned by the gambler-man cowboy hat, the boots, the carefully crafted good-ole-boy bonhomie. Wier could mix it up with any audience, tapping reservoirs of joy, regret, love, and laughter, and make 'em dance in the process.

Success is a relative measure. "I've thought about that question for a long time," he mused as he leaned back and fired up a Vantage blue. "According to a lot of people, I've probably already made it. According to a lot of people I'm a legend. A poor legend," he added with a laugh.

"All I wanted to do was to make one album. That's how it started out. You never really get there, I don't think. If you imagine you do, I think you're fooling yourself." ←

AMA Preview
Jimmie Dale Gilmore

VOL. 8 NO. 28 ★ MARCH 17, 1989

JOHN T. DAVIS

TO HEAR JIMMIE Dale Gilmore sing is to enter into the sensibility of the High Lonesome, a place that echoes with memories of empty highways at night and freight trains rolling towards a distant horizon. When he sings, it is a place where one wants to linger indefinitely.

The West Texas native only got around to releasing his first album, *Fair and Square* (Hightone), last year. But his musical pedigree stretches over two decades, and includes collaborations with some of the most remarkable artists to come out of a remarkable area.

Gilmore was born in Amarillo, but he grew up in Lubbock listening to border radio and watching his musician father who, he recalled, "played in little bands around those little towns."

Not long after he was out of high school, Gilmore had a little band of his own. The Flatlanders, which also included Joe Ely and Butch Hancock, were one of the first groups in Texas to aggressively combine folk and country music. Their one surviving record, an album issued years after the band's demise by England's Charly Records, premiered Jimmie's song, "Dallas," with its yearning line, "Have you ever seen Dallas from a DC-9 at night?"

That song made it onto one of Ely's albums, as did other Gilmore compositions, but for years, the only way to hear the songwriter perform his own material was to track him down to an Austin-area bar or nightclub. That changed with the release of *Fair and Square*. Produced by Ely, the album was calculated to inject Gilmore squarely into the bluesy, honky-tonk tradition of Jimmie Rodgers and Lefty Frizzell. In an era in which country musicians routinely evoke the Byrds when asked to cite their influences, Gilmore still waxes rhapsodic over Hank Williams and Webb Pierce.

"I believe that what I think of as 'real' country, well, the public never really lost their taste for it," he said one time. "But the, um, availability of it suffered for awhile."

The good news is, the more albums Jimmie Dale Gilmore makes, and the more stages he graces, the quicker that shortfall will be redressed. ←

AMA Preview
Two Nice Girls

VOL. 8 NO. 28 ★ MARCH 17, 1989

JOHN T. DAVIS

IT IS AN IMPROBABLE musical geometry that can render three young women into Two Nice Girls. But Kathy Korniloff, Laurie Freelove, and Gretchen Phillips are used to adding up to more than the sum of their parts. Who would have expected that Phillips, an alumnus of an avant-garde band called Meat Joy,

Two Nice Girls' Gretchen Phillips, Kathy Korniloff, Pam Barger, and Meg Hentges at the AMAs, 1991. Photograph by Martha Grenon.

would choose to throw in her lot with two relative neophytes in the persons of Korniloff and Freelove in 1985? Or that their combination of layered harmonies, deadpan humor, and incisive lyricism would command so loyal a following so quickly?

Two Nice Girls is all over the map. When they perform, it may be in the context of a subterranean beer joint (where they may be the only "nice girls" ever to darken the door) or an International Women's Day celebration. They transformed Lou Reed's "Sweet Jane" into a polymorphous slice of heaven; at the same time they were bringing listeners back down to earth with anthems such as "I Spent My Last Ten Dollars (On Birth Control and Beer)."

In order to help their audiences appreciate the lyrical rabbit punch beneath the airy harmonies (and, incidentally, conjure up a little sing-around-the-camp-fire fellowship), Two Nice Girls used to be in the habit of handing out lyric sheets before their sets. And in a quest to learn more about the kind of people they were enticing through the door, the band has run an opinion survey from the stage.

"They said they liked our sense of humor, our free spirits, and our harmonies," said Korniloff, which was a nice reaffirmation.

Opinion polls, lyric sheets—it's damned considerate when you think about it. ◀

AMA Preview
Lou Ann Barton

VOL. 8 NO. 28 ★ MARCH 17, 1989

JOHN T. DAVIS

THERE ARE FEW visions in rock & roll more incendiary than the sight of Lou Ann Barton, trailing smoke, stalking out onstage in a miniskirt you could stick in a highball glass. The look, the attitude—it's all there in the single hip-shot glance she gives the audience before launching a cigarette butt in the darkness with the flick of one insouciant nail.

The look, the attitude and . . . the voice. A buzz saw fueled by honey, it is a voice that can cut a swath through lust and love and the million shades of blue in between. It is a formidable weapon to be placed in the hands of a Fort Worth girl. Even today, there is a lot of Cowtown in the whiskey frosting she puts on words like "time" and "cry" and "man."

That voice has led her to the forefront of the Fabulous Thunderbirds, Roomful of Blues, and an array of her own groups. It has taken her from Fort Worth gin mills to the glittering showcase clubs that spangle both coasts. It was in one of the latter, in Manhattan in 1980, that she captured the ear of veteran blues/soul producer Jerry Wexler, who virtually offered to produce her on the spot. Two years later, Lou Ann

Lou Ann Barton. Photograph by Andrew Long.

debuted with *Old Enough*, on Asylum Records, an album co-produced by Wexler and Glenn Frey. Linda Ronstadt summed up Lou Ann's sonic impact when she observed, "That woman scares me to death."

Unfortunately, Barton got dropped from Asylum during a corporate shuffle, and a follow-up album never materialized. Her personal fortunes went into decline, and a 1986 effort, *Forbidden Tones*, never received the distribution it deserved. Even so, *Rolling Stone*, in reviewing that album, called Barton "the most commanding white female belter to erupt out of Texas since Janis Joplin." ◄

AMA Preview
Doug Sahm &
West Side Horns

VOL. 8 NO. 28 ★ MARCH 17, 1989

JOHN T. DAVIS

OVER THE YEARS, Doug Sahm has worn more masks than Lon Chaney and the Lone Ranger combined. He's been a child prodigy on steel guitar and fiddle, and a San Antonio youth whose infatuation for conjunto music was so pervasive that it earned him the nickname "Doug Saldaña" from his Chicano neighbors. He's been a bandleader on the Alamo City's El West Side, and an international sensation as a faux-British pop star.

He's been a cosmic cowboy riding the psychedelic range, and an R&B revisionist who has helped perpetuate the memory of Lone Star monuments like T-Bone Walker and (during his Duke Records tenure) Bobby "Blue" Bland. Last fall, he found himself on stage singing his 1965 chart-topper, "She's About a Mover," with Bob Dylan in Canada.

Throughout all the guises, only a few things have remained constant: an abiding affection for Big Red soda pop, a passion for sandlot softball, and an unchecked love for all of the southern and southwestern variations of American music. On the cusp of 47, there is little he hasn't played, and less he won't.

These days, Sahm's musical coloration has taken on a decidedly blue tint. After expatriate years in Scandinavia and Canada, Sahm has returned home to release his first domestic record in eight years, *Juke Box Music*, on the Antone's label. True to its name, the album combines contemporary material with Sahmian interpretations of blues material by the likes of Etta James, Johnny Adams, and Glenn Wills.

Call it another mask. As far back as 1968, Sahm was taking a detour from his Sir Douglas Quintet pop career to record *Honkey Blues*, a greasy R&B experiment that prefigured *Juke Box Music* by two decades.

Two stalwarts who have been along for much of the ride have been trumpet player Charlie McBurney and tenor sax man Rocky Morales, together known as the "West Side Horns." They have collaborated with Sahm on his albums for at least sixteen years, weaving blues lines and mariachi sass into the fabric of Sahm's stylistic excursions.

As for Sahm himself, he has been established as a member of the *Chronicle* Music Poll's Hall of Fame. Unwilling to play the greybeard, however, he is touring the country with an R&B revue that includes Antone's Records labelmate Angela Strehli and the West Side Horns. The ostensible aim of the tour is to promote *Juke Box Music*, but it's really all just about moving. ◄

Triple Threat's Stevie Ray Vaughan, W.C. Clark, and Lou Ann Barton at Soap Creek Saloon, 1977. Photograph by Ken Hoge.

W.C. Clark Gets His Due

VOL. 9 NO. 8 ★ OCTOBER 20, 1989

JOHN T. DAVIS

DUSK HAD DESCENDED over the outdoor patio that serves as a beer garden at Grizwald's, a South Austin eatery. W.C. Clark kept his shades on. Clark plays the blues, leavened with dollops of soul, pop, and jazz, but all of it seems to marinate in a blend of honey and pepper. It's pretty without being, you know, *pretty*.

Clark was working his usual happy hour gig at Grizwald's with a truncated version of his Blues Revue: George Winn, his regular bassist, and pinch-hitting drummer Barry "Frosty" Smith-Frost. The combination hardly mattered. There are few musicians of any longevity in town with whom Clark has not played.

Not that any of them were clamoring to join Clark on this night. He was playing to a cluster of the restaurant's regulars, a little less than two-score people in attendance. It wasn't much to show for over three decades of steady work. Some of the musicians he had tutored had gone on to acquire fame and money and the ancillary perquisites that accompany them. Fame and money were not, however, making their presence conspicuous at Grizwald's.

Clark could be forgiven for wondering sometimes if it wouldn't go on like that forever. His might ultimately be a legacy of massive goodwill and small recompense. It might be that his personal orbit might never eclipse much more than the nightclubs and beer joints and restaurants that dot the Austin metropolitan area.

But you never could tell.

FIVE NIGHTS AFTER he played for thirty people, W.C. Clark was preparing to play for 12 million.

If Clark appeared nervous at the prospect, he wasn't showing it. He was standing in a brightly lit dressing room one floor below Studio 6A, which houses the set for the PBS series *Austin City Limits*. Clark was the centerpiece of a swirl of activity around the room. Indeed, he was the focus of the evening itself.

Call it payback. Clark had been the student of one generation of Austin musicians, and had served as mentor to another. Now, some of his former protégés were coming together to perform for an *ACL* episode that was being billed as "A Tribute to W.C. Clark." To Clark, who will turn 50 on November 16, the fete was something akin to a birthday party.

Stevie Ray Vaughan was standing in a corner of the dressing room, regarding Clark with no small degree of affection. He and Clark had formed the aptly named Triple Threat Revue (with Lou Ann Barton filling out the triumvirate) a decade or so ago. "The first time I remember seeing him," the guitarist recalled, "was in Alexander's [barbecue joint]. . . . We were all playing with different people, and we just decided to have a killer band."

> ## Clark had been the student of one generation of Austin musicians, and had served as mentor to another.

"Triple Threat came together in a bank vault on Sixth Street," Clark recalled. "That was where we rehearsed." He glanced around to make sure his mother is out of earshot before he added, "It was hotter than hell in there."

Outside the dressing room, in a foyer by the elevator, Stevie's older brother Jimmie could not recall exactly where he and Clark had first crossed paths. "It was probably around '69, when I moved here," he ventured to guess. "We'd run into him at Ernie's Chicken Shack or the IL Club."

Clark, for his part, was interested in Vaughan and his band at the time, Storm. To put a finer point to it, he was as intrigued as much by the band's complexion as by its music. "I had never seen a complete white blues band before in my life," he said. "They were not really interested in making money, just in learning how to play."

Clark had a money gig at the time, playing bass for Joe Tex. But he moved back to his hometown with alacrity and began sitting in with Storm on occasion. All the while, he was saying to himself, "Something is happening here. I've never seen this thing before . . . Whatever this thing is, I want to understand it. I want to be involved in it."

WHEN HE WAS GROWING UP on his home place between Austin and Pflugerville, Wesley Curley Clark was prepared for life as best his family knew how. His grandfather taught him how to butcher hogs and tend a smokehouse. He watched his mother bake pies and put up vegetables. "There was no way they could know the world was going to be like it is today. They were preparing me for what they knew about the world.

"My music interest comes from listening to my grandmother cooking cakes, washing dishes, working, and humming." He paused in his conversation and emitted a low and mournful note. "Sometimes, to a little boy, it would be so scary, so . . . scary. Soulful scary, until I'd be around the corner, peeking and listening."

His grandmother and mother might have preferred he maintain that respectful distance from music, at least that of the secular variety. His mother, Ida Mae, was raised at the altar of the Old Time Religion, and it took her a long time to accept that her son made his living cheek-by-jowl with painted women and intemperate spirits. W.C. Clark has made music for 34 years, but, astonishingly, his mother never saw him perform for an audience until the *ACL* taping.

W.C. Clark, 1989. Photograph by Martha Grenon.

Clark, though, was seduced early on by the musician's life. At age 16, in 1955, he was standing onstage at the Victory Grill, playing bass with his cousin, L. P. Pierson. "The next thing I know," he said, "I was playing with T. D. Bell & the Cadillacs, and Blues Boy Hubbard & the Jets." He mastered the bass, took up the guitar, and acquired a nodding acquaintance with keyboards and the saxophone.

Now, he said, "I would say my blues is really blues and jazz, progressive blues, or whatever you want to call it."

The nomenclature notwithstanding, Clark's application of his art was sufficient to help inspire the Vaughan brothers. He also worked with Angela Strehli in two of the city's first integrated bands, James Polk & the Brothers and Southern Feeling, in the mid-1970s. He enabled Will and Charlie Sexton—at the tender ages of eight and nine—to cut their musical teeth with him over the course of dozens of gigs at the Continental Club. Throughout it all, he kept his own bands working, up to 200 nights a year. Not bad for a guy who didn't get around to cutting an album of his own, *Something For Everybody*, until 1987.

THEN IT WAS HIS TURN. Stevie Ray Vaughan welcomed Clark to the *ACL* stage with a heartfelt abrazo. They kicked the evening off with a bluesy instrumental, and soon the stage began filling up. There were guitarists on the order of both Vaughan brothers, along with Denny Freeman, Derek O'Brien, Will Sexton, and Clark himself.

There were vocal pyrotechnics, courtesy of Lou Ann Barton and Angela Strehli. Jon Blondell doubled with George Winn on bass, and joined saxophonist John Mills on trombone. Rusty Trapps, Clark's Blues Revue drummer, contributed harmony vocals, while Smith-Frost held down the backbeat. The Fabulous Thunderbirds' Kim Wilson added vocals and cayenne-spiced blues harp as the music made a broken-field run between blues, pop, and soul.

The flashpoint of the evening occurred when everyone shoehorned themselves onto the *ACL* stage for an ensemble version of Al Green's "Take Me To the River." It was the stuff that, you know, dreams are made of.

Clark earned himself a six-pack of standing ovations. He introduced his mama from the stage, and she got a standing ovation. At night's end, the crowd sang "Happy Birthday" to him.

Surely, as W.C. Clark stood onstage, basking in the glow of approval and drifting on the tides of applause, he was being vouchsafed a singular award for a well-spent life.

After all, next week, it would be back to playing for thirty people at Grizwald's again. And playing his usual Thursday night gig at Raven's. Back to all the other one-night stands that keep him revolving around Austin. Back to business as usual. Out of the spotlight tonight, though, it don't get any better than this, right?

But you never could tell. ◄

Lucinda Williams
No Tougher Judge

VOL. 9 NO. 13 ★ NOVEMBER 24, 1989

JOHN T. DAVIS

THE PEN WAS SLASHING with a terrible vitality through the dim light. Back and forth, over page after page, it described a series of X's, eviscerating one song title after another. It wasn't quiet in the *Austin City Limits* control room. Far from it. Studio-quality speakers reverberated titles such as "Passionate Kisses," "I Just Wanted To See You So Bad," and "Changed the Locks."

Lucinda Williams, the author of those songs, seemed to suck the melodies back inside her. There was an avid fixation about her as she crossed out the songs on her set that seemed to negate the music she had just finished making.

The control room was slicked with shadows. The only light came from the bank of television monitors that made up one wall of the room. More than a dozen screens caught Williams from as many angles and flung her image across the room. She watched her pixilated counterpart, far from happy with what she was seeing. Each performance that failed to meet her standards was crossed off her list.

"Well, that's it," she said to no one in particular. "I just wasn't meant to do this. Fine. I'll just go back to L.A. tomorrow and tell my manager that I'm only going to write from now on. This is the last tour I'm doing."

Someone ventured a compliment, but Williams wasn't in a mood to be placated. "Goddamn it," she snapped, "*I* know what my voice is supposed to sound

Lucinda Williams at the Austin Music Hall, SXSW 1995. Photograph by John Carrico.

like. I know when I'm singing good and—" flinging a finger towards the offending television monitor, "—I sound like shit."

Ego junkies have rampaged through the *ACL* studios before. The prima donna is far from an endangered species in the music business. But Williams was not indulging in a flight of temperament, nor unleashing a fit of rock diva pique. It was just her reaction to a night in which the wheel of circumstance seemed to be grinding exceedingly fine.

Lucinda made her home in Austin from about 1980 until 1984. She hit town with a formidable album (her second, *Happy Woman Blues*) on the Folkways label to her credit, but without an excess of worldly goods.

In those years, she was always the woman whose shows at emmajoe's or the Alamo Lounge were imperiled by cars that cratered on the way to the gigs. She was the one who turned up on your couch when her love life turned sour, the one who made a financial tapestry by stitching together a seemingly endless series of day jobs to supplement the money she made performing. She once lost a job as a receptionist at a law firm because, as she reported in a sardonic aside, "They said I wasn't perky enough."

She is, for the record, about as perky as Hamlet. Sweet-tempered, though—and damn, she could sing. She mixed up songs by blues masters like Robert Johnson and Memphis Minnie with original compositions detailing the tribulations of good girls in bad circumstances. Every now and again she would take her boyfriend Clyde in tow and disappear into the vastness of the Acadian country of south Louisiana. A few days or weeks later, you'd see her slender figure wafting around Austin once more, a fistful of andouille sausage in one hand, and four new songs in the other.

Then she moved to Los Angeles, dammit, and fell in love. The resulting marriage didn't work out, nor did a pending contract with CBS Records. None of it seemed to resonate with tragedy, somehow. Williams went about her business, making music and pursuing the brass ring with what appeared to be admirably laconic detachment, just as she had in Austin and Houston and Louisiana and New York. Eventually, the word-of-mouth that her talent cultivated led to a record deal in 1988, with Rough Trade, a San Francisco hardcore label whose cumulative output, prior to her signing, sounded like industrial machinery breaking down.

And yet it worked. Lucinda had met an old buddy from Houston, another Texas expatriate with the improbable name of Gurf Morlix. Together, they produced *Lucinda Williams*, perhaps the most lovingly detailed and fully realized cycle of songs to be released in the whole of last year.

In the ensuing months, Lucinda has received barbed-wire-kisses from any number of critics. She's schmoozed with Letterman and modeled in the "swimsuit issue" of *Spin*. There is talk of a *Saturday Night Live* appearance.

Yet, there was a part of her to which it didn't signify. Inside the woman in the spotlight lived a Louisiana girl who looked askance at the sound and fury. That was the steel magnolia who was savaging her set list after the *Austin City Limits* taping. Never mind that the *Austin City Limits* performance is far more accomplished than she believed in the heat of the moment. Or that the critical hosannas are likely to continue.

"It's a nice feeling to know that I can actually make a living with my songs and not have to depend on performing," she said. "It's hard to get used to it—that you deserve it, and it's okay. It's sort of an uncomfortable feeling in a way. I dunno. You have to learn how to enjoy it."

Then she laughed, a shy laugh, of sorts. "I'm still working on that." ◂

Dancing About Architecture
Liquid Repasts

VOL. 9 NO. 47 ★ JULY 27, 1990

KEN LIECK

IN THE OFFICE OF Louis Meyers, manager of Michael E. Johnson and the Killer Bees (as well as a bunch of other bands that he doesn't talk much about), there are several items of Bee memorabilia and other Bee-related stuff on display. Among them is a small placard, snagged from some forgotten bar, delineating the pleasures of a drink called the Killer Bee. If memory serves, the beverage consists of one shot of Barenjager (a honey liqueur) and one of Jägermeister (a killer liqueur). Eventually, after seeing this endorsement for such a fine concoction several times, I actually ordered one at some San Antonio saloon. While the drink might have proved fatal to someone with less stamina (i.e., someone who's not used to eating food he finds in his car) it simply inspired me to wonder—if other local bands had drinks named after them, what would the potion in question contain? For instance, a Coffee Sergeant would have to be a Club Soda with a tab of acid floating in it, right? In any case, with the help of the usual drunken sots, I came up with this list of fine liquid repasts:

> The Javelin Boot: Trash Can Punch and X (aged 12 years).
> The Bouffant Jellyfish: A 40-ounce Schlitz Malt Liquor with the alcohol removed.
> The Dangerous Toy: A double shot of Jack Black with a Crackerjack prize floating on the top. You drink it blindfolded.
> The Reiver: A fine aged wine with a hole in the cork.
> The Girl in the Nose: A Girl Scout Cookie with a beer chaser.
> The Hand of Glory: Whatever Jim Morrison drank.
> The Hollywood Indian: Ginger Ale—but they swear to God it's scotch . . .
> The Hey Zeus: Anything through a crazy straw.
> The Texas Tornado: Mescal through an I.V.
> The Wannabe: Whatever's free.
> The Fundamental: A thawed-out Coors Party Ball.
> The Al Escovedo: Old Granddad.
> The Randy Franklin: Old Granddad with Grecian Formula.
> The Kris McKay: Well, she heard that Janis Joplin drank Southern Comfort . . .
> The Butthole Surfer: I don't know. Does red or white wine go with a penis reconstruction film?
> The Dirtbag: Who cares? Whatever it is, Davy'll drink it.
> The Twang Twang Shock-A-Boom: Prom punch that "somebody said was spiked."

Another drink that we figured any bartender worth a liquor license ought to be prepared to serve was the Michael Corcoran, a warm beer salted on the rim with—you guessed it—brown biker speed. ◀

ED HALL
LOVE SPOKEN HERE

BONER

Albert, the first LP from this psycho-grungy Austin outfit of stark raving mad ex-art students, had all the directional sense of a blindfolded rat in a flaming maze. The interesting grooves found on a few of the LP's cuts were too few and far between to make the album palatable to more than a few fringe listeners.

Now, here comes the psychedelia, summer of love-themed *Love Spoken Here*. Looking at those colorful kitschy plastic flowers on the cover, you think, "Oh god! More trash from beyond the realm of comprehension!" Wrong! Someone has turned on the lights. Ed Hall actually hits a hard, cerebellum-slicing groove from the very first note of "Pay for Me" and never relents the rhythmic fervor nor intense energy until the tone arm wrestles itself from the final groove. These guys display some wonderful, albeit simple riffs which rival anything that sonic-thrash kings Dinosaur Jr. or Mudhoney can dredge up.

For those who like the Ed Hall of *Albert,* don't worry. In spirit, they're very much the same band that dumped that stuff on the unsuspecting public in 1988. Their lyrics and attitudes are still so bizarre and hallucinogenically abstract that they make Frank from Blue Velvet look like a prime candidate for dinner at the White House. Their sound now is just a lot more coherent and accessible. It's a sound that's making me happy and is sure to widen the band's audience. **JOSEPH P. MITCHELL**

VOL. 9 NO. 49 ★ AUGUST 10, 1990

Pastures of Plenty A History of Willie's Picnics

VOL. 9 NO. 43 ★ JUNE 29, 1990

JOHN T. DAVIS

ON PAPER THE RECIPE didn't look that complicated: Take one cow pasture, one summer day, a dozen or so musical cronies, and one stage. Add beer, and voila—an instant party in the bosom of Texas. There was the heat, of course, but the people were used to baking themselves to a turn in the course of outdoor activities, especially on the Fourth of July.

It wasn't a festival that was germinating in the back of Willie's mind. That word, after the excesses of Woodstock and Altamont, had acquired a bad connotation. What he had in mind was something more convivial, more homespun . . . Something like a picnic.

A real *big* picnic.

1973, Dripping Springs: Wild in the Country

THE LINEUP: Waylon Jennings, Tom T. Hall, Rita Coolidge, Doug Sahm, Sammie Smith, Kris Kristofferson, "and Many Others . . ."

Many were called, but few were sober. According to a newspaper report, almost 50,000 of the curious showed up for Nelson's first one-day flirtation with instant Utopia. Unseasonable rains dampened the days leading up to the Picnic and many feared attendance would be dampened as well. Nelson hastened to assure everyone the rain would stop on the day of the show, except for a brief afternoon shower to cool things off. People bought it, and flocked to Dripping Springs. And Nelson had the added advantage of being correct in his weather forecast.

1974, College Station: The Epiphany

THE LINEUP: Michael Murphey, Jerry Jeff Walker, Jimmy Buffett, Waylon Jennings, Randy Newman, Leon Russell, and a cast of zillions.

This was the watershed; during the three-day Picnic, concertgoers discovered a new sense of collective identity. It was the birth of a regional consciousness that still persists—the national-state of Texas.

MANY WERE CALLED, BUT FEW WERE SOBER.

The heat was stifling, and cars in the parking lot burned like so many holiday sparklers. Wolfman Jack and the crew of the *Midnight Special* television program embarrassed themselves in person and on the airwaves, and the Texas World Speedway became an open-air latrine. None of it mattered. The music was, by and large, superb, and there was that seductive sense of shared recognition. Nelson and the others staked out their musical turf for all to see. Of course, no one made any money after all the bills were paid. Asked if the Picnics were on their way to becoming an annual event, Nelson replied (only half-joking), "I guess so. I'd hate to put 4,000 thieves out of work."

1976, Gonzales: Apocalypse Now

THE LINEUP: Leon Russell, David Allen Coe, Doug Sahm, and a lot of drunks with guns.

The 1976 Picnic was a monument to Murphy's Law and frontier karma. In late May, Nelson said there would be no Picnic. On June 14, he reversed himself and announced another three-day affair, but the Gonzales County judge only granted the promoters a one-day permit. The promoters responded by saying they were perfectly willing to ignore the law and hold the show for as long as they pleased.

A local citizens' group that went under the acronym of CLOD (Citizens for Law, Order and Decency) tried to block the concert. In retrospect, it's a shame CLOD didn't succeed.

One hundred forty-seven people were arrested, one man drowned, three rapes were reported, and there were enough drug-related arrests and car wrecks to fill a court docket for months. Nelson was sued by the concert site landowner, the ambulance service, and the electrical contractor who wired the juice.

That was the year that the good-guy "cosmic cowboy" yielded to the ugly macho specter of the "outlaw." Bluster, swagger, and ego replaced the prevailing social graces, and handguns became a popular fashion accessory.

The music was as rancid as the mood. Concertgoers were treated to the odd spectacle of Leon Russell belting out "Jumping Jack Flash" at seven in the morning. Shortly thereafter, a rainstorm collapsed the roof over the stage and drowned the sound system. The Picnic finally limped to a halt a little more than thirty-six hours after it began. Nelson never even played an entire set. His only appearances onstage came when he sat in with Doug Sahm and Russell.

1979, Pedernales Country Club: The Sound in Your Mind

THE LINEUP: Leon Russell, Ernest Tubb, the Lone Star Records ensemble.

Nelson bought a country club outside of town, ostensibly so he could set his own pars on the golf course. To the dismay of the greenskeeper and several score of outraged whitetail deer, he set up a stage at the head of the ninth fairway and threw the first bona fide Picnic in three years. At last, he thought, he had found a permanent site for his annual blowouts.

No more rented pastures, surrounded by angry neighbors. Well, no more rented pastures anyway. A few of his new neighbors tried to stop the show, but many of them were won over by the day's conclusion.

The music was excellent. Nelson and Leon Russell worked the crowd like tent-shot evangelists, and a new generation got a firsthand taste of Ernest Tubb. The Lone Star artists were also well-received. Unfortunately, the fledgling label had folded in May, plagued by charges of mismanagement and chicanery.

1986, Manor Downs, Manor, TX:
Living in the Promiseland

THE LINEUP: John Mellencamp, Bonnie Raitt, the Beach Boys, Alabama, Jon Bon Jovi, George Jones, X, Neil Young, the Fabulous Thunderbirds, Don Johnson, and more performers (approximately eighty) than Ringling Bros.

Last minute changes of venue (from UT's Memorial Stadium to South Park Meadows to Manor Downs).

Accusations of deceit and bad faith. A talent lineup that changed by the moment. Confrontations with the powers-that-be. Yes, the 1986 fete contained elements all familiar to connoisseurs of Picnics past.

But for the first time in the fourteen years since the Dripping Springs Reunion, there was more to a Picnic than a fajita, a case of beer, and thou. The 1986 affair also did double duty as Farm Aid II, reaching millions of viewers (courtesy of cable channel VH-1's coverage) and raising over $1 million in pledges for Nelson's labor of love.

Thanks to a revolving stage and truncated sets (two or three songs apiece), all of the assembled performers got their fifteen or so minutes in the limelight (or spotlight, since the event ran, in the words of Nelson's farming compatriots, from "can't see to can't see"). If none of the music was overly memorable, that did little to distract from the triumph of packaging over performing that characterized the '86 Picnic. ◂

Willie Nelson, backstage at the Armadillo World Headquarters, 1972. Photograph by Burton Wilson.

97

The 1990s: An Introduction

RAOUL HERNANDEZ
The Austin Chronicle Music Editor, 1994–present

Fuck Emo's

USTIN'S *Slacker* nonchalance seduced the rest of indiedom on July 5, 1991, when Richard Linklater's neo-realist zeitgeist shuffled into art house movie theatres and college campus student unions nationwide. Three months later, Sept. 24, Nirvana's *Nevermind* came out. Joe Ely's "Row of Dominoes" had begun its chain reaction.

Daily occurrence becomes history's march—recorded in dates arbitrarily significant. Between the death of Stevie Ray Vaughan on August 27, 1990, and Doug Sahm's on Nov. 18, 1999, Austin's decade of music ran the gamut of reaction to another band of punks shrugging *Never Mind the Bollocks*. One way or another, everything before and after Kurt Cobain pulled his own Sid Vicious on April 5, 1994, smelled distinctly like "Teen Spirit," in Austin as it is on Madison Avenue.

Once SRV's "Riviera Paradise" (*In Step*, 1989) gave way to Eric Johnson's "Cliffs of Dover" (*Ah Via Musicom*, 1990), and finally the Arc Angels' eponymous 1992 Geffen debut—guitar/vocal duelists Charlie Sexton and Doyle Bramhall II fronting Vaughan's rhythm duo Double Trouble—River City still projected a resolute roots façade despite a long rich history of DIY acts from the Big Boys and the Dicks to Scratch Acid and Butthole Surfers. Putting their best snakeskin boot forward, Lucinda Williams' *Sweet Old World* and Alejandro Escovedo's solo debut, *Gravity*, defined 1992 Austin as much as Hyde Park rents and Las Manitas. That May, an "alternative" lounge opened just off the corner of Sixth Street and Red River.

Campus landmarks (Hole in the Wall), Congressional monuments (Continental Club), and international wonders (Broken Spoke) matched the Armadillo World Headquarters' mythos, a legacy that includes its timber-helping shelter successor Liberty Lunch. When greedy, inept local government razed the latter in 1999, Stubb's wasn't quite yet ready to assume its mantle. Punk pits descended many layers downtown, notably clubs Cave and Cannibal, but only one grungy haven hosted Johnny Cash on the same South By Southwest Thursday that Mudhoney and Jimmie Dale Gilmore fused that so-called grunge with Texas roots existentialism (March 17, 1994). Liberty Lunch hosted Nirvana, but Cobain left behind Emo's.

1994. Daniel Johnston drops briefly on Atlantic Records just for *Fun*, while Kathy McCarty unveils her *Dead Dog's Eyeball* in a jar of his formaldehyde. Future Warner Bros. bubble-buster Sixteen Deluxe forms even as the Fuckemos dupe enough cassettes to force Rise Records' jukebox staple *Fuckemos Can*

Kill You. Soul Hat, representing the Sixth Street evolution of Antone's Fabulous Thunderbirds 1980s (Ugly Americans, Little Sister, Ian Moore), tries Sony's hand at post–Pearl Jam rock with *Good to Be Gone*. Jimmie Vaughan, meanwhile, launches otherworldly blues on the same conglomerate via his solo debut *Strange Pleasure* in contrast to one Sir Douglas Quintet's *Day Dreaming at Midnight* for Elektra Records. Fiddling with banjo traditions, the Bad Livers dig as deeply for their haunting *Horses in the Mines* as Don Walser soars skyward on his unearthly *Rolling Stone from Texas* yodel. Pariah's metallic purgatory: the Back Room. Old school and new school coexisting just as Willie Nelson decreed, in perfect harmony.

Even as the Motards did to the Blue Flamingo what Hilly Kristal occasionally scrubbed off CBGBs, and rabid raconteur Ed Hamell shouted down the Electric Lounge, Austin's salad *days* of the mid-Clinton years weren't solely tentacles off Butthole Surfers basher King Coffey's Trance Syndicate label (Cherubs, Johnboy, Crust, Ed Hall). If alt.country begins at Uncle Tupelo's demise and subsequently Wilco's *A.M.* and Son Volt's *Trace*, both 1995, ATX's golden era of honky-tonk pumped to the oil derrick two-step: Kelly Willis, the Derailers, Dale Watson, Wayne "the Train" Hancock, the Robison brothers, and belle of the ball Libbi Bosworth. (Billy Joe) Shaver became a major label *Tramp on Your Street*, while Jimmie Dale Gilmore spun

gold for Elektra (*After Awhile; Spinning Around the Sun*), Joe Ely rode from *Live at Liberty Lunch* to *Letter to Laredo* on MCA, and Butch Hancock sweetened Sugar Hill before deciding *You Coulda Walked Around the World* in 1997 with Ely producing. Darden Smith, Jimmy LaFave, James McMurtry, Jon Dee Graham, and Texas music baron Robert Earl Keen all also roamed the flatlands.

Before . . . *And You Will Know Us By the Trail of Dead* (1998) became the last in line at Trance Syndicate, and Okkervil River's homegrown bow *Stars too Small to Use* (1999) signaled a millennial Renaissance, Emperor Jones broke the American Analog Set (*Fun Watching Fireworks*) and Spoon scored Matador (*Telephono*), both in 1996. Townes Van Zandt's death New Year's Day 1997 also stamps the year Kacy Crowley (*Anchorless*) and Davíd Garza (*This Euphoria*) surfaced on Atlantic. Fastball throwing platinum for 1998's "The Way" (*All the Pain Money Can Buy*) ties Butthole Surfers' novelty "Pepper" two years earlier on *Electiclarryland*.

Which leaves only 1:39 of Fifties horror movie monster mash grinding a Crampsian encapsulation of Austin's 1990s:

Fuck! Emo's. Fuck! Emo's. Fuck Emo's . . . Fuck Emo's . . . Fuck Emo's.

Forever. ◀

Page 2

VOL. 10 NO. 1 ★ AUGUST 31, 1990

MICHAEL HALL

IN AN INTERVIEW with the *Chronicle* just after his first album came out, Stevie Ray Vaughan was asked why he admired Jimi Hendrix so much. "I can't help it," he said. "He's one of the biggest . . . [and here he paused, trying to find the right word] souls I ever heard. He's one of the most . . . he's as big as . . . he's so big that you can't help it."

That's kind of how a lot of people feel now, trying to come up with the right words to describe what Stevie Ray Vaughan meant to them, what he means still. You stumble for the right words—there've got to be some that say how much he meant to you, to us. You pause and look at the person you're trying to reach, and trail off. . . . They're only words, but maybe Stevie Ray said them best: he was one of the biggest souls we ever saw. And, obviously (more so since he's gone), he was the soul of Austin music.

Like T-Bone Walker, Vaughan created something new, his own brand of shuffle—a rolling, thundering boogie that brought his blues into the modern world.

I suppose I'm like a lot of people who took Stevie Ray for granted the last five years or so, who saw him at the Rome Inn and Antone's in his hungry years and occasionally bought one of his records thereafter, but generally saw him as one who had found his fame and fortune. All of a sudden he seemed to belong to the rest of the world. I was wrong, of course; I would be

Stevie Ray Vaughan on Sixth Street, 1978.
Photograph by Ken Hoge.

reminded of this when I'd hear his brother play in the Thunderbirds or see a band at the Continental with a guitarist doing his best to cop Stevie's riffs, when the man himself would show up at Antone's some night or when he and his band kept winning all those Austin Music Awards.

Still, who would have thought he would become a star of such magnitude? I can remember John Hammond in 1983 saying that Vaughan was going to be huge. This was the guy who discovered Billie Holiday, Bob Dylan, and Bruce Springsteen. I wanted to believe it, but I wasn't the only one who chuckled at the prediction: Stevie Vaughan was the lifer who played for peanuts at the Continental, who jammed for hours at Antone's with his friends and idols, just another raggedy, drug-troubled Albert King fanatic. He was a blues musician; it was the Eighties.

Well, never underestimate the power of one whose heart is wild and true. Like his brother Jimmie Lee, Stevie Ray grabbed the blues and pulled it close enough to him to make it his own. Unlike his older brother, Stevie Ray attacked his guitar like an impatient kid, playing so fast and furiously, twisting the neck until the guitar groaned that it would break, coming up with sounds heretofore unheard; then you would remember that he was still a young man and, Hendrix being in his blood, a rocker.

Sometimes he wreaked too much havoc, played too many notes, too many tricks. But then he would slow it down, hit the sweetest spot and hold it, and you would remember he was first and foremost a blues man, that he was walking in step with his heroes. Like T-Bone Walker, Vaughan created something new, his own brand of shuffle—a rolling, thundering boogie that brought his blues into the modern world.

It's safe to say that Austin would be a very different place had Stevie Ray Vaughan never moved here from Dallas in the early 1970s. Antone's might not have survived; it might never have existed. Half the guitar players in town would be playing bass, or going to night school. The music scene would be several notches dimmer; Austin would be just another music-heavy college town. And we wouldn't be so sad today.

The *Chronicle* would not have had the early hero we did; insofar as we need a vital music scene around to thrive on, the *Chronicle* might not have survived without him. Stevie Ray was our patron saint: we cheered when he signed, we made fun of Bowie, we rooted for his first record (Margaret Moser led us: "Hey hey, Stevie Ray, how high are you on the charts today?"). He was lowdown but earnest, tough yet sweet, all the things we wanted to be.

Stevie Ray Vaughan had so much heart; it carried him through fame, fortune, dissolution, heartbreak, and his physical and spiritual rebirth. You could see it in the little boy's smile he had on the eve of his first major tour; that same smile was there last spring at the Awards show, where in accepting the awards for Musician and Album of the Decade, he once again acknowledged his place in Austin music. That smile said, I'm doing what I love to do, and people love me for doing it; I love this life.

It's easy to forget, or to have missed, just how popular Vaughan was, and is, how many people he reached, how right his brother was when he said to Stevie, long ago, "I may be big around here, but you're going to play on the moon." ◄

AMA Preview
Arc Angels

VOL. 10 NO. 28 ★ MARCH 15, 1991

JOHN T. DAVIS

TWO GENERATIONS of Lone Star musicians came together in a local rehearsal space and emerged as a yearling band with thoroughbred bloodlines. That, at least, is the nutshell genesis of the Arc Angels, a band which had its first gig in November and was on the verge of signing a major label recording contract by the Ides of March.

When one considers the magnitude of the talent involved, it's no surprise that the pace of events has been so swift. Bassist Tommy Shannon and drummer Chris Layton, late of Stevie Ray Vaughan's band, Double Trouble, were set adrift by Vaughan's untimely death last August. At the time, the two were renting space at the Austin Rehearsal Complex on South Congress. So were a couple of other guys.

"Charlie was in the back working on stuff, and Doyle was coming in and out . . ." said Layton. "Charlie" was Charlie Sexton, the charismatic guitarist/bandleader recently returned from a ride on L.A.'s star-making machinery. And "Doyle" was Doyle Bramhall Jr., a young Ft. Worth guitar prodigy whose father was a frequent songwriting collaborator with Vaughan.

"I thought it would be a real interesting thing if the four of us got together and tried to make some music," said Layton. He was right. The Arc Angels landed their first gig opening for Robert Cray on Nov. 30, and mixed newly minted original material and Little Richard covers.

"It wasn't like we said, let's get a band together and have a big career," said Layton. "But all of a sudden it seemed like a good idea. We all have a lot of the same musical sensibilities, and we haven't even scratched the surface." ◂

Arc Angels at the 1990–1991 Austin Music Awards. Photograph by John Carrico.

REIVERS
POP BELOVED
DB

Some people here in Austin seemed to actually like the Reivers' third record, but for this newcomer *Pop Beloved* ranks as a major comeback, their best record since they were Zeitgeist. They still have a sometimes formulaic reliance on their trademarks: the yin/yang harmonies, the slow-building tension of their songwriting arrangements, and the repetitive riffs. Since John Croslin and Kim Longacre are consummate singers together, Croslin is a deft and dramatic songwriter, and those riffs are damn catchy, I'm not arguing at all.

Lyrically it sounds like Croslin came off a roller-coaster of a relationship during the writing of the songs "Over and Over," "Keep Me Guessing," and some of the others. The first two tunes are simply dead-on, single riff pop songs, with Longacre delivering a tough but plaintive vocal on the first, and Croslin handling the vocal chores on most of the second. That song starts off irresistibly, with a thrusting guitar riff bolstered with a little piano and Garret Williams' pounding drums, calms down a little for a quiet bridge, and then kicks back up again.

"It's All One" is something of a masterpiece, a shining example of Croslin's songwriting prowess and the band's extraordinary flair for epiphany-reaching arrangements. A lovely ballad with quiet acoustic guitar, strong melodic support from bassist Cindy Toth, and a flamenco-ish solo from guest Mike Tamas, the song is striking enough that Croslin can get away with awkward lines like "your futon/your cigarettes" and moving enough that when Croslin recites his good and bad memories and then moans, "When I think that I can't take it and I wish that I could leave/stuck in Austin with my heart upon my sleeve" you want to buy him a drink and a plane ticket. But he doesn't really want to leave; the song is bittersweet, sad but hopeful.

Croslin the vocalist may be the biggest improvement here. His deep, dark tone has gotten more expressive when he sings alone, as on "Keep Me Guessing," "It's All One," and "If I Had A Little Time Without You," a musically nasty song of frustration. He's flatter when he sings with Longacre, but that would seem intentional: he's the leveling straight man to her expressive histrionics. Of course, Longacre's voice needed no improvement, and on "What You Wanna Do" and "Chinatown" she delivers performances that you just want to follow forever, with Croslin adding soaring choruses. There are only a few missteps: a moody, almost obligatory instrumental title track, and the album closer "Second Chance," which is simply a decent, bluesy rocker. The rest of the record is perfect.

JASON COHEN

VOL. 10 NO. 37 ★ MAY 17, 1991

RECOMMENDATIONS: TAILGATORS, BAD LIVERS
TEXAS TAVERN, FRIDAY 16

The Tailgators have been playing their Texas brand of wicked Louisiana swamp rock for years, to the delight of critics and audiences all over the world. The disadvantage of this kind of popularity is that Austin doesn't get to see as much of them as we'd like—they haven't played here in months. No matter, come Friday night at the Texas Tavern, they'll be swinging into their lowdown sound with genre-benders the Bad Livers, currently a favorite around town and the *Chronicle* offices. Besides, school starts soon enough. Get down there and get your ya-ya's out.

MARGARET MOSER

VOL. 10 NO. 50 ★ AUGUST 16, 1991

ESTEBAN "STEVE" JORDAN

LA ZONA ROSA, FRIDAY 20

You can have your blues at Antone's, your two-stepping at the Broken Spoke, or your roots-rock at the Continental; my favorite archetypal Austin music experience is conjunto at La Zona Rosa. Steve Jordan, who comes around maybe four times a year, is known as "the Jimi Hendrix of the accordion," not just because of his astonishing physical technique but also because of the range of sound he coaxes out of his box, played through an impressive-looking rack of effects pedals. The result is a conjunto that covers the usual bases—waltzes and rancheras, tearjerkers and party songs—with strong doses of rock & roll electricity and jazz-improv experiments. Plus there's Jordan's onstage character. With his long hair, big grin, and covered eye, Jordan looks for all the world like a shaman, pirate, and angel, ready to tell you stories, play you music, and take you to conjunto heaven.

JASON COHEN

VOL. 11 NO. 4 ★ SEPTEMBER 20, 1991

HERMAN THE GERMAN & DAS COWBOY

BLACK CAT, MONDAYS

It's time to go down the ol' Chisholm Trail once more. A man whose digits dance across a fretboard like methed-up tarantulas, Mr. The German's high-octane mix of beerhall tunes, Link Wray voltage, and Billy Lee Riley–style mania always equals a sloppy good time. His six-string dexterity is truly mind-boggling, his atmospherics could give Jorgen Ingemann ("Apache," you ditz!) pause, and his Kaiser helmet's a true scream. Forget Clapton: Herman the German is our *true* Father Who Art . . . **TIM STEGALL**

VOL. 11 NO. 24 ★ FEBRUARY 14, 1992

TERRY ALLEN

LA ZONA ROSA, SUNDAY 14

As genuine a talent as he is a cult figure, Allen's prolific forays into visual art, theatre, and film have, in the last decade at least, come at the expense of his profile as a musician. Though he regrouped his Panhandle Mystery Band for the Joe Ely Band reunion shows in Lubbock, his live performances remain rare, and it's been years since he played Austin (though you can always catch his son Bukka, who is also a formidable mixed-media talent when he's not behind the keys). He has plenty in common with his flatland compadres—a rigorous intellect, a broad sense of humor, and a ridiculously strong command of color, detail, and imagery—but Allen's concerned with Americana of all kinds (Vietnam, drugs, football, and beautiful waitresses) and all places, not just Texas. The music he's made with Ponty Bone, Richard Bowden, the Maines Bros, and Jesse Taylor strikes me as skewed honky-tonk, with only a little bit of folksiness. At La Zona he'll be joined by Richard Bowden, Lloyd Maines, and whoever else is in the Panhandle Mystery Band (it is a mystery, after all) these days. **JASON COHEN**

VOL. 11 NO. 41 ★ JUNE 12, 1992

LIBBI BOSWORTH AND TUMBLIN' DICE

BROKEN SPOKE, SATURDAY 29

Austin hasn't had a Queen of Country Music in a very long time, maybe not since Marcia Ball disbanded Freda & the Firedogs in the Seventies. Kelly Willis may be the most obvious contender but don't be too surprised to hear the name Libbi Bosworth bandied about, either. Bosworth's road-tested, feisty vocals go a long way toward making her a prime contender for the title in this town. God didn't make honky-tonk angels, but he was awfully close to pure heaven when he created Libbi Bosworth. **MARGARET MOSER**

VOL. 11 NO. 52 ★ AUGUST 28, 1992

Pure Texas Country
Walser Walks the Straight and True

VOL. 11 NO. 24 ★ FEBRUARY 14, 1992

LEE NICHOLS

IT'S A MONDAY NIGHT at Henry's Bar & Grill, the honky-tonk oasis of North Austin, and the crowd here is blessed with the presence of an Austin legend, Jimmie Dale Gilmore. It's a magical evening, the kind that has given Austin its reputation as a wonderland of musical brilliance. An enchanted onlooker leans forward in awe and makes the commentary heard so often before: "Boy, I just love his voice . . ."

The adoring fan isn't referring to Gilmore; he is Gilmore, and he's talking about Don Walser, leader of the Pure Texas Band, and in the words of Bad Livers bassist Mark Rubin, God's Own Yodeler.

It's not an overstated title. There are moments in music that transcend mere entertainment—times when an artist hits on an intangible something that suddenly elevates the performer and audience alike onto another plane, a different reality devoid of time in which all conversations cease and wandering minds become focused on the immediate happenings. A sort of religious experience that, at its completion, elicits cathartic shouts of joy.

Don Walser conducts his services every Monday night at Henry's and produces such transcendental scenes just about every time he raises his beautiful tenor voice into a powerful yodel. The gig has become a weekly appointment for many needing a fix of traditional country music, performed by someone who can do more than simply imitate Ray Price or Bob Wills. Much of his material is indeed covers, but his faithful don't come simply to hear old favorites. Walser himself is the attraction, no matter whose material comes out of his mouth.

Often, that material is his own. Walser has put out two local cassettes of both covers and originals, *Singing Pure Texas* and the recently released *Don Walser Sings More Pure Texas*. Perhaps those aren't the most imaginative titles, but they accurately describe his musical philosophy.

Walser does it right. He can't help it. He learned C&W in a day when radio was somewhat more regionalized and unconcerned with pop crossover.

"I love traditional country," Walser says as he talks in the back parking lot of Henry's. "When I say traditional, I'm talking about the older country. And there's still a few that do it, like Travis Tritt, but for the most part, country music's been taken over by soft rock. If the Eagles were still going strong today, they'd kinda be playing country—and there's not a thing wrong with them, I love the Eagles; I used to play some of their stuff in some of the bands I was in. But traditional country music has lost its niche. It's just not there anymore, and it's going away if we don't keep trying to plug it.

"And the kids love it," continues the gray-haired Lamesa native, who won't reveal his age, but is definitely older than "the kids." "I think if traditional country music is done right, there's a place for it."

Walser does it right. He can't help it. He learned C&W in a day when radio was somewhat more regionalized and unconcerned with pop crossover.

"I guess I've been playing since I been 15 years old. The guy that probably got me started in music was 'High Pockets' Duncan. He was a disc jockey out of KDAV in Lubbock, and High Noon told me he used to do something with Buddy Holly, too. The way they got in touch with me—I didn't have a phone at home in Lamesa—old High Pockets would get on the radio and say 'Anybody over there in Lamesa see ol' Don Walser, tell him I want him to be at such-and-such place at such-and-such time.'"

Walser played around the Panhandle, working many of the same "jamborees" as his friend Hoyle Nix. "I started writing my own stuff, and we recorded a single of 'Rolling Stone from Texas,' and our drummer sent it off to *Billboard*. They rated it four stars; but we were all young and ignorant, and didn't know what that meant. We probably could have gone to Nashville and done some good."

Years later, Walser's naiveté would become Austin's good fortune. He moved here in 1984, not originally seeking a musical career. He began working with Al Dressen's Super Swing Revue and then later formed his Pure Texas Band.

The group has always been loaded with talented musicians to give Walser's voice the ample backing it deserves. Legendary steel guitarist Jimmy Day recently left the band to return to session work in Nashville, and former members of Bob Wills' Texas Playboys have come in and out of the unit. The current lineup now features Herb Rivera, who formerly played steel for Hank Thompson's Brazos Valley Boys, superb bassist Don Keeling ("Skinny Don," as opposed to the more portly Walser), fiddler/guitarist/vocalist Howard Kalish (of Ethyl & Methyl and his own Rightsiders), and

Don Walser and his wife Pat at the Broken Spoke. Photograph by John Carrico.

multi-instrumental prodigy Jason Roberts, a 16-year-old relative of Johnny Gimble.

"There's nobody doing what we're doing right now," Walser says. "Nobody. [We do the] three types of Texas music: cowboy yodeling; honky-tonk music like Ray Price, George Jones, and Marty Robbins; and then you got the Western swing."

That may sound boastful, but he's right. The latter two styles can be found in abundance, but it's hard to find a good yodeler these days, much less one of such superlative ability. ("Most people can't yodel . . . and they ought not to if they can't," he adds with a laugh.)

"Elton Britt did a thing called 'Chime Bells' years ago, and I liked that song and said I've got to learn to sing that and worked at it until I could. Then Slim Whitman did a thing called 'Casting My Lasso,' and I added that, and then I couldn't find any more yodeling in the little town I was in. So I started writing my own."

Had he done better at submitting his stuff to the big leagues, "You" (from *More Pure Texas*) doubtless would have found its way onto the playlists of Price or Robbins. In fact, those two might have been the only ones capable of giving it the proper vocal treatment. As for lyrics, "John Deere Tractor" (from the first tape) could likely earn status someday as a Texas cult classic. While vastly different in style from Butch Hancock, its evocative simplicity illuminates the poor dirt farmer as national hero much like his West Texas compatriot's "Dry Land Farm."

Walser has been a welcome addition to Austin's scene not only for his incredible talent but his unassuming nature as well. When asked about moving on to "bigger and better" things—a lucrative record deal, in the lingo of most local artists—Walser replies, "We're trying to branch out and do better; we're playing one night a month at the Broken Spoke and we're talking to some more bigger clubs." Clearly, this is not a man with stars in his eyes.

But then, perhaps entering the big-business side of music might ruin it. Don Walser is among the last of a dying breed of musician, and not just stylistically—how many modern musicians, or human beings in general, would say something like, "You got to go slow; I don't like to spook other bands and book while they're there, because then that gives them the feeling that you may be trying to take their job. I'd rather stay home than to do that, 'cause musicians ought to be brothers."

He's that thing you heard about but didn't really believe exists—the musician who plays purely because he loves it, with no ulterior motives. ◄

DON WALSER'S
PURE TEXAS BAND
EMO'S, OCTOBER 29

I'll admit it. I didn't go to this show to listen to Don Walser sing. Oh sure, his magnificent voice, backed by one of Austin's finest country bands, is always a marvelous thing to behold, but I was here to watch. And what a spectacle it was. It's not uncommon to see rockers listening to Don Walser. The temporarily closed Henry's Bar & Grill became known in the last couple of years as one of the few places, if not the only place in the world, where punks in leather jackets with spiky purple hair could sit and dance alongside rednecks in Stetsons and ropers without being hassled, and enjoy some fine, traditional C&W.

Even years of being one of the freaks in the middle of the kickers couldn't prepare me for the scene at Emo's. There they were, on one side of the stage, a huge painting of the Flintstones engaging in B&D sodomy; on the other, a typically demented work from Roy Tompkins; and on the far wall, a picture of a psychotic clown holding a smoking gun and another of a nude woman with syringes for hands. And in the middle, five of the goodest ol' boys you can imagine, big Don yukking it up like always and fiddler Howard Kalish looking every bit the truck driver, seemingly oblivious to it all but really loving every minute. David Lynch couldn't come up with something this bizarre.

I expected to see the punks gaping in confusion at this oddity, but they seemed to take the menu of Marty Robbins yodeling, Ray Price shuffling, and Bob Wills fiddling in stride. Instead, I found myself gawking during the first hour. Here in Emo's, Austin's premiere thrash-rock bar, was a table of gray-haired old Walser veterans looking like they had gotten off the bus in the wrong neighborhood, and nearby, some hicks that I swear came straight from the trailer park. They stayed for an hour, but gave way to a young audience that shouted louder approval with every song.

The Rolling Stone from Texas: Don Walser at Emo's.
Photograph by Michael Crawford.

The show was a huge success, and the Emo's crowd deserved the biggest applause for its open-mindedness. If one tried to play thrash at a honky-tonk, they would be met with stony silence, but here, Don and crew were treated like the stellar musicians they are, and a new tradition for Thursday nights was born. Y'all come on out about 7:30pm, y'hear? Wear black, of course. **LEE NICHOLS**

VOL. 12 NO. 10 ★ NOVEMBER 6, 1992

The Bad Livers
Picking the Wide World of Music

VOL. 11 NO. 51 ★ AUGUST 21, 1992

JASON COHEN

IT'S SAID THAT in some realm of the afterlife all the dead rock stars have a band. It sounds like a big mess to me: Sid Vicious refusing to sing with Jim Morrison, Hendrix sounding out of place with Roy Orbison, and Johnny Thunders trying to get Hank Williams to talk to him. It might be better if God (or Satan) appointed one cohesive group of musicians to the divine post. They would have to be able to play a wide variety of instruments. They would have to know every song since the dawn of creation. And they couldn't have a manager or a drummer.

Unfortunately, the only band that might fit that description, the Bad Livers, are not available. Even if they weren't stuck here on earth with us mortals (at least when they're offstage) their schedule (300 bookings last year) leaves little room for other activity. Over the past year Danny Barnes, Mark Rubin, and Ralph White have gone from Saxon Pub and Headliners regulars to a band that can pack both La Zona Rosa and Emo's, from a local secret to a band that can tour the country regularly, thanks to shows in front of thousands of people opening for acts like the Dillards, Michelle Shocked, and the Butthole Surfers (a slot they beat out Nirvana for).

Now they're unleashing their debut record, *Delusions of Banjer* (Quarterstick/Touch & Go), on the world. If the Bad Livers' onstage virtuosity and breadth hasn't already convinced you that playing punk and metal covers is just one facet of these insatiable music lovers, *Delusions of Banjer* will. Aside from a song by producer/Butthole Surfer Paul Leary that even he probably didn't expect to hear performed with tuba, accordion, and banjo, *Delusion of Banjer* features all Bad Livers originals that encapsulate and expand upon the band's vast and seemingly divergent musical heritage.

"A lot of people will come to the gigs and there will be one facet of what we do that they like," bassist Mark Rubin says. "Like, we'll play some old-time tunes and someone goes, 'I like the Bad Livers, they play great old-timey music.' Then another guy will see Ralph play the accordion and go, 'Man, I just love the Bad Livers because they play accordion music.' It's easy for people to want you to be that one thing, whereas in the studio we were very conscious to let ourselves do everything we wanted to do. I have no problem putting our original material up against anything we've ever played."

"The original material sort of drips off the end of playing a lot of really choice old tunes," adds singer and banjoist Danny Barnes. "Classic textbook banjo pieces, or classic fiddle tunes, or standard bluegrass, or even covering punk rock bands."

Delusions of Banjer comes after a long period of label shopping. While the band was flattered by the interest they got from certain esteemed traditional labels, they found that the people at Touch & Go were the only ones who trusted them to be themselves.

"The point that needs to be made," Rubin says, "is we booked those gigs. We manage this band. All those sorts of decisions were ones that we decided for ourselves. We've worked very hard to make this a self-operative, self-enclosed grassroots organization."

Being labelmates with Therapy? and Pegboy might keep the Bad Livers from reaching the traditional audience, but they're used to that. They're also used to confounding "alternative" listeners. "Something that we've known all along is that if you're going to tell the

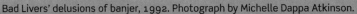

traditional audience to go to hell, you're going to tell the punk rockers to go to hell, too," Rubin says. "You have to cut your own swath if you're going to get anywhere. We like to be confrontational with our audience, if only because we've never been able to live up to anybody's expectations of what we're supposed to do."

In fact, the Bad Livers would be perfectly happy to alienate any single-genre crowd in favor of the only audience that matters to them: the Bad Livers audience. Their own tastes include metal and rap as well as gospel, ragtime, and folk, and they are no more a bluegrass band than they are a thrash band.

"We're like three individuals that have complete other worlds of music which we just happen to share a little bit of," White says.

" WE LIKE TO BE CONFRONTATIONAL WITH OUR AUDIENCE, IF ONLY BECAUSE WE'VE NEVER BEEN ABLE TO LIVE UP TO ANYBODY'S EXPECTATIONS OF WHAT WE'RE SUPPOSED TO DO.

" MARK RUBIN

"This is something that is such a part of our very essence that we'll be able to do it 'til the very end," Barnes concludes. "I don't have to have hair extensions or lose a bunch of weight to do this. I can be an ugly old fucker.

"In fact," he continues with a grin, "that's kind of like one of my goals, to be a cool old fucker who plays the banjo on the front porch. And it's going to happen." ←

Bad Livers' delusions of banjer, 1992. Photograph by Michelle Dappa Atkinson.

SKREW

BURNING IN WATER, DROWNING IN FLAME

METAL BLADE

When I first got my crawly little paws on Skrew's demo around six months ago, I thought it was the best thing I'd heard in hours. "Orifice," the opener on my little boot, throbbed with mangled guitars, Adam Grossman's breathless, snivelling screech, and a nifty Richard Burton sample (from *Equus,* of all things), and it grew more or less weirder from there. Unfortunately, Skrew's Metal Blade release has dropped Burton's rant in favor of, um, sounds like Phil "I'm a Nig, he's a Nig, wouldn't you like to be a Nig, too?" Owen. Bumfest, 1992. Like brethren Ministry, the SkateNigs, and a parasitic host of other like-minded groups, these guys yank their collective acrimony out like a rotted tooth and furiously shove the blackened, stinking result in your recoiling face. Sometimes it works ("Sympathy for the Devil") and sometimes it don't ("Poisonous"). Sure beats Al Jourgensen's latest effort, though. **MARC SAVLOV**

VOL. 11 NO. 52 ★ AUGUST 28, 1992

SKELLINGTON

SKELLINGTON

What makes Skellington good is the collision of its rhythm section's straightforward punchiness with Britt Daniel's skewed pop sense and (justified) artistic pretentions. Daniel still wears his influences on his sleeve (Smiths, Velvets, Pixies, Julian Cope), but he's got a knack for creating something unique out of the marriage of his heroes' idiosyncrasies and his own odd vision and sharp melodicism. This tape captures Skellington with their new guitarist Mike Hurewitz, who contributes the energetic "RXN," while Daniel wrote or co-wrote the other three tunes: the nervous head-trip "Underwater Fuchestra," the quietly bouncy "Pop Gun," and the taut, amusing paean to "Crispin Glover." Of course, now that this new lineup has finally gelled it looks like the band might implode (for young Austin bands, college graduation equals attrition), but even if that's the case, keep an ear out for Daniel's next move. **JASON COHEN**

VOL. 11 NO. 52 ★ AUGUST 28, 1992

A Songwriter's Struggle
The Devil and Daniel Johnston

VOL. 12 NO. 3 ★ SEPTEMBER 18, 1992

JASON COHEN

DANIEL JOHNSTON'S six years away from Austin have been, to say the least, cataclysmic. He's become internationally famous. His songs have been covered by dozens of bands. Homestead Records has reissued three of his cassettes. He's released three new records, and has just been discovered in England. He also spent a good part of the last six years in mental institutions, barely surviving an acid trip that was literally mind-blowing and a widely reported incident that he would sooner forget: believing a woman to be possessed by the devil, he broke into her apartment, frightening her out a window.

Last year his parents moved from West Virginia to Waller, Texas, and now, after a stay in the State Hospital, Johnston is living in Austin again. With the help of a daily regimen of anti-depressants, he's feeling more stable than he has in a long time. In August, armed with a batch of new songs, he went to Dallas and played live for the first time since South by Southwest 1990. The six tough years have definitely taken their toll on him; to look at his great shining moment on MTV, this gawky, grinning kid plugging *Hi, How Are You*, is to barely recognize the much paunchier, graying, but still good-natured and boyish man who will take the stage at Liberty Lunch next week.

"I'm doing a lot better now. I spend most of my time making up songs instead of letting my imagination

The creation of art requires great leaps of imagination; Johnston just has trouble distinguishing between his fantastic mental adventures and his real life.

Daniel Johnston in front of his iconic frog mural, 1999.
Photograph by Todd Wolfson.

113

carry me away," he says. "After I took some acid [just before leaving Austin], my thoughts were just more and more loony all the time, to the point where most of the time I was trying to save the universe from aliens. I had it all figured out. I was in and out of hospitals and some preacher came into the hospital once in West Virginia and handed me a Bible, and I was going, 'I must be in this book. I'm in this book!' And I looked, and it talked about the man-child in the Book of Revelations, and I was like, 'That's me, man; that's me.'"

Johnston punctuates his anecdotes with little laughs and giggles, recollecting his madness with a detailed immediacy that might be useful for songwriting but is a little disarming in person. You want to remind him that this reminiscing isn't necessary, that he's okay for now. It's frightening to imagine him being in total thrall to these scenarios, and rather difficult to respond when he talks about it. However, after he finishes one tale, in which he was a piece of ham pursued by Porky Pig, I have to ask him why Porky Pig would want to eat ham.

"That's a very good question!" he says, surprised, as if delusional fantasies required internal logic. "He's like a cannibal, you know what I mean?"

Anyone who listens to Daniel Johnston, watches Daniel Johnston, works with Daniel Johnston, or writes about Daniel Johnston runs the risk of glorifying his problems, encouraging a freak show mentality. There is also the obvious, inextricable relationship between his illness and his gifts. Artists are generally neurotic, compulsive, and self-destructive; Johnston is just less able to keep it in check and, clinically speaking, more seriously stricken. The creation of art requires great leaps of imagination; Johnston just has trouble distinguishing between his fantastic mental adventures and his real life. Most people go through life collecting layers of emotional armor; Johnston's heart is wide open.

Johnston's tales of good and evil, of God and Satan, of the Holy Ghost and Casper the Friendly

Ghost, might be dark and weird and funny ("Don't play cards with Satan, he'll deal you an awful hand"), but his love songs are perhaps the sustained narrative of unrequited love. "Ain't No Woman Gonna Make a George Jones Outta Me," Johnston sings on the song of the same name, but to a certain extent, a muse called Laurie did just that a long time ago.

"When I met her I was totally gone, I was like the Nowhere Man, totally fried, zoned, lonely, confused, completely out of it, I was just ready to give up," Johnston says. "I went to college at a branch of Kent State and I had this class and I went in there and it was the first class I had and I was like, oh god, the misery of life . . ."

His voice takes on a quiet reverence as he continues. ". . . Then she walks in, and she was like . . . glowing, and she sat down beside me, and all of a sudden I was changed, all of a sudden it was great to be alive! She turned and said hi to me and I said 'Hi, how you doing,' I don't remember what I said, but she was talking to me. Suddenly I was alive and had something to say. And she worked at this store and I'd hang out at the store for about three hours a day just talking to her. She was never rude to me, she never put me down, it was love, it was fantastic. One time I made up these songs just to amuse her, and she said, 'You know, you do that rather well,' and after she said that, I was at that piano every day, bangin' on that piano man. And that's how the whole thing started."

Artistic Vice is Johnston's first real studio record with a band (though Hand of Glory's Bill Anderson and the Texas Instruments back him up on *Continued Story*). Along with some of the more accessible cover versions that have appeared over the years ("Speeding Motorcycle" by Yo La Tengo and the Pastels, "Walking the Cow" by the Reivers and fIREHOSE), it presents Johnston's songs in a most palatable form, the crudeness of his earlier playing and singing replaced by a serviceably bluesy rock band. The songs sound great, the quavering power of Johnston's voice and facile melodies are nothing short of astonishing, and while Johnston is the first person to decry his rudimentary guitar playing, when he gets behind the piano he is capable of both bouncy pop accompaniment and gospel-style mournings. It might be his best record. His music, Johnston says, "is kind of like Bob Dylan meets the Beatles."

The most important thing is that Johnston be able to sing his songs and live his life without any serious recurrences. "I just want to stay out of the hospital, that's goal number one," he says. "I think some people try to be crazy, but I'm not trying to be crazy. I'm just crazy. But I'm harmless, and I'm behaving myself. I have the chance to play out and make a little money and keep on singing, so things are going good." ◄

Dancing About Architecture

VOL. 12 NO. 3 ★ SEPTEMBER 18, 1992

KEN LIECK

IT'S BEEN A BUSY WEEK here at the *Chronicle*'s music wing. I've been getting calls from all over the country (okay, I got one from Seattle and a bunch from around town) noting that "Hey, Nirvana's Kurt Cobain was wearing a Daniel Johnston T-shirt on the MTV Video Music Awards show." "Wow! That Nirvana guy was wearing D.J.'s *Hi, How Are You* shirt on the cover of the *New Musical Express*!" "Whoop! Kurt wore Johnston's shirt at the Nirvana show at the Seattle Coliseum!!" I think we can assume one of two things from this information: either K.C. is a *huge* Dan fan, or wife Courtney Love is way behind on her laundry chores. (Last minute clue: Jason Cohen says that *NME*'s top competitor, *Melody Maker*, claims that Cobain stole the shirt from a member of their staff.) ◄

Dancing About Architecture
Titty Bingo?

VOL. 12 NO. 6 ★ OCTOBER 9, 1992

KEN LIECK

NOT ALL THE LETTERS that arrive at the *Chronicle* offices are whiny. Some merely bear the mark of desperation, as did one recently from a reader who was going absolutely bonkers trying to figure out what was up with all these bumper stickers you see around town bearing the multicolored phrase "Titty Bingo." The reader was not alone in her worries. I can't begin to count the number of people who have asked me about this phenomenon.

Yes, Titty Bingo is a band. Yes, that band consists of notable persons (Jon Blondell, Derek O'Brien, Arlyn/Pedernales Studios' Fred Fletcher, and high-powered attorney Dahr Jamail). Yes, they sell/give away shit-loads of bumper stickers, T-shirts, tank tops, etc. So what's the big mystery? How about this: they only play about once a year, and even then they usually perform at a party or somesuch!

According to Fletcher, the band was formed as a fun "shit-for-brains rock & roll band," with no particularly serious intentions, and one day they decided to have a few bumper stickers printed up. After those caught on, they made a few T-shirts to give out, and people began demanding the chance to buy more. Fletcher says that the stickers can now be spotted in thirty states, mostly by mystified citizens who will never actually see the band (a note on the back of unpeeled stickers merely notes that Titty Bingo is a "garage band," and gives an address and merchandise price list).

As far as the origin of the name, the laughing Fletcher wouldn't say, but did offer that when Willie Nelson wears the band's apparel, he tells folks that it's "a little parlor game they play down in Texas." ◄

DIXIE CHICKS
LITTLE OL' COWGIRL
CRYSTAL CLEAR

Wow! What happened? The Chicks' first record, *Thank Heavens for Dale Evans,* was flat-out dull, a display of bluegrass and western competence, but without any flair. They've done a complete 180, partly because they aim a little more toward the mainstream. Normally that would be a recipe for disaster, but for the Chicks it has broadened their style. They tackle excellent songs by John Ims, Mary Chapin Carpenter, and even Sam Cooke and Ray Charles. Also included is "Past the Point of Rescue," a hit last year for Hal Ketchum. Those songs have subsequently rubbed off on the Chicks' own compositions and, coupled with improved instrumentalism and honey-sweet vocals, make for anything but a sophomore slump. Now, the big question: will the major label that grabs them (as will surely happen) make them dull again? Stick to your guns, gals. **LEE NICHOLS**

VOL. 12 NO. 8 ★ OCTOBER 23, 1992

TISH HINOJOSA
TAOS TO TENNESSEE
WATERMELON
CULTURE SWING
ROUNDER

Tish Hinojosa comments in the liner notes for *Culture Swing* that the past year or so has been "everything but dull" for her. No wonder. The last twelve months have seen the release *Aquella Noche,* the Christmas album *Memorabilia Navidena* (both on Watermelon), and now two more albums, *Taos to Tennessee* and *Culture Swing.* The former is a CD reissue of her first, a cassette-only recording originally released in 1987; *Culture Swing,* on Rounder, is brand new. It's fitting that Hinojosa's first record and her most recent one have been released virtually simultaneously. They give the listener an opportunity to hear both where she's been and where she's going. *Taos,* a crisp, low-key eight-track recording made in New Mexico, reflects a balancing act between the two musical poles suggested by the title—the cultural Cuisinart of the American Southwest and the slicker, more pop-oriented sound of Nashville, to which Hinojosa was making occasional forays at the time.

If the lovely, understated *Taos* shows promise, *Culture Swing* is the fulfillment of that promise. Hinojosa's voice is richer and more expressive, her musical palette has grown (harmonica, saxophone, accordion from Flaco Jimenez on a couple of cuts), and so has the scope of her lyrical concerns. With one exception (Chuck Pyle's "Drifter Wind"), the songs on *Culture Swing* were written by Hinojosa, and they cover a broad spectrum: folk, traditional Mexican music, the relatively straight country of "Louisiana Road Song," the Texas swing of "San Antonio Romeo" (which approaches Bob Wills' "San Antonio Rose" from the other side of the relationship), and delicate, understated tunes such as "Every Word." Jimmie Dale Gilmore suggests in a liner note that Hinojosa's music might be termed "MexTex," but songs like "Rag of the Sun" remain pretty much beyond category. She straddles and crosses borders of all types—cultural, political, emotional—and *Culture Swing* is border music of the first order. **LEE MOORE**

VOL. 12 NO. 8 ★ OCTOBER 23, 1992

WILLIE NELSON
STATE CAPITOL, NOVEMBER 1

Risking a dangerous mixture of church and state, the people of Austin came out on a glorious breezy afternoon to demonstrate their support and respect for two legendary local institutions in need of assistance: the pink-granite dome and the red-headed stranger. Willie Nelson played a 45-minute acoustic set on the steps of the Capitol Sunday to generate promotional material for his *IRS Tapes* and to raise donations for the renovation of the State Capitol building.

What a magnificent photo opportunity: Willie, graying tresses blowing in the breeze, framed by the massive structure of the Capitol entryway and a breathtakingly blue sky, playing his poignant ballads to an awestruck crowd. He performed an entirely spontaneous cross-section of his repertoire that included several tunes from *The IRS Tapes*, as well as jukebox classics like "Blue Skies," "On the Road Again," and "Crazy." Many of the songs, such as a medley of "Family Bible" and "I Saw the Light," turned into gospel-type sing-alongs, with the crowd playing fervent congregation to Willie's southern preacher.

A definitive moment illustrating the devotion of his followers was when he pulled out the haunting war protest, "Jimmy's Road," as the second song. The restless throng that had been chanting his name and hollering requests three minutes earlier now stood transfixed and silent during the entire duration of that stirring number.

It was a great change of pace from the overcrowded and overpriced shows that Willie usually sells out around here. You could tell it must have been a gas for him as well, after playing almost two hundred gigs this year at his Branson, Missouri, dinner theatre. The real thrill was the experience of finding myself standing so near such an almost mythological figure that I could read the ancient signatures on his beat up gut-string guitar. I will probably never witness a more transcendent musical performer at work. The guy is a goddamn genius, no two ways about it. Just ask the hundred or so people he autographed stuff for after the show.

Larger than life, and a little worse for wear and tear, both Willie and the Capitol are two structures that are definitely going to have a surplus of reverent supporters for many more generations. Plus, it's always nice to know that our tax dollars are going to such good use. **PAUL MINOR**

VOL. 12 NO. 10 ★ NOVEMBER 6, 1992

The U List
The Most Notable Austin Underground Bands

VOL. 12 NO. 26 ★ MARCH 5, 1993

THE HORSIES: Unusual, giddy(up!) hodge-podge of brainy art rock, flower child grooviness, Afrobeat, and Beefheart. They're a rhythm derby between current and former members of Joan of Arkansas, Pocket FishRmen, Hand of Glory, Happy Family, and the Muleskinners. **JASON COHEN**

STRETFORD: All they want is Xerox Love, but Pete Shelley keeps parking his butt on the screen. Punkstalgia was never so sweet (or speedy!). **TIM STEGALL**

SINCOLA: This scrappy, three-woman, two-man quintet teeters between divine chaos and sublime pop perfection, mostly due to a complementary guitar tandem (blooze 'n' melody gliding over chord-crunch) and crafty vocal hooks. Even when she's just standing around sipping water, unhinged vocalist Rebecca Cannon exudes a playful presence. **JASON COHEN** ←

THE TEXAS INSTRUMENTS
MAGNETIC HOME
DOCTOR DREAM

David Woody's very spidery guitar riff crawls up your spine the moment *Magnetic Home* opens, and from there on this veteran Austin quartet spits out its fourth strong album in a row. The anthemic "Generation Beat Away" embodies much of what's special about this band: a manically bent guitar solo, the rhythm section burning oil out on Highway 61, singer Woody bellowing "We got no voice and it shows." Life's little and not so little internal contradictions spur TI's songwriting, as always, with articulate bits of anger, insight, warmth, and weariness spilling out all over the edges. Musically they continue to take chances, blending punk rock roots with desert/heartland country and folk, then distorting the whole thing, turning guitar-driven, Dylanesque country rock inside out and applying almost a jazz band's sense of meter and time (check out the astonishing close to "Don't Give Your Life") in the rhythms. Eventually the rest of the world will catch up. **LUKE TORN**

VOL. 12 NO. 27 ★ MARCH 12, 1993

ST-37
THE INVISIBLE COLLEGE
OVER AND OUT

Although it was recorded well over a year ago, ST-37's debut CD is still light years ahead of its time. In an alternative universe where hallucinogens are one of the four food groups, ST-37 would probably rule the hit parade. Back on earth, these longtime stalwarts of the Austin underground provide a rather esoteric mixture of punk fused with the Can/Red Krayola vein of psychedelia. Despite seemingly innumerable personnel changes, ST-37 has succeeded in refining its craft since the days of Dong Huong. This finely layered cornucopia of fuzzy guitars along with synthesizers and tape loops would be a fine musical companion for the next time you freak out and decide to jump naked through a plate glass window. **GREG BEETS**

VOL. 12 NO. 32 ★ APRIL 16, 1993

Psychedelic warlords ST-37, 2002.
Photograph by John Anderson.

STEPHEN BRUTON

ANTONE'S, MARCH 19

Stephen Bruton was instrumental in making 1991 the year of Gilmore, and 1992 the year of Escovedo. By rights 1993 should be the year of Bruton. It's time for Austin's best guitarist/producer to step out from behind Bonnie, Bob, and Kris and show his own hand. If his Antone's showcase is any indication, it should be quite a hand. Leading an expectedly crack band, Bruton showcased material from his upcoming solo album for an expectedly packed house. On one tune the band sounded like a street-tough take on *Infidels*, the next a muscular *Damn the Torpedoes*. Bruton's own eclecticism, like his production, never gets in the way of the music. The thread through it all is the quality of the songs and, of course, Bruton's brilliant sold-his-soul guitaring. "I've Searched the World to Find My Love" shows he's no slouch as a vocalist either, with a dirty-sweet tone out of the Hiatt/Dylan school. This will be the album to look for this year. **MICHAEL ECK**

VOL. 12 NO. 30 ★ APRIL 2, 1993

THE FUCKEMOS
THE FUCKEMOS

SICKE FUCKE

Russell Porter of the Fuckemos. Photograph by Michael Crawford.

The Fuckemos are Austin's brightest new punk band, if punk can be defined as ugly music to compliment an even uglier world. After listening to the Fuckemos debut cassette, I had to suppress the sudden urge to go out and spray paint their name on a church or government building. With all the venom of dateless suburban high school outcasts, this quartet takes listeners on a brutal journey to a land where the streets are covered with severed limbs, bloody sheets, and human waste. Amidst the rubble, the Fuckemos also display their lighter side quite nicely on the soon-to-be-classic "2 Punk 2 Fuck" and the Ramoneseque Nazi fairy tale "Berlin 45." Vocalist Lars powerfully delivers his lyrics through some kind of pitch-shifter that makes him sound a lot like Linda Blair possessed, and the obligatory tape-ending suicide song "Opus Rus" features the greatest Casio solo I've heard since at least 1986. Best of all, the Fuckemos are giving this tape away for free. I only wish I would've had the foresight to hand this tape to the First Lady during her recent visit affixed with a note: "for Tipper."

GREG BEETS

VOL. 12 NO. 35 ★ MAY 7, 1993

THE MOTARDS
STARDOM
MORTVILLE

No band epitomized the raging, fuck-all ethos of mid-Nineties Austin garage punk better than the Motards. They aimed low, but struck hard, liberating pent-up mammalian impulses from Texas to Tokyo. *Stardom* is an odds-'n'-sods collection of 22 singles, comp tracks, B-sides, and other rarities from the local quintet's surprisingly prolific recording career. The disc opens with the Motards' 1993 debut 45, a train wreck of a recording that made the Estrus catalog sound meticulous by comparison. "I'm a Criminal" and "My Love Is Bad" land precariously close to the frothing, contrarian essence of punk, splashing all comers with a sloppy cocktail of beer and bile. The primitive 1994 recording of "Why Am I Even Here?" approximates the sensation of passing out under Suzie Bishop's snare drum, while supremely combative vocalist John Motard kicks out the song's rhythm on your shins. "Unhappy" is a hardcore shiv delivered in a yapping, Dee Dee Ramone–style vocal, while "Nothing Ever Changes" exhibits a murky blues pedigree recalling Poison 13. While *Stardom* can't be expected to best the band's legendary live prowess, it goes a long way toward explaining what the fuss was all about. GREG BEETS

Johnny Motard, 1996. Photograph by Michael Crawford.

VOL. 22 NO. 50 ★ AUGUST 15, 2003

NANCI GRIFFITH

PARAMOUNT THEATRE, APRIL 27

It's been said that every woman deserves to spend one night of her life as a homecoming queen. For Nanci Griffith, after bitter years as a wallflower on the Austin music scene, this April night was a homecoming in every sense of the word. If this Texas exile was a bit too determined to show the hometown folks how good she'd made it, it worked to the crowd's benefit. Everyone from Ann Richards, Emmylou Harris, and guitarist Nina Gerber to Carolyn Hester, Tom Paxton, and John Gorka dropped in to pay tribute, and Griffith rewarded all with nearly two hours of unbroken song.

Exile has always been Griffith's central theme. From the fugitive Mormon wife tearing down the LA freeway in a Ford Econoline to the old lovers who can only dream of returning to Texas one sweet bluebonnet spring, Griffith has drawn strength and inspiration out of being far from home. Everyone had something to add on the subject, with Paxton doing "My Ramblin' Boy," Gorka contributing "The Gypsy Life," and Hester chiming in on the Dylan farewell song, "Boots of Spanish Leather."

In another sense, it was a musical homecoming for Griffith. Her personal choices always seem to spotlight the sense of wanderlust and separation that sits at the heart of the Anglo-American ballad tradition, a tradition that traces in a long and winding line from the piers of Belfast through the Appalachian mountains and into Woody Guthrie.

If there's a weakness in Griffith's act, it's her singing. She'll assault a lyric full-bore even where a gentler touch is called for, as though the hometown girl is still trying to prove something. The difference is vivid when she's trading verses with a seasoned stylist like Emmylou. But the sweet, sad songs themselves generally triumph, and the Blue Moon Orchestra, led by guitarist Pete Kennedy, gives the folky songs a Nashville beat without getting in their way. Effective vocal backup came from the "Estrogen Choir," with mandolinist Lee Sanderfield and singer-songwriter Iris DeMent chipping in on some gorgeous three-part harmonies.

The most dead-on tribute of all to a tough and tender Texas woman came at the very start of the evening, from that shambling bear of a bard, Guy Clark. "It's just as clear as the windowpane," he sang in a short opening set. "She'll survive at all cost."

STEVE BROOKS

VOL. 12 NO. 35 ★ MAY 7, 1993

ERIC JOHNSON

ANTONE'S, APRIL 30

This was the proverbial you-had-to-be-there night. The evening, which raised over $10,000 for victims of violent crimes, built luxuriously over the course of Sue Foley's spare, silky blues, and Chris Duarte's turbulent Hendrix-cum-Stevie Ray Vaughan roar. And while both local guitarists were good, it took Eric Johnson only fifteen minutes to demonstrate beyond any doubt that he's taken his guitar playing to the next level, a level where not only a unique, individual style emerges, but also where a consistently high level of excellence is maintained. At first, Johnson merely added piercing leads to the full-bore backdrop of guitarists Bill Carter and David Holt as they romped through standards "Nadine" and "Willie the Wimp." Even then, however, Johnson's decorous fretwork evidenced a wicked, Duane Allman sting that's not generally associated with the guitarist's mellifluous and airy tone. Still, his leads got sharper and his solos longer and more commanding until he finally exploded like a monster on a ten-minute instrumental that sounded like Duane and Dickey dueling on Sonny Boy Williamson's "One Way Out." From that moment on, it was Johnson's show, and despite his endearing doe-caught-in-the-headlights look of bewilderment, he took center stage and held it. On occasion he'd get mired in a simple blues solo, but Holt would pick up the dropped ball, not missing a beat, and fire off a solo that demonstrated he's not far behind Austin's fair-haired wunderkind. The occasional lapse aside, Johnson clearly proved that impassioned blues are nowhere near outside his realm of expertise and that he truly is one of Austin's finest treasures whose rare club appearances are absolutely priceless.

RAOUL HERNANDEZ

VOL. 12 NO. 43 ★ JULY 2, 1993

TOWNES VAN ZANDT, DAVID RODRIGUEZ

CACTUS CAFE, AUGUST 13

Few events on the Austin music scene are as unpredictable as an appearance by Townes Van Zandt. Depending largely on his sobriety, the great Lone Star candidate for the Dead Poets Society can be either revelatory or deeply painful to watch. As one local songwriter recently remarked to me, "People pay to see Townes die in front of them." Townes, no stranger to his own myth, puts it better than anyone else: "There ain't much that I ain't tried/Fast living and slow suicide."

Then again, I thought during my first extended exposure to Texas' greatest living songwriter, maybe Townes has simply been playing footsy with the abyss all these years. He's gotten down deep enough to send back reports, but never quite meant to lose his hold on the edge.

I had a few of those hopeful thoughts as he put in what one longtime Townes-watcher called the best night he'd seen in fifteen years: two-and-a-half hours of poignant poetry from a man whose throwaways would be career highlights for most songwriters. When he's focused, nobody does the songs better than the gaunt, mournful-voiced man who wrote them. A whole night of Townes had a cumulative impact I'd never

Townes Van Zandt. Photograph by John Carrico.

gotten from catching just a few songs. One breathtaking line tumbled out after another: "Being born is going blind/And bowing down a thousand times . . . The stars for a diamond and the world for a ring . . . I believe it with my blood/If not my eyes . . ." It's the haunted beauty of Robert Johnson's delta, transplanted to the dusty deserts where Pancho bit it.

The Cactus had the good sense to pair Townes with one of the very few songwriters that can survive a toe-to-toe comparison: David Rodriguez, whose newest compositions keep up the quality of the old favorites. Rodriguez's poetic turf is different, as resolutely political as Townes' is personal, but they share a mordant humor and a seeming inability to write a bad line. The highlight of Rodriguez's new songs was "Cisto," a true story of a drummer who died in jail and a Latino neighborhood set to be swallowed in the maw of Bergstrom airport.

Was Friday's concert a lucky accident or a return to the world of the living? Townes himself seemed undecided. "Some would look at this glass," he remarked, "and say, 'Is it half-empty or half-full?' I would look at the glass and say, 'Is it vodka or water?'"

STEVE BROOKS

VOL. 12 NO. 51 ★ AUGUST 27, 1993

At the Starting Gates of the Seventies

VOL. 13 NO. 1 ★ SEPTEMBER 3, 1993

BILL BENTLEY

NIXON WAS OUT OF CONTROL, and Vietnam appeared to be the new Hundred Years' War. Students were killed at Kent State, and paranoia was running rampant everywhere.

Psychedelics were less plentiful, while crystal methedrine and the odd cocaine connections were coming to town. 1970 looked like it was going to suck.

The 13th Floor Elevators were turning quickly into a hazy memory, and the Conqueroo, after cutting bait and moving to California, had also called it quits. The

Jerry Jeff Walker, Roky Erickson, George Raines, and Doug Sahm at Gemini's, 1977. Photograph by Ken Hoge.

Vulcan Gas Company, the virtual center of Austin's new music universe, had definitely seen better days. Co-founder Don Hyde, on the advice of a local vice squad cop, had already gone to the West Coast, and the club at 316 Congress was a shell of its former self. After a great last gasp concert by the onetime, on-site house musician Johnny Winter in March, it was all over but the sweeping up at the Gas Company. Everything was winding down.

Except for Shiva's Headband. It seemed like they were just getting started. They had quickly turned into the city's house band after the Elevators crashed, and thanks to a nice-sized chunk of cash from their recently signed Capitol Records contract, Shiva's was willing to put their money where their music was. With the help of manager Eddie Wilson and a few equally imaginative friends, the band saw the gaping need for a place to hang their headband.

So while the Vulcan Gas Company was passing into legend, the summer of '70 saw excited talk of the opening of a new nightclub—even bigger, even better! And instead of only music, the room would be a vast cultural center, a home away from home for all the hippies and musical hedonists that seemed to take to Austin like rattlesnakes to rocks. The news started the summer with a strong sizzle. Along with a handful of clubs bubbling away in various parts of the city, there was soon to be the mother of all musical centers.

The Armadillo World Headquarters was like a vision: an airy former National Guard armory that someone had turned into a roller rink, with plenty of room to spill over in. As the dedicated crew began the stifling job of auditorium alchemy, Austin was looking to the corner of Barton Springs Road and South First as some sort of soulful savior.

First a former hometown hero decided to pay what would turn out to be one last visit to her old stomping grounds. No artist from Austin had ever made it bigger than Janis Joplin. From being the baby beatnik

THE ARMADILLO WORLD HEADQUARTERS WAS LIKE A VISION: AN AIRY FORMER NATIONAL GUARD ARMORY THAT SOMEONE HAD TURNED INTO A ROLLER RINK, WITH PLENTY OF ROOM TO SPILL OVER IN.

at the early student union folk-sings, she'd put her action in the San Francisco scene and grabbed the brass ring. Being an eternal loyalist, though, she'd come home to sing at her mentor Kenneth Threadgill's birthday party in a field right outside of town. Dressed in drop-dead threads and party pumps, she sat down in a chair, strapped on an acoustic guitar, and announced that she'd be doing songs by "someone you've never heard of, but who you'll be hearing a lot more of someday."

Accompanied by Chuck and Julie Joyce from Threadgill's band, she sang "Me and Bobby McGee" and "Sunday Morning Comin' Down" by newcomer Kris Kristofferson, to nary a dry eye in the audience. A few months later, the first song would be her biggest hit, and Joplin would be dead. That summer night, though, there was a tremendous pride that one of the city's own had gone on to such success yet would still remember her roots by returning a musical favor for Mr. Threadgill. Maybe 1970, and the new decade, wasn't going to be so awful after all.

It only took until August 7 for that fact to become breathtakingly clear. On opening night, Shiva's Headband, of course, topped the bill at the Armadillo, or AWHQ. The room wasn't really ready. There was no beer license, and it was obvious that it was still an embryonic musical mecca, but conditions be damned: Austin had been reborn.

Kenneth Threadgill. Photograph by Scott Newton.

The end of summer, with the kind of heat that turns people silly and runs off the lightweights, was right around the corner. There were plenty of musicians milling about town, and now that there was a sympathetic place to play, River City's golden years were just getting underway. The arrival then of the Oak Cliff blues crew and a particularly soulful singer from Louisiana signaled things were far from over for local bands. In fact, a second generation was starting.

Storm, with Jimmie Vaughan, Doyle Bramhall, Paul Ray, Lewis Cowdrey, and Denny Freeman, were the perfect band to bring a mountain of soul from the unlikely environs of the Dallas area. They realized the irrationality of white players plying their trade there. Thanks to the friendly education of bluesman Bill Campbell on the joys of East Austin's black nightlife and clubs like Charlie's Playhouse, Sam's Showcase, and Ernie's Chicken Shack, they saw that blues not

only had a chance west of I-35, it also had a home among its true believers. What a novel concept: a harmonious and interested city for a music that could barely get arrested anywhere else. By Storm setting up shop in Austin, the word went out and a blues train began to run that would eventually bring a cityful of players (and later, Clifford Antone) to Austin.

In 1972, no one was predicting the onslaught of redneck rock that would become such an albatross a few years later. In fact, nobody really thought twice about the stylistic sonics. Hadn't Hub City Movers started inching in that direction in the late Sixties, with their classic, "The Chicken Song," concerning a farmer dropping acid and setting his chickens free? In some ways, country music's influence was inescapable in Texas, even if all it did was inspire a Texas musician to flat-out reject country. At least with Freda & the Firedogs—and, soon enough, Greezy Wheels, the

Flatlanders, Kinky Friedman, and others—the boundaries of the sounds were being stretched to the snapping point.

The idea that anyone outside Austin would go for this concoction was remote at best, but this was before anyone besides Shiva's Headband even knew what a record company was. It was all virgin territory, and the sheer abandon and sense of near-nihilistic fun to be had either playing or listening to music had the feel of this incredible secret Austinites shared, and nobody wanted to study or talk about it too much for fear the bubble would burst.

IT GOES WITHOUT SAYING that there was next to no money to be made by musicians, but in the early Seventies, it was still possible to live in Austin on almost nothing but air. Take the case of the One Knite. Located in a small room perched precariously above a creek on Red River at the edge of downtown, there was never a cover charge and beer was all but free. Every Monday night Storm played, and it was never a problem to walk in and find a seat. Over on South Lamar, the Split Rail featured Freda & the Firedogs and the more country-influenced groups, for free, of course. And then there was Bevo's Westside Tap Room at 24th and Rio Grande, split down the middle for fraternity-types on one side and university bohemians on the other, and a beer garden in back with live bands like Kenneth Threadgill's.

No talent scouts, no managers, and no booking agents. It's hard to imagine now, but Austin had produced an incredible ecosystem where musicians found places to play and plentiful audiences to play for, without much more of a support system than a few music stores and gas stations to get a dollar's worth of ethyl.

That changed one day in the summer of 1972. George McGovern was running a presidential campaign that, besides being hopelessly lost, was a last-ditch attempt to rid America of Richard Nixon. Naturally, musicians of every stripe were lining up behind McGovern, and when a fundraiser was organized at Zilker Park with the help of a young Democratic Southern pol named Bill Clinton, the usual suspects of Austin bands were rounded up to play, with a couple of surprises. First, Phil Ochs showed up unexpectedly, and, after asking what city he was in, went out to give the city a dose of semi-stardom. He was, after all, a man who had run in the same circles with Bob Dylan and written several classic Sixties protest songs, even if he was soon to take his own life at the end of a rope on the East Coast.

Perhaps much more prophetically, a veteran country singer who had recently moved to Bandera following a fire at his Nashville house showed up for a stirring set. Backed by Bee Spears on bass, Paul English on drums, and Greezy Wheels' Mary Egan on fiddle, Willie Nelson—relatively short-haired and beard-free—brought the small but devoted crowd to silence. It wasn't so much that everyone knew who he was. Remember, this was a left-wing rock & roll event, for a politician being painted as just a few inches short of socialism. Still, Nelson had the goods. He ripped through blues lines on his beat-up acoustic guitar and sang in a beautifully sad voice that spoke of endless loneliness.

In an instant, he created a brand new genre of music, and it only took a quickly arranged booking at the Armadillo to give birth to the cosmic cowboy. The next summer, Nelson put on the Dripping Springs reunion, which he transformed into his Fourth of July picnic the following year. So in a way, it was an even swap: Austin (and America) didn't get George McGovern, but it did inherit an artist with the kind of expansive talents to bring together a whole movement. And Austin was off and running. ◄

Daytrippers Shiva's Headband at the psychedelic Love-In in Wooldridge Park, 1969. Photograph by Burton Wilson.

SHIVA'S HEADBAND EXPERIENCE
TRIP THE PSYCH FANTASTIC

"Above my typewriter is a framed 45 single that is the most important recording in Austin. . . . The single was 'Kaleidoscopic'/'Song for Peace' [by Shiva's Headband]." —Chet Flippo

Those words by rock critic emeritus Chet Flippo mean little today, but in the high and far-off times of the late Sixties, they were engraved in native Texas limestone. Shiva's Headband shaped the image of Austin as a musically creative oasis in unforgiving times. Yet, somewhere between the adulation for the 13th Floor Elevators' psychedelic pioneering and Doug Sahm's enduring Tex-Mex rock, Shiva's Headband missed its rightful place.

Spencer Perskin—his bespectacled stature suggests the Hobbit race—masterminded Shiva's Headband in 1967, one of the earliest progenitors of roots rock in Austin. The quintet, including his wife, Susan, served as house band for the Vulcan Gas Company, and when that venerable venue vanished, Perskin founded the Armadillo World Headquarters with a group of well-chosen friends. Shiva's was the first rock band in Texas to land a major label contract with Capitol for *Take Me to the Mountains* in 1969. For Perskin, it was a canny combination of right-place, right-time, and economic know-how.

"Remember, there weren't very many bands around," says Perskin over some lunch on South Congress. "Austin wasn't what it is now. Now, it's what I wanted it to be then, you might say. We didn't have any competition to speak of. We played fraternity parties back then.

"I emerged as a leader-spokesman because I was better at negotiating business. The band got paid better because I had the nerve to ask for more money. Sometimes we got it. I wish I had what we used to make in '69. We got to where we didn't accept jobs for under $750. We only played weekends and might get paid $1,000 for the night back then."

And what about *psychedelic*, that butterfly elusive term that defies definition? Shiva's Headband fused country and rock well before the cosmic cowboy Seventies and never compromised. The phrase "roots rock" wouldn't become music lexicon until the Eighties. Was Shiva's Headband ever psychedelic? Perskin hesitates only a moment.

"We took a *lot* of psychedelics. But I let the music tell me where it wants to go." MARGARET MOSER

VOL. 24 NO. 50 ★ AUGUST 12, 2005

IAN MOORE
IAN MOORE
CAPRICORN

Texas must be the best and worst place in the world to be a hot-shit young blues guitarist. There's more than enough great players to learn from, but however much you pick up or mature, you're always going to be the "next" Vaughan, Johnson, or Gibbons. For years, Ian Moore's been living proof of Texas Guitarist Syndrome, and, unfortunately, his pair of demos that ultimately landed this Capricorn deal did little to prove otherwise. But something funky happened on the way to the studio. Ian Moore's band caught up to him and many of the same songs that sounded flat on the demos reek of soulful hooks on this record. Furthermore, finding filler that wouldn't sound great on radio is near impossible from a batch of well-penned songs that could singularly please guitar purists and an MTV audience-in-waiting. With a band, songs, the expected soloing, and an unexpected voice probably as good as the picking, Ian Moore is a complete package that in a couple of years should provide a crop of current Texas sixth-grade phenoms with the challenge of overcoming "Ian Moore" syndrome. **ANDY LANGER**

VOL. 13 NO. 8 ★ OCTOBER 22, 1993

MONTE WARDEN
MONTE WARDEN
WATERMELON

KELLY WILLIS
KELLY WILLIS
MCA

With the Wagoneers, Warden emulated his influences; now, he imitates them. This album may be the best thing Buddy Holly ever made; unfortunately, it's supposed to be a Monte Warden album. Now before all of you hypersensitive fans write in angry letters please realize I really do like this. Warden is unquestionably one of the finest songwriters and practitioners of Texas country/rockabilly (now more the latter than the former) in the state. It's just that I'd rather hear Monte Warden imitate Monte Warden. The highlight: "The Only One," a duet with Kelly Willis that is, ironically, the finest single recording of her career. As for the finest collection of her recordings, that would be her new, third album. Willis has finally fully realized her musical vision, even topping her excellent previous albums. She employs the finest songwriters from both Austin's cowpunks (the Robison brothers, Mas Palermo, Libbi Dwyer, and herself) and the nation (Kevin Welch, Marshall Crenshaw, Jim Lauderdale) to push her angelic voice to its limits, sounding fuller and more confident than ever. The clincher is her band, mostly comprised of Welch's Overtones. Highlights here include a duet with Welch and a superb reworking of the Kendalls' "Heaven's Just a Sin Away." With this album, Willis has taken a huge step from being just another great Austin musician to essential listening, the kind of album for which people will still search for a decade from now. **LEE NICHOLS**

VOL. 13 NO. 8 ★ OCTOBER 22, 1993

Let's Go (Back) to Luckenbach, Texas Walker Revisits the Past, But Lives in the Present

VOL. 13 NO. 8 ★ OCTOBER 22, 1993

LEE NICHOLS

"Last week I was thinkin'
Ah, it's record time again . . ."
—"Gettin' By"

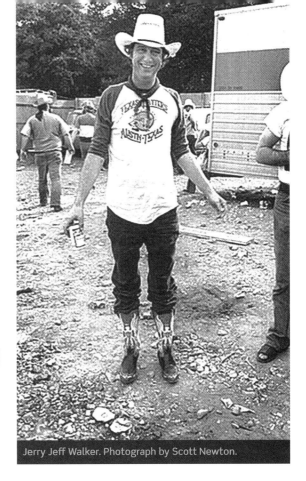

Jerry Jeff Walker. Photograph by Scott Newton.

OFTEN, A SEQUEL is just a bad idea. Sequels to funny movies almost always come off as strained, struggling attempts to revive old jokes. Follow-ups to emotionally powerful novels usually lack the inspiration that drove the first one. Spontaneity, by its very definition, cannot be re-created.

Hence, Jerry Jeff Walker isn't even going to try. Yes, there will be a recorded concert in Luckenbach on Friday night. And yes, it's being held in honor of the landmark album of his career, *Viva Terlingua!*, which also was recorded live in Luckenbach 20 years ago, but Walker and company have insisted, "We are not interested in reincarnating that Seventies era." There won't be any reliving of the past, just a celebration of what was, done in the style of what is.

"When we recorded the first time," Walker says, "we didn't know what we were going to do, so there's nothing to re-create. We didn't even have the songs. I wrote 'Gettin' By' there that afternoon. Gary P. [Nunn]

As Walker says, he wasn't trying to have a career; he was just trying to have a good time.

taught me 'London Homesick Blues' that afternoon, and I said, 'Instead of me learning all the words, you just sing it and I'll sing on the choruses.'"

Face it, that can't be re-created, and with twenty years more experience under his belt, it's questionable whether Walker would want to. The first concert was an adventure. As Walker says, he wasn't trying to have a career; he was just trying to have a good time. In 1973, he was finding that he could have the former by doing the latter, partly under the tutelage of one Hondo Crouch, a rambling old character who had decades of such experience.

"I was drawn to these people who'd done things," says Walker. "Charlie Dunn was a little-bitty bootmaker working in the back of a store, but he was content, he had a purpose in life. And Hondo was someone who I thought was a perfectly charming, great character who was doing neat little interesting things in life and living his own life. We had a lot of fun together."

While hanging around New Mexico, Walker discovered that Crouch had bought "beautiful downtown Luckenbach," as the liner notes to *Viva* call it, and he decided to come back to Texas and join the fun.

"He had a chili cook. He had a domino tournament, and once in a while one of us would pick down there around the store. I think we'd done a couple of those things before the concert; I think Willie did one and I did one, on a little flatbed truck under the trees right there by the town. We would just go down there and hang out. I'd finish a tour, staying in hotels in Detroit and shit, and look forward to going down there and relaxing."

Somewhere in Walker's mind sprang the idea of recording such a session. He had already recorded studio albums and wasn't always pleased with the results. After being channeled through various machines and twisting of knobs, the resulting sound was different from what had come out of his mouth and guitar. A live recording wouldn't allow "screwing around" with the sound. Although retakes would be taped, there was only so much fine-tuning that could be done. Rather than a "perfect" recording, the emphasis would be on capturing the memory of summer nights in the Hill Country.

They probably succeeded even more wildly than they hoped, certainly more than they should have. One of the first-ever mobile recording trucks, run by a company called Dale Ashby & Father, using bad electricity and equipment far inferior to today's, was brought in to make it all possible. With little regard for the technical aspect of things, they produced an album that would rise above anything Jerry Jeff Walker had ever done or would ever do; in fact, it rose above Walker himself to become a defining feature in the "outlaw country" terrain. While he would go on to record several brilliant albums, this was the one that not only boosted his star, but helped swing the spotlight on songwriters Guy Clark, Ray Wylie Hubbard, Michael Martin Murphey, and Gary P. Nunn.

Walker is not kidding himself into thinking he can do it again. The Jerry Jeff Walker taking the stage Friday is not the same rowdy character of the 1960s and early Seventies. Back then, he was a cutting-edge young talent. Now, he is a not-quite-larger-than-life legend. Then, he wrote and sang about getting wasted. Now, he writes about his wife and exercises fairly regularly. Then, he shared a little flat with Guy Clark in Houston. Now, he has a beautiful, swimming pool-adorned house outside Austin.

It's a new Jerry Jeff that might disappoint fans only familiar with his cocaine-snorting past, but, as has usually been the case throughout his career, it's exactly where he wants to be.

"Now," he laughs, "I always tell people I get up feeling like I used to when I stayed up all night, except now I go to bed." ◀

Remembering the Cosmic Cowboy Years

VOL. 13 NO. 19 ★ JANUARY 14, 1994

CHET FLIPPO

Doug Sahm. Photograph by Scott Newton.

YOU ALMOST NEED a flow chart to explain the cosmic cowboy blip in the history of Austin music and music in general: The Vulcan Gas Company begat Armadillo World Headquarters, which begat the marriage of hippies with country music, which begat Willie Nelson which begat Willie's picnics which begat massive audience and media awareness of the movement, which begat KOKE-FM which championed "progressive country," which led to gradual overdose and excesses in general.

For every Jerry Jeff Walker who moved to town and enriched the Austin music scene, there were two or three interlopers and hustlers arriving, until the scene collapsed under its own weight. Cosmic Cowboys immediately predated Nashville's "outlaws" (Willie's next incarnation), who in turn were supplanted by the Urban Cowboys. Music eras aren't as durable as they used to be.

As for exactly what a cosmic cowboy was, this is my mental image of it: it's Doug Sahm in full-scale cowboy regalia at the old Soap Creek on Bee Caves Road, doing an extended rocking country version of the Rolling Stones' "Honky Tonk Woman." And he was only partly kidding. The Cosmic Cowboy, at least as far as the artists were concerned, stood at a crossroad where the paths of Hank Williams and Woody Guthrie and Bob Dylan and Mick Jagger intersected.

As far as the cosmic cowboy fan went, ah, now, that was another matter entirely. I actually wrote in

Rolling Stone in 1974 that "the Austin-style cosmic cowboy is one who wears long hair and a cowboy outfit, drinks a lot of beer and chases it with marijuana or cocaine, likes only country music and gets loud and aggressive in the C&W clubs, has a much-younger 'old lady,' and drives a pick-up with a KOKE-FM bumpersticker." That was dead-on accurate. Those bumperstickers, by the way, were quite famous, and depicted a long-haired kicker roping a goat. (And as far as the beer consumption went: in 1974, the Armadillo was Lone Star Beer's second-biggest account, behind only the Astrodome in Houston. The Armadillo was running through at least 500 fifteen-gallon kegs and 500 cases of longneck bottles a month.)

If the club scene began to get frenetic, imagine the big Willie Nelson picnics: cosmic cowboys magnified by tens of thousands, roaming outdoors under the bare skies, free to do whatever they wanted to do. The 1972 Dripping Springs Reunion, put on by a bunch of Dallas businessmen, was a fairly sedate affair compared with what would come later. At that first gathering, the emphasis was on traditional country, with the likes of Tex Ritter in a suit and Loretta Lynn in a demure calico dress, although the arrival of Kris Kristofferson and his Band of Thieves was fairly cosmic: they were all hair and black suits, with silver

THE COSMIC COWBOY STOOD AT A CROSSROAD WHERE THE PATHS OF HANK WILLIAMS AND WOODY GUTHRIE AND BOB DYLAN AND MICK JAGGER INTERSECTED.

and turquoise dripping off them, and they wore so much leather they creaked when they walked.

The next year, Willie took charge of the progressive country movement and staged his first Fourth of July Picnic at Dripping Springs. The main performers were his choices: Waylon, John Prine, Kris, Charlie Rich, Billy Joe Shaver, Tom T. Hall, Rita Coolidge, and rock star Leon Russell. The latter delivered the festival's sermon in late afternoon by observing to the crowd that "this is the greatest gathering of hippies and rednecks in history."

It was certainly the strangest such gathering. Hours of 100-plus-degree heat and gallons of beer and who knew what else combined to induce shell shock in many persons and some were literally wired out of their skulls and scampering nude up a light tower. The power blew and the older fans began packing their lawn chairs and making their way out of an eerie scene as fast as they could. The half-light spilling over from the stage (stage power being run from a line plugged into an RV) and from an orange glow from fireworks being set off in the distance illuminated a panorama of naked limbs glistening with spilled beer and wine: shrieks and giggles and curses competed with Tom T. Hall's "Me and Jesus." Progressive country was on the map.

The apogee of the Cosmic Cowboy movement came in February of 1974 when Houston radio station KPFT-FM held a benefit (for itself) billed as the "Tribute to Cosmic Cowboys." Posters went up around Houston showing a longhaired cowboy toking a joint and someone from KPFT hyped the event as "Country Bangladesh." The actual show was not bad: nine hours of music in Hofheinz Pavilion by Jerry Jeff Walker, Doug Sahm backed by Freda & the Firedogs, Jimmy Buffett, Billy Joe Shaver, Kinky Friedman, Willie Nelson, Asleep at the Wheel, Don Sanders, Commander Cody, and Michael Murphey. The latter closed his own door on the era when he called Sahm to the stage to sing "Cosmic Cowboy" with him because, Murphey said, "Sir Doug is the original cosmic cowboy."

As for the aftermath, allow me to quote from my journal from an undated day in 1974: Just off the Drag, as I park my car, I run into Michael Murphey, who is on his way to eat at Les Amis. He invites me along, and we sit outside and he interrupts his vegetarian lunch to tell me he's considering moving to Denver.

"Austin is, it's becoming too much of a scene," he says, his beard fairly bristling. "There's hucksters comin' in every day and callin' me up to do this and do that, bogus benefits that'll set them up as local bookers. That's not what I want. I want some peace and quiet. The song 'Cosmic Cowboy' was meant as a satirical song, that's what I intended, but it was taken seriously here. I never intended that it be taken seriously. I wrote that one night at the Bitter End in New York. Jerry Jeff and I were there, playing cowboy in New York and I just kinda made it up and sang it that night as a joke. We cracked up—look at us, we're the cosmic cowboys. It was a lighthearted song. What is a cosmic cowboy, after all?

"It gets under my skin a little bit. Somehow that phrase caught on and people said, yeah, that's what we are and they started wearing boots and huge cowboy hats. It went too far. It's fun to have fun but we came off as Clint Eastwood. Clint Eastwood with long hair. A lot of these cowboys that took it seriously are pretending to be that. They're just rednecks who've let their hair grow a little. They still have that macho thing and they'll beat the shit out of you in a minute to prove it. The longhairs wear boots instead of tennis shoes so that the *real* cowboys will just think they're good old boys."

I leave Murphey (who was wearing hiking boots) and stroll next door to Inner Sanctum, the most popular record shop in town. The Sanctum is packed, because they've brought in tubs of free beer to celebrate an expansion of the store. The bulletin board is full of posters and notices: Augie Meyers at Soap Creek, Tom Rush at Castle Creek, Townes Van Zandt at Saxon Pub, Jerry Jeff Walker at the Country Dinner Playhouse, Billy Joe Shaver at Cherry Street Inn, Waylon Jennings at the Armadillo, and Willie Nelson at Big G's.

Out of the Sanctum, down the Drag. Doug Sahm waves and stops. He's on his way to Oat Willie's to pick up his mail and messages. Huey Meaux has just come up from Houston, he says, to see about possible dates for Freddy Fender. Meaux is back in action after a prison stretch for a Mann Act violation and his first act (after producing the latest Jerry Lee Lewis album) is to issue a Freddy Fender album. Fender, Doug says, will go over great in Austin.

On down the Drag. Rusty Bell, program director of KOKE-FM, this country's first and only progressive country station, is getting a hamburger. He tells me that KOKE, which adopted its present progressive format on New Year's Day of '73, is going great. Sold 30,000 bumper stickers, but the Pulse ratings aren't in yet. KOKE-FM is the local rage, though. Where else could you hear Eric Clapton followed by Maybelle Carter followed by Doc Watson followed by the Dead followed by Sahm followed by Willie followed by Hank Williams?

On down the Drag, Armadillo artist Jim Franklin is overseeing the completion of a mural on the wall of the University Co-Op Store. It's a great panorama of Austin and everyone in town seems glad to see it go up. It's graceful, yet it's crude, in the best sense of the term. But no one here will call it either. They'll just say how they like it.

Franklin tells me it reminds him of the Vulcan Gas Company's proudest days, when the Velvet Underground finally came to town. Franklin lays down his brush to gesture as he talks.

"Houston White [a Vulcan co-founder] didn't want the Velvet Underground," he says. "He said they were just a faggot band. But I finally got them here and they sold out for three nights. It was the high point of the Vulcan's existence. Solid rock & roll for three nights. Sterling Morrison of the Underground liked Austin so much he came back here later to live, like a lotta people do. Austin is like movin' to San Francisco without leavin' home. It's the only place I know where people sit around for hours and talk about how great it is to live here." ◄

Listening to the First "Austin Sound" The Essential Cosmic Cowboy Albums

VOL. 13 NO. 20 ★ JANUARY 21, 1994

CHET FLIPPO

THE FOLLOWING is a highly subjective and opinionated list of what made it to record in the early Seventies in Austin. They are listed by their original record labels. A note to detractors: Willis Alan Ramsey was not part of this, no matter what anyone says (although some of his songs were, as performed by others). Nor was B. W. Stevenson, even though he was an early Hat Act. Nor was Asleep at the Wheel. Shiva's Headband came before. Willie Nelson's *Red Headed Stranger* came after, as did Joe Ely. Rusty Wier was better in clubs than on records, as were a number of people not represented here.

Frummox, *Here to There* (Command/Probe/ABC): The 1969 forerunner for what came later. Steven Fromholz was the true godfather of the movement, the first to really prove that folk music could wear a cowboy hat. This is as well-written an album as you will ever find (some of it co-written with Frummox partner Dan McCrimmon). Listening to this, you can taste the dust and feel the hot Texas sun. Unfortunately, Fromholz never matched this work and was soon eclipsed by the following cowboy.

Michael Murphey, *Geronimo's Cadillac* (A&M): This 1972 album galvanized the burgeoning folkie/progressive community in and around Austin. Murphey built on the gritty realism pioneered by Fromholz and added a seemless, lyrical rockin' country beat, aided by such talented sidemen as Gary P. Nunn and Bob Livingston, who later would do the same for Jerry Jeff Walker before branching off to form the Lost Gonzo Band.

Michael Murphey, *Cosmic Cowboy Souvenir* (A&M): One year later came the album with the rallying song "Cosmic Cowboy (Part One)." Murphey previewed this album onstage in Austin with a string quartet. It was that big a deal. This still stands up very well, after all these years, as does Murphey's first album.

Doug Sahm, *Groover's Paradise* (Warner Bros.): The quintessential Austin album, the true Cosmic Cowboy record. Kerry Awn's cover art is the ultimate hippie vision of Austin. Check out some songs: "Groover's Paradise," "Houston Chicks," "Beautiful Texas Sunshine," "Girls Today (Don't Like to Sleep Alone)."

Sir Doug & the Texas Tornados, *Texas Rock for Country Rollers* (ABC): For "Cowboy Peyton Place," "You Can't Hide Your Redneck (Under that Hippie Hair)," and "Country Groove."

Kinky Freidman. Illustration by Nathan Jensen.

Bobby Bridger, *And I Wanted to Sing for the People* (RCA): The introspective side of the progressive movement. Talking to coyotes.

Bill Neely, *Blackland Farm Boy* (Arhoolie): A true link between "real" country and the progressive movement. Neely learned music at Jimmie Rodgers' knee and ended up in Kenneth Threadgill's group, along with the likes of the cosmic Powell St. John. Sweet Mary Egan from Greezy Wheels appears here.

Greezy Wheels, *Juz Loves Dem Ol' Greezy Wheels* (London): A classic Armadillo cover by Jim Franklin and Greezy Wheels' goodtime sounds.

Alvin Crow & the Pleasant Valley Boys (Long Neck): What Doug Sahm would sound like, had he not become cosmic. Real goodtime music.

Augie Meyers, *You Ain't Rollin' Your Roll Right* (Paramount): Doug Sahm and Augie were Texas' Odd Couple, now and then ricocheting and spinning off side projects. Augie's is a raucous, rollicking, stripped-down Texas Bohemian country rock.

Freddy Fender, *Out of Reach/Fuera de Alcance: Hits by Freddy Fender* (Starflite): El Be-Bop Kid at his best, before he was a country star. This is the way he sounded at Soap Creek.

Jerry Jeff Walker (Decca): His first Austin album, in 1972, notable for "Hill Country Rain," "Charlie Dunn," "That Old Time Feeling," "Hairy Ass Hillbillies," "L.A. Freeway," and "When I Had You."

Jerry Jeff Walker, *Viva Terlingua!* (MCA): Live at Luckenbach, Austin finally goes gonzo with Ray Wylie Hubbard's "Up Against the Wall Redneck," Murphey's "Backsliders Wine," Guy Clark's "Desperados Waiting for a Train," and Gary Nunn's spirited "London Homesick Blues."

The Lost Gonzo Band (MCA): An incredible band, suffering for want of a front man.

Kinky Friedman, *Sold American* (Vanguard): Texas Jewish hip meets Nashville in an album that was so far advanced it's still being deconstructed.

Willie Nelson, *Shotgun Willie* (Atlantic): Willie left Nashville, moved to Austin, became a hippie, and learned about life's possibilities.

Willie Nelson, *Phases and Stages* (Atlantic): More of the same and better. Get a six-pack and sit a spell.

Guy Clark, *Old No. 1* (RCA): The progressive movement is capped by its finest, most sophisticated work.

Various Artists, *For the Record: Austin Country 1973–1978* (Maverick): Worth noting for Marcia Ball & the Misery Brothers, Bobby Earl Smith, the Reynolds Sisters & the New Oso Band, Jon Emery & the Missouri Valley Boys, Joe Gracey (who pioneered progressive country on KOKE-FM), Augie Meyers' "High Texas Rider," his wife Carol's "Meet Me in Seguin," and Doug Sahm's classic "Henrietta." ◄

ED HALL
MOTHERSCRATCHER
TRANCE SYNDICATE

With their latest offering, Ed Hall solidifies their place in the harrowing lineage of Texas psycho rock. Therefore, it makes perfect sense that the first song on *Motherscratcher* pays tribute to the popular legend of Gibby Haynes rubbing himself on Amy Carter's suitcase in an attempt to have the president touch his pubic hair ("White House Girls"). The album is a showcase for guitarist Gary Chester's unique brand of technical wizardry. Larry Strub's bass is appropriately evil, and the lyrics succeed on the band's own twisted terms. Lyman Hardy's mighty drumming could stand to be a little higher in the mix, but that's a moot point in lieu of *Motherscratcher*'s overall consistency. Besides, what other band is thoughtful enough to include almost 24 minutes of esoteric droning at the end of the CD to bring you back down? **GREG BEETS**

VOL. 13 NO. 24 ★ FEBRUARY 18, 1994

DOYLE BRAMHALL
BIRD NEST ON THE GROUND
ANTONE'S RECORDS

That Doyle Bramhall has emerged as a strong song-writer on his own and with Stevie Ray Vaughan ("Life by the Drop," "Hard to Be") seems as unlikely as the path that has led to *Bird Nest on the Ground,* a neatly packaged debut/body-of-work collection the Dallas native just released. Because the tracks range from 1981's "Change It" and "Other Side of Love" from a 1985 Dallas all-star session to vintage tunes like Albert King's "The Hunter" recorded in 1992 and last year's "I Know," *Bird Nest* is a rich, tightly woven patch-work of blues, and all the squares are different ma-terials, some soft, some rough, some smooth. Stevie fans will find the album eerily comforting; Vaughan's style is taken directly from Bramhall's soulful strut. The album's victory and brawn is all Bramhall's, whose dedicated love for blues saw him through many a dark year before its birth; *Bird Nest* is a classic record of modern Texas blues.

MARGARET MOSER

VOL. 13 NO. 27 ★ MARCH 11, 1994

COTTON MATHER
COTTON IS KING
ELM RECORDS

Cotton Mather writes songs less like dudes and more like lads, preferably chaps who at one time lived in the same flat as Elvis Costello or who went for pints at the local pub with members of Squeeze. With *Cotton is King,* their label debut and follow-up to the independ-ently produced *The Crafty Flower Arranger,* the boys have proven themselves to be members of pop's elite school, songwriters who cut through the camp and head straight for the gut, both lyrically and musically.

Granted, boppy, bouncy tunes like "Lost My Motto" and "April's Fool" far outnumber melancholy ballads, but affecting songwriting doesn't get much bet-ter than "New Kind of Trash." The album's lyrics, of course, sometimes whisper, "Love me, I'm so awfully clever," but the wordplay is rarely gratuitously annoy-ing, and the mini-dramas are good for a bit of vicarious pain. While *Cotton is King* hasn't knocked Crowded House's *Temple of Low Men* off any pedestals, it certainly topples any of the overrated bunk being churned out by our local heroes. **MINDY LABERNZ**

VOL. 13 NO. 28 ★ MARCH 18, 1994

JIMMIE VAUGHAN, JOE ELY, BUICK MACKANE
THE BACKYARD, LA ZONA ROSA, HOLE IN THE WALL, JULY 1

It was a night when the slogan came true. Yes, that slogan.

Not much of a stretch to believe a sold-out Back-yard audience was happy to see Jimmie Vaughan after an absence of four years (save for the occa-sional sit-in at Antone's) from local stages. They were ecstatic, and so seemed Vaughan, who, along with an Austin-built road band featuring George Rains on drums and Denny Freeman on piano and guitar, dug his black-booted heels into home turf and delivered the type of two-hour set that's been garnering the band rave reviews all along the tour trail. Proving he's every bit the galvanizing frontman his younger sibling was, Vaughan paced back and forth on the roomy Back-yard stage, letting one long and lean blast of blues after another spill from his guitar. They came silky and fluid, like a person exhaling until out of breath, only where most guitarists would inhale and start a new run, Vaughan just kept playing. Material from his solo debut, *Strange Pleasure,* felt well worn-in

Jimmie Vaughan six strings down at Antone's, 1991. Photograph by Susan Antone.

like soft leather, especially "Flamenco Dancer," which featured a Spanish butterfly intro by Vaughan's guitar tech Rene Martinez and "Six Strings Down," which saw a stool-bound Vaughan accompanied only by his acoustic guitar and his three back-up singers. It was, however, songs from *Family Style* that had the sharpest bite, particularly "DFW" and "Good Texan," which received the loudest reception of the evening when Vaughan, by way of introduction, remarked: "I've been called a lot of things in my life, but when I die I hope I'm remembered as a good Texan." A good Texan, and a one-of-a-kind performer is what that epitaph will read.

Joe Ely's stone will read the same, though for his first local headlining gig since returning from *Chippy* rehearsals back east, the Lubbock Tornado was breathing hell-fire in contrast to the heavenly sounds Vaughan was making. For no sooner had Vaughan finished his set near midnight, than I raced to La Zona Rosa hoping to catch fifteen minutes of his set. Instead, I got a solid hour of Ely, who was egging on guitarist David Grissom when I stepped near the stage. "I always like to have David let loose at least once during a show," said Ely, panting, "and I think he's been holding out on us." With that Grissom ripped into a Booze Weasel live staple, "Lonesome Train," and the locomotive didn't stop for the next hour. "For Your Love," "Settle for Love," and "Whenever Kindness Fails" all got workouts to make Jack LaLanne look like a slacker, and a guitar duel between Ely and Grissom during "Cool Rockin' Loretta" was eclipsed only by a ten-minute encore of "Fingernails," for which Eric Johnson appeared and commenced trading scorching guitar barbs with Grissom.

And if an hour of hurricane Joe served as an encore for Vaughan, then 1 am still left an hour for Buick MacKane at the Hole in the Wall to pick up where Ely left off. Playing to a small, but firmly entrenched crowd, Alejandro Escovedo and the boys put on a power-chord extravaganza to evoke images of AC/DC playing the Australian club circuit in the early Seventies. Orchestra faves "The End" and "Gravity" weighed in more metallic than ever, but it was set-ending versions of Rod Stewart's "Hot Legs" and "Ain't That a Shame" that had more than a few fingers digging into ears to salvage some form of hearing. Through it all, Escovedo loomed large on the tiny Hole stage, joking and generally holding court, casting a presence that any stranger through the door would recognize as sure star power.

Yes, it was one of those nights, one of those nights to close your eyes, click your heels thrice and repeat: There's no place like home.

RAOUL HERNANDEZ

VOL. 13 NO. 49 ★ AUGUST 12, 1994

CHERUBS
HEROIN MAN
TRANCE SYNDICATE

It's a shame that the Cherubs were already history before this album was even done. *Heroin Man* displays much more sonic panache and potential than their debut, *Icing.* Instead of focusing so much on pure frenzy, *Heroin Man* attacks the senses with a new sense of rhythm and discipline probably obtained on the road. The album starts out with an off-the-hook signal that provides a melodic white noise base to the discordance of "Stag Party." The same effect is achieved with static-laden samples and strings on other songs. The raw, Sweatbox Studios production suits the Cherubs sound just fine. The drums don't always come through as strong as they should, but the low end is pure demon-spawn. This is a record that could have established the Cherubs as leaders in their field. Instead, *Heroin Man* is a fitting testament to what might have been. **GREG BEETS**

VOL. 13 NO. 46 ★ JULY 22, 1994

JOHNBOY
CLAIM DEDICATIONS
TRANCE

BEDHEAD
WHAT FUN LIFE WAS
TRANCE

CRUST
CRUSTY LOVE
TRANCE

King Coffey's Trance Syndicate Records established a beachhead for the local label renaissance that has inundated Austin record stores with homemade music. At the same time, Trance has built a worldwide reputation on presenting the lunatic fringe of Texas rock, much like Houston's International Artists label did in the Sixties. With these three new releases, Trance continues to dish out the distinctive Texas weirdness that made the label famous.

That said, it seems Coffey isn't having good luck in keeping bands together after their albums come. First, the Cherubs said uncle before *Heroin Man* hit the streets, and now Johnboy is DOA upon release of their new album, *Claim Dedications*. No matter. Johnboy has produced an album that combines their trademark tight structuring with harmonic, trance-inducing (sorry) guitar assault. Steve Albini does a fine, albeit uncredited job of fattening Johnboy's guitar and drum sound to its full tonal potential. "Driving Reservoirs Up Noses" surrounds you in a glorious grind that evokes shades of the Jesus Lizard and Fugazi. The lyrics seem to be an afterthought, which is just as well since you can't hear them. Musically speaking, though, *Claim Dedications* is as prolific as it has to be.

Dallas' Bedhead offers a pleasant take on a vein of gentle, sleepy pop that goes completely against today's dominant paradigm of underground Texas—non-fans of *Velvet Underground*–era VU, Galaxie 500, or 4AD need not apply here. I admire Bedhead less for their songs and more for their ability to create a sense of warmth and intimacy in the studio. They also have a keen ear for the melodic layering of guitars. Is Bedhead as earth-shattering as some critical ravings might have you believe? Probably not, but when I had a stomachache the other night, I put on this album and managed to doze off tranquilly. That's gotta count for something.

Finally, hold onto your lunch because here comes the second full-length from Crust and it's piled high with coprologic tales of white-trash angst as told by Austin's foremost show band. The only things missing are the worms from Rev. Art Bank Lobby's diaper and the accompanying Zippo for the pyrotechnic display in his pubic hair. Musically, *Crusty Love* transcends previous Crust efforts by fusing a more rock-oriented approach to the band's previously honed ability to make music out of tribal thunder, homemade instruments, and tape loops. One of the most realized examples of this mix can be found on the Guitorgan-laden "Slurpee." Rev. Lobby's savvy for perverse send-ups of traditional values is also a major selling point, as always. This is an album guaranteed to disturb and confound most species of neighbors. **GREG BEETS**

VOL. 14 NO. 2 ★ SEPTEMBER 9, 1994

Kathy McCarty
From Glass Eye to *Dead Dog's Eyeball*

VOL. 14 NO. 3 ★ SEPTEMBER 16, 1994

CHRIS WALTERS

A PIANO BEATS out a simple progression in rapid quarter-note time, instantly irresistible. A woman's voice comes in, her searching alto on the trail of something ineffable:

> *Trying to remember*
> *But my feelings can't know for sure*
> *Try and reach out*
> *But it's gone. . . .*

The chorus is mad poetry about endurance: "I am walking the cow. . . ." Thirty seconds into the first vocal track on Kathy McCarty's *Dead Dog's Eyeball: Songs of Daniel Johnston*, there's little doubt you're in the presence of greatness. Then a blood-quickening cello punches in on the bridge, and there's no doubt at all. Music so elegant and pointed, pleasure so direct, hasn't been heard very often since the heyday of Lennon and McCartney. This is the real thing, something new.

Kathy McCarty felt a similar shock of recognition over nine years ago, when she first heard a tape called *Hi, How Are You* given to her at a gig by a nervous, awkward guy who wanted to open a show for her sometime. Her band, Glass Eye, had surfaced in the Austin wave of 1984, sorta kinda playing Gang of Four to the True Believers' Clash. By 1985, they'd attracted a passionate following, which meant devotees and unsolicited tapes. McCarty threw this one on the pile with all the others she never listened to.

Then the guy showed up at another Glass Eye date, even more nervous than before. He asked if she'd listened to his tape, and he asked again about opening for them. McCarty felt guilty. She told him he could.

After the show McCarty went home and listened to Daniel Johnston's tape. The first song floored her; she couldn't believe somebody had written so honestly about self-pity. The second one impressed her, and the third song was "Walking the Cow." She was hooked. When the rest of the band came over for rehearsal the next day McCarty made them sit down and listen to it. They concurred. Not long afterward, they began covering a few of his songs, beginning the process that became *Dead Dog's Eyeball*.

"'Living Life' was my absolute favorite, and it became a song that I ended up doing when Brian [Beattie, Glass Eye bassist and *Eyeball*'s producer] broke a bass string, which happened frequently," McCarty remembers. "Whenever I broke guitar strings, we always played 'Low Rider' because that has no guitar."

As Johnston went around town pressing a free tape into every hand he shook, it turned out he'd already written over a hundred songs, many of them astonishing. It also emerged that he was a fragile soul, plagued by recurrent manic depression. Over the next few years he was in and out of mental hospitals or taking refuge with his father in West Virginia. Yet his crudely recorded tapes could be unsettling even if you knew none of this.

You can still hear Johnston's history, its despair and its promise, in the naked emotionalism of his singing, in his infectious changes (some lifted straight from a Beatles songbook), and between the lines of his songs. They tell a story about a boy trying to reconcile his impossible romantic yearning and his huge

Kathy McCarty of Glass Eye, 1994. Photograph by Chris Walters.

artistic gift with his wretched place in the world. "If I can't be a lover, I'll be a pest," he concludes in "Grievances," an early song that supplied key phrases and images for many that followed.

Glass Eye broke up around the time of their 10th anniversary in 1993, after a run that left a string of records—*Marlo, Huge, Bent By Nature, Christine, Hello Young Lovers*—graced by exciting, emotionally astringent music. When a major label deal for a new album, *Every Woman's Fantasy*, fell through, the burden of soldiering on became insupportable. McCarty had planned on making an album of Johnston's songs as a sideline to the band; now she found herself free to devote all her energy to it.

"A lot of what I could see and hear in Daniel's work, other people didn't get it," McCarty explains. "Other things got in the way. I want to introduce Daniel to the segment of the population that tends to scoff at him, so they can see how incredibly endearing and beautiful his songs are. There's a lot of his stuff that's so plain it's almost cliché; it's just the way he writes it that makes it real again.

"Other songwriters can appreciate the genius of his songwriting because they know the territory. But the general public, they listen so much to what a record sounds like that often they don't hear the songs.

> " A LOT OF WHAT I COULD SEE AND HEAR IN DANIEL'S WORK, OTHER PEOPLE DIDN'T GET IT.
>
> " KATHY MCCARTY

141

That was one of the things I consciously set out to turn around. I wanted to put the songs into a context where the sounds brought out the virtues of the songwriting, or at least didn't interfere with them."

A lot of bands and soloists have covered Johnston's songs over the years. McCarty wanted to avoid the mistakes she heard in some of their approaches—excessive polishing, "too-beautiful singing," or hooks removed "because they're not familiar, recognizable, music-industry-everyone's-done-it-for-twenty-years-type hooks." Working with longtime partner and (platonic) housemate Brian Beattie on a DAT machine in the garage behind their house in South Austin, she spent ten months making *Dead Dog's Eyeball*. Beattie played most of the instruments and acted as producer; cellist John Hagen, trumpeter Dave Crawford, former Glass Eye drummer Scott Marcus, and others occasionally sat in.

Freedom from studio constraints liberated their imaginations and gave them time to think through every arrangement. Some, such as "Running Water," recorded in a bathroom at the University of Texas to get a faucet-and-tile ambiance, are exact duplicates of Johnston's versions. A few were radically rearranged. "Oh No!" almost sounds like a *Revolver* outtake—pure psychedelia. "Sorry Entertainer" pairs a demented acoustic guitar with Marcus' bashing. "Hate Song," recorded at the Dog & Duck Pub, features McCarty and a bunch of drunken friends (including yours truly) bellowing at the top of their lungs, accompanied by tuba and accordion. Sometimes a purely formal choice makes all the difference, like the sublime synthesizer break that comes out of nowhere in "Museum of Love."

"There are a lot of songwriters who think that if you're writing a depressing song, you've got to turn it around and give it an up ending. Daniel and I both don't feel compelled to do that." ◀

GUY FORSYTH & THE ASYLUM STREET SPANKERS

AUSTIN OUTHOUSE, JANUARY 25

If you think you know Guy Forsyth, think again. The self-proclaimed "master of the single-entendre" has put together an acoustic group made of musicians and actors that will make you long for the days of vaudeville. Mysterious John dances around and holds up signs telling people when to clap. Pops Bayless plays every stringed instrument known to man. Olivier of 8½ Souvenirs plays gypsy guitar. Spoken word artist Wammo jams on the washboard and bells when he's not stepping out to sing the Hank Williams Jr.–esque "I Was Flannel When Flannel Wasn't Cool." High Nooner Kevin Smith plays the stand-up bass, Jimmy Dean whacks on his drum, and everyone pitches in with a kazoo when necessary. Then there's "the beautiful, talented, ambidextrous, sanitized for your protection, do not inflate to over 32 PSI" Christina Marrs. With the greatest voice this side of Bessie Smith and a wit smart enough to keep Forsyth in his place, it's a sin this woman isn't more popular. Whether doing blues, gospel, ragtime, acid country, singalongs, or just kibbitzing amongst themselves and the crowd, these guys kept everyone laughing, dancing, or at least saying, "Huh?" And they did it all without one amplifier. **AL KAUFMAN**

VOL. 14 NO. 23 ★ FEBRUARY 10, 1995

1995 SXSW Picks and Sleepers

VOL. 14 NO. 27 ★ MARCH 10, 1995

TONY CAMPISE: Within the confines of Austin's small jazz scene, it's easy to lose the singular sax/flute talents of Tony Campise. Hell, everyone is lost: Martin Banks, James Polk, Tina Marsh, etc. What you can't lose is Campise's *Ballads, Blues & BeBop* and last year's world-class companion piece *Ballads, Blues, BeBop & Beyond*. With them in your CD player there's no denying that Campise is a big fish in a little pond.

RAOUL HERNANDEZ

IAN MCLAGEN & MONKEY JUMP: Austin has attracted its share of aging rock legends to town, but Ian McLagen is a most welcome addition as he's brought that soulful respect the Brits have always had for the blues. McLagen's gigs around town pack 'em in too, as the ex-Face melds his solid Hammond sound with the best of Austin's blues players. **MARGARET MOSER**

WAYNE HANCOCK: Some people were just born too late; if Junior Brown or Big Sandy had hit their peak 30–40 years ago, they'd be hall-of-famers today, and the same goes for the up-and-coming Wayne Hancock, a modern incarnation of Hank Williams or Little Jimmy Dickens. Looking for *real* country? It doesn't get much more authentic than this. **LEE NICHOLS**

SKATENIGS: The first Austin band to get the attention of the Wax Trax!/Ministry confab, the Skatenigs still rule the regional industrial scene with below-the-belt grind and hypnotic rhythms layered over bellowing vocals. Their endless loops of metalcore machine music have inducted ex–Big Boy Chris Gates into the band's ranks, giving them that supersonic bottom Gates brought to bands from Poison 13 to Junkyard.

MARGARET MOSER

OMAR & THE HOWLERS: Kent "Omar" Dykes and company have been kickin' their "big leg music" around so long that, like the Tailgators, they've come to define the "swamp rock" genre—that hypnotic, Louisiana-bass thump carried by Omar's salty marsh growl. Some listeners evoke Creedence Clearwater Revival, but the Howlers' bayou blues-rock is the Real McCoy, brewed and steeped in Texas honky-tonks and blues bars around the world. **MARGARET MOSER**

MICHAEL FRACASSO
WHEN I LIVED IN THE WILD
BOHEMIA BEAT/ROUNDER

The grand potential hinted at on Fracasso's Dejadisc debut *Love & Trust* two years ago reaches full bloom on this 14-song album that ranges from pure pop to aching balladry to bluesy shadows to razor-sharp rock & roll. From the opening strains of "Tell Mary," one of the most instantly memorable tunes any Austin artist has produced this decade, to the gentle closing touch of "Near and Far," Fracasso has fashioned an album that should elevate him beyond the ranks of local up-and-comers and onto the map as one of the most promising new voices in American music. The centerpiece is his voice, a colorful tenor that shines particularly on such melodically fluid tracks as "Big Sister," "Sleepless Nights," and "One by One." But lyrical creativity is nearly as important a piece of the puzzle here: Fracasso can paint a portrait and tell a story more effectively and originally than most songwriters. Whether this album is a career high or the first of many gems is yet to be seen; for now, it's enough just to bask in the glory of the music.

PETER BLACKSTOCK

VOL. 14 NO. 28 ★ MARCH 17, 1995

SUE FOLEY
BIG CITY BLUES
ANTONE'S

Not to be crass, but let's talk about fuck songs. You know, like how "Scratch My Back" makes you shift in your seat or "Hello My Lover" makes you pull your lover's hips a little closer on the dance floor. Fuck songs are special because they have a blues-based rhythm that courses like hot blood from start to finish, and makes you want to seek out a dark corner to get a little closer with the one you love. On *Big City Blues,* Sue Foley has created a stellar collection of fuck songs, unmatched locally since Lou Ann Barton's *My Lips.* So what if Foley's vocals still waver charmingly; they lend a juke-joint purity to hip-grinding classics such as "Howlin' for My Darlin'," and the post-orgasmic instrumental exhilaration of "Girl's Night Out." Solid musicianship and spare production make it feel like Foley stepped into the past to move forward, with excellent results. This will be one of Austin's best albums of 1995. **MARGARET MOSER**

VOL. 14 NO. 28 ★ MARCH 17, 1995

GUY CLARK
DUBLIN BLUES
ASYLUM

After his mediocre *Boats to Build*, Asylum easily could have dropped Clark. Perhaps his reputation as the essential Texas songwriter persuaded them to keep him; whatever the reason, their faith has paid off. *Dublin Blues* is, with the exception of *Old No. 1*, as fine a work as Clark has ever produced. It's typical Clark, lyrics revolving around salt-of-the-earth simplicity and the joys of just living, a philosophy never expressed more directly than in the Rodney Crowell co-penned

"Stuff That Works," which celebrates exactly what the title implies. And he elevates these "common" things to their proper importance. In one of the finest lines ever written, he says, "I have seen the David, I've seen the Mona Lisa too, and I have heard Doc Watson play 'Columbus Stockade Blues.'" There are a few throwaways here, but when he's on, he's really on.
LEE NICHOLS

VOL. 14 NO. 32 ★ APRIL 14, 1995

THE SCABS
STEAMBOAT, JUNE 12, 1995

In most cases, side-projects are fruitless and pretentious, long on ego, short on entertainment. Somehow, with the pseudo-lounge Scabs, Bob Schneider's managed to balance both vanity and laughs. And oddly, this is good news for the Ugly Americans and their fans in that it allows Schneider the same healthy outlet for hokey angles and solo breathing room he originally used the Ugly Americans for during the Rockhead-era. Just as the Ugly Americans gave him room for wanton discourse on "Dry Humpin'," the Scabs' forays into "Big Butts and Blow Jobs" and "Sir, I Fucked Your Daughter in the Ass" are similarly beyond acceptable Ugly American boundaries. And yet, as offensive as the titles and their companion lyrics may seem on paper, it's Schneider's sharp wit and nonchalant presence within the schmaltzy live texture that makes it more fun and danceable than pathetic and detestable. So if the Kiedis-Schneider comparisons never worked because Kiedis seemed too eager to believe his own hype, Schneider finally proves with the Scabs he's perceptive enough of his own love 'em or hate 'em hype to offer a quick wink of humility. Ultimately, the whole Scabs concept is a joke, but a surprisingly funny one at that. **ANDY LANGER**

VOL. 14 NO. 43 ★ JUNE 30, 1995

Toy Story
Dangerous Toys' Jason McMaster

VOL. 15 NO. 15 ★ DECEMBER 8, 1995

ANDY LANGER

"I JUST CAN'T SING songs or write lyrics about my dick anymore," says Jason McMaster of Dangerous Toys. Clearly, this Jason McMaster is a more mature model than the one who penned "Sport'n a Woody" back in 1989 and explained the song, with a straight face no less, to the national glossy *RIP* as "just a humorous way to deal with a hard-on."

Although the "cock-rock" carnival ride of MTV exposure, major label backing, a gold record, big tour buses, and the arenas to drive them to are now just memories of seven years past, McMaster and the Toys have only recently seen the fruit of their gradual growth: a dark and challenging record, tellingly titled *The R*tist 4*merly Known as Dangerous Toys*. In its light, the "hair-band" connotations simply don't apply anymore. And yet, a record this gloomy and bottom-heavy may still not be an album to send home to mom, though in terms of both lyrical embarrassment and sexual content, it wouldn't have to be sent in a plain brown wrapper, either.

While it may be true that Guns N' Roses broke down the commercial barrier that made it possible for a Back Room act like the Toys to get a national push, the hard rock ghetto the band was immediately placed in wasn't always necessarily fair. The Toys were always more about ZZ Top boogie than Ratt sleaze, and more a playful KISS tribute than a rootsy Tesla. In fact, Ian Astbury of the Cult, who lent actual alternative credibility to the Toys back in 1990 by inviting them to open their Sonic Temple arena tour,

Dangerous Toys' Jason McMaster "Teas'n, Pleas'n" the 1990–91 AMAs. Photograph by Martha Grenon.

may have nailed it best when he said repeatedly that he saw the Austin band as a late-Eighties Texas take on the New York Dolls.

"If tragedy makes a man, or a band, so be it," McMaster says of the recent series of personal problems he's endured, including the death of friend, roommate, and Pariah bassist Sims Ellison; a relationship gone sour; and a rotating Toys lineup that's left only McMaster, guitarist Scott Dalhover, and drummer Mark Geary as original members of the band.

"I suppose you need sorrow in your life before the happiness so you can tell the difference," posits McMaster. "These personal tragedies started me writing songs I was finally feeling good about. I started writing songs in my room with the door closed, where nobody tells you how cool you are or how your hair looks. Perhaps it takes something horrible before you can look in the mirror without primping your hair and putting cover-up over your zits. There was a time I was threatened by change, but it took waiting for a catastrophe, the earthquake before the tidal wave."

The Toys were always more about ZZ Top boogie than Ratt sleaze, and more a playful KISS tribute than a rootsy Tesla.

If the new record is the tidal wave, it could be argued that everything since the Toys' Cult tour has been the earthquake. When Dangerous Toys were signed by Columbia in 1988, McMaster himself had only recently committed to becoming the Toys' full-time frontman—creating local debate when he ended his seven-year stint with Watchtower, a groundbreaking metal-fusion act featuring Billy White and Doug Keyser and sold-out Ritz shows shows paralleled only by the Big Boys and Butthole Surfers.

Less than a year after McMaster made the jump to the Toys, the band was unpacking their gear in arenas, fueled by MTV's heavy rotation of "Teas'n, Pleas'n" and "Scared," both from the band's debut, *Dangerous Toys*. With sales near the 400,000 mark (it would eventually go gold), Columbia began demanding a follow-up only six months after their debut release. Today, McMaster admits that the band wasn't ready to record *Hellacious Acres*, and can only wonder why he didn't have the insight to stand up and say so at the time.

"We were led into the studio by the almighty dollar and the hand that feeds," says McMaster. "Here we were in arena soundchecks trying to write songs, taping jams on the house tape deck so we could write dummy lyrics on the bus. We were on the road and were like kids at the carnival that didn't want it to close. We thought we should have been milking the first record longer. I still believe MTV would have played a third video."

By June of 1991, however, MTV wasn't interested in video from *Hellacious Acres*, marking the start of a waning commercial environment for the Toys' brand of hard rock, thanks in part to Seattle's emergence as a scene. And despite the band getting a second credibility boost by sharing the stage with three of their biggest idols on a summer package with Judas Priest, Alice Cooper, and Motörhead, the tour folded after ten weeks as the summer's biggest flop. A club tour then became necessary just to remind people a second Toys record existed. Columbia dropped its entire hard rock roster soon after, leaving the band back in Austin without a deal for the first time since they began.

"The drop came unexpectedly, and we weren't overly cautious or smart enough to be overly concerned right away. After all, I'd quit Watchtower because the Toys was this anything-goes band," says McMaster, who admits he'd never written a song prior to joining the Toys, mostly because Watchtower's 13/8 time signatures made it tough to write vocal melodies in jazz time.

After a year of writing at home while discovering the major label window was for the most part closed,

Watchtower, the early years, 1986. Photograph by Martha Grenon.

Dangerous Toys signed with Antone's new DMZ label, recording a new record in a month. *Pissed*, a transitional record that featured ex–Dirty Looks guitarist Paul Lidel, traded anger for Eighties attitude and groove for boogie—a nice starting point for a 200-date touring year, but not quite the full evolution *The R*tist* would become.

McMaster says the decision not to replace departed bassist Mike Watson and to simply handle the bass duties himself on the new album has led to something more than just a murkier, bass-heavy record. "I feel better about the material now that I have such a part in it," he says. "Until now I've been a bass player singing without a bass, so now it feels right."

Although the recent shake-up at DMZ has made it even more difficult for this record to earn the widespread recognition it deserves, McMaster says experience itself has allowed him to come to terms with roadblocks like label problems and the haunting reality of being even more underground than Watchtower once was.

"I have close friends [who say] they like this record," he says. "And I know they really do because these are friends of mine that made no secret they didn't like any of our old shit. As for the old fans, the most common e-mail response I get is that they're still letting [*The R*tist* . . .] grow on them.

"Maybe they're confused, but it's a confusion of growth I'm happy to fuel, pour the gasoline for, and strike the match. I just want to be back on our way to being reckless and off-the-cuff again."

In 1996, that probably does mean leaving his dick in his pants. ⬅

SXSW Picks to Click Sixteen Deluxe

VOL. 15 NO. 26 ★ MARCH 1996

MARGARET MOSER

DECEMBER 1994: Sixteen Deluxe is onstage at Emo's. The stage is dark, save for the twinkle of Christmas lights from the band's microphones. The cool blackness of the night reverberates with electric anticipation as the band—oblivious to the transfixed audience—feed off each other's loud, searing cues, serving up huge slices of atmospheric psychedelia. The final chord echoes into the air and a current shoots through the crowd, jolting them into rapturous applause. Glowing from the low pastel twinkle, Carrie Clark turns smiling and looks at the audience, her face as sweet and innocent as a child's, as if to say, "Did we do that?"

The answer, of course, is yes.

Like it or not, Sixteen Deluxe may well be pictured in the dictionary under the definition of "buzz band." When the Austin quartet presented themselves to the world a scant two years ago, they were an unqualified hit. Few local bands, in fact, have ever been greeted with the combination of instant audience acceptance and critical praise as Sixteen Deluxe. The most amazing part of their ascension, however, has been that the band is actually living up to—and beyond—its hype with hypnotic aplomb.

"We had an epiphany early on," smiles bassist Jeff Copas. "This is about being young and having fun."

That's the easy answer. What Sixteen Deluxe has really done is create an aural hurricane of well-crafted alternative pop, where swirling guitars and throbbing percussion meet and embrace. A celebrated fifteen-minute version of Big Star's "Kangaroo," the sonic sound of "Warm Jets," and the feedback lust and exuberance of the lavishly praised single "Idea" go a long way towards demonstrating the band's acid-drenched influences as seen through a soft focus lens.

The transcendental moment in every Sixteen Deluxe show is when the band collectively taps into the adrenal cortex with a guitar drone of seductively fuzzy pop. It's almost nirvana, and it seduced audiences and critics alike from the band's first show. It led to the Trance Syndicate release of their first record, *Backfeedmagnetbabe*, spawned a single that grabbed everyone's ears in "Idea," and won them Best New Band at last year's Austin Music Awards. Though that instant acceptance is a victory of sorts, Sixteen Deluxe is autonomous, even as they're wooed by major labels. When Atlantic Records came sniffing around 16D's labelmates Starfish, the trio told the label to go out and buy their own copy of the CD. 16D defiantly did the same thing.

"After South by Southwest last year, these people would call me at home and say 'I'm such-and-such-from-whatever in L.A. Could you send me a CD?'" Clark looks astounded. "I told them 'No. I can't even afford a postcard.'"

"These are people with *expense accounts* calling us," adds Chris "Frenchie" Smith, Clark's co-conspirator on guitar. Smith pauses and shakes his head. None of the band members seem anxious to call a major label home. They seem downright skittish about it, drummer KC Rhodes commenting, "It's hard to listen to someone who had nothing to do with it sit and break down your song."

For right now, Sixteen Deluxe's "success" seems relative, secondary to the process of developing their

Sixteen Deluxe, 1994. Photograph by Michael Crawford.

DANCING ABOUT ARCHITECTURE:
SIXTEEN DELAYS

"It's just a fucking rock & roll band," says Jeff Copas. "If this means we've blown it, then we've blown it." He's referring to Sixteen Deluxe's decision to cancel a string of concert dates, the release of a single, and the shooting of a video at precisely the moment Warner Bros. had planned to give their major label debut, *Emits Showers of Sparks*, its anticipated big push. Problems for the band were a long time in the works but finally came to a head after the band's April 4 show at Liberty Lunch with Luna. That's when singer/guitarist Carrie Clark admitted that she had stopped attending counseling for her heroin addiction and had resumed using the drug. "She had been trying to get help, and we thought that she *was* getting help," says Copas. "It became obvious to us that the pressure of the band was keeping her from getting better. I'd rather put the brakes on now and have her be alive."

Clark entered inpatient rehab last Friday via the SIMS Foundation for a period that may range from ten days to four weeks. In her absence the remainder of the band is continuing to write new material and work on demos for their next album with producer John Croslin. "It's pretty frustrating for the three of us, obviously," admits Copas, but he says that Warner Bros. has been understanding about the matter and assured them that *Emits Showers of Sparks* is not a "dead album." The label confirmed this with a tersely worded statement that simply confirms the facts of the situation. KEN LIECK

VOL. 17 NO. 32 ★ APRIL 17, 1998

music. After SXSW, the band goes out on tour with 7 Year Bitch for three weeks in the deep south and east coast, then finishes up the last week on their own. A new single, "Reactive" b/w "Kids in America," plus a new 7-inch on Trance produced by Crust, are both due soon, in addition to the four-track demos on which they've been working out their newest material. The labels can continue pitching woo.

"But we won't compromise style," Smith says flatly. Good idea. ◀

JIMMIE DALE GILMORE
BRAVER NEWER WORLD
ELEKTRA

The title does not lie. Gilmore is venturing into territory that only dreamers and outlaws dare to tread. But this is no soma holiday. Gilmore's painting big pictures of big places, mainly West Texas, his homeland as well as that of his heroes Roy Orbison and Buddy Holly, whose echelon he is sure to join if he's not already there. The sound is rough, muddy, and percolating. It desperately churns as if it were trying to remove itself from the bowels of the earth and run naked on the plains. Perhaps producer T-Bone Burnett has found himself a new niche. Burnett's wife, Sam Phillips, gets into the act here, too. Her "Where Is Love Now?" is the most striking track on the album. Its slow, foreboding tempo conjures images of lazy windshield wipers stroking away the rain droplets on the edge of a greenish-gray spring storm on a lonely highway. Gilmore has tapped into something here that transcends genre. This is the place from which the truly great art emanates. There's no turning back now. **JOE MITCHELL**

VOL. 15 NO. 44 ★ JULY 5, 1996

BUTTHOLE SURFERS
ELECTRICLARRYLAND
CAPITOL

It was the best of albums. It was the worst of albums . . . Pretty much what every Butthole Surfers album has been over the past thirteen years: monumental jack-off in the hands of true pros. It's what *Mad* magazine always wanted to be; the rag you threw down in disgust and then snickered at and picked back up— only to throw it down *again*. At its best, . . . *larryland* is "Pepper," a drum-looped nursery-rhyme that works Texas mythology to a level the state's visitors' bureau only dreams about. It's hard to resist, and because radio has swallowed it hook, line, etc., there's no reason to think new kiddie ditties like "Jingle of a Dog's Collar" and "TV Star" couldn't do just as well. At its worst though, *Electric* . . . is "Thermador," something best wiped off the studio console and not thought about. Same goes for "My Brother's Wife" and the French-in-three-easy-lessons muzak of "Let's Talk about Cars." Yet, what connects these studio time-killers with the more obviously commercial toss-offs is an overwhelming sense that the band just doesn't give a shit anymore. The lyrics could be from any cocktail napkin mess and the riffs from any late-night jam session. It seems almost arbitrary. What's that they say about throwing typewriters into a roomful of monkeys and waiting a few hundred years?

RAOUL HERNANDEZ

VOL. 15 NO. 44 ★ JULY 5, 1996

SHAWN COLVIN
A FEW SMALL REPAIRS
COLUMBIA

Using superlatives is like crying wolf. You can't do it too many times before your credibility factor vanishes. Inherent risks be damned. Here goes: *A Few Small Repairs* is the best record released this year. This one nails the routine flawlessly and sticks the dismount without a hop (maybe just a slight equilibrium adjustment with the arms). On the first listen, *Repairs* is enjoyable, like looking at a pretty landscape painting. There's a scenic musical backdrop further decorated with Colvin's airy and sometimes frail but colorful voice. It's passive. It's aesthetically pleasing. But keep listening further and you see this wide variety of emotional characters who are typically passionate, but usually understated so as not to crush you with excess weight. Then you realize you're not looking at a flat, static picture at all, but actually reading a fantastic book into which you are now inextricably drawn. If the tumultuous domestic affairs (specifically her divorce) and any related suffering Colvin may have endured recently were indeed the inspiration for the material here, then, from a listener's standpoint, it was worth it. **MICHAEL BERTIN**

VOL. 16 NO. 9 ★ NOVEMBER 1, 1996

Dead Rabbits
Townes Van Zandt's Insight

VOL. 16 NO. 19 ★ JANUARY 10, 1997

ED WARD

WHEN I GOT A CALL the other morning telling me Townes Van Zandt had died, my first thoughts were on a story he'd told me the last time I'd seen him. He'd been in Berlin for a concert, accompanied by his friend and manager Harold Eggers, who had some business to talk over with me. They'd been sightseeing with their friend and mine, Wolfgang Doebeling, who owns a label that had put out a live album by him, when Doebeling called to say they were ready to get together. I suggested a cafe up the street from me and walked up to meet them.

Van Zandt wasn't in such great shape. An icy shot-glass of vodka stood before him, as well as a basket of bread and butter. Doebeling was trying to get him to eat something and told me that Van Zandt had been real shaky on the sightseeing tour, having to sit down every few minutes because he was so weak.

My business was with his manager, but Van Zandt really wanted to talk. First, he told me a hilarious story about how his habit of stealing Bibles from hotel rooms had come to an end, and then he questioned me at length about what it took to live, legally, in Germany. He pulled a small bottle of vodka from his pocket and surreptitiously refilled the shot-glass, and then, out of nowhere, he started telling me another story:

"I was going through a real bad depression once, and it was like I couldn't get out of bed. I drank some, but that didn't help, and I listened to some Hank, and even that didn't help. I mean, it was real bad.

TOWARDS THE END, HE'D LOSE THE LIGHT AS OFTEN AS NOT.

"So I'd been like this for most of a week, just lying around, and it got to where I had to take the garbage out. My dog was just rarin' to go out. She hadn't been out in a while, and so when I went to the door with the trash, she was right there. I opened the door, and right there, in front of the door, was this little bunny. The dog, she shot out of the door, and I thought, 'Oh, no.' See, she's been taught that the squirrels and the bunnies are our friends, and she's not to mess with

them, but I guess she'd just been cooped up inside with me so long that something wild got the better of her, and before I could do anything, she was out the door, and that poor bunny didn't have a chance.

"Well, I pulled her off of it, and it was still alive, so I yelled at her good and sent her back into the house, and she knew, she just knew she'd done something wrong. I dumped the trash, and went back to the bunny, and it was holding on. So I carefully picked it up and put it somewhere it would be out of harm's way, and got something warm to put on top of it, and went back into the house.

"The next morning, I decided I had to see how that bunny was doing, and I went out there, and, well, I guess I should have guessed, or known, but it was dead. So I got some newspapers and picked it up, and walked over to the trash with that little body, and I just felt so bad, you know. I couldn't blame my dog; she's only a dog. And I couldn't blame myself. It had just happened, that's all.

"And I went back into the house, and I just couldn't get that bunny out of my mind. And all of a sudden, I had this realization. 'Townes,' I said to myself, 'you are one sorry son of a bitch. Here you are moping around the house for days, feeling sorry for yourself, but *what about that bunny*?' You know, I was all wrapped up in my own troubles, but that was nothing next to what had happened to that bunny. And all those sorry feelings I had for myself just lifted off of me like a big stone."

I have no idea why Van Zandt needed to tell that story, but I could see as it unfolded that the need was a powerful one. He shook a bit after he told it, and repeated "What about that bunny" a couple of times. And, after I'd gone back home, I couldn't get the story out of my head either, because I'd seen the effect it had had on the man who told it. I wanted to go back and tell him that the next time he got hit with a depression like that, there were things he could do about it that might lift him out of it without pills or dead rabbits. But I couldn't make the show that night, and I never saw him again.

Van Zandt's insight was a lot like the ones that attracted some people to his songs and his shows, and that makes me as sad as anything. There was a morbidity to some of his songs that was obviously one byproduct of depressions like this. People could watch him onstage, struggling to tell the story—wondering if just this once the genius would break through, or it would all collapse again—and they could think "At least it's not me." Towards the end, he'd lose the light as often as not. All those of us who cared about him can hope for is that although, like the bunny, he met his peace in an awful way, he did, at least, find it. ◄

MISS LAVELLE WHITE
IT HAVEN'T BEEN EASY
DISCOVERY /ANTONE'S

The Sabine River is the hardy creation of nature that knits together the borders of Texas and Louisiana. Though it can rise and swell with rain or run low in the high summer, it never changes direction, ever-flowing into the mighty Gulf of Mexico. Miss Lavelle White might be able to tell you a thing or about the Sabine, having been born in Louisiana but raised in Texas, and if she can't tell you, she can certainly make you hear it. White is blessed with a voice from God—rich and soulful, winding and snaking its way through funky territory. For her second outing on the Antone's label, *It Haven't Been Easy*, that voice flows like the river, warm, liquid blues pouring over a solid bottom of rocky rhythms. You just can't get enough of her classic sound, churning for four decades, steeped in a Sixties Memphis soul tradition but comfortably contemporary. White's songwriting imprint is on nine of the album's twelve tracks, and she wends her way from "Wootie Boogie" to showstoppers "Mississippi My Home" and "Don't Let My Baby Ride" with stops at familiar titles, such as her remake of Eddie Floyd's "I've Never Found a Man to Love" and the late Johnny "Guitar" Watson's "Lonely Lonely Nights." This is dance music, honey, belly-rubbin' blues of the finest kind from one of the masters of the genre. You expect Miss Lavelle White to be good; what you don't expect is that she would be so great.

MARGARET MOSER

VOL. 16 NO. 23 ★ FEBRUARY 7, 1997

Miss Lavelle White at the 1995-96 AMAs.
Photograph by Martha Grenon.

Parallel Universe
El Gato Negro's Ruben Ramos

VOL. 17 NO. 22 ★ FEBRUARY 6, 1998

RAOUL HERNANDEZ

RUBEN RAMOS has existed in two different worlds his whole life. Born Texan, he has lived Mexican. In his world, people speak mostly in Spanish to people with dark skin, dark eyes, and dark hair. They eat different food, have different customs. Though a rock & roll convert at a young age, he sings mostly in Spanish while his band plays music made for south-of-the-border sensibilities. Some call it Tejano, Ramos calls it Chicano. His entire musical career has had little to do with the music business most Americans are familiar with; parallel universes, and never the twain shall meet.

"It's true," nods Ramos. "It's very true. But I can't cry about it. I gotta keep working. I gotta keep doing what I love to do. I know there's racism in the music business—all over. People say it's gone down, but no, it hasn't gone down. It still has a lot."

Take, for instance, the segregation that exists here in lovely, liberal Austin. *¿Qué te parece?* What about that?

"*No me parece*," says Ramos. "I don't like it very much. Very segregated, but I'd rather live here. I love Austin. *Austin tiene todo* (has it all). Has lots of green, lots of trees, lots of grass, water—a little bit of some hills. What else can you ask for?

"San Antonio is a city like no other city in the world, but I'd rather live here. For what I do, it's perfect. I love to jog. There's the most beautiful jogging trail that I've found in the United States. I love to golf. Some of the best courses are around Austin. I wouldn't move from here. I'm very comfortable. Plus it's centrally located for my business."

And business is good?

"Business is good, *gracias a Dios*. Looking for it to get better. I've just started. To me, I'm just beginning. I've gotten wiser. We should have done this a long time ago—gotten serious. Do this the music business way."

Since taking his act to Barb Wire ("three guys in Plano"), Ramos' musical career has definitely been on the upswing: 1996 brought an invite to play the Presidential Inaugural gala, 1997 swept him into the prestigious Pura Vida Hall of Fame, and this year will find Ramos receiving an honor equivalent to being enshrined into the Rock & Roll Hall of Fame: induction into the Tejano Music Awards Hall of Fame on March 7 at the Alamodome. Ramos and his band prove why the next night in San Antonio.

Playing a fundraiser for congressional hopeful Walter Martinez, Ramos and his Texas Revolution take an old-style cafeteria, the Flamingo Ballroom, and turn this staid event with a lot of older Hispanics into a bonafide *rocanroll* show, complete with smoke, light show, and catcalls. The nine-piece band, complete with a quartet of horns, cranks out tunes such as "*Juana la Cubana*" like there's no tomorrow. This isn't wimpy Tejano crap, the R&B is too prevalent, the salsa too pronounced.

In the midst of it all—the smoke, the red, flashing lights—is Ramos, impeccably dressed in a beige suit and sunglasses, shaking a maraca and looking like either a Secret Service agent or a visiting foreign dignitary. These days he admits his voice isn't that great, but when you have a band like his that may not be the point. About thirty minutes into the show, Ramos brings his son Mark onstage, and the two belt out a version of "*Ya Yo te Quiero*" from the new CD, *El Gato Negro Smooth*. Shaking their well-dressed stuff, father and son revel in the family business.

SOME CALL IT TEJANO, RAMOS CALLS IT CHICANO.

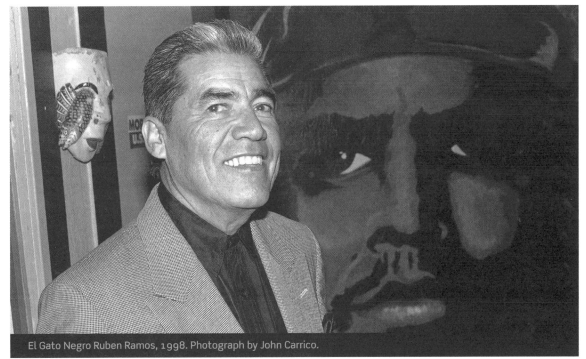

El Gato Negro Ruben Ramos, 1998. Photograph by John Carrico.

"The *Mexicanos* like you to look good. That's what I'm catering to. For a while, we thought, 'Who's gonna play, you or the tie you're wearing?' But hey, we're dealing with the *Mexicanos*, and this is the way they see success. If we get up onstage in short pants and ripped tennis shoes, it's not the same as getting up there in a tuxedo or a double-breasted suit where people are saying, '*Híjole*, they must be good.' These are the people that we're catering to. We're not catering to *gringos*. We're catering to the *Mexicanos*, Latinos."

Catering to them to the tune of 200 nights a year, actually. This has been Ramos' life for almost forty years, the legacy of ten uncles who all played music, the great-grandfather that paid hard-earned money to have them tutored, and the relation before him that made getting a tutor seem more like a necessity than a frivolity. The family legacy.

"I think I'm part of that, yeah," nods Ramos. "My son, Mark, has started to sing. So I see him as continuing that [legacy]. But you know a lot of [*Mexicanos*] have a different concept of music: '*Música es para los marijuanos.*' You know? Like, it's no good. That's a bad label. But that's the concept some people get. You know, *música* isn't any good. And that's another thing I'm proving here.

"See, my uncles were good musicians, but five of them died before my age, from *puro alcohol*—[drinking] every day, every day, every day. I want to show that music is a reputable business—can be a reputable business. That's one of my goals."

Probably a better one than "crossing over."

"It's a *gringo* world," says Ramos without a hint of emotion, his eyes betraying nothing. "That's where I'm at now. I don't say forget the *gringo* world. We gotta do business with the *gringo* world. But as far as me wanting to cross over or wanting to be accepted, fuck it. I have enough *raza*—Latinos—here. I've got the *Cubanos*, the *Puertorriqueños* that come and say, 'Hey man, I liked that merengue you played.' They come back, too, because we play a little bit of their music. Those are my people. I don't need the *gringos* to support myself."

Es verdad. It's true. Let history record this. ◄

Davíd Garza's Musical Manifesto

VOL. 17 NO. 30 ★ APRIL 3, 1998

ANDY LANGER

SOME PHILOSOPHIES are easier to execute than they are to explain or discuss. Davíd Garza calls them the "untalkables," and the local musician says he's driven by three such abiding philosophies. The first, recently appropriated from his guitarist Jacob Shultz, reads like an excerpt from Hallmark's "Inspirations for the Musician" line of greeting cards: "Close your eyes, hit a string—*bend* it—and hope that it's close. Whatever happens, it's perfect. Just keep going."

Garza's second guiding theory is part Nike ad, part slacker slogan: "No expectations." The third and perhaps overriding theory? "Follow the music."

> ## " I'VE ALWAYS ALIENATED AS MANY PEOPLE AS I BRING IN.
> ### DAVÍD GARZA "

"I may die tomorrow and I don't want to say I was doing anything other than what the music told me to do," says Garza. "I've tried before to do what *I* wanted to do and it's not the right thing, but if you try to follow what the music tells you, you and your music will be okay. There's a reason your brain's up here and your heart's down there. They should be separate. And when you start thinking with your heart and feeling with your brain, you're in trouble. I know these kinds of ideas may come off as really namby-pamby, artistic, aesthetic, Oscar Wilde kind of things, but they affect the end thing more than anything else."

In just over eight years of living and playing in Austin, Davíd Garza has followed the music down some fairly diverse paths. Between his tenure with local sensations Twang Twang Shock-A-Boom, Garza's first band and still perhaps his most successful (in terms of hype anyway), and next week's release of his Lava/Atlantic major label debut, *This Euphoria*, the philosophizing Garza has been many things: teen sensation, struggling singer-songwriter, fraternity favorite, road warrior, independent record mogul, home studio wizard, and Time/Warner associate.

To hear his detractors tell it, all these paths have most often rendered Garza directionless, causing him to be insincere, egocentric, and most often, pretentious. In fact, although he and Alejandro Escovedo share both a Hispanic heritage and a thirst for constant reinvention, Garza has mostly been greeted by the locals as the anti-Alejandro; perhaps no local musician has taken on as many challenging personas and gotten more bad press and general resentment for their efforts.

"Austin's special for me," says Garza, "because I don't think I'll ever be respected here. And there's a comfort in that. If I go on to sell X number of records, they'll say I got lucky or Atlantic bought it for me. That's because Austin has known me since I was a dork singing about fishsticks with Twang Twang. How could I be about anything else to them?"

By all accounts, the party least concerned with Garza's local reputation is Lava, a small Atlantic Records imprint with a lot of corporate clout. After a bidding war, Lava signed Garza in 1996, licensing his homespun label Wide Open Records in the process. Yet because Lava's four-person staff spent most of 1997 milking multi-platinum debuts from Sugar Ray and Matchbox 20, they asked Garza to wait his turn in the pipeline, delaying the release of his debut and throwing him a juicy bone instead—the opportunity to place a song on the *Great Expectations* soundtrack. Better yet, Lava consented to Garza's releasing a homemade EP, *The 4-Track Manifesto*, which came out late last fall on the musician's Wide Open imprint.

Not only did the EP's rough edges and anthemic songwriting help reposition Garza musically just in time for his proper national debut, it also made valuable inroads at college radio and retail. Actually, the same could be said about the EP's impact on Atlantic, where label brass were so impressed with *The 4-Track Manifesto* that they urged Garza to add two of the EP's tunes, "Float Away" and "Discoball World," onto *This Euphoria*, declaring the latter tune the album's first single. Back in Austin, meanwhile, the EP's local promotion was intentionally low-key.

"I've taken to carrying [*The 4-Track Manifesto*] in my bag to give them away," says Garza. "It's like, 'Here, I know you haven't listened to me in five years. Take it, free.' Then maybe those people will start coming to the gigs."

Although the success of Twang Twang and the many years Garza has put into developing a local audience might suggest larger local crowds, the singer's post–Twang Twang gigs have traditionally catered to just 350 people. And not just the same 350 people, either; every time Garza has reinvented himself musically, he's pulled in a different 350 people.

"I've always alienated as many people as I bring in," admits Garza. "You can never underestimate that. As soon as you stop thinking there will be turnover, you're dead."

Clearly, different people hated Garza for different reasons. Maybe that he had learned to write and sing in public at 18 didn't help; certainly a glut of sappy love songs sung by a teenager didn't. Nor did the fact that many within the local music scene believed Garza was changing his name from David to Dah-veed (the Spanish pronunciation of Davíd) as some sort of ego stroke.

Even beyond the name issue, there may be yet another culture clash contributing to Garza's local bad rap—his obvious ambition and Austin's reputation for a lack thereof. Before Garza signed with Atlantic, he had already self-released five CDs and three cassettes on Wide Open. Their combined sales? Over 30,000 copies.

At the same time, Garza took his act where he was better appreciated—on the road. Less than a year after Twang Twang had broken up, Garza was already cultivating a regional base that included stops in Dallas, Waco, San Marcos, Nacogdoches, San Antonio, Corpus Christi, Lubbock, and El Paso. Teaming up with other regional acts such as Better Than Ezra, Little Sister, and Jackopierce, Garza's fan base soon stretched well across the Southwest.

If all goes according to plan, it will be more than a year before Garza gets another serious chance to write and record. And while he's admittedly nervous about Atlantic's machinery spinning too fast, or the idea of spending too long between records, Garza says all he can do is follow the music.

"If I sell a million records or sell five and get dropped, that's what the music wanted me to do," says Garza, flatly. "I'm a big believer in fate. What matters right now is that I take things slow; that when I start a song, I start it at the right tempo and sing it the right way, because there's nothing anybody can say or control about that. Live music is the sanctuary and always should be. And I think people forget that just because you're part of the machinery, you can still do the music the way you want."

If Garza is indeed ready and Atlantic's machine is equally ready, wouldn't it then make for the biggest "I told you so" in Austin music history?

"I don't want the last laugh," Garza says. "I just want to keep being able to do this." ◄

JON DEE GRAHAM
ESCAPE FROM MONSTER ISLAND
FREEDOM

There's a lot to be said for the self-discipline of Jon Dee Graham, who waited nearly twenty years to release his first solo album. The most obvious point is that a lifetime of experience will be poured into such an effort, but then Graham's lived more than a few lifetimes. Punk guitarist, New Sincerity rocker, sideman, session man, and songwriter, Graham's *Escape From Monster Island* is the ten-song destination from all those roads, rendered through Graham's words, played out in tender verses, and sung in his tobacco-battered voice. Out there on *Monster Island*, life is for contemplation, though the album is clearly "inspired by and dedicated to" Graham's son; "Soonday" gently invites the listener to "Come to Roy's house" and it's hard to turn down its guileless invitation, especially when he pleads "Don't grow up so goddamn fast/wait a little while for me to get home . . ." The wisdom of two decades is evident at every turn, as Graham has one foot planted firmly in the future and one in the past. It's like stumbling on a well-worn path, reaching down to pick up the rough, unassuming stone that tripped you up, and cracking it open to reveal dazzling crystals inside. MARGARET MOSER

VOL. 16 NO. 47 ★ JULY 25, 1997

Unbreakable: Jon Dee Graham, 1999.
Photograph by John Carrico.

TINA MARSH & CO2 "DREAMKEEPERS"

LAGUNA GLORIA AMPHITHEATRE, JUNE 5, 1998

If there really is an Austin curse, Tina Marsh might say it plagues the capital city's jazz community the worst. As educated a populace as Austin is purported to have, it apparently rejects the notion of jazz as intellectual music, because most local jazz events here go notoriously under-patronized. Knowing Marsh, a musician who believes passionately in her art—jazz—she must have been cursing the curse, her luck, and El Niño when the only rain to hit Austin for what seemed like all spring gathered on the horizon to welcome the Creative Opportunity Orchestra's annual gala event at Laguna Gloria. Only instead of the rain signaling further proof of some mythical scourge, it proved to be a bona fide blessing instead. Bringing the loveliest evening Austin is likely to see until at least October, the afternoon shower not only brought down temperatures into the seventies, it brought out a healthy crowd of locals to experience a show as exotic as Laguna Gloria's Rousseauian grounds. With Marsh in an Egyptian headdress, bedecked in blue, leading an Orchestra that numbered sixteen musicians—as well as Sherri Baby Canon's drum chorus—a cool wind carried the beating of Brannen Temple's drums and an assortment of triangles, gongs, and even bubbles, which signaled a thirty-five-member choir to make its entrance stage left. The first part of composer Carla Bley's suite "Dream Keeper" followed, featuring a Latin-flavored piece from El Salvador, "Feliciano Ama," and Larry Spencer's trumpet. A second processional, children in Mexican death masks, marched across the stage and into the audience as Marsh sang into a headset mike that couldn't compete with her big band, except when she used her voice as another instrument, emitting squeaks and shrieks and something that sounded like Swahili. The fourth and final episode of the piece, "N'kosi Sikeleli Afrika," was probably the strongest, with a third and final processional being just as enchanting and musically disruptive as the previous one. The second set, played in the dark as dozens of children continued their happy pandemonium up top of the sunken theatre, featured Marsh and the orchestra getting down to their time-honored business of avant-jazz with excellent compositions from local composer/trombonist John Mills ("Wish," "Haunted Heart") as well as Marsh's bewitching "Tell Me What You're Dreaming" and her husband Randy Zimmerman's swelling "Pursuit." Laguna Gloria's 10 pm curfew cut the band off rather abruptly, but by that time the evening and event had been a success; it wasn't Wynton Marsalis' "Blood on the Fields"—Marsh's budget being a tiny fraction of Marsalis'—and yet on a night as beautiful as this one, it was every bit as memorable. **RAOUL HERNANDEZ**

VOL. 17 NO. 41 ★ JUNE 19, 1998

BRUCE ROBISON

WRAPPED

LUCKY DOG

There's a big difference between the *Wrapped* that Bruce Robison self-released here in Austin last year and the *Wrapped* that came out several weeks ago on Sony imprint Lucky Dog. Despite the fact that both albums share nine of the same songs, the former could easily be classified a strong Americana singer-songwriter roots affair, while the latter could never be mistaken for anything other than its obvious genrefication: Nashville. And surprise! Guess which one is better? Far better. In fact, not only is the second version of Robison's *Wrapped* head and shoulders above the first, it may also have the distinction of being the purest truest Nashville album released by a longtime local living locally. Adding two new songs, the lead-off Southern evocative, "Rayne, Louisiana" (a duet with brother Charlie Robison) and "Desperately," as well as the best tune from Robison's awkward, self-titled 1995 debut, "Angry All the Time," *Wrapped* sports all the earmarks of classic Nashville: stainless steel studio work (Rich Brotherton, Lloyd Maines, Marty Muse, Gene Elders, Amy Tiven, and Chris Searles—all Austin musicians), expert songwriting, and the singer's trembling tenor. Throw in a true Nashville queen, Robison's wife Kelly Willis, and their duet "When I Loved You," resequence the album leaving its true centerpiece "My Brother and Me" right where it was before at track five, and the only thing wrong with *Wrapped* is the James Taylor factor; neither "Go to Your Heart" or "End Like That" would go missed if their syrup was wiped up. Even that defines *Wrapped* as a Nashville record. Yep, a fine Music Row product, except it bears a familiar trademark of true quality: Recorded in Austin.

RAOUL HERNANDEZ

VOL. 17 NO. 41 ★ JUNE 19, 1998

DALE WATSON

LITTLE LONGHORN SALOON, JULY 16, 1998

Richard Linklater knew what he was doing when he cast Burnet Road as the old main drag in *Dazed and Confused*. The stalwart North Austin artery has maintained a Seventies facade despite the encroachment of the Eighties and Nineties. After all, who needs the hassle and expense of Sixth Street when you can spend Thursday nights with Dale Watson at Ginny's Little Longhorn while knocking back $1 Schlitz and pickled sausage? Watson's jaunty, informal stage demeanor is well-served by the Little Longhorn's

atmosphere. It's almost like having him play in your living room (if your living room has a set-up bar). There's plenty of audience interaction, and calling out requests is encouraged. Want to hear Merle Haggard's "Silver Wings"? Patsy Cline, George Jones, Faron Young? No problem at all. Watson and his band play the role of quintessential C&W jukebox enthusiastically and effortlessly. There are also plenty of Watson originals that hold their own amongst the many standards. I can't imagine wanting to be anyplace else on the planet when Watson plays "Honkiest Tonkiest Beer Joint," a reference-laden paean to the Longhorn. The role of low-key troubadour is custom-fit for Watson's deep, resonant voice and Bakersfield-fueled guitar handiwork. Ricky Davis' steel guitar playing is equally inspiring, and Brian Farriby's drumming displays the subtle restraint of a consummate session cat. It's hard to believe that such a rich, mellifluous sound can come from a corner of the room that's about the size of a postage stamp. Not bad for the provinces. **GREG BEETS**

VOL. 17 NO. 46 ★ JULY 24, 1998

STORYVILLE

DOG YEARS

ATLANTIC

There is no joy in Storyville, and it's not because *Dog Years* is a bluesy rock album. No, it's because *Dog Years* is a listless and soulless bluesy rock album. From the opener, the Will Sexton–penned "Enough," Storyville comes out slacking and doesn't pick things up until the occasionally noisy muscle on "Fairplay," all but two tracks shy of the album's end. By that time though, not even an Al Green cover ("It Ain't No Fun to Me") can redeem this mostly mechanical effort. Even the best groove on *Dog Years,* "Keep a Handle on

It," sounds worn out. And the dulcet acoustic closer "Lucky (One More Time)" is more than offset by the aptly titled "Don't Make Me Suffer." What's just plain sad more than merely disappointing is how much talent there is in the band that's being left on the bench. Storyville has, arguably, Austin's best rhythm section in Chris Layton and Tommy Shannon, and maybe its best rock guitarist in David Grissom (whatever happened to the thick, warm, piercing riffs?). Hell, when singer Malford Milligan was in Stick People he did things that put to shame the rote rockisms that he relies on for Storyville's material. *Dog Years*, an album of veterans dogging it a little too much.

MICHAEL BERTIN

VOL. 17 NO. 46 ★ JULY 24, 1998

BILLY JOE SHAVER
VICTORY
NEW WEST

The first song Billy Joe Shaver sings on *Victory* is an a capella original, and halfway through comes a lyric that serves notice for the album as a whole: "Silent sacred solitude how it knits upon my brow." What follows is a thoughtful, often fierce string of country gospel originals, as Shaver brings his considerable talents to bear on the inner workings of his faith. The result is a simple album filled with unshakable conviction, one that explores the wonders of saving grace while never straying toward the daunting or didactic. The favored subjects are "five and dimers," rough-hewn penitents of the sort Shaver played in

Amazing grace: Billy Joe Shaver, 1998. Photograph by John Carrico.

The Apostle; the favored vehicle is a mix of guileless confession with the gospel truth. "Ain't no way to get around it," Shaver sings, "you just can't beat Jesus Christ." *Victory* is an insistently religious album, and for all of its fallen angels, an insistently optimistic one as well. It is also personal, born of a hard-won faith and spelled in simple language. The album's emotional power is both direct and cumulative, and it's hard not to listen with a touch of awe, regardless of the needlepoint on one's own spiritual compass.

JAY HARDWIG

VOL. 17 NO. 49 ★ AUGUST 14, 1998

BEAVER NELSON
THE LAST HURRAH
FREEDOM

For nearly a decade, no one but the major label weasels who kept commissioning and rejecting Beaver Nelson's demos knew how the local musician's reckless barroom rock translated onto tape. Now, with the release of this long-delayed debut, Austinites will discover that the suits were right: Nelson isn't major-label material, he's too good. His songwriting is too straightforward, too disquieting. His delivery is too direct, too tormented. *The Last Hurrah* is an album for long drives and attentive at-home play, where the full effect of Nelson's clever lyrics and Scrappy Jud Newcomb's conscientious production can seep in. With hardly an underwritten song or lazy performance in the lot, Nelson's *Last Hurrah* sports a now-or-never vitality that perhaps only Jon Dee Graham's *Escape From Monster Island* or Lucinda Williams' *Car Wheels on a Gravel Road* have evinced of late. It's simply that strong of an album. And with any luck, it won't be Nelson's last hurrah after all. **ANDY LANGER**

VOL. 18 NO. 9 ★ OCTOBER 30, 1998

All the Pain Platinum Can Buy

VOL. 18 NO. 15 ★ DECEMBER 11, 1998

ANDY LANGER

"HERE TODAY, GONE LATER TODAY."

It's hard not to notice that in separate interviews, months apart and fully outside each other's earshot, Miles Zuniga and Joey Shuffield both quote the same music industry dictum as a way of explaining what keeps them going when they're already going around the clock.

Standing out from the platinum pack is almost as difficult as going platinum in the first place.

"Anytime I start to lose focus, I remind myself of being in the van and wondering if my day job was going to take me back six weeks later," says Shuffield, Fastball's drummer. "I know we can be replaced immediately. If we drop our guards for a second, the million bands inches behind us get to move forward."

Even with those nameless, faceless replacement killers on their trail, keeping focused isn't always as easy as it looks. Since the Austin trio's smash single "The Way"—arguably the most notable radio hit of 1998—started its ascent up the pop charts last February, Fastball has not only surfed Jay Leno's couch on *The Tonight Show*, they've been interviewed by seemingly every media outlet in the country, and crisscrossed the nation with everyone from Art Alexakis to

Everclear. Oh, and they sold a million records, too. Not bad for a local band that couldn't get arrested at the Hole in the Wall back in January.

"We're not taking this for granted," says the group's guitarist, Zuniga. "It's the music business. It's not like I invented Liquid Paper or some kind of drug that cures cancer and I've got the patent. The nature of this business is you're here today, gone later today."

Exactly what being "here today" will ultimately earn the band, Fastball's going platinum, a feat in and of itself—the last Austin act to go platinum with a new release was the Fabulous Thunderbirds in 1988, and before that Christopher Cross in 1981—isn't nearly as interesting as what it actually takes to *sustain* a platinum album. You want numbers? Forget units sold and dollar amounts for income derived thereof. Try instead the number of tasks that a touring platinum act like Fastball must accomplish on just one three-city swing through Washington, D.C., Philadelphia, and Boston on the band's current tour:

1 meet 'n' greet dinner
3 club performances
3 acoustic performances for live audiences
3 radio/retail meet 'n' greets
7 radio interviews
8 phone interviews
9 public performances of "The Way"
10 public performances of "Fire Escape," the band's current single
11.5 traveling hours between D.C. and Philadelphia, Philadelphia and Boston
39.5 combined hours of work that appear on the official itinerary
72 possible hours to complete all of the above

"There's no way to really prepare for all this," says the man who penned "The Way," Tony Scalzo, of Fastball's day planner for the last year. "I'd heard from other bands about all the promo stuff, interviews, and radio stops, but nobody can really know what it's like until they're there. But there are those who are willing to do it and those who aren't. I think those that are have a little better chance of being around for the long haul."

Undeniably, Fastball is a band willing to make that promotional commitment. Just as they know their run of success could end tomorrow, they also know that standing out from the platinum pack is almost as difficult as going platinum in the first place. In Fastball's new world order, the opportunity for casual radio listeners to connect a name to a face or an artist with a song is an opportunity to make a legitimate fan. To that end, it's the same routine in every city: One of their label representatives picks up the band somewhere between 9–11 am, loads them into a Blazer, Suburban, or Town Car, and takes them on a guided tour of the city's radio market.

For the next ten hours, Fastball will devote its time to servicing radio—offering interviews, wacky station IDs, acoustic sets, and private performances to stations that have supported "The Way" or its follow-up, "Fire Escape." If it seems that a Fastball tour is as much about radio as it is about live performances at night, it's because it is.

"Everything is about exposure," says Zuniga. "If you stop at a radio station on the way to a gig, you're being exposed to so many more people than could ever hear you at a venue. It's like a virus passed through the subway system: It's capable of infecting so many more people than if you just coughed on them." ◄

Fastball. Photograph by Michael Lavine (courtesy of Hollywood Records).

165

Drake Tungsten and His Boy Skellington

VOL. 18 NO. 21 ★ JANUARY 22, 1999

RAOUL HERNANDEZ

DRAKE TUNGSTEN and Skellington have the drop on Britt Daniel. Two minor toughs from the Spoonman's nefarious past, Tungsten and Skellington hold all the answers. Naturally, they've vanished. *Poof!* Haven't been seen in a Hoffa's age. These ill-mannered thugs will sing Daniel's story like failed pledges at a frat-house hazing inquiry. Find the Thin Man, gumshoe, Tungsten and his boy Skellington, and all the clues fall into one keyhole, unlocking the mystery of Spoon's *A Series of Sneaks*.

This much we know for sure: A cloak-and-dagger bludgeoning of the "alternative rock" sort, Spoon's second LP was unquestionably one of the most dan-

A SERIES OF SNEAKS IS DOWNRIGHT DIABOLICAL.

gerous weapons in Austin's musical arsenal last year. Menacing the listener with a mouthful of sinister insinuations, accusations, recriminations, *A Series of Sneaks* steals along the shadowy side streets of an urban nightmare, leaving behind what one sleuth called "a trail of intrigue, confusion, and a lot of unanswered questions."

The songs are short, jagged, a hail of riffs raining down over a clanging, clamoring sonic backdrop that sounds like industry in decline. Daniel's voice, as both the group's singer and songwriter, barks ominously as if through the sole, century-old loudspeaker in Big Brother's holding cell. *A Series of Sneaks* is downright diabolical.

Under the interrogating glare of the media spotlight, asked how *he* would describe *A Series of Sneaks*, Britt Daniel—smart, cagey—flinches, blinks two or three times, then slumps. Slap him again.

"Uhhh?"

He trails off. Long trail. Like the back nine at the Sahara Country Club. Nothing to do now but take five, maybe. An early Beatles album plays in the background, but the barren walls of Daniel's mostly deserted Hyde Park apartment couldn't care less. They look the other way. Get my cigar clipper.

"Uh, it's real rock."

"Real rock"? Is that some kind of a joke, smart guy? You trying to be funny? Go on, mouth off some more. See what that gets you.

"How do I describe it? I don't know. I don't know how to describe it. I'd probably go into how we recorded it. It took a long time to record. It was a tortuous process. I wanted *A Series of Sneaks* to be more like the *Soft Effects* EP, which was done real thrown off, done real fast. We didn't put a lot of thought into it, and then it turned into something that I really, really liked, and was really proud of. You know, I wasn't expecting much from it.

"But then with *Series of Sneaks*, maybe because we knew it would be an album, or maybe because we had more time and money and were doing it in a real studio instead of just in John's [Croslin] garage, we ran into problems. We were thinking it through too much."

Finally, some answers. Not very good ones, but at least he hasn't dummied up. During their relatively short recording career, Spoon's musical missteps have been few. Formed in late 1993, the group, originally Daniel and Greg Wilson (aka Wendel Stivers) on guitar, Jim Eno on drums, and Andy Maquire on bass, was a compelling one from the very start. Releasing a four-song vinyl debut in May '94, *The Nefarious EP*, Spoon quickly caught the eye of Hole in the Wall regulars and the ear of the local press with their taut sound and tight songs. In 1995, Daniel and company signed

Spoon, circa 1994: (l-r) Jim Eno, Britt Daniel, and Andy Maquire. Photograph by John Carrico.

a recording contract with the hippest of hip New York indie labels, Matador. A one-way ticket down Easy Street, right? Not so fast.

By the time Spoon's Matador bow, *Telephono*, hit the streets in 1996, Wilson was long gone and Maquire's legal representation was demanding one-third of the group's advance and publishing royalties following the bassist's acrimonious split with the band (she got both as per the original agreement with her bandmates). Filling in for the interim, *Telephono* producer and longtime local musician in good standing John Croslin toured extensively with the band in support of a full-length debut that garnered generally positive press when not being derided for being a Pixies tribute. Daniel loves that one, though he's too polite to bristle.

Not *Telephono*. It bristles. With "real rock." A bashing good time with big production values that don't betray its origins in Croslin's garage (or its $3,000 price tag), *Telephono* comes over the wire like a call to arms, easily one of Matador's more commercial releases. From the relentless demand of the opener "Don't Buy the Realistic" to the *High Voltage*–era AC/DC intro of the album's first single, "All the Negatives Have Been Destroyed," *Telephono* just plain rocks, three of the album's best tunes originating on *The Nefarious EP* in rougher versions, including the slightly Pixilated "The Government Darling." The album sold all of 3,000 copies.

Typical, that story. Ugly as an ex-wife. Yet Daniel and Eno could at least take comfort in one thing: Spoon had made a major leap in the music industry arc of becoming a viable recording venture, going from local artists putting out their own product to national league hopefuls on a marquee indie with major distribution. Now it was time for a follow-up. That's when Daniel turned up Drake Tungsten and his muscle Skellington.

Born in Galveston 27 years ago, raised in Temple, Daniel grew up in a household rocking to the Beatles and rolling to the Stones, his dad a neurologist father of five who collected guitars even though he wasn't really a practitioner of the instrument ("He was the kind of dad that would wake up and turn on the stereo real loud in order to wake everybody up," says Britt). When he moved to Austin in 1989 to attend UT, Britt tried his own hand at playing guitar, starting a band whose sound landed somewhere between the Beatles' tuneful pop and the Stones' swagger: Skellington.

Quick to local recognition, Skellington ('90–'92), featuring "the very Fripp" guitar stylings of Travis Harnet (Tik-Tok, Futura), was the gleefully "real rock" precursor to *Telephono*-era Spoon. The songs evinced Daniel's typically droll melodies and *Skellington, Skellington Rex*, and *The Town's Gone Dry*—all cassettes—sold the band to those close enough to hear the buzz. The last tape evokes none other than Tom Petty & the Heartbreakers on the first song, before the second, "Bowhead," makes its declaration loud and clear: "You pull me up to tell me I'm Tom Petty and expect me to swallow my pride." Better still is the demo of a song found at tape's end, "Loss Leaders."

A snappy, upbeat acoustic number, "Loss Leaders" is one of those songs that makes you sit up and start asking questions like, "Who wrote this?" Five years later, when "Loss Leaders" appeared on 1997's *Telephono* follow-up, *Soft Effects EP*, it was the best song on the five-song swirl, only now it was a little slower, a little spacier. Like its four companions on the *Soft Effects EP*, "Loss Leaders" was a departure

from most everything on *Telephono*. It was pop to its core, pop of the variety proliferated by Spoon's Matador labelmates, Guided by Voices. Bob Pollard pop: four-track, home studio songs that yield nothing but melody after irresistible melody. Drake Tungsten–type meanderings, found on a 1996 self-released local cassette and single sounding suspiciously like another thin, blonde warbler. Tungsten, Skellington, *Soft Effects EP*. Bingo. *A Series of Sneaks*.

"I've always written songs like the ones on *A Series of Sneaks* and *Soft Effects*," says Daniel, giving up his alter-ego Tungsten. "It's just I hadn't done them with Spoon. I hadn't done them in a band. I have four-track stuff backlogged since 1989 that does a lot more things than just the upbeat rock that is *Telephono*. The other stuff was always just me by myself, and when we put together *Soft Effects* and *A Series of Sneaks*, I was taking those more experimental things, things with different styles or different speeds, and doing it with the band."

The album is so raw, full of black eyes and bruises—a busted, bleeding nose.

"Usually, the song would be written, and then a week before we went in to record the song, I would do a four-track version of what we were gonna do, and I would come up with ideas for other instruments or hand-clap parts or whatever. For whatever reason, when I was coming up with this album, I really wanted stuff that was different, that would make you wonder what kind of instrument that is, or 'How did they do that?' So basically, I would just do it at home, and we would re-create it in the studio.

"When it gets down to it, I was just trying to make it more exciting for me. And our manager at the time, when he heard the demos for *A Series of Sneaks*, he promptly fired us, because it wasn't anything like *Telephono*. He told me that my songwriting had taken a real step backwards. And this was coming at the time when we just started mixing. I wasn't sure how the record was turning out, and I was very sensitive about what it was sounding like. All of a sudden this guy who manages the Goo Goo Dolls, Pat Magnarella, says that.

"At the time, it really hurt my feelings, and I thought, 'Man, we're making a shitty album.' But the way I look at it now, that's an assurance that we had improved and maybe it wasn't gonna sell a million copies, but we were doing something. In other words, maybe it was a good thing that the manager of the Goo Goo Dolls didn't like it—that we were doing something he couldn't get."

True enough. Problem is, it would have been swell if the record label that put out *A Series of Sneaks*, Elektra, one of the Big Five Mafia families—hehem, major labels—had "gotten" the album. They didn't. So they deep-sixed it.

After the *Soft Effects EP*, Spoon had the option of releasing another album on Matador, but by mid-1997, Daniel was having other ideas. Working on a new album with a new bassist, Josh Zarbo, Daniel felt worn down by persistent indie snobbism that had labeled Spoon too commercial for Matador. Having had the band's profile raised by its association with Matador and two strong releases, Daniel, Eno, and Zarbo let some of the big labels sniff around. One of them, Elektra, under the guise of A&R rep Ron Laffitte, had been humping Spoon's leg for quite some time, and that fall, amid much hesitation and indecision, the blushing Austin band said "Yes."

The following February, 1998, album now completed, Spoon put pen to paper, and with shaking hand, signed over its dowry for two albums "firm" and the option of Elektra picking up another four. By the time April arrived, however, at which point *A Series of Sneaks* came out to the best reviews of the band's career, something was already wrong with the marriage. The first thing to go was the band's benefactor and courtier, Laffitte. Spoon followed in August,

> ## "
> ## MAYBE IT WAS A GOOD THING THAT THE MANAGER OF THE GOO GOO DOLLS DIDN'T LIKE IT—THAT WE WERE DOING SOMETHING HE COULDN'T GET.
> ## "
> **BRITT DANIEL**

dropped only four months after they had been signed. Get rid of the one guy that backs you and there's no one left to watch your back, is that it?

"Yeah," nods Daniel, "but they didn't really back us to begin with, and even a couple of months before the record even came out, [Laffitte] stopped taking my phone calls. I honestly feel like I've known two people when I think about him: the guy that I knew before, and the guy that I knew, like, almost right after we signed. Not even after we signed, but after we told him we were going to sign is when it started taking two weeks to get my calls returned."

In the *Chronicle*'s boiler room several days later, under much duress, both Eno, 31, and Zarbo, 25, the Attractions to Daniel's Elvis Costello, admit they still can't believe how fast the house of cards fell.

"No one would have ever known that a VP of Elektra, who had been chasing us for a year-and-a-half, who was totally excited about our band, would ever just flake out and get fired from the label," says Eno incredulously. "There was no indication at all that that would ever happen. That's why it's laughable. We never thought anything like *that* would happen."

Your worst fears, eh kid?

"This was *worse* than our worst fears," confesses Daniel. "To tell you the truth, this was beyond any bad scenario we thought about when the band was thinking what label we should go to. We never thought we would get dropped before this record was even done being worked. It just never entered our minds. Maybe we were naive. We could see maybe not getting another record if things didn't go well, but the way they dropped us, less than four months after it came out, it really just knocked the wind out of us. We had these tours we were supposed to go on; all of a sudden we didn't have money to go."

Eno nods. Austin's answer to Charlie Watts, a flawless timekeeper and energetic accenter of his band's guitarist—with whom he hooked up in a post-Skellington almost-roots trio called the Alien Beats—it's Rhode Island native Eno who fronted the capital for Spoon's *A Series of Sneaks* with money from his well-paying day job; he moved to Austin from Houston in '92 to design microchips for local techies Cadence Designs Systems, an organization Eno is very grateful to for allowing him plenty of time off for touring.

"There's nothing we could have done about what happened to us," shrugs Eno. "Oh, well."

If only the Spoonman saw it that way.

Britt Daniel is convinced that Elektra president Sylvia Rhone's decision to drop Spoon, after she had personally promised Daniel his band wouldn't get dropped if Laffitte walked the plank, is somehow his fault. That he "blew it." Forget the politics of the music industry at the corporate level. Forget the subjugation of art at the expense of commerce. Forget every morally corrupt facet of the music business. You're right, Daniel, this was your fault.

"I'm grateful for what I've got," he says with conviction. "But, at the same time, I do feel like we blew it. I feel really bad about the way things happened with Matador. Working with those people meant so much to me personally, and I really feel like we blew that situation, and I guess I just have to look at it as a learning experience."

Uh, oh. Poor sap. You know it's spiraling downward when they chalk it up to "a learning experience." It's

no wonder Daniel tries to call off the interview an hour before its scheduled start. What's there to talk about? Daniel looks depressed though he swears he's not; he says his friends are concerned.

No, he insists, he's pulled through the whole ordeal in pretty good shape, even though he lost his record deal, broke up with his girlfriend, and had no place to live in the latter half of 1998. He's hopeful about the fact that Vapor Records will be putting back into print the now-deleted Elektra title, *A Series of Sneaks.*

A new 7-inch on Merge, "Anticipation" b/w "Headz," high quality leftovers from the *Sneak* sessions, also gives Daniel cause for cheer, as does the thought of a projected 45 for later this year: "The Agony of Laffitte" b/w "Laffitte Don't Fail Me Now." That puts a faint gleam in his eye, one that almost makes you forget that Daniel's gotta be more than a little gun-shy after his last hunting accident.

Zarbo, who moved to Austin in June for Spoon, isn't having any.

"I don't think we blew it," he says decisively. "No. I'm gonna get flogged later for saying this, but I don't think we blew it. I think we made the best decision we could make under the circumstances, and I think it was completely out of our hands."

That's right, Daniel, listen to me and listen good. In the soul-selling business of music, where the artist might as well be making sneakers in some Asian rice paddy, good albums are never lost—they just become cult favorites until one day, God willing, someone like Kurt Cobain comes along and covers three of your songs on a multi-platinum MTV special. Longevity and perseverance: the Glass Keys.

"Look," says Daniel wearily at my final query. He reaches over and turns off the interrogation lamp, smoothing his rumpled clothes, gingerly running his fingers over his various welts and bruises. "I can't be absolutely deadpan honest with my interior emotions and predictions about what's gonna happen in the future, because I don't know, and there's a lot more at stake—there's other people involved with what Spoon has become.

"But this is my prediction on the way things are going to happen with Spoon. I don't think another label is just going to swoop down and offer us another deal. If we are to survive, then we're going to have to make a record the way we always have—make it ourselves, fund it ourselves—and then have an album that's really good and turns people on so much that they'll want to put it out after it's made.

"I can come up with a lot of great songs. That's why I started a band, that's what turns me on about rock music."

Precisely, agrees the rhythm section. In fact, they look a little bewildered when asked about Spoon's future. What future? It's just business as usual.

"Britt's gonna keep writing good songs, and there's gonna be another good record coming up here," says Eno.

"It's just a niche in Spoon history," exclaims Zabor.

Hear that, Britt, another chapter that's read and buried, but never forgotten. Just like Drake Tungsten and his boy Skellington. *A Series of Sneaks* solved.

1999 SXSW Picks and Sleepers

VOL. 18 NO. 29 ★ MARCH 19, 1999

THE CORNELL HURD BAND: Californian-turned-Texan Cornell Hurd may be sorry he ever coined the term "Left-wing swing" to describe his own wry, wisecracking Western style, but here in the press, we're eager to up the ante: Subversive country. Call it what you like, the music of Hurd's band is as pure a two-stepping experience as you can hope for in the sawdust glory of South Austin's venerable Broken Spoke. **MARGARET MOSER**

PONG: Austin, Austin, rejoice! Ed Hall is back. Remember Ed? The finest singer-songwriter on the Trance Syndicate roster? You know, author of *Gloryhole*, *Motherscratcher*, and *LaLa Land*. The big lumbering dude with the club foot and hunched back. You know, one of the best acts in Austin? Well, now he's back, with his buds Gary, Larry, and Lyman. And another guy. Oh happy day! We've been waiting for this since Larry moved back from Thailand. Now the gang's all here. Ed? We missed ya. Bad. **RAOUL HERNANDEZ**

TRISH MURPHY: Although this Austin songstress hurled a ton of buzz at last year's South by Southwest, it took until just last month for her to ink a deal with local indie Doolittle Records. She follows her self-released and critically acclaimed *Crooked Mile* in June with an as-yet-untitled set produced by Jim Ebert. **ANDY LANGER**

MONTE WARDEN: As both a Wagoneer and solo artist, Monte Warden has been Nashville's perennial next big thing. That said, Warden has never seemed more poised for country stardom than now; his Asylum debut of divorce-inspired tunes just hit stores and has radio written all over it. Best of all, the release of *Stranger to Me* means Warden's getting a chance to return to the stage where his songs and good-boy charm seem to shine best. **ANDY LANGER**

SOULHAT: Earlier this year, Austin's Soulhat put out its first post-Epic release, a six-song EP that serves as their first recording without founding guitarist Bill Cassis and their last with original bassist Brian Walsh. Despite the lineup changes, Soulhat is arguably just as vital and quirky as ever, thanks in large part to frontman Kevin McKinney's wickedly offbeat lyricism and legendary drummer Barry "Frosty" Smith's still-unyielding sense of groove. **ANDY LANGER**

SCRAPPY JUD NEWCOMB: Jud Newcomb is a side-man with so many local Austin acts such as Toni Price and the Resentments, it's amazing he finds time to perform solo. When he does, he attracts Austin's best singer-songwriters, who find his guitar playing as smooth and lean as he is long and tall.
MARGARET MOSER

EPHRAIM OWENS: Trumpeter Ephraim Owens is a prominent figure in the solid crop of young jazz players in Austin, and this showcase at the historic Victory Grill is part of the Dial Tone Records showcase, with whom Owens is currently negotiating for his first jazz recording under his name. Owens mixes original compositions with wonderfully styled takes on standards, and with vocalist Yashi Vaughn in the lineup, the range runs from funk to free form.
CHRISTOPHER HESS

DAMNATIONS TX: With *Half Mad Moon* (Sire), the Damnations TX are poised to take over the world. The album is an outstanding collection of songs that inject rock & roll lifeblood into folk and country structures, beautified by the vocal harmonies of sisters Deborah Kelly and Amy Boone, and bolstered by Rob Bernard's rock-perfect guitar and banjo work. The live show is even better, and this outdoor appearance will surely be one of the conference highlights.
CHRISTOPHER HESS

HOT CLUB OF COWTOWN: In the tradition of Django Reinhardt and Stephane Grappelli and their Hot Club of France, this Texas country version of European jazz with bass, guitar, and violin is sophisticatedly swinging and always a good time. **CHRISTOPHER HESS**

SUPEREGO: Besides offering incontrovertible proof that nice guys rock, Superego deserves your respect for the often thankless, but just as often glorious, task of closing Hole in the Wall's Sunday Rock & Roll Free-for-All going on five years now. It's not easy re-inventing yourself week-in, week-out, but the reason Paul Minor, Jon Sanchez, Andrew Duplantis, and Erik Conn pull it off is because whatever else they've got going on, they can just cut loose here for a couple of hours. **CHRISTOPHER GRAY**

remember Gerry's songs." And they were right, because *The Cause of It All* is all about songs; Van King penned all ten tracks, and while all but a few play out like boarding passes to the Mothership, each is just as faithfully funky as anything Jammin' Oldies is spinning. In fact, Van King's signature song and *The Cause of It All*'s raucous centerpiece, "I've Just Been Funkafied," already screams early-FM radio classic. Best of all, Van King's not bumping alone. Whereas conventional wisdom and a smaller budget might have recorded Van King and his bass as a Sixth Street field recording, *The Cause of It All* features a large and similarly Funkadelic-inspired set of session players, with each guitar line and each horn chart meticulously arranged Detroit/Casablanca style. The result is an album of first-class, old-skool funkateering: brilliantly short on unnecessary innovation but long on ultra-catchy choruses and surprisingly well-executed groove. Who'd of funk it? **ANDY LANGER**

VOL. 18 NO. 34 ★ APRIL 23, 1999

GERRY VAN KING
THE CAUSE OF IT ALL
AARON AVENUE

Since Gerry Van King (aka "The King of Sixth Street") is without a doubt Austin's highest-profile busker, he's also widely regarded as mere amateur night entertainment: funk for the drunk, live music for people who can't commit to paying cover, a tourist curiosity. During South by Southwest 98, it took a couple of those tourists to figure out what local "Picks & Sleepers" pundits hadn't: behind Van King's P-Funk medleys lies a damn fine songwriter. Ft. Worth's Aaron Avenue Records threw a record deal in the local musician's bass case that year, declaring in *The Cause of It All*'s liner notes that they "couldn't remember any of the showcase bands we saw in 1997, but we could

BROWN WHÖRNET
BROWN WHÖRNET
AUSTIN MUSIC MAFIA

Austin's foremost cut-and-paste avant-punk collective taps the same anarchic grace as the speed-away perps on *World's Scariest Police Chases*: you don't know which way they'll turn next. Having established their proclivity for devouring an endless array of musical styles, Brown Whörnet's latest release is an exercise in reining in the superlatives. The album begins engagingly with "Working Song," a mechanical, tension-building spiral that sounds like your local TV news theme on Judgment Day. Then it's on to the jaw-dropping prog-punkisms of "Arsenio's Fat Black Ass '98," a song appropriated from the late, great Big Horny Hustler. "Variations on the Pope" promenades

Gerry Van King, the King of Sixth Street.
Photograph by Michael Crawford.

through all your favorite speed-metal-deathcore clichés in under two-and-a-half minutes before dumping you cold into the Middle Eastern–flavored rhythms of "Danse Raja." The band also revels convincingly in German synth-pop decadence ("Cutting Myself in the Mirror"), Carl Stalling–style music for circuses ("Puffy Upper"), and all night jazz-funk workouts ("Pash the Gaseous Pecan"). With just the right amount of both ambition and concision, this powerhouse is Brown Whörnet's strongest and most enjoyable work to date.

GREG BEETS

VOL. 18 NO. 34 ★ APRIL 23, 1999

MC OVERLORD
HOUSE OF FUNK
LORDSHIP ENTERTAINMENT

Questions: What kind of hip-hop album does a guest list from the Steamboat side of town, zero booty calls or odes to weed, and a distinct lack of Ruff Ryder posturing make? And would his *House of Funk* be a place worth kickin' it in? Answers: A damn good one and damn right. As has been the case with his previous self-released local discs, *House of Funk* finds Austin's MC Overlord possessed of mad lyrical skills equal to his physical stature, like Eightball, Big Pun, or Goodie Mob's Cee-Lo, with rhymes clean enough for his little nephews to rap along. He's an entertainer, so when he says "Bounce Yo Ass," this experienced local club security man is 86ing playa haters, not issuing a strip joint directive. As far as crews go, he's shouting out the Good Lord and his family. Producer Yoggie gets his props too, well-deserved for his rubbery, funkacized grooves; there are even some nifty, deep-soul background vocals from Patrice Pike, Malford Milligan, and Lisa Tingle, of all people. The album's a bit long (74 minutes), but name an album since Nas' *Illmatic*

that isn't. So one final question: Could such positive, life-affirming rapping possibly be embraced by today's materialistic, mack-heavy hip-hop mainstream? MC Overlord's answer: "Tell Dr. King we've all got dreams."

CHRISTOPHER GRAY

VOL. 18 NO. 48 ★ JULY 30, 1999

THE DERAILERS
FULL WESTERN DRESS
SIRE

What goes around comes around. Back in the Sixties, the Beatles lionized Buck Owens, and George Harrison's early guitar lines smacked of Carl Perkins' licks. Owens and other country artists, in turn, adopted ideas and themes from Sixties pop. After all, Sixties pop was all about the hook, and the Derailers are chock-full of them on their fourth full-length. Listen to *Full Western Dress* and hear echoes of *Rubber Soul*, Johnny Rivers, the Grass Roots, the Monkees, and maybe even a little Gary Puckett. *Full Western Dress* finds the local honky-tonkers still assimilating the Bakersfield sound, but stylistically they branch out farther than ever. "Just to Spend the Night with You" and "Whatever Made You Change Your Mind" tap deeper into Sixties AM-radio veins than anything they've done previously, while the atmospheric "Longing" wanders into Chris Isaak/Roy Orbison territory. Buck himself sits in for one song and the band throws in a cover of the oldies-radio chestnut, "Then She Kissed Me." There are two strong singers and fluid Telecaster specialists in the band who can pull it all off flawlessly. Producer Dave Alvin has achieved a rich-sounding mix while avoiding the overbearing, bombastic sound that prevails on country radio. Sharp harmonies, inventive playing, great songwriting; "Crossover country" doesn't necessarily have to mean "insipid."

JERRY RENSHAW

VOL. 19 NO. 5 ★ OCTOBER 1, 1999

Destruction as Beauty . . . And You Will Know Us by the Trail of Dead

VOL. 19 NO. 6 ★ OCTOBER 8, 1999

GREG BEETS

ALTHOUGH THEY'LL never have to upstage the Who like Hendrix did at Monterey, . . . And You Will Know Us by the Trail of Dead knows their way around the art of breaking apart. The Austin quartet's propensity for destroying instruments amid a swirling panorama of noise and sweat has garnered them favorable feedback in crannies throughout the international underground music circuit.

Unlike thickheaded doofs who just want to fuck shit up in the name of cool, Trail of Dead girds their mayhem with a fervent desire to break through the superficial barriers separating audiences from performers in order to bring about that elusive but pristine moment of collective, frenzied transcendence.

"Not to be overly philosophical, but I think you can get to the point where you're not thinking," says guitarist/drummer Jason Reece. "You're not trying to be one thing or the other. You're just playing and whatever happens just happens spontaneously. There's no preconceived notion or motive. You're not even directing it."

Trail of Dead's new album, *Madonna*, sacrifices just enough of that onstage spontaneity to bring the artistic merits of the music itself to the forefront. The

. . . And You Will Know Us by the Trail of Dead, 2005. Photograph by Aubrey Edwards.

end product of this slight refinement is one of the most engaging and fully realized rock albums to come out of Austin this year. *Madonna*'s vaguely cinematic structure captures a wide range of emotions, from poignant woe ("Clair de Lune") to frothing anger ("A Perfect Teenhood"). A nonstop wall of guitars rises and falls with the changing moods. At only one point on *Madonna*, between "Flood of Red" and "Children of the Hydra's Teeth," is there no sound at all. The rest of the album never stops humming, unless you count the space between the last song and the obligatory secret track.

"Rather than release something that is thirteen tracks of this band's music, one song and the next song and the next, we've always tried to have an album that is conceived as one piece," says Conrad Keely, who also switches between guitar and drums. "It's one piece of music. And I don't even think this record reaches the apex of what we might do in the future as far as taking that theme further."

"We have angry songs, but then we also have some softer, mellower parts, too," contends Reece. "Everyone has a full range of emotions, and I think these songs reflect a full range of emotions, from angry to beautiful to happy to depressed."

It all comes back around to the band's inclination to use whatever it takes to break through the boundaries between themselves and the audience. Dancing one's way back and forth across the thin line that separates chaos from order is risky, but nothing good comes without risk, artistically or otherwise. Trail of Dead gleefully embraces that risk and wrestles it to the floor, much to the delight of paying customers.

"We do what we do with enthusiasm," says Keely. "If a three-year-old kid is running around the house enthusiastically and he happens to knock over a plant, you can misinterpret that as aggression, but it's not aggression. We're out there having fun." ◀

Wasted Days, Wasted Nights
The Soap Creek Bombers

VOL. 19 NO. 13 ★ NOVEMBER 26, 1999

JOE NICK PATOSKI

AND THEN THERE was the night Doug Sahm brought Freddy Fender to Soap Creek in early 1974. Five years earlier, Doug had paid homage to the onetime Elvis of the Rio Grande Valley on his back-to-Texas-roots opus, *The Return of Doug Saldaña*, with a greasy, soulful version of "Wasted Days, Wasted Nights" that began with three piano chords and the echo-drenched voice of Doug saying, "And now a song by the great Freddy Fender. Freddy, this is for you, wherever you are," before charging into three minutes of South Texas soul climaxing with Rocky Morales' torrid sax solo.

IT WAS THEN I REALIZED HOW REALLY STRANGE AND EXOTIC EL WEST SIDE OF SAN ANTONIO AND THE WORLD OF SIR DOUG REALLY WERE.

It turned out that Fender, née Baldemar Huerta of San Benito, was actually in Corpus, living in obscurity and semi-retirement following a string of rock & roll hits recorded in the Fifties, including "Wasted Days"; Doug had seen him play a San Antonio drive-in at the peak of his popularity and was mightily impressed. He didn't witness Fender's rapid decline, culminating in an extended term in Louisiana's notorious Angola prison

The Texas Tornado Doug Sahm, 1974.
Photograph by Burton Wilson.

for the crime of possessing two marijuana cigarettes. By the time Doug did his shout-out, Fender was working as a mechanic, attending Del Mar College, and playing bars and cantinas on weekends, mostly for spare change and pleasure.

"Wasted Days" was a frequent request at Soap Creek, where Doug functioned as house band in the early Seventies while living in a rented mansion a couple hundred yards down the road. For all the hype the Armadillo received, Soap Creek was really the nerve center of the fresh new Austin music scene, nestled way back in the cedar breaks a quarter-mile down a dirt road off Bee Caves Road back when Westlake was still more or less open country. If the cops had any intention of messing with the unusual breed of hippies hanging out at the club, there was plenty of warning.

It was after one too many requests, then, that Doug went looking for Freddy and found him. A gig was booked with Freddy as the headliner and Doug as the opening act, assuring the low-ceilinged room would be packed.

I showed up in the afternoon, hoping to get an interview, but Freddy wasn't around. I did find Rocky Morales and Richard Elizondo in an old Mercury parked by the club, both of them passed out from a round of drinking Mad Dog 20/20. I woke them up and gave them a ride to a convenience store because the Merc's battery was dead. Richard, a hunchback dwarf who drummed and could sing Dean Martin better than anyone I've met before or since, introduced himself by saying "Gimme four"—his left hand lacked a thumb—and launched into a manner of speech I can only describe as his own language, punctuating the conversations with "eh eh's" and "que que's." It was then I realized how really strange and exotic El West Side of San Antonio and the world of Sir Doug really were. The Mad Dog purchased at the convenience store wasn't bad either.

Freddy finally showed up after dark, visibly nervous and apprehensive. He wanted to play, but he was clearly uncertain about the venue and the clientele, no matter how much Doug reassured him. When showtime rolled around, Fender returned dressed for the occasion in a long-fringed leather vest—his interpretation of hippie fashion; only the matching blue outfits with flared bell-bottoms worn by Steve Jordan and Rio Jordan, another special guest act who appeared at Soap Creek at the behest of Sir Doug, were cheesier. (I later learned for all their sartorial futility, Jordan's entire band had been tripping on acid that night.)

Doug and his band warmed up Freddy by doing their usual thing, working himself and the audience to the "all-buttered-up" stage by 10 pm, a full two hours earlier than normal. When Fender finally jumped onstage, his eyes had that frozen, deer-in-the-headlights look, telegraphing the message, "Where the hell am I and of all people what am I doing here?"

The start of his set was sprinkled with pop and country standards of the moment, a smart tactic that typically pacifies a Holiday Inn lounge audience, but exactly what the crowd didn't want to hear. Freddy got more comfortable when Doug joined him onstage, and finally loosened up—no doubt influenced by taking a band break and accepting rolled gifts of kindness from strangers—and then proceeded to wail away in the Heartbreak Key, his distinctive tenor voice in beautiful form. While reeling off his old hits like "Crazy Crazy Baby" and yes, "Wasted Days, Wasted Nights," punched up by Rocky Morales' sax, Freddy even tore off some surprising guitar licks that gave Doug a run for his money.

It was a breakthrough for Freddy Fender. Within a year, one of the songs he sang that night, a sugary ballad called "Before the Next Teardrop Falls," shot up the pop and country charts to the No. 1 position simultaneously, followed by a new version of "Wasted

Days, Wasted Nights." In other words, if not for Doug Sahm, Freddy Fender probably would still be working on cars back in Corpus, wondering about what might have been and never was.

So Doug, this one goes out to you, brother, wherever you are. You're one beautiful cat. ◀

The 2000s: An Introduction

CHRISTOPHER GRAY

The Austin Chronicle Music Columnist 2003–2007;
Houston Press Music Editor 2007–Present

T'S FUNNY. Since July 2007, my most regular contact with Austin comes both musically and digitally, via satellite radio. Sirius XM Radio has one whole station based around Willie Nelson; honky-tonker Dallas Wayne does his four-hour DJ shift on Outlaw Country from Austin ("The Big D in the OC"); and local indie bands, most notably Okkervil River and Spoon, are all over indie-rock channel SiriXMU. Close my eyes and it's like I'm back at Emo's or the Broken Spoke. Almost.

A decade ago, Austin was already an important music city and budding digitopia, but nothing like today. In the notoriously bicoastal entertainment and multimedia worlds, it's the only city in Texas that matters to both the taste-making class of music bloggers and hardwired establishment bodies such as the Recording Academy—i.e., the people who give out the Grammys—as well as being probably the leading southwestern center for film and TV production, graphic design, and, neither last nor least, Web development.

Austin put a good deal of its chips into the dotcom pot early on, and despite a sizable hiccup around 2001 and 2002, that bet paid out—financially, civically, and culturally. Somebody somewhere figured out how to send reams of computer data through telephone lines, and Austin hit the big time. And because the musical and digital classes were always tight-knit—musicians working day jobs at Apple;

dotcom millionaires dropping into Antone's—its musical profile likewise went through the roof. Of course, the rise of the Austin City Limits Music Festival to national prominence didn't hurt, but with increased development came higher rents and changes to the scene like 2005's city-wide smoking ban.

Back when people were still getting used to near-foreign phrases like "logging on," Austin musicians and its more tech-savvy music fans recognized the Web's potential at the exact same time. As the music business made its often ungainly transition into the digital age, networking (both on- and offline) became more important than ever, something for which both South by Southwest and its host city were already in prime position to reap the benefits.

Anytime an Austin band or musician sent me a "friend request," I clicked yes, no questions asked. After all, I already knew about ninety percent of them, but only then did I truly realize how huge the music scene had become. There were *hundreds*. After about six months on MySpace, it was threatening a thousand. Though it's both more Luddite-friendly and more tedious, Facebook is no different.

I got used to checking out my musician friends' pages—often people I had partied with the night before, slept on their couches, given or gotten a ride home, was still up with the next day—and seeing comments from people in places I'd never heard of on top of pictures posted by someone living two streets over.

The social havoc wreaked by the Internet had the odd effect of making Austin, and especially the music community, both more cosmopolitan and more insular.

After only eighteen months in H-town, visiting Austin seems odd. All the new skyscrapers downtown, condos on the Eastside, retail/residential developments on South Congress—offline, a lot of the city is unrecognizable. Now the Austin I know is the one I see on MySpace and Facebook. Not a day among the mosquitoes, freeway chases, and sold-out AC/DC shows goes by when I don't think about Austin. And thanks to technology—and satellite radio—not a day goes by when I can almost convince myself I never left. ◄

Where the Shadows Are Deepest
In Search of James Hand

VOL. 19 NO. 36 ★ MAY 5, 2000

CHRISTOPHER GRAY

QUESTING IS SOMETHING of a lost art, especially now, when it's not even necessary to leave the house for groceries. For someone who must have seen *Monty Python and the Holy Grail* at least a hundred times in his youth, the hope of one day setting off in pursuit of an elusive, faraway quarry was never terribly distant.

This particular quest has its genesis a couple of months back, when local indie label Cold Spring Records released *Evil Things*, an absolute gem of a country album. Its author, James Hand, surfaces occasionally to play the Broken Spoke ("He's got that Hank Williams–type charisma," Spoke owner James White says), but otherwise his profile is that of your average CIA operative.

A call to the label turns up a phone number, plus the information that Hand is not actively promoting the record. In fact, says label publicist Jennifer McGuire, he's pretty much disowned *Evil Things* altogether. Dave Biller, who produced the album, uses the word "disappointment" rather than "disowned."

Calls are placed to the Hand residence somewhere within the 254 area code. The first goes something like this:

"Is James Hand there?"

"No." Click.

A couple of days pass, then another call:

"Can I speak to James Hand, please?"

"Which one?"

"Uhhh . . . the country singer?"

"He's not here."

This time, I'm able to leave a message. A few more days go by, but there's no word from Hand. Another call:

"Is James Hand there?"

"Which one?"

"The singer."

"Oh, is this the guy from the paper? I still haven't seen him."

It rapidly becomes clear I must track down Hand in person, only without the first clue where to start looking. Casting about for some sort of plan, it dawns on me to look in the phone book, which reveals area code 254 to be in the southern half of the old 817 Fort Worth/Waco region.

A rental car is procured, and after a few loose ends at the *Chronicle* are tied up, the quest is under way. The journey north is uneventful. An hour-and-a-half after departing Austin, I exit I-35 at FM 2118, the main east-west thoroughfare of "The Czech Point of Central Texas," known to census-takers and rural-route deliverers as West, population 2,515.

West takes its Central European heritage seriously; the name of most local business establishments—eateries, antique shops, even glass-cutting—contains some sort of Czech reference. There's Kolacek's Kolace Kitchen, the Nemecek Brothers Meat Market, and Czech Point Collectibles, to name a few. The Czech Stop gas station sits right off the highway, and also specializes in various baked goods. Numerous publicity stills, from Reba McEntire and Martina McBride to the Picket Line Coyotes and Ted Roddy's Tearjoint Troubadors, line the upper reaches of the walls. After a much-needed trip to the lavatory, I head to the counter for even more-needed Camel filters.

James Hand at the Broken Spoke, 2000. Photograph by John Carrico.

"You look really young," says the clerk. "Do you get carded a lot?"

I ask her if she knows James Hand.

"You mean Slim? The singer?"

Bingo.

"I know who he is. He's out at Wolf's bar sometimes. Turn right at the stop sign, go past the railroad tracks, and it's on the corner on your right."

Wolf's is right where she said it is, but Hand is nowhere to be found. It's getting late, so I retire to the Every Day Inn on the outskirts of Waco for the night.

Up and at 'em Tuesday; first stop, Wolf's. Proprietor Joe Wolf is sitting alone at the bar watching the midday news. Yes, he knows Hand, "ever since he was a little kid." Wolf says he used to have a place where young Hand would come in and sing Hank Williams songs, and tells me about a club where the Bouldin used car lot is now that Hand worked at for about a decade. His brother was even on Slim's football team at West High.

"He knows him a lot better than I do, but he's playing golf in Austin today," Wolf says, adding, "I haven't seen [Hand] in about six weeks."

After lunch at the Czech Stop, I cross the highway to take a picture of the West city limits sign. On a whim, I duck into the nearby beer joint Shadowland. A sign over the bar says "Everybody looks good at Shadowland," and two guys are busy installing a new air conditioner. The stocky older one, Bud Craig, says Hand is a "helluva good guy" and that if I wait about thirty minutes, "this fella'll be here who knows him real well." The younger guy turns out to be Shadowland owner Aubrey Gerik, who won the bar in a poker game.

Sure enough, half-an-hour-later, scrub-clad Buck walks in.

"I went to all three of his weddings," he laughs, "but I wasn't ever the best man."

He plays a couple of songs off Hand's first CD, *Shadows Where the Magic Was*—a staple of the Wolf's and Tokio Store jukeboxes—and explains the origins of the singer's nickname: "He's just always been skinny, I guess." A bit nonplussed that I'd come all this way virtually unannounced, Buck makes a quick phone call to the Hands. Twenty minutes later, who should stride through the door but Slim his own self, trailed by his bull-riding son Tracer. After a bit of small talk about wrestling, Slim agrees to sit for an interview. Mission accomplished. Quest complete.

AUSTIN CHRONICLE: *Tell me about the new album.*

JAMES HAND: I love it. I love everybody on it. I think everybody was the greatest thing in the world.

AC: *Have you lived here your whole life?*

JH: Not yet. So far.

AC: *Did you always want to be a country singer?*

JH: Ever since I was a kid.

AC: *Do you mostly just play around here?*

JH: Yeah, I play here. I played at the Shadowland last Saturday night. There's people that say I don't want to play anywhere else; that's not true. To me, I don't see no sense in playing Pocatello, Idaho, where nobody knows who you are, just to say I've been on the road. Hell, I drove a truck for most of my life, I've been everywhere. Why go somewhere where nobody knows you? That's why I signed a record deal with Cold Spring, so I can get some distribution.

AC: *It seems like your songs are pretty autobiographical.*

JH: Yeah, I don't see how a fella can write about something he ain't never done. How do you sing a song you don't believe in?

AC: *Do the songs come pretty naturally to you?*

JH: Yeah, yeah.

AC: *Have they always?*

JH: Mmm-hmm. I wrote one the other day called "What We've Done to Us," like, "It ain't what I've done to you, it's not what you've done to me, it's what we've done to us." And I wrote one, I don't know, yesterday or something, about "Livin' for You Is Killin' Me." You take a fella who gets up every day with the birds singing and the sun shining, a guy who kisses his wife goodbye and goes to work. I don't see him writing a song like that. People say I love misery. I don't love misery. I love a girl that don't love me.

AC: *Would you say you've had a hard life?*

JH: I'd say I've made it hard on myself.

AC: *In what way?*

JH: In a way that I wouldn't want to blame anybody else for.

AC: *What was it like growing up around here?*

JH: I had a wonderful childhood. My family, we're a very close family. I went to high school here at West, know everybody in town. My whole life is right here.

AC: *Was it ever important to you to be a big star?*

JH: Yeah, sure. I think that anybody that ever plays wants to be a success at it . . . I play probably way less than any other, but the fact is, if I were a star making money, there's no obstacles that you couldn't do for your family or your friends. Money to me takes obstacles out of life's highway. You don't take those obstacles out so you can drive faster, you take those obstacles out for people that you love. It's hard to be broke and see your momma and daddy living on $950 a month. That's why I would want to be a star, to have money. Not for me. I don't give a rat's ass about me. I promise you I don't.

AC: *Do you think you still could be big?*

JH: I think my window of opportunity is closing pretty fast. I know that I'm a dinosaur. I can see some high-powered record producer, they look at me and look at my songs and say, "This guy's good, but he's born too late."

AC: *But you think you can only do your music one way?*

JH: A man feels something special for every song he writes. I don't think you could take my music and destroy it any way you did it. People, like it or not, if it's selling or not; people have the basic human emotions: they love, they hate, they love, they hate. You can't deny how you feel in your own heart. Now whether you like to hear Metallica sing about a broken heart, or you like to hear me sing about a broken heart, eventually, somewhere back down the line before all the music, the amplifiers, the instrumentation, the contracts, the people that have anything to do with the music, somebody had to sit down somewhere all alone and say, "God, why are you against me? What have I done? What can I do to ease the pain?" and scribble something down on a piece of paper.

You start that when you're about 12 or 13 years old, and it's the only outlet you have from losing your mind. Then, you get to be 47 years old and you wonder why I didn't get a job like everybody else, why I didn't do something with my life other than chasing a dream until it led me off the edge of a cliff. So when I say I sing because I got to, it's not because somebody's got a gun pointed at my head, it's 'cause that's what God put in me, and I think it would be a terrible waste if, even in my death, something didn't happen to some of my songs. I just don't believe God put me on earth to be a complete failure, but then I don't

believe he put me on earth to be Elvis Presley either. Who knows what a failure is? In certain people's eyes right now, I'm a complete and total waste, a failure.

AC: *What about in your eyes?*

JH: I think I'm probably pretty much a failure.

AC: *Do you think you would have been happier if your life had turned out to be more stable?*

JH: I don't know. I've never had that opportunity. Most people get in and out of relationships, it's almost like shuttin' the door, you know: "Well, that's behind you, don't worry." I don't have that chip in my mind that allows you not to worry. How do you not worry?

AC: *What do you think about the idea that a lot of the best music comes from a broken heart?*

JH: Like when you're happy, you want to hear happy songs. When you're sad, you want to hear sad songs. It oughta be just the opposite. If in the next instant somebody walked in and said, "Okay James, I'm gonna take care of all your debts, take care of your family, give you money to live on, all you gotta do is sing and keep writing songs," that's probably as close to heaven as I'll ever get. But you know, in an interview, you don't want, "Please let somebody read this so I can be a superstar." That's bullshit. That ain't what it's all about. Like if the *New York Times* called you right now, you'd go, wouldn't you?

AC: *Probably, yeah.*

JH: So, as a journalist, you don't want to be stuck out interviewing people like me the rest of your life, do you?

AC: *I don't know. This is pretty close to what I want to do. I want to find people that nobody else is really writing about and tell their story.*

JH: [laughs] You found one. ◀

SLAID CLEAVES
CACTUS CAFE, FEBRUARY 1

Lo and behold, sometimes nice guys do finish first. It makes for better songs if they're battered, bruised, and trod upon, though; no art without pain and so forth. That gulf between art and real life was an acoustic country mile wide Tuesday, as certified nice guy Slaid Cleaves launched his excellent new Philo album *Broke Down* to a roomful of appreciative friends, family, and fans. Tupelesque opener "Horseshoe Lounge" peeped some poor schmuck peeling labels off longnecks and lamenting, "I sit and think about you every night." The album's title track visited wedding bands on the bottom of Lake Pontchartrain, and "One Good Year" counseled, "Grace ain't so easily found." Things really got dark with a spare "This Morning I Am Born Again," Cleaves' turn at a *Mermaid Avenue* posthumous Woody Guthrie collaboration, and "Cold and Lonely" conjuring the existential dread of vintage Townes Van Zandt. The second set, heavy on *No Angel Knows,* was somewhat brighter, thanks in part to the litany of lemons in "Skunk Juice." *Broke Down* producer Gurf Morlix, previously coaxing shady, snaky leads out of a hollowbody electric, added sweet steel tears to Hank Williams' "Long Gone Lonesome Blues" and "Kaw-Liga." Finally, in introducing "Don't Tell Me" as "my wife's favorite song" from *No Angel,* Cleaves demonstrated conclusively, as he had all night, that the subjects of his songs and the man singing them could not be further apart.

CHRISTOPHER GRAY

VOL. 19 NO. 24 ★ FEBRUARY 11, 2000

VALLEJO
INTO THE NEW
EPIC/CRESCENT MOON/550 MUSIC

Twenty-four seconds is all it takes for Vallejo's major-label debut to bloom. "Welcome to my room with a view," intones leather-pants-wearing A. J. Vallejo on the album's explosive title track, classic rock guitars booming like KLBJ-FM through your JBLs. "I hope you'll stay for a while." It's an invitation worth accepting, especially if you keep that car-radio dial tuned to local frequency 93.7, longtime home to a beefy, Texan guitar sound as high and rock-solid as the walls of a local Sixth Street live music venue once known as Steamboat. "*Hola, bienvenidos,*" reaffirms Vallejo's "Classico," one of an album's worth of solid, readymade drive-time anthems. If the subtle, percussive Latin mulch of "Someday" doesn't evoke Tijuana's favorite son overtly, "La Famila" obviously traces its musical heritage to the Grammy-winning guitar guru who fused Tito Puente and psychedelic blues. "Modern Day Slave," with its undeniably great riffs and hooks, would sound perfectly at home sandwiched between ZZ Top, Stevie Ray Vaughan, and a Schlotzsky's commercial. Phat, modern, and *muchos cojónes*, like thirty years of classic rock radio. **RAOUL HERNANDEZ**

VOL. 19 NO. 51 ★ AUGUST 18, 2000

Songs of Innocence and Experience
The Gourds Kiss the Winged Life as It Flies

VOL. 20 NO. 4 ★ SEPTEMBER 22, 2000

CHRISTOPHER HESS

THE BATHROOM in the Steamy Bowl is a place that prompts a good stirring of intellect. The fleeting nature of earthly beauty and happiness, and the necessity of an artist's understanding of temporal pleasures are spelled out with calligraphs in a coloring book for all who take a seat.

"He who binds himself to a joy does the winged life destroy, but he who kisses it as it flies lives in Eternity's sun rise," for instance, is credited to one "William Blake Fruitcake."

It's here, or more accurately, at the Steamy Bowl, that the Gourds were born. It's a dumpy little house set back from a small residential street on the north side of town, a shack being slowly consumed by the gigantic crepe myrtle trees that linger over it like doting relatives. Especially in this blistering Texas summer, the place takes on the role of turgid incubator, a crooked little hothouse where music and words germinate and flower into song or wilt, crumple, and dissolve back into the earth.

Jimmy Smith, bassist and songwriter for the Gourds, lives there. The place has been home to the band since its beginnings in the summer of 1994. The Gourds have since passed through a celebrated infancy and a rocky adolescence and grown into one of the most revered bands in Austin, all under the eaves of Smith's unsteady cottage. Used to be the walls of the small main room were covered with wisdom from a Sharpie, drunkenly scrawled stretches of poetry, lyrics, and drawings that would spring from or lead to inspiration. This is all very much the hallmark of a band starting out—excited, energetic, and armed to the teeth with songs and more songs.

"We used to have a thing we called bottle night," explains guitarist Kevin Russell, "like that line from 'Grievin' and Smokin.'" We'd all bring a bottle of Irish whiskey and drink our asses off all night. Just the guys. We'd get drunk and play music and write all over Jimmy's walls with a marker. All kinds of poetry and art went up all over the walls. Those bottle nights were when a lot of stuff would happen, a lot of music came about. . .

"It's not the same with us now," he laughs. "We don't drink like that anymore, do those kinds of things. But for a while, it was that way. That house has everything to do with the Gourds."

Our man William Blake writes, "Those who restrain their desire, do so because theirs is weak enough to be restrained." From the outset, the Gourds were not likely to fall into this trap. Their music was a blender grinding country, blues, folk, swamp boogie, and enough rock & roll together to keep it from becoming any of these, and in the early days, the abundance of creative power kept the whole thing barreling ahead. Then, in 1995, came a shot on KUT's *Live Set*, which they turned into a tape that, for a while, blared from stereos and loudspeakers in bars and coffee shops across the city.

The following year would be even bigger when Mike Stewart, who later produced the Gourds, brought some executives from the Dutch label Munich Records to the band's South by Southwest showcase.

Before the group knew it, they were making their first album for them. For that, they headed out to Laurels Ranch, a 600-acre spread in the Hill Country between Fredericksburg and Comfort owned by the family of Russell's wife Robin. The ranch provided a comfortable atmosphere where the band could stay for a couple weeks at a time without a studio meter running, a fact that contributed to the easy, natural sound of the Gourds' debut, *Dem's Good Beeble*.

"*Beeble* is a document of the infancy of the band," says Russell, "of when we were first starting; it has that naive quality, lots of space in it. It's a strange record, a lot of people love it. It has that feel, a real fresh thing about it. *Beeble* just happened, and Mike Stewart was there to capture it."

About this same time, Keith Langford hooked up with two sisters named Deborah Kelly and Amy Boone in a band called the Damnations. They were loosely connected to the Gourds, as Smith had played drums

The Gourds, 2000. Photograph by John Carrico.

for them before, and Kevin is married to Keith's sister.

"Those were the innocent days," recalls Langford. "The Gourds were the shit; they were going to Europe, and they were playing great, every night. We had this little band called the Damnations and people liked us too, 'cause we were kind of like the Gourds but a little different. It was so good back then. Then, the bomb hit."

In 1998, the Gourds released their second album for Munich, *Stadium Blitzer*. From the outside, the album—more sonically ambitious than *Beeble* and more far-ranging in the writing and the instrumentation—and the tour that followed were smashing successes. Inside the band, however, there were problems.

"We looked for someone to market *Blitzer* in the states, and we got Watermelon/Sire," says Russell. "That was a rush deal. I wish we would have looked around. If we'd have talked to Mark Rubin, he would have told us what was happening with Watermelon. We wouldn't have done it."

Watermelon went bankrupt and thereafter had lots of music by lots of bands and the money that came from them tied up in court. The release of *Stadium Blitzer* was held up initially, and the Gourds have yet to see a single penny from that or its follow-up EP, *Gogitchyershinebox*, which features the infamous cover of Snoop Doggy Dogg's "Gin and Juice."

For South by Southwest 98, the Gourds were offered a second showcase, late on Sunday night at the Hole in the Wall. Robert Lee, a local poet and friend of Russell's, informed him that a friend of his, Max Johnston, would be in town for the annual music conference and that they should play some music together. Russell extended an invitation through Lee, and Johnston showed up at the gig, fiddle in hand.

"He came and sat in, and it was great," grins Russell. "I never imagined playing with somebody who played like that, even though I always imagined having

a multi-instrumentalist in the band. The guys were sort of like, 'No, we don't want to upset the chemistry,' and I was like, 'Shit, our chemistry is nicotine and alcohol, my friends.'"

Johnson joined for the recording of the *Blitzer* follow-up, *The Ghosts of Hallelujah*, and with little practice and an almost complete unfamiliarity with the new batch of songs, he turned in some instrumental performances that not only add another whole dimension to the Gourds' sound but elevate it to an entirely new level. The fiddle featured on "Up on High" is just as stunning as the fiddle he laid on Uncle Tupelo's "Slate," which is to say, world-class.

"More than any other band I've played with, I'm allowed to be myself," enthuses Johnston. "They encourage me to be in the band, to be a fifth member of the band, not just a side guy. I've enjoyed being a side guy, all these amazing people I've played with, but I just kind of floated around. But what I've created with the Gourds is no one's creation but mine."

The Gourds, as they stand now, are a more cohesive unit, technically stronger and more aesthetically powerful than they've ever been. They've also found a new home at Jovita's, the South Austin Tex-Mex eatery and *casa* for down-home music. They pack the place most Saturday nights, digging into a well of songs so deep it seems bottomless, drawing on an instrumental arsenal that leaves their legions of fans reeling, over and over again.

Their new album, *Bolsa de Agua*, is a solid showcase of their new existence. They have embraced the "winged life," as the walls of the Steamy Bowl's latrine have implored them to do for so long. The grip has remained loose, but change and joy have remained constant and intact.

Meanwhile, the music just gets better and better. ◄

SHEARWATER
THE DISSOLVING ROOM
GREY FLAT

The term "maturity" is bandied about often when discussing songwriting. It's generally considered an asset when a songwriter, whether Dylan, Van Zandt, or Elliott Smith, has an accumulation of experience to draw upon. Shearwater's local debut, a collaboration between Will Sheff of Okkervil River and Jonathan Meiburg of Kingfisher, wears the sincere and allegorical clothes of such sage craftsmen proudly, but leans more toward the confused coming-of-age adolescent perspective, in the process supplying more questions than answers. Then again, who needs answers when the questions are as elegant and emotionally charged as these? *The Dissolving Room* is a rough diamond of intimacy, adorned with flourishes of violin, accordion, harmonica, and pedal steel complementing the acoustic guitar and banjo base. Sheff and Meiburg trade vocal duties, with Meiburg's smooth, often-falsetto tone contrasting Sheff's more haggard delivery. "Ella Is the First Rider" demonstrates why Sheff's lungs have been likened to those of Will Oldham, though Sheff can actually *sing* in a conventional sense, while still conveying the trail-dusty despair of the badlands. His "Sung Into the Street" and "Little Locket" paint prosaic portraits of uncertainty, the latter peppered with whispery instability. Meiburg's unforgettable "Military Clothes" follows the lead of nostalgic pedal steel work into a picaresque setting where one fateful day a young man's life changes suddenly like the tide of the seasons. A riveting debut. **MICHAEL CHAMY**

VOL. 20 NO. 33 ★ APRIL 13, 2001

RAY WYLIE HUBBARD
ETERNAL & LOWDOWN
PHILO

In the past decade, Ray Wylie Hubbard has become one of the best singer-songwriters of our time. Since 1992, he's released a series of albums, each more impressive than the last, with songs and stories that are pensive, witty, and filled with vivid imagery, all hung on musical frameworks either spare and sensitive or no-holds-barred rockin'. All leading up to *Eternal & Lowdown*, his latest and greatest. This marks the first time Hubbard has worked with producer and guitarist Gurf Morlix (Lucinda Williams, Slaid Cleaves), who blends his bluesy guitar style and economical backdrops with Hubbard's lyrical vision to create pure magic. Between the rapid-fire Dylanesque delivery of spirited opener "Three Days Straight," the clanking and clattering gambler's lament "Mississippi Flush," the swampy blues of "Weevils," down to the tired and dusty "After All These Years," Hubbard weaves a spell that recalls past musical gurus such as Lightnin' Hopkins and Townes Van Zandt, yet remains true to his own singular voice. Particularly poignant is the gospel-inflected "Didn't Have a Prayer," which finds Hubbard singing in a voice quivering with emotion, an undoubtedly autobiographical account of his struggle with life's many demons: "I need to get me, I got to find me, I got to have me, a little peace in my heart." Such moments of naked honesty are rarely revealed by any artist, yet *Eternal & Lowdown* is filled with flashes of equal intensity. A gem. **JIM CALIGUIRI**

VOL. 20 NO. 44 ★ JUNE 29, 2001

Those Magic Moments On the Eve of His Club's 26th Anniversary, Clifford Antone Remembers the Masters

VOL. 20 NO. 45 ★ JULY 6, 2001

MARGARET MOSER

FOR A MAN WHOSE DAYS begin and end in a cell at the Federal Correctional Institution near Bastrop, inmate No. 22656080 still has a firm grasp on the outside world. Federal facilities have a reputation for being summer camps next to state prisons and local jails, but that's like saying a kick in the face with a jackboot is preferable to a spike heel. Prison is prison.

Clifford Antone began serving his four-year sentence for conspiracy to possess with the intent to distribute more than 1,000 kilograms of marijuana and money laundering just days before his club's 25th anniversary show last year. He's allowed some privileges, and can keep in telephone contact with Antone's record store, the nightclub, the record label, and his sister Susan. Calls are limited and subject to phone availability, but Antone stays in touch regularly with all.

In an anniversary year dedicated to late Houston guitarist Clarence Hollimon, Antone spoke from prison about the club's twenty-six years of magic moments. It may well have been politic of him to avoid addressing his present circumstances, but it is also 100% Clifford to focus on musical memories and his club's colorful history—especially considering John Lee Hooker's death just two days earlier.

"I remember John Lee Hooker," Antone begins. "He called me in 1975 for a gig at the club, and I set him up. Later, he would call me and come visit, like a vacation, not even to play. That's how close we were.

"It was a hard time for blues," he continues. "The hardest time was right around '75. That's why we became so close with Jimmy [Reed], Clifton [Chenier], Muddy Waters, Willie Dixon, Walter Shakey Horton, and Sunnyland Slim. Some of them had never been to Texas. Some of them no one wanted anywhere, and here's this club of kids devoted to the blues. It just blew them away. The musicians would drive up and come in and ask, 'Where's Mr. Antone?' and I'd say, 'That's me.'

"'Where's your father?' they'd ask.

"'He lives in Port Arthur,' I'd tell 'em. 'Why?'

"'Who owns this place?'

"'Well,' I'd tell 'em, 'I do!' And they'd just start laughing. Just some kid, you remember. We were just kids.

"It was magic. I don't think the city of Austin really comprehends how important that was. There's not even a plaque on Sixth Street to say we were there, all those people were there. Stories are written about the history of Sixth Street and don't even mention us. Maybe it's like the music itself and will take 100 years for them to appreciate it, appreciate all these people.

"I've been the luckiest man to know all those blues musicians. Angela Strehli helped me through so much of this, her brains helped everything. All the great musicians from the Eastside inspired me at the club— Blues Boy Hubbard. You remember Ural DeWitty, the drummer from the Jets. DeWitty might have been the best drummer in Austin and never got any recognition.

Home of the blues: (l–r) Eddie Taylor, James Cotton, Snooky Pryor, Clifford Antone, and Jimmy Rogers, 1985. Photograph by Susan Antone.

"I'VE BEEN THE LUCKIEST MAN TO KNOW ALL THOSE BLUES MUSICIANS."

CLIFFORD ANTONE

Outside of Bobby Bland, I never heard anyone who could sing better. And drumming—he was an artist of a drummer, playing so beautiful.

"There's a lot of young kids out there doing it, like Rusty Zinn, Johnny Moeller, the Keller boys; all music needs support, but these very talented kids need it too. Rusty Zinn sounds like he was playing in Memphis for Sun Records in 1950. Johnny, nobody can burn like that kid. He's got the heart like Stevie had, about the only one I've seen with that kind of heart. Johnny's so quiet and bashful, just a sweet kid and sometimes those kids get overlooked.

"The talent pool in Austin is just wonderful. Bob Schneider, the Scabs, I love 'em. The Vallejo kids, it's good to bring them all to one place to play. Even Lucinda Williams, I love that girl.

"Sue Foley's either 100 years ahead or behind, I'm not sure which. Sue could have come up with Robert Jr. [Lockwood], Little Walter, or the old blues cats in Chicago. One of the few who knows how to play the blues correctly. Look at everything they call blues today! When she and Derek [O'Brien] are backing Kim [Wilson], it's too much. It's so good to have younger musicians mixed with the older ones.

"I was lucky also in my association with the younger generation of the Seventies: Jimmie, Stevie, Kim . . . Seeing Jimmie Vaughan play that many times in my life is like *whew*! He's as superior a musician as there is, another one folks don't realize what an artist he is.

"I watched [Jimmie] play slide with Muddy Waters and saw Muddy's head just *turn*! Muddy loved Kim Wilson too. Watching Stevie Vaughan and Denny Freeman every week with Paul Ray & the Cobras, seeing the Thunderbirds back then with Lou Ann, Angela . . . All that, I think about at anniversary time. I could write a book about it, and I'm going to.

"My message is the same one I've had all these years: Turn off the TV, get out and support live music. The object is to put money in the pocket of the musicians, support live music. People in Austin are spoiled to so much good music, but when it comes to the blues, there aren't that many masters left." ◄

TCB
PROFESSOR ANTONE

Quick, name a UT course where a typical pop-quiz answer is former Johnny Cash sideman Earl Poole Ball. That would be "The Blues, Race, and Social Change," and while the title sounds typically academic, the instructor doesn't, because he's Clifford Antone. A former Longhorn himself, the blues' local namesake is in his first semester of teaching the Sociology/American Studies class, which meets twice a week to examine the social impact of R&B and rock & roll. A discussion on music and prejudice leads Antone to recount his own long-haired experience: "We would be standing on Guadalupe and frat boys would drive by and throw bricks at us." Future meetings will cover Atlantic Records, Chess Records and Chicago blues, Motown, and New Orleans, and Antone isn't discouraged when only two people in the room have heard of Jimmy Reed. His job is done, he says, "If one kid is inspired to go buy a Muddy Waters CD who didn't know who he was."

CHRISTOPHER GRAY

VOL. 23 NO. 24 ★ FEBRUARY 13, 2004

Clifford Antone. Illustration by Nathan Jensen.

One More for Her Dale Watson Writes His Grief

VOL. 20 NO. 48 ★ JULY 27, 2001

JERRY RENSHAW

COUNTRY MUSIC and grief go hand in hand. Hank Williams set the standard, but soak up some of Roy Acuff's hardscrabble hillbilly laments or Johnny Cash's ruminations, and you'll soon feel the weight of their burdens. Even Ray Price's smooth, urbane love songs are often steeped in melancholy. Loss, loneliness, and anguish are the core of the greater country music catalog, the seeds of "I'm So Lonesome I Could Cry," "Tonight the Bottle Let Me Down," and countless others.

Dale Watson's *Every Song I Write Is for You* follows this pattern. It's an album of deeply personal and intense love songs, written for a woman who is gone forever. Through its songs, it's easy to trace all the steps of Watson's grief: anger ("I'd Deal With the Devil"), denial ("One More for Her"), guilt ("If I Knew Then What I Know Now"), and acceptance ("Angel in My Dreams"). There are no truckin' songs or honky-tonkers on *Every Song*. It's purely about someone trying to come to grips with a horrific tragedy, and it's painful to hear Watson's soul exposed in such a way.

The events leading up to this tragedy began in April 2000, at which point the local honky-tonk ace's life had come to a crossroads. For starters, his marriage of nine years was coming to an end, made even more painful because the couple's two young daughters were involved.

"It happened for all the usual reasons," says Watson. "Being a working musician, gone for two months at a time, not home very much, and things just sort of deteriorated."

Things were also in transition professionally. Watson's relationship with HighTone Records had soured, leaving him in search of a new label. It was about this time that Watson met Terri Lynn Herbert, a young lawyer with the Travis County Attorney General's office. He was hardly thinking in terms of new relationships, but then that's often how couples couple.

"She was a real firecracker," Watson recalls. "She'd always come to shows at Ginny's or the Broken Spoke and see bands, come out to support them. And she'd always pay the cover charge rather than expect to get in on the guest list. That just wasn't her."

On December 28, Watson checked into an Austin hotel with the intention of ending his pain for good.

Herbert's legal specialization was in the Victims' Services branch of the AG's office, but she had also been exploring entertainment law, lending her services to a group of lawyers doing pro bono services for musicians. In the recent past, she had helped negotiate a record deal for Seth Walker and helped Matt Powell find his way out of a bad one.

She and Watson hit it off at a birthday party for Powell, and things were rolling immediately. It was only a month or so after the singer's separation from his wife, but things progressed quickly. Herbert met Watson in Spain for a series of gigs, and soon the two were talking about marriage. Their plans were cut short last September 15.

That evening, Herbert was on her way to meet Watson at a gig in Houston when she lost control of her car and was killed. She hadn't even made it to I-10; the accident occurred on Highway 71.

"The DPS said she fell asleep at the wheel, but that wasn't Terri," reflects Watson. "She wasn't

wearing her seat belt at the time, which also wasn't like her. I think she was fishing around the floorboard for her cell phone or a CD or something when she left the road, then overcorrected when she saw what was going on and rolled the car. She was banged up pretty badly and was dead at the scene."

Through a series of crossed signals and unfortunate timing, Watson didn't receive the news from Herbert's mother until hours afterward. Though devastated, he continued to play his scheduled gigs. In a horrible irony, his first gig after his fiancée's death was at a wedding.

"That wedding gig was pretty rough," notes Watson. "Everyone wanted to know if I felt up to it, and I suppose I could've just canceled it and everyone would have understood. Still, that just didn't seem like the right thing to do."

As the reality of Herbert's death sank in, Watson went into that blackest of emotional states, haunted every moment since first getting the news. It was as though time was standing still, and every day was September 15. To make matters worse, the two had squabbled that day, burdening Watson with guilt as well as grief. He was unable to sleep, and took to sleeping pills and alcohol to numb the pain.

"I want to apologize for that period," he says now. "I may have said or done some things to people then that I wouldn't have ever done otherwise, but I was really just out of my head for a long time there."

At the same time, the songs for *Every Song I Write* were coming together whether he wanted them or not; for the most part, they were proving good therapy for what had happened. Indeed, "You're the Best Part of Me" was written and performed at the wedding following Herbert's death. No amount of songwriting, pills, or alcohol was filling the gap left by his fiancée, though, and on December 28, Watson checked into an Austin hotel with the intention of ending his pain for good.

Despite Watson's efforts to cover his tracks, his road manager Donnie Knutson sensed something was up, and tracked the singer down. He found Watson semiconscious from a combination of sleeping pills and vodka, and had him rushed to the Brackenridge emergency room. Several days later, the singer was transferred to the St. David's Pavilion counseling center, and between the hospital and the SIMS Foundation, Watson was deemed a likely candidate for a neurological therapy known as EMDR.

Within a few weeks of his EMDR therapy, Watson started letting go of the guilt associated with Herbert's death—those nagging doubts that maybe he could have done something differently to prevent her death. The songs on *Every Song* trace the progress of Watson's recovery, like a before-and-after perspective on the EMDR sessions. His songwriting morphs from grief and loss to an appreciation of the time they had together and the ways his life was enriched by knowing her.

To start, Watson put out a 10-song version of *Every Song I Write Is for You*, with proceeds from the sales going to the Terri Herbert Foundation, a scholarship fund for children of single moms (Herbert's own situation). Soon, hoping for a wider audience and more donations to the foundation, Watson started shopping the album to various labels, on the condition that whoever put it out would also release his upcoming *Live in London* and *Christmastime in Texas* albums.

Eventually, the package deal was picked up by Nashville's Audium Records. Chances are they were swayed in part by the incredible response Watson's homemade version of the album generated. E-mails to Watson's Web site from people touched by the new songs were plentiful and heartfelt. From one Dallas fan: "You make me wish I'd known Terri Lynn Herbert, and pray that I can find one of my own. I don't know you and you don't know me from Adam, but hell, I sure do wish you the best as you fight this battle, and I've added you to the list of people I pray for when I'm driving through Texas thunderstruck by the vast expanse of sky and clouds and pure sunshine."

Dale Watson sits in the dining area of his sparsely furnished condo, sipping coffee while a Johnny Bush 8-track plays softly in the background. The gray in his hair has thickened over the past couple of years, and the weary look in his eyes has deepened. His physique looks more wiry than before, and a couple of his tattoos are beginning to fade.

He recalls how he took a flight last month and stopped dead when he saw a woman a couple rows in front of him. From behind, her hair looked so much like Herbert's that it gave him a bad start. This is the kind of thing that still happens constantly in his life.

"I was taking a shuttle bus from the airport," recounts Watson, "and started talking to the driver. Somehow we started talking about what happens after someone dies, what there is beyond this life and where we all go. She said, 'Well, I think when you die, that's it. Your life is just over and your soul doesn't exist anymore.'

"I thought, 'Well, then you've never lost anyone close to you yet. Just wait, and when that happens, you'll think differently.'"

Nobody comes out on the other side of an experience like Watson's the same person. The loss of someone close is something everyone faces sooner or later, each with their own way of coping. Like Dale Watson, we must all find a way to pick ourselves up and carry on. Country music is there for you when the time comes. ◀

THE WEARY BOYS
THE WEARY BOYS

Were this 1946 instead of 2001, flour companies throughout the South would have beseiged the Weary Boys with offers for radio programs and promotional tours. They might have even helped elect a governor. Unlike BR5-49 or Split Lip Rayfield, Austin's Wearies fervently ply their grandfathers' music without a trace of smug retro irony, like they really do rehearse barefoot in the back of an International Harvester, not in the garage getting high and listening to Flatt & Scruggs. It's the vocal harmonies that give them away, lending a familial, otherworldly resonance to Bill Monroe's "Dark as the Night." Equally strong are their instrumental chops, relentless on "Clinch Mountain Backstep" and properly reverent on "Rock of Ages." As a matter of fact, lead guitarist Mario Matteoli's originals ("Lose One More Baby," "Pick up the Steam") nestle among songs simply credited "Trad."—including a barn-burning "Freight Train Blues"—with no appreciable interruption of continuity, lyrically or musically. Perhaps it's time we had a second look at those birth certificates, o' Weary "Boys."

CHRISTOPHER GRAY

VOL. 21 NO. 7 ★ OCTOBER 19, 2001

Welcome to Deadwood: The Weary Boys, 2005.
Photograph by Aubrey Edwards.

OKKERVIL RIVER

DON'T FALL IN LOVE WITH EVERYONE YOU SEE

JAGJAGUWAR

Like Neutral Milk Hotel's *In the Aeroplane Over the Sea*, Okkervil River's sophomore LP launches immediately into a coming-of-age story, balancing poetic lines with an undeniable emotional investment that sustains itself over the course of the entire album. Okkervil River and frontman Will Sheff are inspired, as is NHM's Jeff Mangum, by the folk tradition of telling a story by song. Opener "Red" is a strummed tale of emotional ruin and a mother's pain. The pedal steel and harmonica of "Kansas City" form the sad, twangy shuffle that has won the band comparisons to Will Oldham's Palace. Sheff goes full-tilt at all times, infusing each word, each phrase with a splash from the cauldron of passion lurking beneath. At key moments, that passion bubbles over and Okkervil River hits full stride. "Westfall" is a tale of high school murder, beautifully spiked by Zach Thomas' mandolin, and is also the band's biggest-sounding song thanks in part to the veteran production of Brian Beattie (ex–Glass Eye). Beattie brings in old pal Daniel Johnston for a memorable duet on "Happy Hearts," like the rest of the album equally giving of trust and sincerity and suspicious of its reciprocation. As fine as it opens, *Don't Fall in Love* finishes up even stronger, with "Okkervil River Song," an accordion-fed instant classic about the Northeastern countryside that lingers in the air long after the last of the recorded bird chirps that cap this fine collection. **MICHAEL CHAMY**

VOL. 21 NO. 21 ★ JANUARY 25, 2002

. . . AND YOU WILL KNOW US BY THE TRAIL OF DEAD

SOURCE TAGS & CODES

INTERSCOPE

This is bigger than all of us now, this unwieldy thing called . . . And You Will Know Us by the Trail of Dead. From its opening salvo, *Source Tags & Codes* proves to be a very special album. "It Was There That I Saw You" reveals Keely as an anglophiliac tunesmith of the first order, his best Damon Albarn clashing with a massive barrage of screaming sonic majesty. As the tune settles in, swelling strings make their regal presence known, as they do throughout the album. A staticky segue feeds perfectly into "Another Morning Stoner," another Keely masterstroke. Neil Busch's taut, sneering "Baudelaire" kicks up the rock factor, which explodes with Jason Reece's punk rock "Homage." Keely's there to pick up the shards, and on "How Near, How Far," craft them into something elegant, powerful, and beautiful. Reece's machine-gun drumming thrusts Keely's distorted dreamtime melodies into the realm of the unforgettable. "Days of Being Wild" holds all the rock fury we expect from this Austin quartet, and the newfound focus we'll expect from now on. "Relative Ways" is the jewel in the crown, the "Teenage Riot" of this *Daydream Nation. Source Tags & Codes* is an album that absolutely cannot be ignored.

MICHAEL CHAMY

VOL. 21 NO. 32 ★ APRIL 12, 2002

1,000 Musical Kisses How Patty Griffin Went from a Flaming Red Folkie Living with Ghosts to a World-Class Kisser

VOL. 21 NO. 37 ★ MAY 17, 2002

DAVE MARSH

SOMETHING TRANSFORMED Patty Griffin this spring. You could hear it in her show at Jovita's during South by Southwest, where the local singer-songwriter debuted her new album *1000 Kisses* with a performance that hushed the crowd, except for rapturous response between numbers. Her phrasing's freer, her onstage demeanor more confident. She radiated enthusiasm back at her fans. Coming offstage, she glowed like a gymnast who had just nailed a difficult landing.

Griffin no longer records for A&M, the arm of Universal Music Group for which she made four albums, two of which got released. She's much more comfortable on ATO, which is owned by Dave Matthews and distributed by BMG. She's also stopped trying to prove she's a rocker, although she convinced the hell out of a lot of us with her second album, 1998's *Flaming Red. 1000 Kisses* establishes a new guise for Griffin's old persona and is a tour de force for a singer's singer,

which would be true even if "Rain," "Making Pies," and "Be Careful" weren't among the best songs she's written.

Griffin's songs are so good, in part, because they're crafted to be sung, a departure at a time when many vocals get croaked out as afterthoughts to tunes written as hangers for clever but cumbersome lyrics. It's not that Griffin sacrifices sense to sound—she's too good to have to make such choices—it's just that her music is so, well, musical. Her performance on "Be Careful" turns those two words into an anthem, and not with a shout. Griffin sings them so delicately that the listener can't avoid feeling the consequences of careless behavior with fragile souls.

Griffin is a tough-minded social observer and a romantic visionary.

When she brought *1000 Kisses* to Joe's Pub in New York City last month, the process had gone even further. Griffin has often seemed as insular onstage as off, wrapped in her own world, turning and stretching through songs as if possessed by a Natalie Merchant dervish. Not now. She's slowed her signature song, "Flaming Red," from punk belligerence to pop purity and surrendered to the transformation.

Or maybe that's backward. Maybe this intensely personal song that she once issued like a threat (even to Dixie Chicks audiences when she toured with them) can calm down because she's found greater mastery of her music. Either way, there was Griffin, tossing her long red locks—not lost in herself, but instead locked into sounds that shone through her.

It was much more compelling visually than her insular movements ever were. She looked free and vivacious. A friend of mine who's seen many of Griffin's shows put it best: "She never let herself be beautiful before."

GRIFFIN HASN'T CHANGED all *that* much. Her songs remain gems of downhearted observation, sung in a voice that still defines sad. Or maybe just lonesome. Yet before she's anything else, Patty Griffin is a singer.

"Songwriting tends to come out of what I need to sing—the sounds that need to come out of my body," she says. "It's the feel of the thing, the way it feels to sing."

What kind of singer is more of an issue, and has been since *Living with Ghosts,* Griffin's first A&M album from 1994. The LP's songs were first recorded with elaborate arrangements by producer Nile Rodgers. "The production was beautiful, but I feel like I played a really smart part in it," says the singer. A&M hated it, but loved the demos, so Griffin proposed using the demos as the album, which with some slight touch-ups (mainly redoing vocals) was what they did. The result married intimate, intelligent songs to intimate, intelligent vocals.

Ghosts built Griffin a reputation, but it also created the illusion that she was a folkie. The follow-up, *Flaming Red,* opened with a punk flare-up that seemed designed to negate the idea that she was a folksinger. It was recorded by a rock producer, with band arrangements that gave it an updated classic rock feel.

"I always felt like I was a rock singer," says Griffin. "It was all I listened to. I felt like, 'Don't call me a folksinger.' I never meant for those songs to come across like that. It kind of stuck you out in the field with all the daisies.

"Now, I don't care."

Identified today as a kind of alt.country singersongwriter—Americana, in a pinch—Griffin has sung on albums by Ray Wylie Hubbard, Eliza Gilkyson, Emmylou Harris, Jon Dee Graham, and Julie Miller; she fits right in with the legends. She's also developed a fascinating live collaboration with Michael Fracasso, one of the few artists who can match her vocal prowess.

Then there's the growing catalog of songs Griffin has had covered: Emmylou Harris did two on *Red Dirt Girl* and one on her duet album with Linda Ronstadt; Reba McEntire, Bette Midler, and Martina McBride have also found Griffin songs that work for them. Most notoriously, the Dixie Chicks did "Let Him Fly" on *Fly,* which sold nine million copies.

What's really important about all those associations, other than giving Griffin income and exposure, is what they say about her stature among her peers. Gilkyson put it well: "People work their whole careers trying to find the creative sweet spot that makes music genuine. But Patty doesn't have to try to tap into the wellspring . . . She *is* the wellspring."

GRIFFIN IS A TOUGH-MINDED social observer and a romantic visionary, a combination that seems naturalistic in songs like "Moses," "Not Alone," "One Big Love," and "Be Careful." In this, she resembles no writer more than her favorite, James Baldwin, albeit without eccentricities of rhythm. As for songwriters, there's some of John Lennon's wit and rage in her, some of Springsteen's Catholicism and gift for compressing character and narrative. She expresses feminism with more clarity and less hostility than Joni Mitchell managed, although songs like "Forgiveness," "Christina" and "Nobody's Crying" show the influence of *Blue.*

These are the kind of songs that good singers want to record, and for the writer that means both recognition and a living. The record business is another matter.

At A&M, bad luck beset Griffin at every turn. The debacle that was the first version of her debut led to great critical success, and the ensuing solo tour began building a fan base and admirers in the press. *Flaming Red* increased both. If she had been operating in the classic rock era, the label would have been primed for the third album. Instead of A&M being poised to capitalize on the gains she'd already made, she was facing a last chance. In fact, after the merger with Universal, there was no A&M at all. Its artist roster became part of Interscope, headed by former record producer Jimmy Iovine.

Though Griffin delivered the album in 2000, it wasn't until last March—the very week of South by Southwest 2001—that Interscope told Griffin she was being dropped from its roster.

That Saturday night, offstage at Fracasso's Cactus gig, Griffin reported ebulliently, "They finally gave me my release. I'm free now." She had never sounded happier.

"I had all these songs floating around that weren't pop enough for Interscope and also some songs I loved to sing, even though I didn't write them," Griffin says. "And I am a singer."

Griffin accepted an invitation from guitarist Doug Lancio to come up to Nashville and record in his home studio. She cut the whole of *1000 Kisses* there— except the title track. The band included her current live group (Lancio, cellist Brian Standefer, keyboardist and accordionist Michael Ramos) plus bassist Dave Jacques. Mix engineer Giles Reaves added a batch of percussion; a few others stuck their hand in, notably Emmylou Harris on "Long Ride Home."

The recording took a week, at the end of April 2001. They did two days of vocals, three of overdubs, and mixed. The album was done. According to everyone but Michael Ramos. He called Griffin and told her there was a Spanish ballad she absolutely *had* to sing. Griffin, who doesn't even speak Spanish, told Ramos she'd come over, but "I'm not going to do the song." Then she heard it.

She might have written the lyric herself. In translation, it says: "Encountering your love I lost my faith and that gave me my reason to live. I lost my heart on the 1,000 kisses that I left on your lips. It might be a sin and it might be insane, but I have to keep loving you until my heart comes back."

"Mil Besos" fit so perfectly that it became the title track of the album. It will stand as one of the great crossover performances of her generation, a song she sings with control and passion. It is one of the hallmarks of her art that Patty Griffin doesn't seem to care whether she wrote the song or not. She inhabits it, either way. ◀

Paradise
Alejandro Escovedo and His Velvet Guitar

VOL. 21 NO. 43 ★ JUNE 28, 2002

RAOUL HERNANDEZ

DOWN THE I-35 CORRIDOR, hot, excoriated, eternally reconstructing two-lane death alley patrolled by dueling semis, hang a right at New Braunfels just outside San Antonio. Take 306 out past Purgatory Road, past roadside vultures frenzied on carrion, another right at the American Legion outpost. Up the hill. Stop at Canyon Lake.

At a green cabin on concrete stilts, park in the turnaround b-ball court by the boat gear. All the trees can't hide the aqua expanse below, nor three levels of observatory on this matchbox house. Tarps, towels, fishing poles, fins, and water sandals lay strewn about the hillside like victims of last night's beach party massacre. Conquistadors once told of this oasis hidden in the wilds of Central Texas.

"We went to get the kids," reads the note tacked to the front/back/side entrance, the scent of Sharpie still hanging in the air. The kids in Austin. "Be back shortly. Make yourself at home—food in the fridge. Lake is yours . . ."

Two splintery flights descend from the mainframe level out onto a third-deck satellite landing. Losing no wind on the steep climb back to the verdant shanty, a Cape breeze wafts through the screened-in porch that opens onto deck *numero dos*. Like the afternoon tranquility, it pulls up shy of the sliding glass door into the living room. Inside, a shutter somewhere, loosened to the elements, sounds insistently against the chalet. This, in turn, is drowned out by the dwelling's bohemian rhapsody.

While Patti Smith stampedes her newsprint *Horses* up the staircase, the True Believers call out *loteria* imagery from a frame behind the couch. Beefheart, Bowie, and the Velvet Underground sun themselves on the windowsill next to the entertainment center armoire, the Ramones idling nearby. A black-and-white snapshot of San Francisco's Nuns, teetering on a stack of maps and legends that cover the dining nook table, trumpets punk's original Prince Valiant bangs. DATs, discs, record store displays—in these gypsy digs, the volume knob is broken off on ten without the stereo being on.

And music is only half the spectacle. Here, the random clutter of everyday life competes with non-existent decibels. For every reel-to-reel tape player, there's a clothesline of paper cutouts stretched overhead. For every acoustic guitar and pair of wilted cowboy boots, a half-dozen bathing suits. Bats, gloves, and an autographed baseball card of Roberto Clemente testify to a faith as binding as Catholicism or Buddhism, both of which have turned this homestead into a home altar. Lady Madonna and Shiva weep and wave on every wall.

Words and pictures are their own religion, from Kipling's *Kim* and Federico García Lorca's torn verse to Mappelthorpe and a small basket of Kodak moments under the *Nuggets* box set. A photo book, full of dark-eyed Mexican women and defiant Mexican men, in San Antonio fifty years ago, flips through like a movieola.

A doorway hung with beads and one final ascent are all that separate the upstairs loft from the rest of the castle. The grownups have their own shower, their own turntable and records, their own upper deck on which the vista reveals itself like the Mediterranean. Exhale. In the crammed kitchenette directly beneath the royal bedchamber, on a vertical scrapbook doubling as the refrigerator, this bedraggled rock & roll resort suggests its ideological antecedent.

"Nobody starts off to play an instrument with the idea of making money," reasons Keith Richards on a glossy tearaway. "You learn the guitar because you have this burning desire."

Nellcote. The Riviera villa where the Rolling Stones family circus rolled a music history seven (the hard way) in the basement of the guitarist's exile domicile. A metaphorical stone's throw from Canyon Lake.

Shine a light in the turret and wait for the man.

IN THE REISSUE OF *Gravity*, Escovedo's liner note describes the period following the suicide of his wife Bobbie LeVie as a "deafening roar." In the 10 long years between said cataclysm and the release of his

most successful solo album, last year's striking *A Man Under the Influence*, Escovedo remarried, had two more children, cut a half-dozen albums, and was diagnosed with hepatitis C. He turned 51 in January.

"Everything led up to this record from *Gravity*," says Escovedo, sitting up in the chaise lounge recliner on the top perch of his leased arbor. "*Gravity* was a *really* important record for me on many levels. Emotionally and musically. Ten years later, I've been through a lot more. It hasn't been easy. It's been a lot of work,

Real Animal: Alejandro Escovedo, 2008. Photograph by Todd Wolfson.

and I've done nothing but struggle all the way. It's important we never gave up."

Casualties include his marriage to former Pork rock queen Dana Smith, and an Austin residency of twenty years. On *la otra mano*, his health checks up as "good." This October, producer of an altogether different half-dozen, Escovedo, and girlfriend Kim Christoff, are due their first *esquincle*—the names Marseilla, Sha Shai, Maya, Paloma, Paris, and Juanita have already been embodied.

Given his growing siredom, it's propitious that *A Man Under the Influence* has been Escovedo's best-selling album to date; sales hover in the vicinity of 30,000, with projected sales as high as 50,000 by year's end. The connective tissue between best and bestseller, *Gravity* and *A Man Under the Influence*, is tenuous at best.

"*Gravity* is a real desolate album," states Escovedo. "Kind of like de Chirico, the Spanish surrealist, with those empty streets. *A Man Under the Influence*—to me—is like an Alejandro Jodorowsky film. Very intense, but colorful. Like something happening inside a carnival. Angst and drama within this really colorful setting."

A Man Under the Influence of what?

"I wrote a song on the record that was a tribute to Townes [Van Zandt]," explains Escovedo, "The one, 'I'll follow you around, I'll follow you down.' I once read an interview he did in *Musician*, with a blues man, an older man. They were talking about channeling the blues—how important they were as channelers of those emotions. Townes to me was always one of those artists that was possessed with it. I don't think he could intellectualize exactly what was happening to him chemically and spiritually as he was writing these songs and singing them. *Man Under the Influence* is about being addicted to that search for beauty and truth. Love, art."

But yours has always seemed less of an obsession than a case of possession—by the music.

"That's what I was trying to get at with that song about Townes. A man possessed. You are possessed by it. Right now, at this point in my life, after having done this thirty years almost, there's nothing else I would ever wanna do. I would never trade anything for what I've done musically. I'm one of the luckiest human beings on the planet. I got to see so much in my life musically, and be so close to it because of my brothers. I was really fortunate.

"At the same time, when you choose to follow the life, to chase whatever it is—like a gambler—you're possessed. And it's sweet sometimes, and it's extremely painful a lot of the time . . .

"Everything that happened after Bobbie died was just so . . . crazy. Just craziness. Like not even being able to feel anything for so long. Not being able to make any sense of anything for a long, long time. It took years. Really, took years.

"Those ten years [between *Gravity* and *Man*], it's probably taken the last year or two for me to make sense of everything that's happened to me. Seriously. It's taken a long fucking time."

"WHAT'S MY NAME!?" Escovedo prompts Ava.

"Mr. King of Rock & Roll!" parrots Ava.

Escovedo, thigh-deep in the lake, breaks into a toothy grin and winks at 10-year-old Paris, who's prowling behind the family cat on shore.

"That's right," intones the patriarch. Wet, his jet-black hair slicked back, the last thing Escovedo calls to mind is a road-dependant musician overseeing his family on a sunset swim.

"Pedro!" protests Kim. Alejandro is actually Escovedo's middle name.

Soon he has them all scrubbing algae off the underwater steps leading down in the water.

This is Escovedo's obsession. On the way back to the lodge he whispers, "See why I never wanna leave this place?" He and Kim hope to buy these two acres.

As the clan changes to go to the store, Escovedo pops a tape into the VCR and flops into the love seat in the living room. Silent home movies: His parents' *luna de miel* in Monterrey, Alejandro as Gene Autry Caballero circa 1956 at a family reunion, a street parade in downtown S.A. With one schizophrenic cut, suddenly it's 1964–65, Huntington Beach, and Escovedo is hanging ten. He watches transfixed as waves wash over the boards and the surfers wash over the waves.

"To be a Mexican surfer was a bizarre thing," he'd said earlier. "Especially in the early Sixties, because all these groups in high school were like low riders, greasers, whatever they wanted to call us—spics— then jocks, and surfers, who were kinda like jocks, but were predominantly white kids who could afford surfboards.

"Or Hawaiians, who would come over sometimes. They thought I was Hawaiian. See, I've got one of those faces, where no one really knows who the hell I am—what nationality.

"Yet if I go to Saltillo, hey man, they know exactly where I'm from. Do you know that there were Mayan ruins around that area? Monterrey and Saltillo? My dad would always tell me, 'We're part Mayan, part Yaqui [Indian]. I'd go, 'Mayan?' And he'd go, 'Yeah.'"

Escovedo's caught a breaker.

"Man, dig this. I had to go to school in Southern California as a kid. You know what they called me? Alex. The teacher would say, 'I can't pronounce this . . .' So years later, here I am a recording artist for Rykodisc, and radio promotions is trying to get my record played on the radio. The music directors are calling up and saying, 'We can't pronounce this name, how do you expect us to play this record?'

"My first record comes out, *Gravity*, where's it filed? World Beat, Latin, Salsa. Everywhere but rock. When I was in Rank and File, we played a big show at the Hollywood Palladium. I went out for a walk on Hollywood Boulevard, came back, knocked on the front door. They said, 'Hey man, the kitchen's over there.' 'I'm fucking playing, man.' It's still everywhere.

"My attitude is so different now. I'm not afraid to rock in their world. I remember Javier, Rhoda, and I, driving from Georgia, where we were making the True Believers record, to Louisiana, where we had a gig. We got pulled over and the first thing he said was, 'Y'all speak any English?'

"That's what [my song] 'Paradise' is about, going through Germany, and they think I'm Vietnamese."

Hear the wolves a howling
The crowd it claps for more
And I thought I heard you praying
It's just the closing of the door.
—"Paradise"

Paradise has multiple meanings. ◀

DEL CASTILLO
VIDA
SMILIN' CASTLE

Part old-world "gitano," part new-world flamenco, with generous shots of rock and blues and a twist of soul, Del Castillo brings it all together in *Vida,* the group's vibrant second album. If the flamenco rhythms of "Los Caballos" or the giddy "Yiddish March" don't nab you, their spectacular delivery will. The fierce guitar licks from brothers Mark and Rick del Castillo lead the way along with throaty vocalist Alejandro Ruiz. Completing the package is blood-pumping percussion by Rick Holeman, Mike Zeoli, and bassist Albert Besteiro. In the hands of lesser talents, the music might be novelty, but in Del Castillo's capable hands, the results are rich, multilayered tunes. "Sueños Madrigales," "Mi Gitana," and "Por Qué?" in particular render the new-old fusion in sublime fashion, peaking in ecstatic crescendos. Even those tunes seem restrained, however, when compared to *Vida's* bonus track, "Barrio Blues," which will leave you limp. If *Vida* is proof, Del Castillo's road to fame will be as short as an I-35 entrance ramp.

BELINDA ACOSTA

VOL. 22 NO. 9 ★ NOVEMBER 1, 2002

SXSW Picks to Click Gary Clark Jr.

VOL. 22 NO. 26 ★ FEBRUARY 28, 2003

MARGARET MOSER

ON A HOT SEPTEMBER afternoon last fall, Gary Clark Jr. took bows to thunderous applause. His set at the Austin City Limits Music Festival had blistered like the sun, blues channeled from Alberts, both Collins and King. With less than six years of experience, Clark has played happy hours, opened for Bobby "Blue" Bland at the Victory Grill, sat in at Antone's with Calvin Jones and Pinetop Perkins, and released a self-titled album nearly a year ago. At Zilker Park that afternoon, he stood facing the future, tall and proud in the moment, 18 years old.

Tonight, Clark is seated on a chrome barstool on the minuscule stage at Joe's Generic Bar as the clock ticks just past 8pm, Sixth Street time. People start trickling in as Jay Moeller and Matt Farrell set up their drums and keyboards, respectively, while Clark tunes. It's not unusual for James Cotton or Jimmie Vaughan to stop and sit in at these gigs. Clark accepts such acknowledgement graciously, a smile on his dark, handsome face.

"I appreciate hip-hop and DJs and that stuff, but blues is what I play," states Clark. "I like Albert and Freddie King. Elmore James. I like Howlin' Wolf's voice, but I can't sing like him. I listen to Marley a lot, Motown, Stevie Wonder. When I was young, my parents would put on a Jackson 5 record. I used to think I was Michael Jackson; I'd dance. I was about four and tried my hardest to get everything right."

If Gary Clark has the future written all over him, he's that way with permission from the past. The

Gary Clark Jr., 2003. Photograph by John Anderson.

SXSW Picks to Click Los Lonely Boys

VOL. 22 NO. 26 ★ FEBRUARY 28, 2003

BELINDA ACOSTA

LOS LONELY BOYS are the kind of guys that make Mexican mothers coo, "Ay, *mi'jito*. I want you to meet my sister's daughter's cousin!" In gringo-speak, that means the brothers—Henry, Joey (Jojo), and Ringo Garza—are good boys with jobs, rooted in family.

"Our *familia*, our culture—we hold on to that," says the eldest, Henry, prior to a Steamboat gig. Or maybe it was Jojo. The brothers tend to finish each other's sentences. When they really get going, they launch into a hilarious schtick that comes from spending way too much time together and watching way too many mobster movies. You had to be there.

Unless it's all a well-spun act, the boys *are* as they seem: close-knit, hardworking brothers who've been paying their dues, rocking and wailing in venues across Texas and beyond: "Music is in our blood, it's thick."

Their musical apprenticeship comes from their father, Ringo Sr., a musician who played with his seven-brother *conjunto* group, the Backroads. Convinced of his brood's talent, Ringo Sr. moved the family from San Angelo to Nashville, where the boys spent their formative years backing their father, playing mostly country music. As the boys matured musically and literally, Ringo Sr. stepped back and let Los Lonely Boys evolve into their own groove.

And groove they do. Just when you hear a whiff of Santana or the ghost of Stevie Ray Vaughan, they streak into their own *onda* with heavy doses of rock &

strapping, silver-haired bassist tuning up with him is Bill Campbell, 58, who led wide-eyed transplants like Stevie Vaughan and Doyle Bramhall to Eastside blues joints like Charlie's Playhouse and Ernie's Chicken Shack in 1970. Through him Clark is directly connected with the heart of Austin's musical history.

"I believe in Gary," confides Campbell. "He's the real deal. His playing is natural and honest, and he's as ate up with it as any I've ever seen. Plus, he's a distant cousin of W.C. Clark."

Back at Joe's, the small room fills up with a Saturday night audience as Farrell and Moeller slide into "Good Night Irene." Campbell hits a bottom note that makes Clark look over and grin. The guitarist has a lot to smile about: Tonight Gary Clark Jr. turns 19 years old.

"I don't want to be famous," Clark confesses. "I just wanna play." ◀

roll and rock en Español. And to hear them deliver the Texas blues ("Baby, I'm from Texas . . ."), damn—it's like ice water on a hot *Comal*.

A couple of demos are floating around, and a 1998 self-titled CD is now unavailable. That will soon change.

"It was Willie Nelson's nephew we met first," says Jojo about their well-publicized "musical adoption" by the legendary Texan. "He showed Willie a tape of us, and we invited him to a show at Momo's . . . and he came!"

That encounter gained an invitation to play Nelson's Farm Aid Concert and other gigs. Nelson opened his Pedernales Studio to the boys, where they'll begin recording their first serious CD with producer John Porter (Keb Mo, Taj Mahal) in March. In the meantime, Los Lonely Boys call San Angelo home.

What would they be doing if they weren't doing music? The same blank look crosses all three of their faces.

"Flipping burgers, digging ditches—yeah, they make good money. . . . Being with the kids and our family . . . there's always PlayStation!"

Then, with an honesty that comes from knowing you're living your destiny, "Hey, we just like to play."

Los Lonely Boys, 2003. Photograph by John Anderson.

Bright Lights, Inner City

When Austin's Eastside Music Scene Was Lit Up Like Broadway

VOL. 22 NO. 44 ★ JULY 4, 2003

MARGARET MOSER

"THE COTTON CLUB was down on 11th Street, just off I-35, coming east right before you get to Ebenezer Baptist Church, at San Marcos Street," remembers Ernie Mae Miller. "They had nice bands there—Duke Ellington, Count Basie. It must have been the Forties when it got torn down, when I was a kid. Right next door was the Paradise Inn. They had a jukebox, but every now and then, they'd bring in a band.

"My mama would tell me, 'Now, y'all go to BYPU,' the Baptist young people's group, 6 o'clock Sundays. So we'd go into Ebenezer, then out the back door and down to the Paradise. My mama came by there with a switch one time, switched me all the way back home. I just wanted to hear the music!"

And it was the music that shaped Ernie Mae Miller's life. The 76-year-old native was a band student at L. C. Anderson High School, Austin's black high school of the day, which was named for Miller's uncle. Back then, she was known by her maiden name, Crafton, and played baritone sax. At Prairie View College, she joined an all-girl, big-band revue known as the Prairie View Co-Eds, who traveled the country playing army bases, camps, and USOs, even hitting hot spots in New York City.

Afterward, Miller returned to Austin, traded the baritone sax for piano, and by the Fifties, had established herself as a solo musician and singer, in part because her husband didn't care for her touring with male musicians. Miller crossed racial lines early, playing clubs patronized by whites such as Dinty Moore's and, in more recent years, nearly every hotel bar in town. Miller's most famous gig ended its 16-year run in 1967 at the New Orleans Club on Red River Street, then considered the western end of the Eastside's 11th Street entertainment district.

"At the New Orleans Club, I played downstairs, and the 13th Floor Elevators often played upstairs," recalls Miller. "One night it rained, and the place got flooded. That night I'd bought a brand-new pair of red suede shoes. You had to walk down about six steps to get to the club, and that night I had to walk—slush, slush—across Coke cases through the water, while upstairs was the Elevators with people dancing.

"I sure did like those shoes."

IN A DARK, POORLY documented corner of Austin's memory, it's pure speculation to suggest that the town's fabled music scene started in the jazz age of the Twenties. It's quite possible, however, that young Duke Ellington loaded into Austin's Cotton Club at the same time that Louis Armstrong was polishing his trumpet in preparation for his well-documented gig at the Driskill Hotel. Jazz was so pervasive at the time that it was being incorporated into country and western music and called Western Swing.

The presence of active military bases at Bergstrom and Fort Hood (then Camp Hood) meant soldiers on the town every weekend. Documents on and of the time imply that the rowdy atmosphere led to scrutiny by the city and subsequent regulation. By Ernie Mae Miller's recollection, the Cotton Club and Paradise Inn were closed by the end of the Forties.

Meanwhile, Huston-Tillotson College's jazz programs were in full swing, the Apostolic Church at

Ernie Mae Miller, 2007. Photograph by John Anderson.

Comal Street and Blackberry offered teen dances, and a place called the Black Cat on 12th was popular, but not until Johnny Holmes opened his Victory Cafe on V-E Day in 1948 did the scene revive. By the time the cafe moved a half-block toward town as the Victory Grill in the Fifties, other clubs like Tony Von's Show Bar—previously the Black Cat—were booking live music, too. As Henry "Blues Boy" Hubbard looks back on it, "The Victory Grill was it," but changes were afoot.

"I was playing piano with a trio at the Victory Grill about 1956," says Hubbard, 69, "when Tony Von had a jazz group at the Show Bar that wasn't drawing so well, and he invited me to get on guitar. We got a group together—no name, just a group—and within a week, the house was packed, and no one was at

the Victory. I went up to the Grill on a Friday not long after, and it was only the people that worked there sitting around looking at each other."

By the late Fifties, East 11th Street and its jog up 12th was Austin's musical destination, much as Sixth Street is now. "Lit up like Broadway," is how some describe the snaking blocks of clubs that attracted jazz, blues, and R&B players of every caliber. The military brought Hubbard to Austin, stationed him at Bergstrom AFB, and there he stayed. In addition to the Victory and Show Bar, Hubbard and company played after hours at places such as Cheryl Ann's on Webberville Road, near the outskirts of town. It was a good time to be young and in the swing of things; the unlikely benefit of segregation was the tightly knit black community that thrived in East Austin.

By the late Fifties, East 11th Street and its jog up 12th was Austin's musical destination, much as Sixth Street is now.

"During the time we played at the Show Bar, Charlie Gildon bought the place," explains Hubbard. "He bought the whole block there: barber shop, cleaners, liquor store, shine parlor, and the club. And when he bought the place in 1958, he called me and said, 'I got part of your band, and they want to make you the bandleader.' Charlie and his wife wanted it to be a business and wanted a name for the band. So I said, 'Why not the Jets? I'm a jet mechanic at Bergstrom.' And that's how it came about."

PAY ATTENTION WHEN Allen "Sugar Bear" Black emcees at Antone's. He's been a fixture at the club since the Seventies; he walked into its original location at Sixth and Brazos Street with former Show Bar owner Tony Von to promote Johnnie Taylor and stayed for the next three decades. The tall, handsome man may stand at the door of Antone's as a greeter of sorts, but he's a direct link between today's downtown blues scene and the glory days of the Eastside.

"I was a youngster in 1965, going to Charlie's Playhouse," recounts Sugar Bear. "I saw bands like Al 'TNT' Braggs, Tyrone Davis, and Albert Collins, but mostly it was Blues Boy Hubbard and his Jets on the weekends. It was basically a Blue Monday club for blacks, but on Friday and Saturday nights, it was 95 percent white kids from colleges and the University of Texas."

The presence of a young white audience on the Eastside had been building since the late Fifties. Hubbard theorizes that the proximity of the neighborhood to UT was the crucial link.

"The fraternities wanted somewhere to go every week," he states. "Here's a club on the Eastside that's all black, and it turned all white. I wasn't surprised to see it—if you'd seen how the kids were going on over that music. . . . When we'd kick that first number, they'd be on the dance floor and wouldn't leave. They'd dance when we weren't even playing. They just couldn't get enough of it.

"The blacks on the Eastside would come to Charlie's and get turned away. Not exactly *turned* away, but no room to sit. The fraternities reserved tables for twenty, forty, fifty, and the Playhouse was full before we'd even kick off. The white college kids were spending more money than the black kids because they had more money. It got to the point that blacks on the Eastside coming from the projects were getting mad at Charlie because of that. But Charlie was looking out for Charlie."

The impact of a moneyed white audience bolstered East Austin's economy. Hubbard saw the changes from a businessman's point of view as well as an artist's: "Sam's Showcase was the only other club to give competition to Charlie's, really. W.C. Clark was playing with me then and would say, 'Well, Charlie's paying $10 a night, but Sam is paying $12.' So he'd end up going to Sam's and play with Major Burkes for a while.

"So Sam and Charlie got together on what they wanted to pay the bands. Sometimes, the musicians would get tired of the same crowd and jump the fence to play another club. The grass always seemed greener. But next thing you know, they were back with me. Until 1970, Charlie had one heck of a business."

Mississippi-born Lavelle White was already a veteran musician based in Houston when bookings brought her to Austin in the Sixties.

"I came to Austin to play," she says, "and I played a gob of clubs: Charlie's Playhouse, the Derby, Good Daddy's, Sam's Showcase, the Victory Grill. Joe Valentine had a club, too. There were a lot of clubs there and really in the swing, you know? They were really doing it.

EASTSIDE MVPs

SINGERS AND MUSICIANS WHO MADE THEIR MARK IN EAST AUSTIN BEFORE THE SEVENTIES.

- → MARTIN BANKS
- → T. D. BELL
- → ERBIE BOWSER
- → MAJOR BURKES
- → WIMP CALDWELL
- → BILL CAMPBELL
- → W. C. CLARK
- → MEL DAVIS
- → URAL DEWITTY
- → WELDON GENTRY
- → HOSEA HARGROVE
- → DUCK JENNINGS
- → A. J. MANOR
- → JEAN MANOR
- → PAT MURPHY
- → PAT PATTERSON
- → L. P. PEARSON
- → JAMES POLK
- → GENE RAMEY
- → MATTHEW ROBINSON
- → ROBERT SHAW
- → LOUIS THOMPSON
- → JOE VALENTINE

"Ernie's Chicken Shack—that was a rockin' place, and I was a rockin' girl. That place was so jumpin', and the best food—mmm, mmmh—you ever ate in your life! That fried chicken and fish was just mouth-watering. It was really hoppin', I'm telling you.

"Everybody went there, every weekend night. You could hardly find a place to sit. Dancing and music. Gambling going on in the back room, yes there was. They had bootleg liquor and Blues Boy Hubbard & the Jets. It was wonderful."

AS QUICKLY AS IT CAME, the scene went. By the early Seventies, the Victory Grill had closed, as had Charlie's, Sam's Showcase, and the IL Club. Ernie's Chicken Shack served its bootleg liquor and hosted the Jets after hours until 1979, when Gildon died. Nearly every one of the musicians interviewed cites the same ironic factor in the decline: integration.

Integration isn't the only reason given; drugs, crime, and the changing times played their part as well. Today, the limestone structure known as Symphony Square stands where the New Orleans Club was located, and to look up the block from there toward I-35 is to see how successfully a bit of architecture can affect a culture. The interstate that quite literally divided the city was, as Harold McMillan says, "symptomatic and not causal."

McMillan moved to Austin in the late Seventies as a student and musician, and his experiences as both led to the founding of his local preservation organizations, DiverseArts and the Blues Family Tree Project.

"Once the desegregation legislation happened," says McMillan, "like the Voting Rights Act, black folks had a false sense of victory. We assumed that when the laws changed, we could go all over Austin and do whatever it is we do—see music, eat wherever we want. No need to do business just in central East Austin, because investment will come here, too, and it'll be just fine. Instead, especially in businesses and clubs, it started to die off."

For veteran musicians like Lavelle White, the memory of the Victory Grill in its heyday clashes with today's reality. She bluntly states there's no place in Austin for her to play any longer and talks of moving away after her new album is released this summer.

"If you're a skinny white boy with a guitar, you got a gig," she asserts. "But no one wants to see a black woman with talent."

Without rancor, Blues Boy Hubbard agrees.

"Lavelle is right," he says. "I was lucky back then; I got with Charlie, and Charlie's living was me. He hired me in '58, and I played for him 'til he died in '79. Every week. But the other black musicians didn't have a place to hang their hat for ten years. The club owners kept coming and going. Get a band to a club for a year, someone else buys the club, maybe he don't want a band.

"Then I went to the Austex and the Continental Club, the Opera House, Steamboat. I met Steve Dean, Clifford Antone, Chuck Geist from Hut's, C-Boy, and Hank Vick, and these guys all kept me working, opening for Bobby Bland, John Lee Hooker, the Fabulous Thunderbirds. I played the Guadalupe club for a month one time, playing to a lot of college kids, just like the old days at Charlie's Playhouse."

There's an arch over the entrance to 11th Street from I-35 today, and it's a bellwether of new hopes and old dreams. Drive up 11th Street and the revitalization is evident in refurbished buildings, construction, and a cleaner look to the area. Everyone agrees it's a positive step for the neglected community: Build it, and maybe the people will come.

Yet the frustration in Lavelle White's voice is understandable. In her mind, the Eastside's musicians are still relevant and should have a place in the music scene on both sides of the interstate: "It's time to make people wake up and smell the music. That's my new saying: Wake up and smell the music." ◄

BLAZE
AURAL KARATE
BUTTER VAT

Jazz is forever misconceived as unapproachable, far removed from mainstream popular music. Yet jazz has always kept its ear to the street, having already achieved equity in hip-hop, electronica, and DJ culture. For drummer Brannen Temple and his increasingly confident local jazz ensemble Blaze, the leap between genres is an easy one. By now, their fresh sound is well on the funky side of the spectrum, and with the addition of NickNack on turntables and various sonic effects, their third album is a blast. While Temple, long one of Austin's best drummers, keeps things firmly in the pocket, trumpeter Ephraim Owens and saxist Michael Malone man the frontline with some terrific playing, soulful and deeply satisfying. They, along with bassist Marc Miller, provide the basic ingredients upon which the intertwining effects shine like brass. Not every tune employs electronic gadgetry; two effective cross-cultural collaborations find the earthy sounds of tabla on "Sultan Williams" and sweet pedal steel guitar on the ballad "Septeletwan," both instruments dancing intimately with Owens and Malone. Likewise, former pianist Steven Snyder augments the relaxed, late-night ambience of "The Invisible." A fixture on the local jazz scene, Blaze has evolved remarkably over the course of three releases. With *Aural Karate*, they've taken a giant step forward with a sound as hip as now. **JAY TRACHTENBERG**

VOL. 22 NO. 48 ★ AUGUST 1, 2003

Waking the Dead
Okkervil River's Will Sheff and Centro-matic's Will Johnson

VOL. 23 NO. 2 ★ SEPTEMBER 12, 2003

MELANIE HAUPT

IT'S NOT SO HOT that you notice, but the ants in Oakwood Cemetery are unbearable. It's almost as if they're protecting the dead, enacting an unrelenting and painful punishment on any who'd dare linger on consecrated ground.

Nonetheless, tarry is what these two men do, perched as respectfully as possible on an ancient monument, surrounded by other gargantuan gravestones bearing the poignant legends "Mother," "Father," "Our Baby Daughter." Together Okkervil River's Will Sheff and Centro-matic's Will Johnson hold court amid the dead in a museum dedicated to absence.

"Not many people have shown up to a show of mine with a copy of Proust under his arm," says Johnson of Sheff, recounting their mutual love of things literary.

Sheff's infectious laugh burbles loudly. "I was making a quixotic attempt to read *Remembrance of Things Past*," explains Sheff, "which I read the first two-and-a-half books of. But it was getting like, 'Alright, I've read about how the light fell on the banister for the past 35 pages now; I'm ready to move on to the next second in time.'

"That was a funny show, though, because you were playing in a fake bedroom that was part of a set at the Hyde Park Theatre."

"It was a teenager's bedroom," recalls Johnson, "and I can't remember what poster was on the wall. . ."

"Bob Marley," interjects Sheff.

"And there was a mid-priced Dillard's comforter on the bed in a very teenaged pattern with a lot of squares that reminded me of what I slept under as a teenager," explains Johnson. "I was kind of inspired by it. I should've run with the 'home' theme."

"You should've started the show with the lights down," cries Sheff, eager to take the ball and run with it. "They come up, and you're lying in bed, then you get up, lift some barbells, and be like, 'I just got a good idea for a song!'"

Together Okkervil River's Will Sheff and Centro-matic's Will Johnson hold court amid the dead in a museum dedicated to absence.

"I think we're on to something," chuckles Johnson.

As their easygoing banter suggests, both musicians are friendly and affable. It's here in the bone yard that both Wills have met to talk about their bands and the dozens of convergences that their careers continue to make. The latest overlap is the shared release date of Okkervil River's third album, *Down the River of Golden Dreams* (Jagjaguwar), and Centro-matic's seventh, *Love You Just the Same* (Misra).

Okkervil's latest platter is already widely regarded as their strongest to date. With the band's rootsy Nick Cave aesthetic, the album is dark and spare, the lyrics often violent. The Austin quartet explores the pained space that separates two people, whether between estranged lovers or a dying parent and grieving child. Sheff, a *Chronicle* Screens contributor, possesses

Will Sheff of Okkervil River and Centro-matic's Will Johnson in the graveyard. Photograph by Todd Wolfson.

cinematic sensibilities, manifested here in a barren, blue-and-gray-hued landscape; the poetry is beautifully accompanied by his gently intuitive bandmates.

Johnson and Centro-matic, while dabbling in similar subject matter—that of absence and lack, a yearning for something not quite nameable—works with a broader palette of colors on *Love You Just the Same*. Those same spaces are filled with melodic bouquets of sound and buxom drum lines, all punctuated by Johnson's scratchy voice. While the delivery is a bit different, the message coming from both acts is essentially the same. The two frontmen are inclined to agree.

"I think it's real natural," says Johnson. "I think these bands fit quite well together."

"It seems to me that Will and I have a lot of stuff in common," says Sheff in between ant bites and sips of wine. "I love Will's writing, and it's certainly been an influence on me."

Johnson nods. "I get the feeling, and shut me down if I'm being totally wrong here," he says to Sheff, "but speaking personally, I'm just as influenced by writers as I am by songwriters. We chat about books every now and again, and just get into the wonder of place and setting and character-building and Faulkner and his wizardry up in his crystal palace."

Sheff laughs his agreement.

"Most of my favorite art, as dark as it is or as sad or scary or fearful or whatever the case may be—it could be a character in a story or a character in a song or whatever—I think has a sense of humor to it as well," expands Johnson. "It takes itself with a bucket of salt in a serious moment.

"And I think when you combine the two, it can make for really great moments. Really ugly stories or really grotesque stories with pretty music set to them has always been wonderful to me; that you can filter it through that light and still have a sense of humor about the grand scheme of things, is quite important, I think. And valuable."

Sheff is more to the point. "I guess like making fiction out of things that are real."

On the strength of their respective new albums, they make up part of that group of interesting new voices making honest, passionate music that more and more people want to hear. Which brings us to the other reason why we're here this afternoon in a giant old cemetery: to talk about the future.

"I plan to be a corpse sometime in the next sixty years," jokes Sheff. "I think Will and I are similar in that we continue to work on shit far in advance. I spent all last month working on the new Shearwater record [Sheff's side project], so there's a certain level where I don't care about the Okkervil record because I'm worried about the Shearwater record.

"That's my favorite way to work right now, just try to be working on the next thing when the last thing comes out so that I don't find myself with a lot of downtime to get self-conscious about the next stuff. I find that to be really barking up the wrong tree, thinking self-consciously."

"I think that's a very fortunate situation to have, working on the next record while one's coming out," Johnson muses. "Our band for its entire existence has played catch-up. For the first time in a long time, I'm really excited about the fact that I don't really know what Centro-matic is going to do next.

"I'm very much excited about recording a record with our band that's a little bit more spontaneous. I think half the wonder of music is uncertainty, and I always embrace that because it's an absolute challenge."

Perhaps that's the secret to success: embracing uncertainty in the face of death, life's one absolute certainty next to the wrath of the Texas fire ant. ⬅

SCOTT H. BIRAM
LO-FI MOJO
KNUCKLESANDWICH

Recorded live on KVRX Feb. 2, Scott H. Biram's *Lo-Fi Mojo* is so anachronistic it's almost cutting-edge. It's easy to imagine Biram hunkered over some bulky microphone in some bottomland basement instead of an award-winning college radio station, even easier due to the singer's fondness for material that predates inventions like, for instance, the radio. To wit, "White House Blues" isn't about the current administration's malfeasance; it's about the McKinley assassination. Filtered through Biram's mouthful-of-dirt vocals, traditionals such as "Spoonful" and "Real Cocaine Blues" aren't fusty at all. "Titanic" and the glorious "We Shall Be Free" inject just the right amount of gospel spirit, while songs by Mance Lipscomb, Rose Maddox, Fred McDowell, and Woody Guthrie all crackle and pop with Biram's contagious energy. Exactly how much Biram has absorbed is evident in *Lo-Fi Mojo*'s two originals: the sauntering, carefree "Wreck My Car" and "Truckdriver," a frenzied, chased-by-the-devil shout-out to "all them truck drivers down there at Dorsett's 221 in Buda, Texas." Talk about mojo: Less than two months after recording this album, a head-on collision with an 18-wheeler—near Buda, no less—sent Biram to the hospital, multiple surgeries, and an ongoing convalescence. The forces stirred up by such archaic hoodoo can be unpredictable and cruel, but as Biram dodges those hellhounds on his trail, he winds up doing more damage with an acoustic guitar and harmonica than Jack White's entire seven-nation army. **CHRISTOPHER GRAY**

VOL. 23 NO. 2 ★ SEPTEMBER 12, 2003

Born on the Fourth of July
To the Moon and Back with Explosions in the Sky

VOL. 23 NO. 8 ★ OCTOBER 24, 2003

MICHAEL CHAMY

A SURGE OF LIGHTNING flickers as thunder cracks above the rumble of molten lava.

"I see in your eyes the same fear that would take the heart of me."

Golden-tousled Midwesterner Chris Hrasky beams, saturated with the sheer gravity of the *Lord of the Rings: The Return of the King* trailer glowing on the Power Mac in front of him.

"The day may come when the courage of men fails."

Michael James removes his headphones and looks up from the Pro Tools workstation, surveying the scene momentarily.

"When we forsake our friends and break all bonds of fellowship."

In the dining room, Munaf Rayani and Mark Smith take a break from the small wooden *Scrabble* blocks and peer in at the last alliance between elves and men.

"But this is not that day!"

No, it isn't. This rainy Wednesday afternoon is, however, the last chance for the members of Explosions in the Sky to lounge around Rayani and James' north Central Austin headquarters before leaving on a weeklong tour of Japan, a last chance to be awed by

Explosions in the Sky's 10-year anniversary at Stubb's, July 4, 2009. Photograph by Sandy Carson.

small, homely things before surrendering to the exotic allure of the Far East.

For these four best friends, the little things count most. Behind every game of *Scrabble*, every pickup game of basketball on the Eastside, the Austin quartet catches a glimpse of humanity. It's this deep obsession with life's countless moments that defines the music of Explosions in the Sky, a series of wordless, guitar-hewed epics so visceral they've moved people to tears.

"I don't know how it is for other bands, but for us, we're full-fledged living out a dream," exclaims guitarist Rayani, at 22 the most wide-eyed of the group. "There have been so many times where we just stop and go, 'What are we doing here?' We're in Vienna, Austria. We're in Taipei, Taiwan. We're in New York City. For me, that's the biggest paycheck."

The road to Taipei, though, has been fraught with peril for these four well-meaning boys with small-town upbringings. And never more so than when the band released its superlative sophomore missive *Those Who Tell the Truth Shall Die, Those Who Tell the Truth Shall Live Forever* in early September 2001. Explosions, martyrdom, and September 11: the ingredients for a shit storm if there ever was one.

THIS PLANE WILL CRASH TOMORROW

The CD insert of *Those Who Tell the Truth Shall Die, Those Who Tell the Truth Shall Live Forever* is illustrated with the bold, crayonlike image of a biplane whose searchlight is fixed on an angel. Unfolding into three sections, the booklet reveals the angel isolated on one side, "help us stay alive" stamped beneath. On the opposing flap, the plane flies over a warning: "This plane will crash tomorrow."

The string of coincidences surrounding the band, its artwork, and the destruction of the World Trade Center was surreal, and they came back to haunt them on the band's first European tour that December. James, the group's bassist, was detained at the Amsterdam airport, told he was a threat to security. James lied about the band's name until the officer asked why "this plane will crash tomorrow" was written on his guitar. Somehow, a copy of the disc got the band past that sticky hurdle.

That October, a pair of shows with the even more grimly named Austin rock moguls . . . And You Will Know Us by the Trail of Dead at NYC's Knitting Factory produced more anxiety.

"You walked out of the Knitting Factory, down to the end of the street, and you could see the cranes, lights, and wreckage," says Explosions' drummer Hrasky.

The show went off without a hitch, as did the rest of the band's first full-scale tour, an unforgettable baptism of fire.

Mercifully, Explosions in the Sky's music serves as an unquestionable boon to any healing process. Though their neo-classical rock peers in Scotland's Mogwai and Montreal's Godspeed You! Black Emperor paved the way for the Austin band's success, Explosions in the Sky have forged a brand of instrumental rock that's a thousand times more lyrical, whispering and breathing more than it screams and shocks. Explosions are lost souls in the middle of the smoke and ash, firemen pulling people out of burning buildings, humbled immigrants watching chaos unfold on their TVs.

"We're more hopeful and romantic," posits Rayani. "That's what we bring to the table that those guys sometimes don't. I think we're all looking at the peak of the mountain, but from different parts of space."

MIDLAND IS NOT A COLD DEAD PLACE

From the vast West Texas skyline they came, three friends—Rayani, James, and Smith—arriving in Austin from Midland, Texas, one by one between 1996 and 1998. Here, they picked up guitars in an attempt to capture the sounds and scenes running through their heads. Hrasky landed last, in 1999, taking refuge from the similar stupor of Rockford, Ill.

"Wanted: Sad, Triumphant Rock Band" read the flier he posted in a local record store on a last-ditch effort to find something worthwhile in Austin before giving up on Texas completely and moving back to Illinois. Answering the summons, the Midlanders forged an immediate bond with Hrasky. With his dramatic, military-march beats and cymbal sprays, Hrasky was the missing ingredient.

"The stars lined up," attests Rayani. "For us to find each other, it saved our lives. If I wasn't doing this, I don't know what I'd be doing—probably boring, pointless shit just to get through the day."

The band's identity didn't really coalesce until July 4, 1999. They had been invited in studio for KVRX's *Local Live*, performing under the unbecoming moniker of Breaker Morant, and it was there they cut "Remember Me as a Time of Day," an early-morning tracer of uncomplicated beauty that remains one of their best works. The composition also marked Explosions' recorded debut, appearing on volume four of the college radio frequency's compilation series. When the group left the station, they could hear fireworks downtown. Hrasky made a remark about explosions in the sky, and the words resonated.

Three years, two albums, and one controversial autumn later, it was time to follow up the awe-inspiring *Those Who Tell the Truth*. Cash and concentration began to wane, and it soon became clear there was only one place to go. Back to the open skies and quiet nights that first stirred the music and its makers. Back to Midland, Texas, which had become a ghost town with the departure of their friends and families.

They worked uninspiring day jobs just so they could play by night in the basement of an office building. The sessions were interrupted by treks out to the quietest, most remote spot they could find, a long string of sand dunes called Monahans Sandhills State Park.

"It's like a desert," motions Smith. "You can go out there and not see one city light, not hear a thing. We'd go out there and talk, bring a jam box and listen to music."

"It's like another planet," swears James. "It was like we were on the moon."

Accordingly, their reservoir of sound began to replenish. Soon, the band had the five multisplendored movements that make up *The Earth Is Not a Cold Dead Place*, which refines the band's sharp dynamics, while leaving intact the restraint and simplicity that made their locally distributed debut, *How Strange, Innocence*, and *Those Who Tell the Truth Shall Die* so endearing.

"For the first time," Smith offers, "it actually sounds like we want it to sound."

FIRST BREATH AFTER COMA

It starts with a single chime of consciousness, the thump-thump of a heartbeat. Then, suddenly, the conscious mind wakes. A single-note melody unravels, taking its first tentative steps into rediscovery. A wondrous, chin-scratching pause presages a shimmering double helix of intertwining guitar lines that mark an onrushing flood of memories.

Narratives like this, which describe only the first half of "First Breath After Coma," the 10-minute opener of *The Earth Is Not a Cold Dead Place*, are the only way to convey the visual power of Explosions in the Sky's music. They're the musical equivalent of psychology/art primer *Drawing on the Right Side of the Brain*, forming a vivid mental picture that's completely free from the crude mental crayons necessary to translate word into meaning.

"Whatever images one of us will say, we hear it the same way," explains Rayani, describing the band's songwriting process. "If Mark says, 'This makes me think of a 12-year-old kid falling in love with a 13-year-old girl for the first time,' we all hear what that sounds like, and we write around it."

"I think that the main example on this record is 'Six Days at the Bottom of the Ocean,'" says Smith of the unfurling collision course that anchors *The Earth Is Not a Cold Dead Place*. "It was written around the story of the *Kursk*, the Russian sub that sank to the bottom of the ocean. We were imagining what it was like to be those men at the bottom of the sea, trapped and desperate, running out of oxygen. [The song] gallops, getting faster and more intense until it just stops, and you breathe your last breath."

At an Explosions in the Sky performance, any song could just as well be a short film. James spends the entire show in an odd stupor, going long stretches with his eyes closed, and others with eyes agape as he jerks back and forth, relentlessly pounding the bass. Rayani is generally either swaying uneasily from left to right, knees slightly bent, or he's kneeling onstage in what begins as a ploy to adjust some pedals but quickly becomes some sort of spiritual crouch. Hrasky is lost in a world of drum heads and cymbals, while Smith toils away on the left side of the stage, seemingly absorbed by all that's happening around him.

"All of us get so lost while we're playing that I truly don't know where I am," claims Rayani. "We've ended shows where we're just toppled over on each other. When that last note ends and I look up, it's like I haven't been there the whole time."

Whether onstage, on album, or in their living room, the natural chemistry of these four minds radiates a collective conviction and palpable warmth, a constant reminder that the Earth is indeed not a cold dead place.

"These guys are my favorite musicians in the world," declares Rayani. "And before we're a band, we're best friends. When we come back from tour, we stay away from each other for a couple of days, just to kinda settle.

"Then it's right back into sitting around with each other, doing nothing. Playing *Scrabble*." ◀

TIA CARRERA
THE NOVEMBER SESSION
PERVERTED SON

The next best thing to "Layla" is "The Jams" disc on the 3-CD *Layla Sessions* box set from 1990. On it, five unreleased jams from Eric Clapton & the Dominos and the Allman Brothers—all over ten minutes, two nearing twenty. Have tape, will roll—a shredder's delight. On their 70-minute debut, Austin's heaviest psych rock trio, Tia Carrera, pulls out its own five jams, only this improvisational summit meters out more like Hendrix firing up his axe while the Melvins pour kerosene on it. As ripe as his *Electric Ladyland* reverb is Jason Morales' deep down Sabbath tones, which aren't nearly as plodding as Tony Iommi's. Erik Conn's Bonzo bash, meanwhile, waits coiled at every turn, bassist Andrew Duplantis in a bottom-end funk to land them all in the spank factory. The between-jam studio chatter only adds to the miasmic stew that is *The November Session*. And this isn't even half of what the three-man conflagration is capable of live. Nearly fourteen minutes of "Doom" shudders like iron spasms, while thirty-four minutes of closer "J. Bankston Manor" is like the Allmans' "Mountain Jam" on Mount Fuji during an eruption. Tia Carrera will have you on your knees, begging darling please. **RAOUL HERNANDEZ**

VOL. 23 NO. 9 ★ OCTOBER 31, 2003

GRUPO FANTASMA
MOVIMIENTO POPULAR
AIRE SOL

Geographically, culturally, and linguistically, the Latin hemisphere is enormous. Austin's Grupo Fantasma should be enormous too, if for no other reason than to incorporate the myriad flavors of Latin music: rumba, salsa, Tejano, cumbia, ranchero, etc. Proficient in these styles, this local 12-piece also bulks up with rock, jazz, reggae, and funk. In weaker hands, this many influences might become a soggy mulch of sound. Have no fear; on their second album, Fantasma's elements—bass, horns, percussion, guitars, and vocals—move in harmony like the eighteen wheels of a speeding semi. With extra hauling power, there's plenty of room for cameos from the likes of Jamaican-style toaster Ragah El, turntablist DJ Baby G, and Los Super Seven crooner Ruben Ramos, who offers a definitive "Oye Mi Cumbia." Opener "Peligrosa" introduces the ensemble's dangerous cumbia beat, while "Vida Guerra" piles salsa syncopation ever higher, until a *tres*-flavored guitar solo breaks through. Closer "Ya No Puedo" ends on a high note, built on a caliente *Combat Rock* circular beat. Lyrics may be en Español, but you don't have to speak Castilian to understand deep groove, hip-spinning rhythms, glowing horn work, and surplus cojones. With *Movimiento Popular*, this enormously talented Latin juggernaut jumps to world class. **DAVID LYNCH**

VOL. 23 NO. 32 ★ APRIL 9, 2004

GILKYSON
BATTLED
HER OWN
NIGHTMARE
AND LIVED
TO WRITE
THE TALE.

Lioness in Winter
Eliza Gilkyson, Purring, Growling, Roaring

VOL. 23 NO. 35 ★ APRIL 30, 2004

MARGARET MOSER

ELIZA GILKYSON has found her voice, and at 53, it's only getting stronger. It's grown from a whisper to a roar within her lean, lioness frame and emerges regally live and on LP. The lengthy journey to this point has lasted most of her life and seen her flit from genre to genre, shedding images and names. She's metamorphosed from a cocoon of wildly divergent influences and become a woman with a distinctive sound and style. Her most recent album, *Land of Milk and Honey*, is the third in a row of milestone recordings. The journey to this point hasn't just been long. It's been emotionally battering. And worth it.

"I was a hippie who turned into a back-to-the-lander, who turned into a parent, who turned into a New Age person, who turned into a totally betrayed and grieving person, who's landed and is doing OK."

Gilkyson is more than "doing OK" on a Friday night, splaying her claws on the political carpet during her Cactus Cafe show for *Land of Milk and Honey*. Under the shadow of a war that's increasingly being compared to Vietnam, Gilkyson takes the folksinger's traditional role as the voice of dissent.

"I played at a private party in D.C. to a bunch of Republicans. Halfway through the night, I was like, 'Should I . . . ?' 'Could I sing . . . ?' 'Can we do . . . ?' But these were, like, the people who are voting for W! *Fuck* you people!"

She grimaces and strums her guitar.

"I already got my first hate mail. Maybe I need to build a *fucking* fence around my house. Install a *fucking* intercom at the gate. Get a big *fucking* dog. The hate letter ended with, 'Have a nice day.' He didn't mean that!"

The chuckles rise and die down again as she introduces the band: Mike Hardwick on lead guitar, Jeff Plankenhorn on guitar and mandolin, Glenn Fukunaga on bass, and son Cisco Ryder on drums. Later, they're joined by cellist Brian Standefer, but now, with a nod of her spiky blond head, the band slips into Greg Brown's "Sleeper." A spotlight hitting the high sheen on her acoustic guitar creates an animated reflection on the club wall, like foxfire darting about a dark forest.

Eliza Gilkyson wasn't born in a trunk, but she grew up close to the microphone. Her father Terry Gilkyson was a successful songwriter; his mother was a composer, too. Brother Tony Gilkyson of X is an in-demand guitarist, and sister Nancy was a vice-president at Warner Bros. Records for twenty years. Her son Cisco plays drums and percussion for her; he and her daughter Cordelia sing on the new album.

Back in her living room, Eliza Gilkyson sits forward from her comfortable position in the armchair, hands outstretched, reiterating her unhappiness with the war in Iraq and the state of the world.

"I'm inspired by people like Al Franken, Michael Moore. People who went on record a year ago when we were going to war and who were accused of being un-American, publicly threatened through letters and humiliated. I thought those people were so brave in going out against the war, using their right to free speech. I was so inspired that's what I want to do with my life now, with this record."

Gilkyson is well aware of the pitfalls of going on record with an anti-war position and that, like Marcia Ball, she might become a target on right-wing Web sites. She took great care that the social commentary on *Land of Milk and Honey* was balanced aesthetically. For Eliza, style was as crucial as substance.

"I didn't write some political rant and throw it out there," she explains. "I like it to be musically satisfying, so you don't just hear the lyric, you feel something. I think we did that with this record."

The fragile balance of life is ever present in her music, and she maintains that equilibrium fiercely. In talking about "Separated," from *Land of Milk and Honey*, she's adamant that the song is not as much about grieving for a breakup as it is about "being separate, the sense of feeling separated from everything—and everyone—around you."

When Eliza Gilkyson sings "Beauty Way" from *Hard Times in Babylon*, there's no doubting the veracity of her lyrics:

I felt the lights on the big, big stages,
the fire burning in my soul.
I've had those nights where my guitar rages.
It's not something you control, little darling.
It's not something you control.

Hard Times in Babylon came out in 2000, following a decade of intense growth. Her output in the Nineties crystallized on 1997's *Redemption Road* and '99's *Misfits*. The titles were prophetic, not just about her music.

The end of the Nineties brought an end to relationships and the death of her father. Redemption meant hard times for the misfit. It also meant a new level of expression. *Babylon*'s opener "Beauty Way" fit AAA radio like a dream; Gilkyson's voice was beginning to be heard, and it had something to say.

In 2002, she followed *Babylon* with *Lost and Found*, garnering even more critical kudos. She was looking for her place in the market and found it with songs like "Welcome Back," "Angel and Delilah," and "Easy Rider." *Lost and Found* was even more introspective than its predecessor, clearing the way for her to expand her musical vision. In "Riverside," the singer alluded to her dismay at the state of the world, more fully vocalized on *Land of Milk and Honey*.

Hard Times, *Lost and Found*, and *Land of Milk and Honey* were all produced by Mark Hallman, who owns the Congress House Studio in South Austin. The two have worked together for more than 20 years. It's a complex relationship, equal parts personal and professional.

"When you've walked a lot of miles with somebody and had experiences with them, it comes through in your art," says Gilkyson. "There's a depth, because you know each other really well. He knows when my vocal is right. He knows when to ask for more. I completely trust him."

Hallman is not surprised at Gilkyson's butterfly-like emergence.

"I knew how good this period would be before we recorded *Hard Times in Babylon*," he reveals. "I heard those songs at the Cactus, and I couldn't believe the difference. They were fantastic; she was jumping to another level. She had really arrived. I think the death of her father has a lot to do with those changes. She may not see it, but I see it as a catalyst for her finding out who she is. She's able to take her pain, her angst, her frustration, and put it in a way that cuts to the bone."

A way that sometimes leaves scars.

"Ballad of Yvonne Johnson," from *Land of Milk and Honey*, extracts an emotional price from Gilkyson. She breaks down in tears and sobs while talking about it, overcome by the inhumanity Johnson suffered. Gilkyson channels a memory of her own, a memory of rape committed on her. She knows the violation, the fear, and understands the coming-back process. In writing about Yvonne Johnson, Gilkyson battled her own nightmare and lived to write the tale.

"I started to feel like I can't just stand by [while] things that are really important to me are falling apart or being threatened. The demise of what so many of us have been dreaming of and working for most of our adult lives. And the music is really reflecting that." ◄

THE MEAT PURVEYORS
PAIN BY NUMBERS
BLOODSHOT

Breaking up is usually bad for bands. Luckily, the Meat Purveyors aren't like most bands. Calling it a day after Bloodshot let fly two platters of driving rural acoustics sutured with urban darkness, Austin's Meat Purveyors reformed, offering up 2002's gleeful *All Relationships Are Doomed to Fail*. With TMP's speed-freak strumfests, tear-in-my-40-ouncer ballads, and peculiar covers, some might tag *Pain by Numbers* as more of the same old shit. If so, this shit is as sweet as Tupelo honey, because the punkgrass outfit pulls it all together here—vocals dripping with unfettered abandon, slapping, picking, and fiddling with furlough-from-the-state-hospital urgency, and mando trills as quick-n-smooth as a neat glass of batch bourbon. More importantly, originals such as the title track stand tall with covers of Loretta Lynn, Fleetwood Mac, Dusty Springfield, and Johnny Paycheck. "I'd Rather Be Your Enemy," a left field cover of troubled experimentalist Boyd Rice, is even faster, and fun, like riding a runaway horse—bareback and naked. Thanks, gals and guys, for breaking up. And congrats on your best album yet. **DAVID LYNCH**

VOL. 23 NO. 48 ★ JULY 30, 2004

High Baptismal Flow In Search of Austin's 13th Floor Elevators, Music to Carry You to the Next Life

VOL. 23 NO. 50 ★ AUGUST 13, 2004

MARGARET MOSER

THE WORDS FLOATED into my dreamworld, twisting and sliding throughout eight ethereal minutes of the 13th Floor Elevators' "Slip Inside This House." I stared at the ceiling of my humid bedroom. The electric blue of the Indiglo clock said 3:20 am. I'd fallen asleep with *Easter Everywhere* on repeat and it haunted my sleep like the hapless student in H.P. Lovecraft's "The Dreams in the Witch-House."

The initial descent began benignly enough: an e-mail query from former Austinite Joe Trybyszewski asking if the *Chronicle* had any interest in an interview he'd done with Tommy Hall, lyricist and visionary of Texas' pioneering 13th Floor Elevators. The offer was tantalizing. As the primary creative source of the band, Hall and Elevators vocalist Roky Erickson rank in the highest order of songwriting teams in rock & roll history. Erickson's story is part of Austin lore, but the Elevators as a band are elusive. An interview with Hall could change that.

The Hall Q&A was indeed intriguing, yet the subject wanted more. Gathering sources and tracking information took nearly seven weeks of phone calls, phone interviews, e-mails, out-of-town trips, and repeated listening to music that has been in my consciousness for almost forty years. Trapped in the Elevators, with the lyrical promise of something better deep within, the effort was revelatory, exhilarating, and gratifying.

Here was a band that was conceptual before the term applied to the form, egalitarian in both thought and deed, and alternative in the truest sense of the word. And the irony, as Clementine Hall modestly puts it, is "the 13th Floor Elevators didn't even get to be mighty enough to fall."

KINGDOM OF HEAVEN

In 1966, Texas still had a black eye for being the scene of the Kennedy assassination three years earlier. The Lone Star State had no hip standing, certainly nothing to suggest it was the breeding ground for a musical revolution all its own. Buddy Holly was long dead, and even Doug Sahm's Sir Douglas Quintet had made their mark in the guise of mod longhairs from Britain. Yet, deep in the heart of Texas, something was happening, and no one knew it better than the 13th Floor Elevators.

The Elevators originated in 1965, incubated out of a confluence of ideas espoused by a University of Texas philosophy-turned-psychology major named Tommy Hall, who recognized the sonic power of rock & roll and its potential as a vehicle for change. Dylan had given songwriters permission to take the message of protest music and apply it to a nonprotest context that challenged the status quo. Hall sought to form a band capable of melding that style and substance.

"I wanted to do what Dylan was doing, playing rock music, but with serious lyrics," states Hall. "Everything I wrote was inspired through my taking LSD."

He found the musicians in two places. The first was the rhythm section of a cover band from the Texas Gulf Coast known as the Lingsmen. Bassist Benny Thurman, drummer John Ike Walton, and guitarist Stacy Sutherland all hailed from Central Texas but found playing beachside concession stands like the Dunes in Port Aransas to their liking.

Nevertheless, it took little convincing to lure them to Austin for something better.

Eighteen-year-old Roky Erickson was singing for a popular local group called the Spades. He'd written their marginally successful single, "You're Gonna Miss Me," which landed the band a regular gig at Austin's Jade Room, one of several hot nightspots of the day. Folk, blues, and rock were the prevalent sounds of the day as Kenneth Threadgill, John Clay, the Jets, and the Waller Creek Boys (featuring a young Janis Joplin and Powell St. John, who later wrote many Elevators songs) played around town.

Tommy Hall, struck by Erickson's charisma and blues-shouter vocals, invited him to join the unnamed band. Not much hesitation went into the decision. John Ike Walton remembers, "We went to Tommy's house. Tommy got Roky over and we were jamming. Next thing, we're playing at the Jade Room."

Though time has sanded specifics, it seems the band fell together easily, with one little hitch: Tommy Hall played no instrument. He was the band's guru and songwriter, along with Erickson, but the other members pushed him to participate musically. As a solution, he picked up the jug, an instrument popular with folksingers and hillbilly bands. "Electric jug" they dubbed the instrument, and born was the band's signature sound, a fey, fluttering noise that percolated through their electric call to arms. With Hall performing and an immediate local following, the Elevators had nowhere to go but up.

REVERBERATION

The Psychedelic Sounds of the 13th Floor Elevators exploded at the end of 1966. With "You're Gonna

Never say goodbye: Roky Erickson, 1974.
Photograph by Scott Newton.

In addition to "You're Gonna Miss Me," Erickson co-wrote four other tunes on the record ("Roller Coaster," "Don't Fall Down," "Reverberation (Doubt)," "Fire Engine"), as well as the ballad "Splash 1" with Clementine Hall, Tommy's wife. Hall and Sutherland composed "Tried to Hide" and "Thru the Rhythm," while Powell St. John, who soon joined Mother Earth, wrote "You Don't Know (How Young You Are)," "Kingdom of Heaven," and "Monkey Island." Austin artist John Cleveland designed the pyramid-and-eye album cover and adapted it into the logo on John Ike Walton's drums.

The album reverberated with a depth and lyrical meaning, appropriating the word "psychedelic" for a musical context. Hall's liner notes reflected his interest in the philosophical writings of Alfred Korzybski, Peter Ouspensky, and particularly G. I. Gurdjieff, famous for his "who am I?" musings.

The lyrics of Hall's songs also reflected his immersion in enlightened schools of thought, worlds apart from what was emanating out of the day's transistor radios. "You're Gonna Miss Me" went No. 2 in Austin, No. 1 in some California towns, and No. 56 nationally.

It's not enough to spin back Austin's clock to the mid-Sixties and say life was simple before the technological evolution. Nothing was simple in the middle of a cultural revolution that both united and divided the country. The space race was on, civil rights were being advanced, and feminism and gay rights were becoming social issues.

The lingering image of Texas as a state unfriendly to hippies wasn't far from the truth. Austin was no

Miss Me" as the opening salvo and cover art unlike any seen before, psychedelia was born. Stacy Sutherland's guitar launched the song with four-chord muscle that distinguishes it as one of the greatest tracks on a rock & roll album. Ever. John Ike Walton and Benny Thurman swept in on drums and bass, accompanied by Tommy Hall's jug producing the fluttery pulse that bewilders first-time Elevators listeners who say, "*What* is that *sound*!?" Then came Roky.

Roky Erickson's hellfire holler thunders on "You're Gonna Miss Me," a primal scream summoning shrieks and whoops adapted from the Little Richard tunes and R&B covers that were staples of the era. (An Elevators live recording from San Francisco's Avalon Ballroom that same year features covers of the Beatles, Solomon Burke, the Kinks, Chuck Berry, and Buddy Holly, all arranged with electric jug.) The song's two minutes and 31 seconds are electrifying even today; imagine the jolt of consciousness it was to the world in 1966.

less oppressive, with hippies often venturing out in numbers, for safety. Clementine Hall recalls seeing "Powell St. John bruised and beaten up, because some guy jumped out of a station wagon with a baseball bat and beat him up, just for walking down the street with long hair."

The Elevators found themselves a constant target of local law enforcement. Clementine Hall talks of "directional microphones on us, outside our house." The band was watched, taped, followed, and eventually busted repeatedly, and it made the news every time.

"They busted the Sir Douglas Quintet in San Antonio and us in Austin on the same night," remembers John Ike Walton. "It was on the news. My father saw me getting busted."

The band had been heavily into LSD and other methods of mind-expansion since their inception. Tommy Hall viewed acid as a tool and led the band through group trips, as both a bonding process and one of self-discovery. A growing number of youth across the U.S. and UK shared the band's search for meaning and enlightenment, but the nexus was the Left Coast's Bay area. Coincidentally, the vibrant youth scene there starred a number of Texpatriates, including Powell St. John, Doug Sahm, Janis Joplin, plus Dave Moriaty and Jack Jackson, who helped found Rip Off Press, and Chet Helms, who ran the Avalon.

Walton says the band "got out of Texas after the bust, went to California, and started writing stuff out there." The Elevators basked in their moment of glory, rubbing shoulders with their peers in Moby Grape and the Grateful Dead. They headlined shows at the Avalon and pursued enlightenment, but friction plagued the band in the form of drugs, particularly speed.

"One of the things that upset Tommy most was speed, amphetamines," states Clementine Hall. "I remember Stacy saying, 'But Tommy, I've never felt love being poured on me like when I take amphetamines.' Tommy would say it was evil, bad for you, and Stacy would say, 'But I need to escape to the place where

I am loved.' Benny liked speed for other reasons, not because he felt warm and mushy but because he could think faster and accomplish more.

"Tommy would say, 'The philosophy behind the righteous drugs is that they're drugs that have been used for centuries by Indians—peyote, mushrooms, marijuana, and by extension LSD. We don't use escape drugs, ever. We do not use pills or any addictive drugs. If you take them for pleasure, they become psychologically addictive. Nobody takes LSD for pleasure. It teaches you way too much about yourself.'"

Changes were happening within the 13th Floor Elevators by 1967. Ronnie Leatherman replaced Benny Thurman on bass. He and John Ike Walton stayed with the band long enough to record "She Lives (In a Time of Her Own)" and "I've Got Levitation," but neither was happy with the band's direction.

"Tommy's philosophical approach became offensive to John Ike and Ronnie," says Walton's replacement Danny Thomas. "They wanted to keep playing music as journeymen musicians, like they did in the early days of the California trip when they made such a big hit at the Avalon and Fillmore."

The band's Houston label, International Artists, called them back from California and wanted them to begin work on a new album. In the midst of the Summer of Love, John Ike Walton and Ronnie Leatherman left the 13th Floor Elevators.

EASTER EVERYWHERE

Thirty-seven years after its release, *Easter Everywhere* remains the 13th Floor Elevators' most completely realized effort. *Psychedelic Sounds* was the bellwether of things to come, but *Easter Everywhere* was a stunning and revelatory work, as slyly conceptual as anything that came after it.

In contrast to what psychedelia was coming out of and turning into—standard blues-rock with lengthy guitar solos and special effects—*Easter Everywhere* rose as a seamless mix of rock with Middle Eastern elements and, of course, the ever-mesmerizing electric jug. "Slip Inside This House" remains a musical wonderment, carried by Tommy Hall's metaphysical lyrics and Roky Erickson's hypnotic chant-vocals, sung with a messiah's conviction.

Drummer Danny Thomas, a North Carolina native attending Trinity University, and fellow San Antonian bassist Danny Galindo were players steeped in Southern R&B. In the same way the Lingsmen plugged in as the rhythm section behind the creative leads of Tommy Hall and Roky Erickson, Galindo and Thomas made the transition from the already-recorded "She Lives (In a Time of Her Own)" and "I've Got Levitation" to eight other songs that comprised *Easter Everywhere*.

Thomas' glistening percussion and Galindo's weighty bass gave the Elevators a fuller, weightier sound on *Easter Everywhere*. Powell St. John's ethereal "Slide Machine" and Bob Dylan's "It's All Over Now, Baby Blue" were the only nonband songs included; Hall, Erickson, and Sutherland, meanwhile, had hit their strides in various combination. Clementine Hall was brought in to duet with Roky on "I Had to Tell You," their harmonies charmingly naive. The result was amazing to all.

"Five of us in a new lineup, so we looked at each other perplexed, wondering what the others would have to put on the table and how the mix would work," recalls Thomas. "It was a big challenge. Frank Davis and Lelan Rogers [*Easter Everywhere* recording engineer and producer, respectively] were able to synthesize it rather than leave the band in fragments. Things would get pretty jagged on occasion, and they would make sure things got resolved, mostly between Tommy, Roky, and Stacy.

"It was an evolving process, each one was pulling in a different direction because each had a different skill and different styles. Lelan put his weight behind making sure that Tommy's direction was the direction

13 SIXTIES TEXAS BANDS YOU DON'T REMEMBER

1. The Sparkles
2. Virgil Foxx
3. Electric Rubayyat
4. The Outcasts
5. Sweet Smoke
6. Lemon Rhinestone
7. Water Brothers
8. Midnight Riders
9. Knight's Bridge
10. Endle St. Cloud
11. Lost & Found
12. Fever Tree
13. Liberty Bell

13 MID-SIXTIES TEXAS 45S

1. "I Fought the Law," Bobby Fuller 4
2. "The Rains Came," Sir Douglas Quintet
3. "Woolly Bully," Sam the Sham & the Pharaohs
4. "Western Union," Five Americans
5. "Hot Smoke & Sassafras," Bubble Puppy
6. "Splash 1," the Clique
7. "Bottle of Wine," the Fireballs
8. "I Have Thoughts of You," Neal Ford & the Fanatics
9. "I Never Cared for You," Homer
10. "1 to 3," the Conqueroo
11. "So Many Times," Sweetarts
12. "Face to Face," Zakary Thaks
13. "Nighttime," the Chayns

VOL. 24 NO. 50 ★ AUGUST 12, 2005

the band was taking. That's part of what made Roky disillusioned with the project.

"Roky was a really good rock & roll frontman, who would've been satisfied to let the philosophical message go in order to just rock out. But Tommy insisted we use this vehicle. We had gotten attention with 'You're Gonna Miss Me,' and Tommy thought we should use our high visibility to answer questions our generation was asking. Lelan saw the wisdom in that.

"Most of *Easter Everywhere* was Tommy's lyrics, in conjunction with Roky. Tommy and Roky roomed together, so there was a lot of collaboration. Tommy would write lyrics as poetry first. And we would have pasteboard boxes full of loose-leaf paper. He'd present them to Roky, who'd do his best to come up with a basic arrangement to fit the meter.

"Roky would make suggestions about changing the lyrics and then it would be presented to us, the rhythm section—Stacy, Danny, and Danny. And it would go through more refinement. Once we had the chord changes, we knew what the style of the song would be, and we'd go about arranging it.

"It was a collaborative process—there wasn't a single lyric Tommy didn't run past the band, 'Are you comfortable with this? If not, tell me.' And sometimes they would be four, five, six months in revision before they got recorded. He's a fantastic person."

SLIP INSIDE THIS HOUSE

The final recordings made by the 13th Floor Elevators were *Live* and *Bull of the Woods*. The former LP is little more than a collection of studio tracks with an audience dubbed in, but *Bull* is a notable effort that stands on its own.

Roky Erickson's deterioration was such that his contribution to *Bull* is limited, while Hall's spiritual participation also diminished. After repeated busts and harassment, the 13th Floor Elevators' direction was clouded and unclear, yet Stacy Sutherland stepped forward as a formidable and underrated talent in the band. He'd been writing and co-writing songs for the band since *Psychedelic Sounds*, and his guitar playing developed a distinctive crystal jangle style. *Bull* stands as Sutherland's legacy to the band whose sound he was crucial in creating.

What happened to Roky Erickson, who declined comment for this story through his younger brother Sumner Erickson, is well-documented. After several busts and hospitalizations in the late Sixties, he began a slow decline into undiagnosed schizophrenia marked by periods of remarkable recordings, including the immortal "Two-Headed Dog" b/w "Starry Eyes" single of the mid-Seventies. Bad health and illness kept him reclusive until the recent intervention of Sumner. Under his brother's care and with proper medical attention, Roky has made an impressive recovery, attending shows, making public appearances, and getting his driver's license.

Reminded that Tommy Hall, now living in San Francisco, doesn't want to talk about music or the Elevators, but insists on talking philosophy instead, Thomas defends his bandmate.

"Philosophy *is* Elevators stuff," stresses Thomas. "That's the way he was then, he's still the same. He's not a musician. Never has been. He feels terrible about it, and he hates it when we remind him of it."

In the end, the secret of the 13th Floor Elevators is the all-seeing eye of the pyramid, the invitation to slip inside the cosmic house and open your mind. Corny? Perhaps. Yet, the original power of rock & roll lay in its promise to carry the listener to places unknown, music to carry you to the next world. It was a powerful message then, and it remains powerful.

"And anytime I get the chance to espouse the message of that generation," Thomas swears, "I take it." ◀

POR VIDA ALL-STAR TRIBUTE CONCERT

PARAMOUNT THEATRE, NOV. 4

Wrapping at the four-hour mark, half-past midnight on Thursday, the all-star Alejandro Escovedo tribute concert played out just as its primary organizer Heinz Geissler had hoped. "Like *The Last Waltz*," Escovedo's manager said last month at the Austin icon's triumphant return to local stages after a two-year layoff due to hepatitis C. "Not literally, of course," Geissler quickly corrected himself, but the Band's last hurrah at the Fillmore in 1976 proved an apt analogy nonetheless. True, the Por Vida guest celebrants weren't quite as Mount Rushmore as the Band's (Bob Dylan, Muddy Waters, Neil Young, Van Morrison), but then those fellows probably never experienced Escovedo's marching guitar army, the True Believers. Or Rank and File, the Nuns, and most importantly, Escovedo's solo act of musical self-immolation. If they had, said stone faces might have moved mountains like Velvet Underground founder John Cale opening this night with a trio of commandments. Opener "Look Horizon" sounded Carnegie Hall, regal, Cale's clanging piano pushing his bottomless voice. "We've got four more years," announced Cale, "and this song's good advice." With that, he summoned "Fear" ("a man's best friend") as if Tuesday's electoral tragedy was 9/11 all over again. Electrifying. The String Quartet backed the glowing guest of honor on a song, one of only three numbers Escovedo performed on all night, then strung up his "Crooked Frame" with wily instrumentalism. Ruben Ramos, backed by the show's music director/glue, Charlie Sexton, gave the same tremulous interpretation of "13 Years" as that on the *Por Vida* album, followed by a pair of Latin ballads with his own band that brought the rooster cries from the Paramount's rafters. Los Lonely Boys' slow, thick chug through Escovedo's "Castanets" shook out better than on disc, Henry Garza's midsong atmospherics all too brief, while their own "Heaven" had the audience down front on their feet. Calexico's *Por Vida* tune, "Wave," plus their Sergio Leone–like "Crystal Frontier," blinked off the intermission, after which proceedings moved swifter with acts on for two songs then gone. Like Sexton, Davíd Garza's musical support throughout the evening, on acoustic guitar and backing vocals, was subtle but invaluable. Nick Tremulis' buoyant Calypso through Escovedo's KGSR smash "Velvet Guitar" gave way to Butch Hancock ("Everybody Loves Me"), Jon Dee Graham ("Helpless"), and Tres Chicas ("By Eleven," "Rhapsody"), all of whom provided strong, and in the case of the Flatlander (Townes Van Zandt's "No Place to Fall"), inspired lead-in to rock & roll scholar, author, and Patti Smith axe-grinder Lenny Kaye, whose street hustle on Escovedo's "Sacramento & Polk" ripped into "Sister Ray" territory. A song he wrote on the plane ride down, "Stuff You Leave Behind," romped like a Woodstock-era campfire classic. That left Escovedo's niece, Sheila E. (her father Pete Escovedo was a no-show), and her Keith Moon finale on "Ballad of the Sun and Moon," graced by her "favorite uncle." Said patriarch demonstrated that favor by polishing off the evening with a six-guitar plow (Sexton, Graham, Tremulis, Garza, Kaye) through his own *Por Vida* capper, "Break This Time." **RAOUL HERNANDEZ**

VOL. 24 NO. 11 ★ NOVEMBER 12, 2004

Mighty Fine
Jesse Dayton, "Country Soul Brother" No. 1

VOL. 24 NO. 17 ★ DECEMBER 24, 2004

CHRISTOPHER GRAY

Jesse Dayton, 2004. Photograph by Todd Wolfson.

WITHOUT EVEN REALIZING IT, most people have a stock word or phrase they use to punctuate conversational pauses. With Jesse Dayton, over a Lone Star at Ego's, there's a "know what I mean?" nearly every other sentence. Of course, at no point during the conversation is his meaning anything less than clear. Quite the opposite.

Dayton's fourth album, *Country Soul Brother*, came out three weeks ago on Stag Records, the label he co-owns with his manager. "I'm waiting for somebody to slam me, so I know I did something different and cool," he says, smiling but not joking. "You gotta piss somebody off. If you don't piss off the traditionalists, you're not doing anything new and exciting."

It's hard to piss people off when your album sounds like a near-flawless fusion of Jones boys George and Tom. Now 35, Dayton hasn't worked as anything but a musician in a decade, and he's worked his East Texas ass off. His perpetual touring has won over crowds waiting to see Social Distortion and X, and fostered devoted followings on the West Coast and in the Midwest. His raw talent so impressed Doug Sahm he recruited Flaco Jimenez and the West Side Horns to join him on Dayton's 1995 debut, *Raisin' Cain*. Dayton and Sir Douglas also shared an acquaintance with infamous Gulf Coast mogul Huey P. Meaux and a mutual passion for the national pastime.

"I got to go to a game with him and Clifford Antone in the Astrodome," says self-professed baseball nut Dayton, who has since sung the national anthem at then Enron Field, now Minute Maid Park. "It was awesome. I just listened to him and Clifford talk about stats the whole time."

The other, most important thing Dayton and Sahm have in common is an innate understanding that the divisions between country and R&B, rock and soul, Cajun and conjunto, or any sort of indigenous Texas music are negligible. *Country Soul Brother*'s title track trades off between banjo and B-3. "Moravia" transplants Memphis rockabilly to the Rio Grande Valley. The cocksure "Tall Walkin' Texas Trash" outfits punk rock swagger in Wranglers and a pearl-snap shirt. "All Because of You" weaves Cajun accordion around honky-tonk steel. Full-bodied horn charts on "It Won't Always Be Like This" and "Just to Get You off My Mind" establish a direct line to swampy regional legends Cookie & the Cupcakes, who hailed from just across the Louisiana line from Dayton's old stomping grounds.

"I didn't grow up on just country music," he explains. "I listened to a lot of black music as a kid. I would just as soon listen to Otis Redding as George Jones. I think they're both the same. It bums me out when people don't get that. I want them to take the stick out of their ass and loosen up a little bit."

Dayton is as proud as he can be of his Golden Triangle roots, which are intertwined with some of the area's other prominent musical figures. His dad went to high school with George Jones. He met Clifford Antone when the Port Arthur–raised nightclub impresario gave the 17-year-old five records from the trunk of his Lincoln Continental. Dayton's first real gig was at the Old Beaumont Cafe in downtown Beaumont, opening for Paul Ray's Cobras featuring Angela Strehli and Stevie Ray Vaughan. "My mouth was on the ground," he recalls. He was the only student at Beaumont Charlton Pollard High (BCP to locals) driving over to Houston to see the Clash. Before he graduated, he was taking gigs wherever he could get them, and has been ever since.

"If you're banging your head against the wall and not making any money doing your art, yeah, maybe you should get a day job and quit," Dayton says. "But I haven't had that problem yet. I guess what I'm saying is, for all the people out there in Texas that are thinking for themselves, I'm your guy. I'm the guy you want to go see."

Know what you mean, brother. ◂

BANJO & SULLIVAN
THE ULTIMATE COLLECTION 1972–1978
HIP-O

Beatlemaniacs have the Rutles, headbangers have Spinal Tap, and now sister-screwing NASCAR fans have Banjo & Sullivan. Straddling—and I do mean straddling—the fine line between parody and tribute, B&S's *Ultimate Collection* is X-rated twang so lasciviously convincing it hardly matters that the duo never actually existed. For the record, they're pickin' and singin' lambs to the slaughter in Rob Zombie's new movie *The Devil's Rejects,* voiced on LP by Austin's Jesse Dayton and a crew of local session ringers. It amounts to Dayton's last album, 2004's *Country Soul Brother,* filtered through the average issue of *Hustler,* or a peep show into B&S's tawdry, albeit fictional, existence. "Dick Soup" documents their tendency to get booked at male-only venues, "Honeymoon Song" details a smorgasbord of S&M far removed from regular "country boy sex," and "I'm at Home Getting Hammered (While She's Out Getting Nailed)" examines differing interpretations of trailer-park nuptials. So while the Dukes of Hazzard may be the hot hillbillies du jour, Banjo & Sullivan are worth a yee-haw or three—and a nice long shower afterward.

CHRISTOPHER GRAY

VOL. 25 NO. 1 ★ SEPTEMBER 2, 2005

CAROLYN WONDERLAND

SAXON PUB, JAN. 13

With a Groucho-esque waggle of her slender brows, Carolyn Wonderland tossed the red mane of hair matching her Les Paul and looked over her rhinestone guitar strap. Smiling to her band through a curl of cigarette smoke, she nodded her head as they slipped into comfortable blues rock. "I've been standing still for hours," she sang plaintively, but those are just words. Carolyn Wonderland has done anything but stand still since leaving Houston, with a passel of awards and enough critical acclaim to load a semi, and moving to Austin, where her profile is considerably lower. That might be partly by choice, for Wonderland is said to have put down the bottle and focused on her music. At the Saxon, she was in high spirits with a bottle of water and a hold on her music that was joyous to hear. She talked in wry sentences about the songs, revealing little of herself and no mention of Bob Dylan, who invited her to jam with him not long ago. When she blisters the guitar and cocks her head fetchingly to sing her songs like "I'm Innocent," she stands in the good company of Sue Foley, Debbie Davies, and Bonnie Raitt. But when she whistles, as she does with disarming ease on another of her compositions "I'm the Man," or picks up the trumpet, she's one of a kind. It's partly her voice, coming from some place dark and painful when singing Bo Diddley's "I Can Tell." It's partly the band groove of Cole El-Saleh, Jon Blondell, Scott Daniels, and Charlie Prichard. And it's partly just her sinewy presence. "This is the title track from my CD *Bloodless Revolution*," she leaned into the mic and announced her last song of the night. And with no chains and only guitar muscle, Carolyn Wonderland released her captive audience.

MARGARET MOSER

VOL. 24 NO. 21 ★ JANUARY 21, 2005

When I'm 64
The Road No Longer Beckons, but Austin Does

VOL. 24 NO. 23 ★ FEBRUARY 4, 2005

MARGARET MOSER

IN HIS NEAT APARTMENT on South Congress, Joe Willie "Pinetop" Perkins sits in an easy chair with two fishing poles propped in the corner behind him.

"I'm deef," he says, pronouncing the word like "reef," tugging on his right ear, and cocking his good left ear toward the speaker. That limits interview conversation with him to a great extent.

A mahogany end table stands before him, on it a silver ashtray, and Perkins' ever-present, well-shuffled deck of cards. On the wall leans a black upright piano lined with awards and plaques honoring his 91 years on Earth. Being in the presence of genuine blues royalty is an awe-inspiring experience, especially when he offers little nuggets from his past without prompting.

"I played with Muddy Waters eleven long years. I got along with him pretty good until he got a booking agent who started taking all the boys' money. The whole band quit."

Perkins pushes himself out of the easy chair and walks a few steps to the piano. His fingers are unusually long and exceedingly tapered, with perfect oval nails the color of sliced almonds. They dance across the ivory keys with a little less deftness than before, but the notes are solid and resound in the small apartment and out the sliding glass door, opened on this unseasonably warm day. He begins to play a rollicking blues number and accompanies himself singing.

"I like that," he tells himself. "Mmm hmm."

Pinetop Perkins, 2008. Photograph by Todd Wolfson.

One of Perkins' trademarks is his hat. A collection of them lines the wall above his piano and follows around the corner to the next wall. Fedoras, dress hats, even a Stetson.

"People give me the hats," he explains, waving a hand in their direction. "I buy them. Women give them to me."

He chuckles at his last sentence.

"I've traveled to places I can't recall the names of—here, there, overseas. My favorites are the ones where I make the most money."

That last comment is qualified by the travel he does these days in his own honor. He played Washington, D.C.'s Lincoln Center last month and will receive a Lifetime Achievement Award from the Grammys in addition to being up for an award. Ironically, he's competing with fellow Austinite James Cotton.

"He got paid $10,000 to play for Jimmy Carter at the White House once," laughs Perkins' de facto interpreter, Clifford Antone. "He liked that!"

The pianist's days are spent resting comfortably. The television is always on for company. The constant presence of friends like Antone and a caregiver means he has someone to watch over him. He settles back into his chair and reaches for the deck of cards.

"I play cards. I like to go fishing and play blues, but I don't do it on the Lord's day. It made people happy, but I hope the Lord will forgive me."

The Lord should forgive him. Perkins refined and carries on a boogie-woogie sound as informed by barrelhouse piano as gospel, having performed with musical greats including Waters, Robert Nighthawk, Earl Hooker, and B.B. King. Life takes on a completely new meaning when the future is here and now, and tomorrow is a question mark. When friends and family are gone, and time plays mean tricks with hearing and slows the fingers maddeningly, Pinetop Perkins has the answer.

"Turn the music up a little louder." ◀

THE CRACK PIPES
BEAUTY SCHOOL
EMPEROR JONES

While the gristly heart of the Crack Pipes' sound still beats out a liberating testimonial of chicken scratch boogie punk, *Beauty School* finds the veteran Austin quartet trying on a slew of additional idioms as well. The Pipes' fourth LP kicks off with the shuffling, country blues title track, which transforms into electric, harp-fueled mayhem midway through. In the church of vocalizing Right Rev. Ray Pride, "Beauty School" is where the Almighty power washes sinners of earthly hang-ups and lets love flow unimpeded. You can hear the love start gushing in the garage soul grooves of "Sexy Pepsy" and "Make-Out Party," while "Let My Heart (Rest in Peace)" breaks it down like James Brown at the Apollo circa 1962. The cinematic warble of "East Side Injections" and the elegiac dirge of "I Was So Worried About You" reveal the Pipes' penchant for overcast experimentalism. The dark mood continues through "Greensboro," a blues-based account of the 1979 Greensboro Massacre. Finally, the exquisitely stringed reprisal of the title track, arranged by Chris Black, delivers us back to the light. *Beauty*, indeed. GREG BEETS

> VOL. 24 NO. 34 ★ APRIL 22, 2005

The Crack Pipes, 2005. Photograph by Mary Sledd.

SPOON
GIMME FICTION
MERGE

Like no less than Wilco, Spoon has yet to release a mediocre album. Where 2001's Merge debut, *Girls Can Tell*, stripped Spoon's jagged edge down to its bassline, follow-up *Kill the Moonlight* reapplied a subtle layer of ornamentation while elongating the groove. Like Wilco's *Yankee Hotel Foxtrot* into *A Ghost Is Born*, Spoon's fifth full-length finds further symbiosis between Britt Daniel's emotional obfuscation and the band's spare, uptown backbeat, then looses drummer Jim Eno to metronome the rest. Five of *Gimme Fiction*'s first six tracks, on which Daniel steps outside his constricted romantic obsessions and into those of "The Two Sides of Monsieur Valentine" and "Sister Jack," all but erase the memory of previous Spoon compositions. Deliberate, demanding, and distorted opener "The Beast and Dragon, Adored" might just embody *t-h-e* ultimate Spoonful. The Scissor Sisters would mortgage their falsies for Daniel's "I Turn My Camera On," with its disco falsetto, while the cinematic drama of "My Mathematical Mind" and its sonic rough-up feels like a song that had been waiting to be born into the rock canon. Similarly rumbling, "The Infinite Pet" piano is more pronounced, swaggering, as are the twisted, knobby knees of "Was It You?" standing out from *Fiction*'s back-end beatific headphones delight. Gimme shelter, gimme gimme shock treatment. *Gimme Fiction*. **RAOUL HERNANDEZ**

VOL. 24 NO. 37 ★ MAY 13, 2005

Ribbon on the Highway The Other Side of Jimmy LaFave

VOL. 24 NO. 36 ★ MAY 6, 2005

DAVE MARSH

HERE COMES JIMMY LAFAVE. Maybe he's walking onstage to sing or slipping into the back of the Cactus Cafe to hear an old friend. Maybe he's walking up your driveway. The setting makes no difference. He's Jimmy LaFave wherever he goes.

He's about five ten, neither slender nor chunky. Wears a chambray work shirt over a T-shirt and jeans. A blue beret tops him. He doesn't wear it like a French intellectual. He wears it the way UN peacekeepers or Green Berets wear theirs. Either way, that cap's not gonna budge. On his face, a goatee and a slight grin. His sideburns are long, and a little dirty-blond hair peaks out from under the beret. A pendant bearing the image of a bison hangs around his neck.

You'd expect to find boots on his feet, but he's almost always wearing sneakers. LaFave greets just about everything in life with immense casualness. He looks like a truck driver, the kind of guy who might take on some impossible task: Get these oil rig parts from Stillwater to some place up in Montana and do it by tomorrow night, no matter how often you have to leave the highway and go cross-country. He looks like the kind of guy who'd make it on time too, Lynyrd Skynyrd or AC/DC blasting all the way, wisecracking cynically at the truck stops where he flirts with just enough intensity and manners to have all the waitresses primping when they see him walking in from the parking lot.

LaFave can get to the heart of ballads because he has such a magnificent sense of time.

Jimmy LaFave used to have that job, driving for his father, who was a parts supplier, first based in Wills Point ("that's in Van Zandt County," the singer points out), then in Stillwater, Okla., where his family relocated. LaFave's still got a long-hauler's instinct for wisecracks, though since getting married, the flirting's toned way down. Driving is part of what defines him. He says he does a lot of his best writing out there, picking up images from road signs, for instance, because he once heard Bob Dylan did that.

EMOTIONALLY YOURS

Here's the catch. There's this other Jimmy LaFave. That cynical exterior masks a remarkable degree of empathy and good taste.

This LaFave pops out of that carefully maintained dishevelment when called upon by the master of his fate, who is, to an amazing extent, Jimmy LaFave himself. When a friend needs a boost, LaFave turns on his warmth, not necessarily charm, just plain and powerful empathy. All his friends say something similar to Bob Childers, LaFave's songwriting mentor: "Jimmy's a really sensitive guy, but he spends a whole lot of time making sure nobody knows it."

"Singing is very emotional," allows LaFave. "You get obsessed with a lot of stuff. There's a sense of loneliness you have as an artist. That's why I close my eyes when I sing, because I like to go somewhere and find that place in everybody."

LaFave's notoriously generous with other performers, especially up-and-comers. He's had a hand in some significant careers—Abra Moore and Michael Fracasso come to mind—beginning locally by co-hosting open mics with Betty Elders at the long-departed Chicago House on Sixth Street, which uncovered a lot of talent, including Todd Snider.

For the past couple of years, he's led the Woody Guthrie roadshow (Ribbon of Highway, Endless Skyway), whose cast includes Childers in the role of narrator (inevitable given his quintessential Okie accent), locals Fracasso, Eliza Gilkyson, and Slaid Cleaves, as well as Sarah Lee Guthrie and Johnny Irion, Joel Rafael, Ray Bonneville, and the Burns Sisters.

Together with Nora Guthrie and Val Denn, LaFave put together the show, based entirely on songs and writings by Woody. He makes no star turn, ensuring the show isn't about anybody but its subject, an atmosphere that creates the sort of musical community Guthrie loved, onstage and off. LaFave is currently completing production on a Ribbon of Highway album, a live set culled from 45 to 50 hours of recordings.

Empathy is why, even though LaFave pens most of the songs on his albums, he's best known as an interpreter of other people's material. He's one of the few contemporary singer-songwriters who work covers into their sets because they belong there—because he loves them and they're well-suited to his singular voice. He's got a gritty midrange, a thrilling ability to hit high notes, phrasing so adept that he can sing quasi-art songs like Jimmy Webb's "The Moon's a Harsh Mistress" as easily as "Oklahoma Hills" or "Have You Ever Loved a Woman." His is a pronounced vibrato, uncontrolled, but he can still shake a note 'til it almost breaks.

His forte is ballads; there's no other singer in Austin, or Americana, who can do as much with a ballad, whether written by him or someone else. His version of "On a Bus to St. Cloud" caused its writer, Gretchen Peters, to say that although she knew it was her best song, she hadn't understood it completely until she heard LaFave sing it. The version on his 2001 LP, *Texoma*, revels in phrasing so legato you can't tell if he

Jimmy LaFave, 2005. Photograph by Todd Wolfson.

really intends to come in behind the guitar. He luxuriates in the space created by the song's rhythms, even
while recounting a tale bounded by madness and
suicide.

LaFave can get to the heart of ballads because he
has such a magnificent sense of time. He commands
the stillness between phrases even more than the lyrics themselves, which makes it seem as if every line
is being uttered for the first time, after due consideration and from a place deep inside.

Maybe that's what makes him such a fine interpreter of Dylan songs, having recorded eighteen
(by my count) since his 1992 debut, *Austin Skyline*,
including "Positively 4th Street," "Emotionally Yours,"
"Girl from the North Country," and "Buckets of Rain."
He hasn't just run through them, either. No one, not a
single singer, has ever sung Dylan with as much grace

and insight as Jimmy LaFave. There was a haunting
night at the Cactus Cafe a few years ago, when he
dedicated a song to a close friend who had just suffered a genuinely tragic loss of a loved one. He sang
"Emotionally Yours" as if it were his best friend who'd
been killed, and he sang it not only without flaw but
from deep, deep inside what the words mean. Sitting
there in the dark, you could forgive yourself for thinking it was the first time anyone at all had sung those
words to that melody.

IT TAKES A TRAIN

Blue Nightfall, his first new album in four years, came
out this spring on Red House, the Minnesota-based
label whose roster counts veteran singer-songwriters
Eliza Gilkyson, Greg Brown, John McCutcheon, and Guy

Davis. It's his seventh album, but the first on anything that might be described as a real label. More than ever, this other LaFave can be heard in the songs on *Blue Nightfall*, all but one of which is an original.

"Don't want to get out of this car, I just want to drive and drive," he sings in the opening lines of the title track, then goes for it all: "Into the fading light, and pretend I'm alive." With spare accompaniment by keyboardist Radoslav Lorkovic and a pulse rather than a beat, LaFave comes to territory mined by Bruce Springsteen and Patty Griffin and stands shoulder to shoulder with them, largely because, like them, he's as devoted to performance as to writing.

The gain can be attributed to that four-year layoff, or more precisely, to the events that resulted in it. They began while LaFave was still touring behind *Texoma*. Barb Fox was pregnant, and she and Jimmy decided to get married. (He'd had a brief first marriage back in Stillwater.) But the same squeamishness that made him a vegetarian made Jimmy jumpy about being present for the child's birth. So he was in Montreal when Fox bore their son, Jackson, on May 12, 2002.

Jackson clearly changed his father's life, and in every way, the change was positive. LaFave kept working, but he only went out for a week or two, occasionally three, not the long rambling stints he did before his son was born. He wanted to be home for those first few years. He wasn't in any hurry to make an album: "I did what I always do, make an album when I have twelve good songs and I'm ready." One more crucial thing happened: His mother was diagnosed with cancer.

When Bob Childers wrote "Elvis Loved His Momma," he tapped into one of the secret truths of rock & roll:

They're *all* mamas' boys, from Elvis to the Beatles. LaFave fits the mold, and he has more reason than most. His mother led gospel gatherings up until just before her death. She bought Jimmy his first guitar using green stamps. When she was entering the final phase of illness, he didn't waste any time.

"I got Jackson and put him in the car and we just drove straight through to Stillwater. I was just in time. I got to spend a day or two there, and I got to play her my version of 'Revival.' She loved it when I sang that song in my shows, and it was so important to play the record for her."

She passed away in her sleep a day or two later, but her absence can be felt in any number of songs on *Blue Nightfall*. The most notable is again "Rain Falling Down." If the first two-thirds of the song are about a parent filled with joy at first sight of his child, the last verse comes from the grownup child who's dreading the big hurt about to come. The unifier is heartbreak.

In uniting those two halves—the child and the man, let's say—Jimmy LaFave steps forward as a much more complete artist. He's always had talent and never lacked for vision, but his songs now reflect a sense of purpose that hasn't been there before.

Jimmy LaFave never went out of his way for stardom. From the beginning, he's been concerned with self-expression and integrity. This goes to the heart of his self-confidence. He's always felt that being the best version of himself was plenty. So he says, with pleasure and not a hint of sarcasm, "I lead a pretty good life." A beat. "I don't sleep on people's couches anymore."

There will always be two Jimmy LaFaves. It's as natural as needing to laugh as well as cry. ◂

Whut It Dew
Mixtape Mechanic DJ Rapid Ric

VOL. 24 NO. 38 ★ MAY 20, 2005

ROBERT GABRIEL

DUBBED THE MIXTAPE MECHANIC, Austin's DJ Rapid Ric is building a lengthy lead out in front of the premier purveyors of impeccably blended mix discs. His latest effort, *Whut It Dew 2*, is hosted by Texas hip-hop legend Bun B of UGK and features a litany of exclusives from a Texas rap scene so absolutely scorching that reporters from MTV and *The New York Times* have been leaning far, far back in a southwestern direction to absorb the heat.

Drawing from a pool of artists that includes Slim Thug, Paul Wall, Mike Jones, Chamillionaire, Z-Ro, and Austin favorite Bavu Blakes, Ric's forte is mixing seemingly divergent individuals into a cohesive team working toward a common goal. As resident mixer on KDHT Hot 93.3, Ric recognizes his position as an influential opinion leader.

"I feel obligated to help aspiring rappers from my region," nods Ric. "That's something I learned from DJ Screw. Having skills on the tables is one thing, but providing opportunities for the people around you, that should always be the top priority."

Growing up in Del Rio, Ric Almeda cut his teeth spinning at a club his best friend's father owned just across the border in Ciudad Acuña. He played Jay-Z and Outkast for local high school kids and West Texas college students, which led the young DJ into the sound design of mix tapes.

"In clubs, people are more interested in getting drunk and hooking up than they are in music," he

The mixtape mechanic DJ Rapid Ric. Photograph by Aubrey Edwards.

explains. "But with a mix tape, people are taking a piece of you home with them. That leaves no room for mistakes. Since there were no radio stations in the area playing rap music and we spent so much time in our cars, mix tapes became an important vehicle for what was hot.

"Where I'm from, the whole society is based on drugs. It's like the ghetto in South Houston in that there's no hope. Either you sell drugs or you're out of the loop. As a result, way too many people I grew up with wound up missing or dead. My own father has been in a Mexican jail since I was in fifth grade. The irony of it all is that many of the Norteño artists that are hugely popular in Del Rio are telling the same sort of stories that gangsta rappers like N.W.A. tell. Los Tigres del Norte have so much in common with hip-hop. They just happen to be fat, 40-year-old Mexican guys."

Relocating to Austin in 1999, Ric augmented his studies at UT with a free-fall into the local DJ fraternity. Along with an internship at KQBT the Beat 104.3 and scattered gigs on Sixth Street, the enterprising strategist worked on refining his mix tape repertoire.

"A lot of mix tapes don't have any real mixing on them, just a bunch of shouting by the DJ host. It really stood out to me at the time that [Austin's] NickNack was doing his *Bside Blends* series, which made me want to do the same sort of thing except with strictly Southern music."

Zeroing in on local artists including Bavu Blakes, Dok Holiday, Basswood Lane, Mirage, and Smackola, Ric's *Austin Powers* mix CD eventually landed in the hands of Paul Wall of Houston's seminal hip-hop imprint, Swishahouse. Eager to help Ric with access to the H-town scene, Wall recognized the Mixtape Mechanic as just that.

"He's a phenomenal DJ, one of my personal favorites," enthuses Wall. "His song selection, remixes, cuts, and scratches are off the hook."

Chamillionaire, with ink still on his fingers from a lucrative signing to Universal Records, reiterates the accolades. "Rapid Ric is one of the fastest rising DJs in the South right now, and it's mostly because of the skill he brings to his art form."

The ability to land unreleased tracks and one-of-a-kind freestyles from the depths of the uncharted seas of the Houston rap scene certainly helps. Then there's that extra disc you'll often find in a Rapid Ric jewel case, which sports the "Chopped Up Not Slopped Up" duplicate of the cover mix courtesy of yet another Swishahouse stalwart OG Ron C. The ideal promotional tool, Ric likens mix tapes to movie trailers. *Whut It Dew 2*, for instance, transports hits like the Game's "Dreams" and T.I.'s "Motivation" into Texas territory by stacking drawled verses from Killa Kyleon, Bun B, and Gritboys over their tweaked instrumentals.

Nestled up closer to the roots of hip-hop adventure than its counterpart the LP, mix tape CDs might just be the avant-garde faction of contemporary rap.

"Look how Jimi Hendrix made what was at first considered weird music only to have it widely appreciated later," quips Ric. "Well, for those who are now sleeping on all of this incredible Texas music just because it's being presented by way of an alternative format, here's to someday having them all come around." ◀

TEE DOUBLE, THE LONE STAR L.P.

MUMBO JUMBO

"I rep my city like an elected official," pronounces Tee Double, re-emerging from Austin's hip-hop underground with his most accomplished work yet. His tenth album over the course of a decade, *The Lone Star L.P.* steers clear of stereotypical expectations with the declaration, "This isn't that same old Southern image. I got my own sound, no need for us to mimic." Emphasis on sped-up vocal hooks and whispered punch lines point to Tee Double shadowing the style of Chicago's Kanye West, but it would be difficult to fault the local MC and producer of such engaging efforts as "Official" and "Changes" for simply being so damned dope. Plus, the album's lead single, "Feel the Vibe," along with its Robbie Hardkiss remix, sounds more like a successful Young MC resurrection than anything even remotely Roc-A-Fella-related. ROBERT GABRIEL

VOL. 23 NO. 32 ★ APRIL 9, 2004

MC BAVU BLAKES AND DJ BABY G
BLAZING SADDLES

An alliance long past overdue, locals MC Bavu Blakes and DJ Baby G bond like Crazy Glue on their *Blazing Saddles* mix disc. Reinforcing some of Blakes' originals, an armory of black-market instrumentals are freestyled with verses altering their intent. Dispersing his quick-witted baritone amidst brief vocal stabs culled from Scarface's "Recognize" and Devin the Dude's "Anything," Blakes juxtaposes himself as an unsigned veteran standing alongside the most respected figures in Texas rap.

Showcasing the versatility and prowess of an entire trans-Texas fellowship as formulated by two of the state's most sought-after underground assets, *Blazing Saddles* defines a moment in time within the deepest recesses of hip-hop. As Baby G spreads a canvas across the cave walls of convention, his lyrical counterpart fills in the blanks as to what role he's currently playing. "It's Mr. Blakes comma space to the capital B, a Kanye South-West for the rap industry."

ROBERT GABRIEL

VOL. 24 NO. 38 ★ MAY 20, 2005

SMOG
A RIVER AIN'T TOO MUCH TO LOVE
DRAG CITY

In downtown Houston's Sam Houston Park, surrounded by some of the most imposing skyscrapers in North America, is a small cedar cabin. Thought to have been built in 1823, then moved to the park sometime thereafter, its only name is "The Old Place." Bill Callahan, aka Smog, might as well be this cabin. His *A River Ain't Too Much to Love* burrows deep into the collective unconscious of American song, its nameless river a site of reflection ("Drinking at the Dam") and escape ("Running the Loping"). This river is, as many others before it, a place of great beauty, hidden strength, and spiritual rebirth: "Say Valley Maker" equates death with a dried-up river, while "Rock Bottom Riser" uses the river as a way to both cast off and reforge familial bonds. Flush with vivid imagery of abandoned wells, thorny brambles (sometimes tangles with pornographic magazines), and sleeping horses, *River* also weaves subtle social comment ("I Feel Like the Mother of the World"), an ancient folk song ("In the Pines"), and playful humor ("The Well") into its rich rural tapestry. Callahan may be new to Austin, as per the wry "I'm New Here," but musically, he and his *River* dwell in the Old Place. **CHRISTOPHER GRAY**

VOL. 24 NO. 44 ★ JULY 1, 2005

VOXTROT
RAISED BY WOLVES
CULT HERO

It's a perfect Sunday morning. No work, no plans, no obligations. The sun is just peaking in from behind a white linen curtain, and all you hear is the hum of the AC. Suddenly, back-up singers pop in from the hallway like an episode of *Six Feet Under*. You hear the hi-hat in the living room, guitars jumping in with quick measures. "First you fade into the background—wouldn't even call me—had the nerve to leave me. Go ahead and love me." This is Voxtrot: a superstar baby band providing the soundtrack for your cable-ready exuberance. The 3-year-old Austin quintet has bloomed into a dance-pop steamroller poised to flatten every Bravery and Killer in its path. An EP on par with platinum acts, *Raised By Wolves* is 23 minutes of glorious jangle. The title track and Smiths-laden "The Start of Something" are only warnings of the resilience of "Missing Pieces." Top-billed on *Wolves,* "Missing Pieces" is an anthem for the disenfranchised, a moral mix of contemporary Canadian mishmash and nostalgic Manchester bounce. Ramesh Srivastava rides Jonathan Richman over the "Long Haul," while "Wrecking Force" is the end credit roller: a song that wraps up all emotion with streamers and confetti of delight.

DARCIE STEVENS

VOL. 24 NO. 48 ★ JULY 29, 2005

Making Biscuit
Punk Icon Randy "Biscuit" Turner Serves Art 24/7

VOL. 24 NO. 51 ★ AUGUST 19, 2005

MARC SAVLOV

A MODEST FRAME HOUSE in South Austin sports a wealth of year-round yard art. A clutch of oversized scorpions guard the screened-in front porch, and the trees in the backyard rain oddities. Not one but two prominently displayed "No Solicitors" signs are affixed to the front door.

Inside, there's an entirely different reality. Walls are covered floor to ceiling with a laff-riot of psychedelic artworks, from garish paintings and improbable collages to dioramic displays featuring dissected baby dolls. It's not so much a house as a state of mind.

Welcome to the inner playscape of Randy "Biscuit" Turner, one-time frontman of storied Austin funk-punk-skate rock legends the Big Boys, as well as Cargo Cult, Swine King, and current member, with Houston's the Slurpees, of the Texas Biscuit Bombs.

Turner's musical legacy has spread far and wide since its Eighties heyday, drawing into its orbit punk peers and progeny such as X's Exene Cervenka, Fugazi's Ian MacKaye, and Jersey spookster Glenn Danzig. Yet the artist-in-residence known as Biscuit is at least another lifetime more than the sum of his musical resume.

It's that seemingly ceaseless stream of madfunkateer artwork as much as those growly punk rock pipes that has ensured Turner's enduring notoriety amongst the underground's forever fickle

Randy "Biscuit" Turner. Photograph by Todd Wolfson.

cognoscenti. Those explosions of Bizarro World hi-jinks, frosted in daubs of blinding, Tokyo-esque neons and chockablock with cheerful chaos, have done as much to keep Ausin weird as anything else the city has ever birthed.

And the bearish Turner, exuding a wickedly youthful charm so utterly devoid of pretense or posturing, presides over it all with the bemused bafflement of a vaguely naughty schoolboy who's just been elected class president.

THE GOOD OLD DAZE

If you're of a certain age and mind-set, if Austin's legendary Drag-bound punk club Raul's stirs beery reptile memories at the base of your brain, if fun, fun, fun is more than just a noun in triplicate, Turner needs no introduction. For latecomers, and there are many, this is the Biscuit bio in brief: Born with a bang in post-war Gladewater, Texas, circa '56, Turner "got art" at an early age.

"Growing up, my mother encouraged me a lot," he says. "She was born in 1921 when Betty Boop was popular and she could draw Betty Boop like nobody's business. When the kids were going crazy, all four of us, she'd say, 'Let's draw!'"

Following a stint at East Texas State University, Turner hightailed it to Austin, where he "immediately began to hang out with the beatniks, drink wine, and learn how to roll joints." For its part, the local music scene was shifting from psychedelic to cosmic, the Armadillo World Headquarters open and longhairs flocking to town for cheap weed and cheaper rents.

"I got a place over by the university for $45 a month," he recalls. "About a week after I moved here, they had a big music festival out where the old baseball park used to be by where the UT art building is now. I remember it was the Allman Brothers, It's a Beautiful Day, Pacific Gas & Electric—all for $3, with

people rolling joints outside in full view. I just thought, 'God, I'm in heaven; this must be Mecca!' It was a wonderful time for me because suddenly I was surrounded by my kind of people, who reassured me that I wasn't nuts and who immediately gave me the encouragement to start being as weird as I wanted to be.

"Austin opened me up to the vastness of other people like myself, people I could really trust artistically and with my soul. People who would reassure me that I'm not crazy, that who I am is okay, and that the most important thing is to be happy. And I think moving to Austin showed me that right away."

Fast forward a few years and suddenly there's another cultural bang: the Sex Pistols, the birth of the Austin punk scene, and campus-area freak nexus Raul's, now the Texas Showdown. It was an electric camaraderie of amps, vinyl trousers, and hair your mother wouldn't be caught dead in. Its reputation attracted name bands not just to the club but to Austin.

"I went to see the Ramones," remembers Turner, "and the Police at the Armadillo World Headquarters, the Runaways with Joan Jett, and a lot of early influential bands that were of that genre of music that was beginning to gel into punk rock and New Wave. You could really tell that something was going on, things were changing. There were people laughing and dancing, whereas previously, Austin had been pretty much all cosmic cowboy–style stuff, with everything painted in saguaro cactus green and not much else."

Turner's response to the DIY renaissance was to form the Big Boys with skateboard pals Tim Kerr and Chris Gates. He proved a natural frontman, sporting outlandish getups (a suit made of Baggie-wrapped sandwiches!) and possessed of a distinctively melodic and bluesy howl that recalls ex-Austinite Janis Joplin if she'd gargled volcanic sand as a whiskey chaser.

"I'm not sure that there was necessarily that much more creativity at that point," reasons Kerr, "but it

The Big Boys in the early 1980s. Photograph by David Fox.

seemed like a lot of creative people got together at this one certain time, kind of like they did in the early Sixties with the beatniks. And that included music, art, writing, fanzines, anything—it was pretty much the kind of a scene where you were urged to participate instead of just sitting back and watching it go by."

Of the Big Boys' enduring popularity, Turner couldn't be more proud. "I really think it was because we were totally off the wall," he posits. "We could have been generic and screamed and yelled like MDC or D.R.I., but instead we chose to do funk and stranger things. Tim's use of a radio on 'Sound on Sound' [from 1983's *Lullabies Help the Brain Grow*] is one of our most talked about songs to this day—people love that song—and he did that with a junky old international band radio."

Like Les Amis, Inner Sanctum, Liberty Lunch, and the Varsity Theater, the Big Boys and Austin Punk v 1.0 is long gone. "That really cool thing you missed," is recalled fondly, more often than not, by those present at its noisy, raucous birth and raised to iconic status by those who weren't even born yet. Tempus fugit, things change, and after a glorious six-year run, 1980–1985, the Big Boys packed it in after one final, infamous night of sheer chaos, both onstage and off, at Liberty Lunch. Acrimony ensues, but this is not that tale.

GAUD IN HEAVEN

Turner, exhaustively creative, forged on with both music and art. He formed the short-lived band Cargo Cult before hitting his musical stride with the punk-performance-artstravaganza Swine King in the Nineties, an eight-plus-member outfit recalled as much for their outrageous stage props, costumes, and theatrics as their gorgeously chaotic musical output.

Throughout it all, Turner's artwork developed from a hodgepodge of found objects and cut-and-paste imagery into something else entirely, a world unto itself, made up of toy-box discards, swirls of acrylic and neon-gaudy temperas, dust storms of glitter, shattered mirror balls, and glue-gun assemblages served poppin' fresh from the Biscuit's inexhaustible inner oven. Man, art, and artist had become inseparable, and you couldn't help but stare and stare and stare.

Describing Turner's staggeringly original artworks without wearing out Rodale's *Synonym Finder* can be a tough job for anyone, even close friends who've had years to bask in the Biscuit E-Z Bake art-kiln.

"I'd call it carnivalesque," says X/Knitters founder Exene Cervenka. "It's ironic and it's funny. He's also one of the kindest people I've ever known. He's such a good person. And his house is the best art gallery in town."

Another of Turner's old-school comrades, Gary Floyd, of the Dicks, tackles the Biscuit mystique by simply calling it overwhelming: "When you stand in his house and you're in the middle of all of it, you simply can't concentrate on one single piece because your eye will catch something else immediately. It's brilliant."

MAD METHODS AND SIMPLE JUNK

Creating new art out of found objects is as old as art itself, or at least as old as your local Goodwill, but Turner's mad methods are unique and affecting in ways that aren't seldom encountered outside of uneasy 3 am dreamscapes.

His fluid, sometimes ominous artistic confabulations comprising what most people would take for junk, too raggedy even for the rummage sale—flambéed toy soldiers, deconstructed doll parts, intimations of Kennedy-era prosperity side by side with images of the malformed, misplaced, or misunderstood—are the giddily overt expressions of that inner Biscuit, the one who, when he spies an evil clown under his bed, doesn't turn tail and run the other way. Instead, he invites the Bozo up topside to help scour his treasure trove of neat stuff, dreaming up new and better ways to view a reality that, let's face it, isn't living up to its childhood promise very well these days.

"It's my world," states Turner, "and sometimes I retreat to it knowing full well that beyond that front door right there is horror and destruction and death and mayhem. But I know I can't control any of that, and so this little world that I've created here, well, I can barely control that, too, but it's much more fun.

"I'm very saddened by the pain in the world and overjoyed at the mundane. That sly grin that people have. I can cry in a moment for people's joy, and I hope that reflects in my art—every facet of life's existence, the sad, the gothic, the funny-as-heck things that I do. A lot of it is planned out, but often it's free-form, mainly because I've got twenty-odd double-stacked boxes which are labeled on the side 'Toy Chaff.'

"And I'll pour a box out on my bed and look at all the little plastic legs, arms, dice, chickens, shrubbery, airplanes, and then suddenly I'll have six airplanes battling a Barbie who's got a Mexican wrestler's head out in front of a picture of a Baptist church that I cut out for the background.

"I love juxtaposing all that together because it's not real. It's a world I created that people seem to think is really funny. And I'm honored completely that anyone would laugh to start out with, much less at my artwork. Because that's what I've always tried to do: give people something to laugh about and also give 'em that tilt of the dog's head, that little 'Huh?'"

Terms of Engagement
Deconstructing James McMurtry in Five Easy Steps

VOL. 25 NO. 2 ★ SEPTEMBER 9, 2005

ANDY LANGER

1

There's fear and loathing in Crawford, Texas. You can see it in the brake lights of James McMurtry's Ford truck. Even in more civil times, before this sleepy farm town became home to the president and ground zero for protest of the war in Iraq, the back roads south of the city's center weren't easy to navigate. They're dusty and treacherously unpaved, without a street sign or speed limit marker in sight.

To stop or not to stop? That's the question, at a forced left turn, where a series of temporary stop signs suggests one thing and a Texas state trooper, blocking a gate that's presumably the back entrance to President Bush's ranch, suggests another. Mc-Murtry splits the difference and rides the brake, not quite stopping, and definitely not ignoring the police presence.

"It seemed weird to stop," admits McMurtry, who's now made the two-hour drive from his home in Austin to Crawford three times. "If I didn't stop would they have chased me down? I didn't know what to do. It's Crawford. There's potential for a tense situation up there."

James McMurtry, 2005. Photograph by Todd Wolfson.

There's also the potential for a standing ovation—if you're playing the right song—and McMurtry has that song. Onstage at Camp Casey, the Crawford vigil organized by Cindy Sheehan, whose son Casey died in Iraq, McMurtry ends a 30-minute performance with the song that earned him his invitation to play, "We Can't Make It Here." Clocking in at just under eight minutes, it's an alternate state-of-the-union, a scholarly commentary on the economy, the war, and arrogant leadership.

"Stark and wrenchingly direct, this may be the best American protest song since [Bob Dylan's] 'Masters of War,'" wrote author Stephen King, who downloaded the song from McMurtry's Web site, where it was hastily posted a week before the 2004 presidential election.

From a stage literally sixty feet from the gated front entrance to Bush's ranch, McMurtry busted out the song's money shot: "Get out of that limo and look us in the eye. Call us on the cell phone, tell us all why." For a crowd gathered expressly to lobby the president to a sit-down with a grieving mother, a line written close to a year ago couldn't have been more prescient. In return, the audience offers McMurtry serious applause and scattered tears.

"I like that people are connecting to it," says McMurtry, who's put a new version of the song at the center of his new album, *Childish Things*. "But not why. They're identifying because they're in bad shape. I got a letter the other day from someone in North Carolina. The factory closed, and now Wal-Mart's paying them half with no benefits. I didn't make this stuff up, it's out there.

"And Cindy Sheehan's a fanatic? No. She's a mother that lost a son. Around election time, there was a saying going around: 'Silence is complicity.' It started to make sense to me. I didn't want to be silent or complicit anymore. Take a look around. We can't afford to be."

2

AUSTIN CHRONICLE: *Your signature, songs sung in character, seems more like a literary device than a songwriter's device.*

JAMES MCMURTRY: It's easier for me. It's always how I start songs. If I had to write everything from my own personal voice I wouldn't be writing much. I suppose I have a voice, but how many songs can you write from it?

AC: *So which comes first, the character or the idea for a song?*

JM: I don't specifically set out to write characters. They come out of the lines I hear. I hear a line and think, "Who's singing that? Who's telling me that? What kind of person would say that?" Sometimes they're characters that don't necessarily reflect my own opinion. A cool rhyme might not reflect the original idea. Then you have to be okay with that line coming out of your mouth for years on end. People are going to blame you if they don't like it.

AC: *With some of your characters, that's not an unlikely outcome.*

JM: Early on, I wrote a song called "Safe Side" for the *Candyland* record. It's from the point of view of a tight-assed Anglo tourist going across the border. I softened the last verse because it got pretty out there. Even so, Tish Hinojosa told me, "I got friends in the Valley that want to know what the hell you mean." Damn. I don't *mean* anything; I'm just trying to write a song here.

AC: *Sometimes those songs wind up seven or eight minutes long. Two songs you're best associated with, "Choctaw Bingo" and now "We Can't Make It Here," are long.*

JM: John Mellencamp told me early on to get the chorus quick and not make it too long. Like it was law, except what about a song like "Like a Rolling Stone"? It's a million years long and has no chorus. Stephen King owns a radio station in Maine. They played "Choctaw Bingo," and it was their most requested song of 2004. It's ironic radio worries so much. Radio doesn't want a song that long because there's only so many minutes to broadcast between commercials. I think listeners care less.

AC: *Sometimes rules just don't apply.*

JM: Or maybe they still do. But I'm 43 years old. I don't care so much anymore.

LIKE HIS FATHER, NOVELIST LARRY MCMURTRY, JAMES' EARLY WORK ALSO USES SMALL TOWNS AS A MICROCOSM OF AMERICA.

3

Aside from "We Can't Make It Here," *Childish Things* isn't overtly political. "It's about people, not politics," says McMurtry of the album. That's also true of the songwriter's first six albums. From his Mellencamp-produced debut, 1989's *Too Long in the Wasteland*, to the pair of albums McMurtry cut post-Columbia for Sugar Hill, it's the defeated and the idealists, the cranky and struggling, that take front and center. Like his father, novelist Larry McMurtry (*Lonesome Dove, Terms of Endearment*), James' early work also uses small towns as a microcosm of America. "You can get your mind around a small town," notes the singer.

While his tales of life across what he calls "Level-land" often sounded like Tom Waits gargling a book-case full of sociology textbooks, McMurtry says he's always been careful to focus on the effect of geography on people, not their politics. In 1997, he told this paper that politically driven songwriting is for "hippies on a soapbox trying to save the world. I don't think that's what songs are for."

All that changed with the 2000 election. McMurtry says he believes the election wasn't won by popular vote, but by voter intimidation and outright fraud at the polls. While he was once a card-carrying member of both the NRA and ACLU, the avid outdoorsman and gun-owner has left the NRA behind. "It became clear to me after a while that my money wasn't going to supporting my gun rights, but instead towards scaring gun owners into voting Republican."

Before long, McMurtry began utilizing the best pulpit he had, the stage. On last year's *Live in Aught-Three*, there's a clip of a stage rap titled "Max's Theo-rem." What begins with an explanation that "Level-land" was written with the unabashedly communist Texas novelist Max Crawford in mind expands into a Bush-baiting rant on the president's pronunciation of "nuclear."

"I knew it's the song all the Bush people were coming to hear," McMurtry says of the tune Robert Earl Keen covered in 1997. "So one time I did it in Plano and a woman got really mad. She said, 'Don't slam Bush.' I told her I would if I wanted to. She came back a little later with a sign that said 'Keep Politics Out of Music.' They tried to run her off. I said, 'No, she can stay if she wants to.' Then some girl kind of playfully tried to snatch the sign away, and she turned around and got the girl in a headlock. Security threw both of 'em out. It was our first catfight in front of the stage. Ever.

"But I thought it was odd: 'Keep Politics Out of Music'? I guess that's okay if you don't listen to Woody Guthrie and John Lennon. Or Steve Earle."

4

AC: *How much of what you do is a reaction to being the son of a famous novelist? You honor him by writing, but not in the same way he does.*

JM: I tried to write like he did for a while. I don't take to prose. It requires a different attention span. Every so often I'll scribble a page of prose, but I don't really know what to do with it. I think it's because I don't read. I'd like to be better read. But, I don't know, I'd like to do the work to get there. Larry is an avid reader. Always was. I didn't read so much. I listened. And a lot of people claim there's some kind of genetic connection. I'd have to question that because nobody ever said that about him. There's no writers in his background.

AC: *Like your father, you write so much about geography. You spent much of your childhood on the move, from Texas to Virginia and back. As an adult you've lived everywhere from Arizona to Alaska.*

JM: Moving around gave me perspective. I was generally on the outside looking in. You pick up on things that people who've lived there all their lives might not notice anymore. A friend of my aunt's told me a story about us riding around when I was 3 years old. I looked out the window and said, "Wow, look at the sunset." They said they'd never noticed it before. To me that's the best part of North Texas. The ground is not that pretty, but the sky is amazing. How they could miss it is beyond me.

AC: *Outsiders aren't always the happiest people in the crowd. Are a lot of your characters lonely and unhappy because you were?*

JM: No. They were unhappy because they were. If you drive around a lot and look through the windshield, you don't see a whole lot of happy people. Mostly you see beat-down unhappy people—far more beat-down and unhappy than I hope to ever be and certainly more than I've ever been. I can't imagine the misery of some of these people. I see it on their faces, and I can't fathom it. I just can't.

5

Six days after his appearance at Camp Casey, McMurtry is sitting at the bar of the new Enoteca Vespaio deconstructing what went wrong with his set. From the crowd, it didn't look like there was much to critique. "Choctaw Bingo" and "We Can't Make It Here" killed. The gig also marked the first time McMurtry shared a stage with his sax-playing 14-year-old, Curtis. Only "Rachel's Song," McMurtry's disturbing tale

of a hard-drinking single mother from 1995's *Where'd You Hide the Body,* seemed flat. Don't think its author didn't notice.

"My son and Steve [Earle] play to a crowd; I tend to play *at* a crowd," he offers. "I have to coax myself into actually trying to connect. It's the mistake I made during 'Rachel's Song.' I played at them. Maybe if I'd have figured out how to play to them they might not have fallen asleep like they did."

That McMurtry is taking notes on his sets, even a low-pressure, unpaid gig like the one at Camp Casey, marks the beginning of a new stage in his career. Buoyed by the critical success of last year's live album and the steadily growing crowds for his weekly residency at the Continental Club, McMurtry has come to believe he could be the rare singer-songwriter with a live show as his best calling card—if only he focused less on the music and more on the audience.

"It sounds simple, but you have to use the crowd's energy if you really hope to connect," he explains. "That's something that doesn't come easy for me. I've had to learn it. And relearn it. I'll forget it and say, 'Next week I've got to look at them more.' Eye contact is a big deal, but I'm kind of standoffish by nature."

Standoffish may be an understatement.

"Aloof? Lazy? I've heard it all before. When you're out there and onstage, you can't expect to have total control of your image," reasons McMurtry. "That's not even the point. It's like a song. A song is as much about the listener as it is the writer. What's a song about? Well, what's the song about to you? I guess I just don't want people to have too much information about me. It's not necessary. Anybody that cares enough is going to have more fun making it up anyway. What's it do to the music? The music is the music no matter who I wind up being." ◄

Static Between Stations
American Analog Set Is "Set Free"

VOL. 25 NO. 3 ★ SEPTEMBER 16, 2005

DARCIE STEVENS

ANDREW KENNY is slight but stoic, his hands barely grazing the strings of his guitar as he coaxes lyrics from the microphone with a voice so calming it opiates. Ever so gently, his imagery takes flight, gliding over sea and sky, creating rhythm out of syllables. Once Kenny crumpled under the weight of his eloquence, but now as a veteran songwriter, his tunes are poetry. He stretches and recoils with the cool brisk flow of the drums, pulsating as the bass hums to itself. He's surrounded by family onstage, and that's only one testament to the soundness of American Analog Set.

The limestone wall of Club de Ville begs for the band's silhouettes on this hot August night. It's a low-key reunion, one where the parents are invited and the kids don't mind. All the sounds blend together graciously, with decibels so contrite that a low roar replaces the distinctly separate instruments.

In and out of albums—*The Golden Band*, *Know by Heart*, *Promise of Love*—and emotion: pain, pledge, love, longing. It's the quietest an AmAnSet crowd has ever been, beginning the moment the five band members quietly walked onstage to the first chords of "Fuck This . . . I'm Leaving," an opener if ever there were one. The final song on new LP *Set Free* is more motivation than rebellion. AmAnSet isn't particularly rebellious in the classic sense.

"Immaculate Heart" moves percussionist Sean Ripple to bounce. Behind him, Lee Gillespie is hunched over the bass, his back all that's visible. Mark Smith flogs the skins with brushes as Kenny descends a length of dissonant chords that seem destined. Craig McCaffrey's black-rimmed glasses barely peek over his double-stacked Rhodes keyboards, the song ebbing and flowing with the rhythm of a midnight locomotive.

As the groove of "New Drifters II" lulls the crowd into a euphoric trance, some begin to drop off. And so kicks in a typical Analog Set show: hardcores up front, chatterboxes in the back. It's become law over the last decade. You can't escape the talkers. Still, Kenny's face is smeared with that sly, peaceful grin; the thoughts skipping behind his closed eyes must be merciless.

The hat trick lies in *Know by Heart*'s closer, "We're Computerizing and We Just Don't Need You Anymore." It begins innocently enough, vibes echoing monotonous strumming. No bass is heard, but slowly the volume rises, as Gillespie fades in additional layers of sound on his four-track until all eyes are on the stage. Who knew the lullaby act could reverberate with the burn of a thousand steam engines? ◀.

Starry Eyes
Roky Erickson
Is Back

VOL. 25 NO. 18 ★ DECEMBER 30, 2005

MARGARET MOSER

ROKY I

"One of the great rock & roll singers stood on the stage with his arms crossed. He uncrossed them and crossed them again. He yawned. Then he sang a verse of one of his songs, 'Don't Slander Me.' His once mighty voice was thin and couldn't quite reach all the notes. He turned his back on the audience between verses. He looked beat. It was 1993, and Roky Erickson and his backing band were performing at the Austin Music Awards."
—*Texas Monthly*, December 2001

If not that night's performance itself, this description from longtime local writer and musician Michael Hall seared a disordered image of psychedelic pioneer Roky Erickson into the imagination of followers and readers alike. Small wonder: in 1993, Erickson was losing a vicious battle with schizophrenia, all but doomed to a lifetime of substandard living and mental illness.

More than a decade later, Roky Erickson is the very picture of Austin's sly, laid-back, and plugged-in populace. Call it a comeback—*the* comeback, perhaps.

It began in earnest this spring, at South by Southwest. Performing with veteran garage rockers the Explosives at Threadgill's Ice Cream Social, anchoring a SXSW panel on the 13th Floor Elevators, and taking in *You're Gonna Miss Me*, a documentary on the legendary group at SXSW Film, not to mention signing copies of the photo book *Easter Everywhere*, music's 58-year-old third eye was everywhere.

That was only the beginning. 2005 also saw him play eight more gigs, including August's benefit for Jon Dee Graham's son Willie, several other shows with the Explosives at Threadgill's, and at the Halloween Masquerade a Go-Go. Then there was his September appearance at the Austin City Limits Music Festival.

Erickson's euphoric rise in the Sixties as lead singer of the 13th Floor Elevators is a tale of mythic proportion. Forget San Francisco: The Elevators were the original proponents of psychedelic music, here in Austin, Texas. The drug busts and forced hospitalization that followed destroyed the band and began Erickson's terrifying descent into three hellish decades of mental instability and frighteningly good recordings. Well-meaning friends and his mother, Evelyn, stepped in to make him well, but it wasn't until his younger brother Sumner intervened that Roky came back into focus.

Like someone who's been awakened from a long, disturbing dream, he walks cautiously through his newly reclaimed life. But make no mistake, Roky Erickson is back.

ROKY II

"This is the most nerve-racking thing I do," sighs Sumner Erickson as he straightens his brother's Gibson, on loan from the company, on its stand. "I set up his guitars."

Amid the chatter and good cheer of Waterloo Records' annual Christmas party at Donn's Depot, Sumner prepares Roky's gear for a set with the Explosives. Guitarist Cam King and drummer Fred Krc settle into their places while Chris Johnson tunes his bass. A Waterloo employee approaches Sumner with an envelope for Roky and one for the Explosives.

As Evelyn Erickson, petite and pretty in black pearl velvet, sashays through the crowd, Fred Krc is handed

CALL IT A COMEBACK—*THE* COMEBACK, PERHAPS.

the band's Waterloo check by Sumner. Krc clasps him with affection. It's time to go pick up Roky, who doesn't hang around before or after performances.

Picking up Roky is part of Sumner's job as Roky's legal guardian. The duties are enormous and require not only legal responsibilities but personal sacrifices. Roky's not the ghost he was a decade ago, but he's set in his ways. Routines are important to Roky, who doesn't tour or play out-of-town gigs yet. Roky makes his own decisions, though, points out Sumner, noting he didn't know his brother quit smoking cigarettes until recently when he overheard him telling a friend.

It's a 15-minute round trip to fetch Roky and bring him back to Donn's. Along the way, the brothers make small talk. Roky spent the day as he often does, watching the Cartoon Network. He's pleased to be

the subject of a story again. And he's most concerned with getting to Amy's Ice Creams after the set.

Hopping aboard the section of Donn's that was once a boxcar, Roky settles into a seat in the corner. He's wearing a dark shirt and a Southwestern print jacket, his long dark hair combed back from his face. A white napkin spread on the table before him holds three "communal cookies" on it. They're triangular gingerbread cookies, pyramid shapes with white frosting eyeballs in honor of the evening's musical guest, but Roky doesn't eat them. There's a childlike innocence to his expression, yet his eyes—clear, light blue—are sharp. They don't miss a thing.

He's quiet save for the occasional reply to a question. No, he's not cold. No thank you to drinks. No food. A smiling nod acknowledges a couple on the

Starry eyes: Roky Erickson, 2005. Photograph by Aubrey Edwards.

dance floor who are grinning in his direction. Sumner waves at him through the crowd. "It's time."

No one stops him as he heads to the band and hoists the Gibson over his shoulder. Partygoers crush toward the front as he strums a chord, its electric sound reverberating in the air. He looks back at Krc and Cam King, who both give the high sign. Under photographs of Elvis, Dolly Parton, and Kenny Rogers, Roky strikes the opening chord of "It's a Cold Night for Alligators."

The audience howls, pushed together and undulating as one vibrating mass. Evelyn stands on her toes, not able to see until the front row parts. Spying Roky standing only feet from her, she beams with maternal pride as the song ends. Then she looks down, mutters about her panty hose, and gives them a yank. Roky launches into "White Faces," then "The Interpreter" and "Bermuda."

"Thank you" are the only words he speaks between songs.

His voice is in excellent form tonight, as is his playing, like the music itself: tough, confident. Guitar rock from any era, played with experience and verve, has no expiration date. Neither do these songs. It's been that way all year, each show better than the last. The Austin City Limits Music Festival set was a milestone, yet every gig is important to Roky because it's a step away from the haunted past and toward a bright future. The opening jangle of "Starry Eyes" fills the room, and the crowd issues a deep sigh of pleasure, mouthing the well-known lyrics, melting into applause at the end.

As the band tears into "You're Gonna Miss Me," Roky's voice takes on the unearthly yowl that forever defines him a master vocalist. He basks in the glory of his signature song and its relentless beat. It closes the short set, but the audience won't let him go. "I Walked with a Zombie" is the encore scrawled on the song-list, but someone requests "Creature with

the Atom Brain" and Roky complies. The song, unrehearsed, hits the mark to its final ringing note.

After the cheering dies down, Roky signs a few autographs and chats with well-wishers. His face glows, obviously pleased with the attention. Music rises in the club. It's the Rolling Stones' "Sympathy for the Devil." Roky slips out of the bar and into the clear night, only one thing on his atom brain.

ROKY III

"That was one supercharged crowd!" Sumner crows enthusiastically, driving toward Amy's. "It was so cool of you to play the request! Awesome, brother!"

"Uh huh," Roky's voice is noncommittal, but he's clearly buoyed by the show. He and Sumner count performances in 2005 and come up with ten. The two are still reminiscing about Roky's most public year since the early Nineties as they walk into Amy's and order malts.

Next stop, Magnolia Cafe. Roky is a creature of habit, living in a manner that makes him comfortable and puts him at ease with the adulation accompanying in public wherever he goes. Sumner makes a well of syrup in his pancakes as he talks about his life with and without Roky, who sits silent but is all ears. Sumner, younger by 18 years, was three when Roky's first band, the Spades, released "You're Gonna Miss Me" b/w "We Sell Soul" in 1965 on a local 45. He missed the 13th Floor Elevators' halcyon days, growing up instead amid Roky's frequent hospitalizations and subsequent fractured life. Sumner, like Roky, was a gifted student and musical prodigy.

Music took Sumner down a very different road, however, one that led to a 20-year-plus stint as principal tubaist with the prestigious Pittsburgh Symphony Orchestra under the direction of André Previn. Sumner was reaping the benefits of life as a classical musician when his brother's friends in Texas decided Roky

Roky Erickson. Illustration by Nathan Jensen.

Sumner moved Roky to Pittsburgh, continuing his orchestra duties while making sure Roky was away from old habits and monitored for medication. Roky spent just over a year there, got his teeth fixed, and returned to Texas on his birthday in July 2002. Sumner followed in 2004.

The youngest Erickson brother is rightfully proud of his contributions to Roky's recovery, noting that Roky has a driver's license for the first time in decades, owns a car, and voted last year. Sumner's also protective of his mother, Evelyn, insistent that their relationship was twisted in the media after the battle for Roky's guardianship almost five years ago.

A familiar four chords explode through Magnolia's sound system. It's "You're Gonna Miss Me," but it takes Roky a moment to realize it. Buttermilk pancakes are quite distracting.

ROKY IV

"Sorry about your car."

Two nights later, Roky examines the gaping hole in my Mazda's dashboard, where some ratbag ripped out the stereo a few days earlier. He locks the door and buckles his seat belt.

He likes listening to the radio, specifically BOB FM and its familiar mix of old favorites. The radio is usually on at his apartment, even when the television is playing, a throwback to the days when he kept a cacophony of electronic media blaring simultaneously to drown out the voices in his head. Today, the volume is no longer head-splitting; the radio's by the kitchen, while the television's in the living room.

Roky clucks sympathetically as we pull up alongside Waterloo Records and park in front of Amy's. He strolls inside and stops below the chalkboard display of ice cream specials. There it is: The Roky, drawn in red and green chalk with a pyramid to suggest the Elevators' first LP cover, and advertising his beloved

needed family support beyond Evelyn's efforts. Roky's teeth were bad, and he was suffering, living in government subsidized housing off Social Security. Roky's friends contacted Sumner and legal machinery began to crank. On June 13, 2001, after a five-month court battle that pitted him against his mother, Sumner was declared "Guardian of the Person and Estate of Roger Kynard Erickson."

sweet cream ice cream malt. Sumner's inside, too, waiting for us. Three malts are ordered. Roky paces in anticipation.

"Are you coming to Threadgill's with us?" Roky quizzes Sumner.

"No," says Sumner, digging his hands into the pockets of his jacket. "I've got a party to go to."

Roky's head bobs in assent. The photographer arrives, as do the malts.

"I'd like to see the two of you posed back here," I indicate the exit stairs at the back of Amy's as the camera setup begins.

"Do I have to sit on the steps?" asks a skeptical Roky.

"No, not if you don't want to, you can stand."

"I'd rather stand." Roky's expression changes. "Then I want to be photographed by the cow." The wall opposite him features a brightly painted cow.

"We can shoot you by the cow."

The brothers Erickson are posed in different positions as the photographer snaps away.

After a few minutes of stiff demeanor, Roky and Sumner relax. Sumner flashes a V with his fingers behind the head of his brother, who grins at the antics as the camera flashes repeatedly. In that moment, all the troubles and pain of years gone recede in the play of a pair of boyish siblings.

ROKY V

"Look."

Roky leads the way out of Amy's to the front of Waterloo Records. He plants himself before the huge poster advertising the Shout! Factory anthology, *I Have Always Been Here Before*.

"Were you happy with the collection?"

"Yes, I really liked it."

Two of his CDs are on display in the E section, and we thumb through the bin inspecting the other titles. "I don't know the songs on this one very well, except 'Starry Eyes' and 'Don't Slander Me,'" I confess while examining *All That May Do My Rhyme*. He gives me a sideways glance. "You would if you heard them." He's probably right.

"The Elevators are over here," he beckons, already a few aisles away. We need not search; a CD copy of *Easter Everywhere*, the band's second album from 1967, lies askew atop the T section.

"Is that a sign?" I tease Roky.

"Yes." He slides *Easter Everywhere* back into the stack.

"That's got my favorite Elevators song on it," I tell him. "'Slip Inside This House.' What's your favorite Elevators song to sing?"

Roky gives me a wily look, the gleam in his blue eyes starry.

"'You're Gonna Miss Me.'" ◀

Winter's Wolves
The Sword's Land of Ice and Snow

VOL. 25 NO. 23 ★ FEBRUARY 3, 2006

AUDRA SCHROEDER

METAL IS ABOUT IMAGERY, the warrior, the virgin, the beast, the secret handshake that binds the mystical to the big riff. This dark vision of the past, this obsession with mythology and the epic battle that's hellbent for leather and personified by thundering drums, marks the oeuvre like a numeric birthmark hidden under the hairline.

Black Sabbath, Motörhead, Iron Maiden, Metallica; it's an image that still frightens parents and guardians while altering the minds of teenagers immersed in dog-eared issues of *Heavy Metal* magazine and *Led Zeppelin IV*. Yet the decibels, the marching guitars, and throat-shredding bellows remain paramount, having long ago spawned some kind of monster. They birthed bands like Austin's Sword, whose debut full-length, *Age of Winters*, was conceived in a sweaty *Heavy Metal* haze.

"It was a big influence on me as a teenager," admits singer/guitarist JD Cronise. "I still read an issue every now and then, but like so many things, it just ain't what it used to be."

Neither is metal. We all know what happened to many of those bands as they veered toward the heady hair-metal days; one day the pyrotechnics guy

The Sword: (l-r) Bryan Richie, Kyle Shutt, Trivett Wingo, JD Cronise, 2009. Photograph by Sandy Carson.

SEEK AND DESTROY
THE SWORD'S SLICE OF METALLICA

BY TRIVETT WINGO
DEC. 17/18: THE FORUM, LOS ANGELES

Night One: So the night before, Lars had been sending me these text messages about wanting to party. I guess I got excited, because before the show had even ended, I had consumed at least half a bottle of Jägermeister on my own. I got kind of belligerent and was somewhat rude to a guy I later learned was Jon Theodore of the Mars Volta (a drummer that totally blows my mind). At some point, I was with Lars, Dave Grohl, Jon, and I can't remember who else when Lars says: "OK, the top five drummers are here! I'm number one; Trivett, you're number two; three [points to Grohl]; four [Theodore]; and five . . ." I don't remember who that last one was as I was beginning to black out at this point.

I tell Dave about my Nirvana cover band, In Dudero, to which he chuckles and replies, "Who are you again?" Next thing I know, we're on Dave Grohl's "Grohler Coaster," a limousine bus that he rents to take people out on the town partying. We're headed to some bar called Red Rocks, but before we get there, all the Jäger kicks in (not to mention the scotch, the beers, and whatever else), and I start spinning. We pull up to the place, and I start barfing immediately and pass out on the floor of the bar. Real classy. Apparently, at some point I'm lying on Dave's lap, and he's babysitting me. I must have been really pathetic.

Eventually I ended up back at Lars' hotel, where I actually threw up in my cupped hands while we were checking in. Woke up totally confused and took a cab back to the Forum, spewing out of the cab on the way there.

After our set, Lars drops by our dressing room to check on me and fill in the blanks a little bit. Apparently, right before I went nonverbal, I was drinking a mixture of Jägermeister and Champagne, which I spilled all over my pants as I became totally incoherent. So the moral of the story is: Don't mix Jägermeister and Champagne, especially if you get nauseous on Grohler Coasters.

VOL. 28 NO. 19 ★ JANUARY 9, 2009

just didn't show up. Such is the nature of evolution. This time last year, Cronise, guitarist Kyle Shutt, bassist Bryan Richie, and drummer Trivett Wingo were rocking shorter 'dos here in River City. Now, the locks are longer, facial hair more abundant. It's only natural: the Sword's slab of sound embraces that, hearkening back to metal's fat grooves and Thin Lizzys, the fantastical and the mammoth. In such company, nothing beats a killer 'stache.

You don't have to be Norway's chief divinity to hear *Winters* as a highly literate endeavor.

Age of Winters descends on Valentine's Day and the buzz has already infected the blood of innocents. The album's guttural guitars and Cronise's overlord vocals carry the story of gory battles and horned goddesses over a seismic rhythm section. The titular imagery is there, of course; the Sword's handle bows to metal's warfare-obsessed history. The riffage is also there, just as sharp. The blade goes deep.

Cronise and Wingo knew each other from Virginia, playing together in a band called Ultimate Dragons. Shutt and Richie, meanwhile, were veterans of Texas bands united by a love of Zeppelin. Over the course of their initial live forays, the foursome fine-tuned the songs that eventually made up *Winters*, revising them ever so slightly over periods of time. After a spring tour with Trail of Dead and the Octopus Project, they got to work in earnest, and by summer were circulating a three-song demo as their rough draft. In October of last year, the band began recording the album at Folkvang, Richie's home studio.

"Doing it at my house, we were able to tweak it a million times," he says. "We were a little worried that [the label] might not accept it, being that I didn't go to school for that. I don't have thousand-dollar equipment."

Cronise produced the album, Richie engineered it, and Wingo is currently the Sword's manager. They recently finished filming a video for "Winter's Wolves" in Staten Island. While the band won't divulge the fantastical plot in store, they confirm that the sun-up-to-sundown shoot was cold, "grueling, and brutal." The day of principal photography, the forecasted snow froze everything over.

"It was exactly what we wanted," Shutt laughs.

Richie takes it a step further: "Odin was on our side."

You don't have to be Norway's chief divinity to hear *Winters* as a highly literate endeavor. While Robert Plant preached of Valhalla bound to Greek and Celtic folk and Sabbath moaned of the apocalypse and "atomic rage," the Sword's vision falls somewhere in between, even quoting William Butler Yeats in the liner notes. Razor-sharp prose such as "Twilight written in the runes of crones" and the barked alliteration of "Harken to the howl of the huntsman's hounds" fill the purist's notion of the metal tradition. The Sword's just reshaping the mold.

"Some are metaphorical, some are allegorical, and some are just fantasy," Cronise explains of his lyrics. "I'm very interested in mythology and folklore; *Age of Winters* draws from Norse/Germanic mythology and folklore and Arthurian legends, although there are other sources as well. There are similar references and imagery found in various songs. It's not a concept album, but it's definitely meant to have a cohesive feel."

Over the last year, packed shows at Emo's and Room 710 have made the battle scars of Cronise's lyrics seem real. It's an assault—slow and calculated, sweat mixed with black, charred riffs creating a narcotic spell, amps piled high like weapons. Divide and conquer, then an ascent unto the right hand of some faceless god holding a giant bong of truth.

We are all slaves to the almighty riff. ◂

The Black Angels rest in peace: (l-r) Alex Maas, Christian Bland, Kyle Hunt, Stephanie Bailey, and Nate Ryan, 2008. Photograph by John Anderson.

SXSW Pick to Click The Black Angels

VOL. 25 NO. 27 ★ MARCH 3, 2006

AUDRA SCHROEDER

IT'S NOT OFTEN that a band's performance can actually make you feel like you're having a flashback. Such is the dark charm of Austin's Black Angels.

Their descent has occurred rather fast since forming locally in 2004. Singer Alex Maas, guitarist Christian Bland, drummer Stephanie Bailey, bassist/guitarist Nate Ryan, keyboardist Kyle Hunt, and drone manipulator Jennifer Raines gigged around town, and rumored marathon multimedia performances only added to their red haze. The grainy video element gives their live shows an eerie glow that might cause the aforementioned hallucination, but their lysergic tones and feral rhythms are what pull like quicksand.

Last year saw the release of their four-song EP on Seattle's Light in the Attic Records, an album that birthed their love child: clean, minimalist tones dosed with Brian Jonestown Massacre's psych adrenaline. Their debut full-length, *Passover*, out in April, channels the spirit of some dusty Texas roadside, drunk on peyote and howling at the moon, much like another psychedelic parent.

"We love the [Velvet Underground]," nods guitarist Bland. "They represent the evil side of the Sixties. While most other bands were singing about flowers and love, they were singing about heroin and death. They were singing about real things, nothing was candy-coated."

And *Passover* is anything but. It's a heavy, dirt-caked, war-is-hell opus of drone, Maas' strident voice rising and falling like a napalm bomb. The title even references a verse from Exodus 12:12–13: "The blood was a sign to the death angel to pass over their homes." From the viscous blues of "Black Grease" and ominous guitar scrape of "Manipulation" to Maas drawling, "You gave a gift to me in my young age / You sent me overseas, put the fear in me" on plodding opener "Young Men Dead," it's definitely, well, dark.

"I can see where people would think that, but we just sing about real life," Bland explains. "Our world is a dark place. It's not like we try to be dark. We're all happy people, but we just see things from a skewed perspective, I guess."

The themes of war and destruction are myriad on the album, but so are questions of love, death, values, and whether our generation is as fucked as our parents'. The Black Angels are channeling something higher.

"The entire album parallels what's going on now with what happened in the Sixties," explains Bland. "The Vietnamese war is about learning from our mistakes so that we don't ever fall into the trap of a second Vietnamese war, which the current war in Iraq is panning out to be. I don't see us as being completely political; we sing about life and truth, and politics just happens to be one facet of that. We do have a message, and it's one of getting people to open up their minds so they can let everything come through."

Texas psych is rising again, and it's a bad moon. ←

Get in the van: the Riverboat Gamblers, 2006. Photograph by Aubrey Edwards.

Rattle Me Bones
Mr. Wiebe Goes to the Chiropractor

VOL. 25 NO. 34 ★ APRIL 21, 2006

CHRISTOPHER GRAY

NEVER LET IT BE SAID that Mike Wiebe hasn't suffered for his art. In fact, the Riverboat Gamblers singer suffers on a daily basis. Years of hyperactive frontman behavior—whipping his head around, climbing amplifiers and rafters, diving into the crowd, Chaplin-esque pratfalls—makes great entertainment, but has left him with chronic aches and pains, frequent headaches, trouble sleeping, and worse.

"I got a pretty bad laceration in New York here," he says, pointing to a wicked scar on his right forearm. "I fell on a pint glass and gashed it bad. It took seventeen stitches. The cab driver took me to [NYC charity hospital] Bellevue, and it took them six hours to see me. There were gunshot wounds, and some guy had burnt his top lip off on a crack pipe."

He's also had a few concussions from "knocking into stuff" (mostly his bandmates' guitars).

"It's not like a GG Allin let's-hurt-ourselves kind of thing," insists Wiebe. "Really, it's like a dozen shows out of hundreds."

To better fathom the physical toll of those shows, the *Chronicle* arranged for Wiebe to consult with local chiropractor Dr. Cynthia J. Schade at the Active Life Chiropractic Clinic on West Sixth Street. After taking his measurements (six foot three inches, 167 lbs.) and watching a brief introductory video on the basic tenets and history of chiropractic, a discipline founded in 1895 and based on locating and correcting "interferences" in the spinal column, Dr. Schade begins her exam.

Early on, it's fairly obvious Wiebe has plenty of interference. Dr. Schade's measurements reveal his left side to be an inch higher than the right. "If these muscles are drawn up here, it's going to pull the shoulder blade up. Same with his ears. See how his left ear is a little more forward than the right?"

Dr. Schade has Wiebe do a series of bending and stretching exercises resembling calisthenics. His right sacroiliac joint, which connects the bottom of the spine to the pelvis, is "not moving at all," likely due to his trademark pratfalls, long hours of sitting in the Gamblers' van, and the repetitive motion of his day job washing dishes at Spider House. She calls this "a hitch in his get-along," which often leads to lower-back and leg pain.

Wiebe's sharpest pain comes when Dr. Schade probes the area where his neck meets left shoulder blade. It's swollen and inflamed, and the muscles are bunched up in a knot. Wiebe says it's plagued him since last summer's Warped Tour. When she raises his head, effectively straightening out the vertebrae, the pain eases considerably. It's the same sort of ailment that befalls people who get whiplash in a car accident, and frequently causes headaches.

Until Wiebe can get his neck X-rayed, Dr. Schade recommends he put ice on his neck and do exercises to smooth out the muscles (basically tucking his chin into his throat). Like all too many musicians, Wiebe has no health insurance, though he says he's considered applying for the Health Alliance for Austin Musicians. The X-rays will run about $60.

A week later, Wiebe says he's decided to get them. To pay for it, he says, "I'm just going to work an extra shift." ⬅

JON DEE GRAHAM
FULL
FREEDOM

Jon Dee Graham's a notoriously fire and brimstone kind of guy, so it's no surprise *Full* boasts more references to thick smoke and heavy rains than a homeowner's insurance policy. And yet, the twisted beauty of this South Austin fixture's fifth album is that it's both his darkest and most optimistic. It's a set where deadly low-water crossings ("Swept Away") saddle up to fortune-cookie giddiness ("Something Wonderful") and where even his shadiest characters are just a woman's touch away from salvation. Take "Remain," it's *Full*'s warmest ballad, but pretty it ain't: "Cigarette ash everywhere/I'm already gone, even when I'm there." There are tunes for pallbearers and partiers, and more often than not, they're the same ones; these are songs built around characters and relationships so bad off things can only get better. While *Full* is a songwriter's album through and through, just as vital to its success is Graham's performance. There's not a clever guitar solo shoehorned in for clever's sake, and where his nicotine-stained voice was once a liability, here its subtle highs and lows gouge as deep as the words he's written. *Full* isn't a bad title for an LP that runneth over with songs so memorable and smart, but when you consider just how much gravity they carry and how high they're stacked, Jon Dee Graham's *Greatest Hits* might have worked just as well.

ANDY LANGER

VOL. 25 NO. 34 ★ APRIL 21, 2006

CHARANGA CAKEWALK
CHICANO ZEN
TRILOKA/ARTEMIS

Chicano Zen is sublime. From start to finish, it delivers a jaw-dropping rhyme of memory, spirit, and clear-eyed reality. While Michael Ramos—Cakewalk's master musician—leans toward electrified cumbias, here he dabbles with a variety of Latin rhythms, bending, zapping, and shape-shifting to create a blazingly distinctive sound. *Chicano Zen* begins with the wonderful title track, an invocation of Chicano cultural icons, starting playfully, then skillfully gliding into a driving pulse. And it only gets better, thanks in part to Lila Downs, Becca Rodriguez, and Martha Gonzalez, who lend their seasoned vocals, as do Ruben Ramos and Patty Griffin in the enchanting "No Soy Feliz." Davíd Garza, Luis Guerra, Max Baca, Celso Duarte, and others sit in as well, adding perfectly calibrated vocals and instrumentation. "Gloria," the most conventional song on the album, is as close to an old-school ranchera as you'll get, until it reaches its intoxicating bridge, where (as Ramos writes in his liner notes), "the accordion, violin, and cello have a three-way conversation." With *Chicano Zen*, Charanga Cakewalk improves on its prior outing by creating something to talk about. **BELINDA ACOSTA**

VOL. 25 NO. 37 ★ MAY 12, 2006

I Saw the Light
The Night Clifford Antone Died

VOL. 25 NO. 39 ★ MAY 26, 2006

MARGARET MOSER

IT LOOKS LIKE A TYPICAL Tuesday night at the Broken Spoke's twice-monthly Hardcore Country show. Alvin Crow and his all-star lineup, including the venerable Austin honky-tonk's owner James White, reach into their buckskin bag of traditional country and make Hank Williams sound MOR.

Pinetop Perkins, who'll be 93 in July, shuffles inside the club with Roslyn, his gregarious caretaker. At his usual table—the large round one in front of the makeshift bandstand in the neon-lit front room—he tips his tan cowboy hat and smoothes his white shirt. Reaching for the bag of CDs he sells at every show, he holds up three, splayed like a deck of cards. This is how Perkins supports himself these days. Camille, one of the youngest patrons at the Spoke, passes the white plastic tip jar around.

"Better tip or she'll cry," Crow warns. "And if that don't make you tip, she'll cuss you out."

What's not typical on the night of May 23 are the long faces on the patrons, many in tears. There's an empty chair by Pinetop where Clifford Antone always sat. Yes, the club owner—whose worship of the blues guided his life—unabashedly adored the Broken Spoke and, in the last few years, spent nearly as much time at the country dance hall as he did downtown at his namesake club. With indie rock bands playing Antone's tonight, Clifford's friends knew where he would've come, so the Spoke is filling with mourners.

Clifford Antone. Photograph by Todd Wolfson.

"This is one of Clifford's favorite songs by one of his favorite artists," Alvin Crow drawls. "He'd always get up and sing it with us."

Alvin nods, the dreadlocks under his cowboy hat bouncing, and with James White at the mic the band cranks up Hank Williams' "Hey, Good Lookin'."

Clifford Antone died only hours before the show, and the Hardcore band plays Doug Sahm and Slim Harpo in his honor. Now, it's time to move the show into its non-Nashville course with Hank Thompson's "Wild Side of Life" segueing into Kitty Wells' "It Wasn't God Who Made Honky Tonk Angels."

Clifford would have loved it. ◀

SOUND TEAM
MOVIE MONSTER

CAPITOL

As its title suggests, the major label debut from Austin's apocalyptic pop collective Sound Team is both cinematic and fierce. The keyboard-driven sextet's compulsive zeal for an ever-changing array of sonic textures dances on the edge of falling overboard, yet it always reined in before devolving into gee-whizardry. This volatile concordance between carnivorous forward vision and pop convention builds its way toward a heady, vibrant sound that feels alive and unsure. Although *Movie Monster* emerges from an aural epicenter cratered somewhere near the cusp of Reaganism, Sound Team's jet-setting approach reaches backward and forward from there, touching down in Brian Eno's Berlin, Joy Division's Manchester, and Arcade Fire's Montreal, among other destinations. The esoteric title track taps out a semiharrowing, synthesized dystopia, but "TV Torso" sounds torn from an after-hours dance party held in the shadow of Pershing missiles aimed at the Eastern Bloc. Somewhere in Hollywood, there's a movie crying out for songs like that. **GREG BEETS**

VOL. 25 NO. 41 ★ JUNE 9, 2006

TCB

VOL. 25 NO. 42 ★ JUNE 16, 2006

CHRISTOPHER GRAY

DARK PLACES

Graham Reynolds' score to Richard Linklater's *A Scanner Darkly* will literally make your skin crawl: the film's first scene has tiny aphids swarming all over an animated Rory Cochrane, as Reynolds' skittering strings and eerie chimes replicate the paraniod ickiness to a "T." The music is often barely discernible, a toss-up between real and imaginary, just as the characters' subservience to a hyperaddictive drug known as Substance D has them constantly questioning their sanity. The special rotoscope animation, which Linklater first used in 2001's *Waking Life*, took more than a year to finish, affording Reynolds and his small army of musicians ample time to refine their ideas. "We experimented with all sorts of different sounds and gradually morphed it into what it is now," says the Golden Arm Trio mastermind. "The individual cues came from different places," he adds, citing Linklater's fascination with *Last Tango in Paris* and a stopgap version that scored several scenes with Radiohead songs. (A few remain in the film.) For his efforts, Reynolds and his girlfriend got to attend *Scanner*'s premiere at the recent Cannes Film Festival and the afterparty on a six-deck yacht featuring marble bathrooms and a private concert by the Rev. Al Green. "It's pretty much out of the realm of what you can dream up," Reynolds says.

The Greatest Gift When Scratch Acid Scorched the Earth, an Oral History

VOL. 25 NO. 53 ★ SEPTEMBER 1, 2006

GREG BEETS

THE AFTERNOON HIGH tops 100 for the umpteenth straight day. Lawns are tinderbox brown. Traffic is at a standstill. Nerves fray; minds curdle.

It's a beautiful day for a Scratch Acid reunion.

From 1982 to 1987, Austin's Scratch Acid roared with unrestrained ferocity while landing their kicks with precision. Between vocalist David Yow's theatre of confrontation, Brett Bradford's jagged guitar spirals, and the rhythmic lockdown of bassist David Wm. Sims and drummer Rey Washam, the quartet created a monstrous, lashing sound that influenced bands long after their breakup.

Scratch Acid's most direct descendant was the Jesus Lizard, formed in Chicago by Yow and Sims with guitarist Duane Denison and drummer Mac McNeilly. The Jesus Lizard parlayed their springboard from Scratch Acid's sound into a major label deal and a Lollapalooza slot in 1995. Scratch Acid also counted many of Seattle's prime movers among their most ardent fans, including Soundgarden's Kim Thayil and Nirvana's Kurt Cobain, the latter of whom once listed the band's 1984 debut at No. 7 in a Top 50 ranking of favorite albums in his journal.

Yet even if they hadn't been the link between Nick Cave's Birthday Party and Sub Pop, Scratch Acid remains one of the quintessential Austin punk rock bands, literally throwing themselves into performances and generating enough mad fever to blow up a blast furnace. Austin has changed a lot in two wild and wooly decades, but on a late summer afternoon, Scratch Acid still makes perfect, visceral sense.

The band played just 146 shows in their five-year run. Their initial EP and sole full-length, 1986's *Just Keep Eating*, were released on a plucky local label called Rabid Cat. A final EP, *Berserker*, appeared on Touch & Go in 1987.

Having turned down reunion opportunities in the past, Scratch Acid agreed to play Touch & Go's 25th anniversary celebration in Chicago as a gesture of gratitude toward T&G head Corey Rusk. With that booked, an Austin gig was only natural. Given how much Scratch Acid informed the musical groundswell that birthed Emo's, having them play the club's 14th anniversary is a particularly rich stroke of kismet.

The saga begins as the Eighties dawn, Austin's population is about 350,000, a few hundred of whom have kick-started a vibrant punk rock scene in the wake of the headline-grabbing 1978 riot at Raul's, instigated by Huns singer Phil Tolstead's punk-on-cop kiss. One person influenced by those headlines was David Yow, well-traveled son of an Air Force fighter pilot and recent high school graduate.

DAVID YOW: One Halloween, a friend of mine and I went to Raul's to see the Huns play. We'd read in *Rolling Stone* about the time the police showed up. That completely changed the way that I thought music should be presented.

BRETT BRADFORD: Austin was a city with a small-town atmosphere. For some reason, the underground music scene just took hold and exploded. That whole "go start your own band!" thing was for real.

DAVID WM. SIMS: I went to Austin High. I probably went toward being in a band to get away from the high school experience.

BB: I moved from Dallas in the fall of 1980 and put up a poster at Inner Sanctum Records saying "guitarist looking for band." There was this guy behind me who said, "Oh, we're looking for a guitarist." I turned around and saw this crazy looking guy with blue hair. It turned out to be Chris Wing of Sharon Tate's Baby. I started playing with him and then we picked Rey up as the drummer.

REY WASHAM: The suburbs of Dallas were very un-cultured and stale and safe and white. When I moved from there to Austin, a whole other world opened up to me. I started going to UT and met some friends there who knew a lot more about music. They turned me on to the Ramones, and it just went on from there.

CHRIS WING, Sharon Tate's Baby/Jerryskids vocal-ist: We did tons of acid. Austin had a great flood on Memorial Day 1981. We were practicing and trying to think of a new name. Brett said, "Let's be Jerryskids." We were weak in spirit, so we said okay. Then we stopped practice and said, "Let's go out and save lives." That's what we did. We actually did save a cou-ple of lives during that flood. We would come across scenes of disaster and pull people out of stranded cars with torrents of water washing down around 51st and Guadalupe where the creek rises. We were all tripping like madmen.

DY: It didn't occur to me to be in a band, but with the whole do-it-yourselfness of punk rock, I thought, "Shit, I'll play drums or bass or something." Next thing you know, I was playing bass in a punk rock band called Toxic Shock. We did Ramones/Sex Pistols kind

Scratch Acid backstage at Stubb's, 1998: (l-r) David Yow, Rey Washam, Brett Bradford, and David Wm. Sims. Photograph by John Anderson.

of punk rock. Nothing too thought out. We were making posters for it way before we had the band.

STEVE ANDERSON, Toxic Shock vocalist: We played a couple of times together, then I split the band. The Butthole Surfers opened for us at our first show. Everybody showed up to see this poster band play at Club Foot. We were being spat upon and beer was being thrown on us. There was a mezzanine around the stage and people were throwing trash down on us. They'd been waiting for a year to fuck with us.

DWS: David and I were roommates. We had a house at 51st Street and Avenue H. That was where we lived when Scratch Acid started. Jerryskids had broken up and I think Brett and Rey invited David to play bass in a band they were starting. I just kind of made a pest of myself by showing up and acting like I was in the band until I was.

While Scratch Acid began rehearsing in 1982 as a quintet with Toxic Shock's Steve Anderson on vocals, David Yow on bass, and David Wm. Sims on second guitar, the California hardcore of Black Flag and the Circle Jerks was the underground sound du jour. Having embraced the weirder, artier sounds of groups like Public Image Ltd., and the Birthday Party, the new band eschews the loud, fast rules of hardcore as everything they don't want to be.

DWS: The big compliment among those bands was "You guys are really tight." Being innovative and weird had taken a back seat.

RW: We all just started hanging out, listening to music and drinking beer. David [Yow] would make these fliers with his weird art and we'd put them up.

DY: At the time, so many Texas bands were not only cool to listen to but really, really cool to watch: The Dicks, the Big Boys, the Butthole Surfers. There were a lot of them, but those three in particular.

BB: To me, the Big Boys and the Butthole Surfers were like going to church. It was a religious, spiritual experience for me.

DWS: We made long lists of two-word combinations and settled on Scratch Acid. We wanted something evocative but nonspecific, something that indicated an atmosphere but wasn't bogged down with word-play or specific allusions.

BB: We wanted to be our own favorite band. That was stated, and it came to be.

Scratch Acid played its first show at Studio 29 on Jan. 20, 1983. The band only performed three instrumentals because they dismissed Anderson by booking the show without telling him. "The decision they made was the right decision," says Anderson, who remains friends with the band. By the time Scratch Acid made its proper debut on March 10, 1983, at the Skyline Club, Sims was on bass and Yow was the frontman.

DWS: The bill was TSOL, the Big Boys, the Butthole Surfers, and Scratch Acid. We made $20.

BB: Somebody had passed out 100 half-hits of acid to anybody who wanted it. So there were a lot of big eyes. It was pretty interesting. I'm not advocating that, but everybody seemed to have a good time.

DY: I was throwing up all day. I was terrified. But I think it was fun. I always got nervous before shows. It would usually go away about three or four seconds into the first song. I really liked the music in the band, so I could kind of get lost in it. That helped a lot. That and drinky-poos.

In July 1984, Scratch Acid entered Austin's Earth & Sky Studio to record their eight-song debut. Between the sledgehammer surf psychosis of "Greatest Gift," high-desert horror of "El Espectro," and the eerie string arrangement that drives "Owner's Lament,"

Scratch Acid remains the band's most potent recorded distillation.

STACEY CLOUD, Rabid Cat Records: Laura Croteau had started Rabid Cat by signing the Offenders, and when I came on, we wanted to do a record with Scratch Acid.

RW: I remember when we first went in to track that record at Earth & Sky. We played live and went back to listen to it and I was like, "Fuck, man! Is that how we sound? That's pretty interesting!" I'd never really heard David sing because we usually practiced with a shitty PA, but when I heard him track that first song, I was like, "Goddamn, that's pretty cool!" We all looked at each other with these big shit-eating grins and started laughing.

BB: I wrote "Owner's Lament" and thought it would be cool with strings. David Sims' girlfriend at the time played viola, and we got some other people from the UT music department. Rey wrote out a string section. I'd always loved cello, and there was a part where I had a guitar solo, so I asked the cellist if he could come up with a solo to go in the solo. He listened to it once and then ran the track. What's on there is what came out of his head, totally improvised and on the spot.

DWS: Other than trying to go on tour, we left the promotion to Rabid Cat. I don't think we were astute enough to realize how important it was to promote a record. But Rabid Cat did what they could.

SC: It was kind of like being blind and walking through a forest. We were just taking one day at a time, and hindsight is 20/20. You can't blame them for wanting to go to Touch & Go because, hell, I would. That was the label of the time to be on.

Although Scratch Acid was Sims' first band and Yow's first turn as lead singer, the group quickly developed

a riveting performance aesthetic. As the EP made its way around the country via fanzines, college radio, and word-of-mouth, the band mounted short tours to the Midwest and the East Coast. In 1986, they opened for Public Image Ltd., illustrating the pitfalls of meeting your idols.

RM: Sims was just rock solid. He didn't move very much. He never smiled. Rey was totally intense on the drums, holding everything together. Then you had Yow and Brett, who were completely crazed. Yow was unbelievable. You'd go and marvel at how he could give up his body with so little regard for his physical well-being. Brett was playing these crazy-ass parts, and you never knew if what he was doing was intentional or not, but it sounded really good.

DWS: There were two shows that we played on consecutive weekends. David hadn't shaved or cut his hair in awhile, and he did this Jesus getup and played part of the show on a cross he built. The next weekend, he cut his hair and shaved almost all the facial hair off and did the show as Hitler. He had the brown shirt and armband. Some people weren't happy about it.

DY: The Ramones played the Back Room one night when we played at the Cave Club. I was backstage after finishing our set and there was a tap on my shoulder. I turned around and it was Joey Ramone. He said, "Nice show, David." I tried to keep my cool and act like it was no big deal. I said, "Oh, thanks a lot, Joey. How was your show?"

Scratch Acid's final months were packed with higher highs and lower lows. Touch & Go released *Berserker*, and the band embarked on its most ambitious tour, venturing to Europe and the West Coast. They enjoyed a particularly warm reception in Seattle, where legend has a young Kurt Cobain being denied entry to their sold-out show. Despite the recognition, the quartet grew more frustrated with their career trajectory, as well as each other. The frustration finally boiled over one night in Minneapolis.

DY: The venue we played in Seattle was crazy sold out. People who couldn't get in were pressed up against the wall outside trying to listen. Those inside were spilling onto the stage. It was cram-packed, crazy, and really fun. I think a lot of the bands that got really big and popular were into Scratch Acid. There was a guy having problems getting in. I went outside and someone said, "Hey, this guy is having trouble getting in. Can you put him on the list?" I said sure. It ended up being Mark Arm from Mudhoney.

BB: That last tour, where we were out for three or four months, made everyone tired and irritable.

RW: When we went to Europe in 1986, we spent Christmas Eve playing to one bartender and one drunk person at the bar.

DWS: Rey and Brett had a big fight onstage in Minneapolis and Rey left the band at the end of the tour.

BB: Rey and I had a blowout. I wouldn't call it a fight. There were no fisticuffs or anything like that, but we had a disagreement. I'd been drinking a little too much before the show. I didn't feel that I was messing up, but he didn't like that I was drunk.

RW: I still loved Brett and I always will, but you work with someone that closely and it's really hard. You let egos get in the way. I started letting my expectations take control. I wanted Brett to be this certain type of person and certain type of musician. I was asking him to be something he wasn't. It was stupid ego bullshit and it blew up onstage one night.

DY: I think we only had a few more shows. We got home, played one more show in Austin, and that was it. ◀

GHOSTLAND OBSERVATORY

ZILKER PARK, SEPT. 16

Any lingering hopes of a midafternoon nap harbored by the kiddos were obliterated almost as soon as Ghostland Observatory took the stage. In a tight pink muscle shirt and circulation-threatening jeans, Aaron Behrens looked not a little feminine sweating away under a humid sun—which is not to say that even with his hair in plaits, the high-singing dude ever lacked *huevos*. In short order, the Austin-based Observatory single-handedly boosted the threat of global warming to the red zone. During a pulse-pounding, hour-plus workout that would make RuPaul blush, Behrens slung a guitar, popped, rocked, and writhed like a snake on a stick, while bandmate Thomas Turner proudly wore a powder-blue cape and showed what it means to be a hometown superhero. Bringing the mix to the max with bone-crunching synth, the duo likewise laid to waste any divisions you might mistakenly imagine persist between rock and disco. Having displayed face-melting mettle on a dozen tracks, including the trash-talking "Sad Sad City" and spaced-out jam "Stranger Lover," both off 2006's *Paparazzi Lightning*, the dance party was too soon over—and, somehow, a new day was just beginning. **DAN OKO**

VOL. 26 NO. 3 ★ SEPTEMBER 22, 2006

Year of the Squirrel Ralph White's Old, Weird Americana

VOL. 26 NO. 14 ★ DECEMBER 8, 2006

AUDRA SCHROEDER

Ralph White, 2006. Photograph by Aubrey Edwards.

ON A DREARY Wednesday night in October, there are four people inside the Parlor on North Loop, including Ralph White. Patrons walk in for pizza, a Lone Star or two, and then continue on their way. A dazed man with a backpack wanders in, then out, then in again, clutching a copy of the local *Fugitive Post*.

Next to the entrance, White sits oblivious, eyes closed, his hat tossed down in front of him as a tip jar. There's a song about murder. The next one's about death. This one's about conspiracies. There are Syd Barrett covers, "Terrapin" and "Long Gone," taken down from hallucinatory heights on the banjo to be baptized in the Delta. Later, he sings of "sycamore leaves and mustang vine," and it rolls off his tongue so languidly it's almost obscene.

This is the fight or flight experience of a performance by Ralph White, a fugitive from old, weird America. He certainly channels the past, but his path of least resistance has been well-traveled by the ghosts of his craft: Bill Monroe, Dock Boggs, Charlie Bowman. He fiddles with traditional Cajun band the Gulf Coast Playboys. He did time with Austin's premier bluegrass punks the Bad Livers. He played fiddle and accordion in traditional French/Cajun group Bourée Texane. He cites religion upon witnessing a Lightnin' Hopkins show as a child but just as hungrily devours African ostinatos and traditional mountain songs. Years ago, an ethnomusicologist friend turned him on to tapes of African music featuring mbira and kalimba, two instruments White now plays live.

"I wanted to play something original like that stuff but didn't want to become what I called an '-oid'— someone who plays one type of music and gets it down really good," White explains in a pleasant Texas twang. "For some reason the music I play is kind of crooked, as far as playing guitar chords. I'm not very taught as a musician, and at first I was kind of embarrassed of it being like that, but now I don't try to stop it from happening. I like the idea of learning something wrong and letting it evolve into something different. A lot of my music is just me playing a melody I couldn't figure out."

The 54-year-old often has a difficult time putting his music into words, and perhaps it's always been that way. The Bad Livers' Monday night Saxon Pub residency became legendary, whether for their covers (notably Iggy Pop's "Lust for Life") or manic energy, but their sound was still as hard to pin down as a buttered-up hog.

When White left the Livers in '96, he began toying with a solo career. Since 1999, he's amassed an impressive collection of traditional instruments and has been "obsessively" playing banjo and kalimba, a small, thumb-plucked instrument. Live, he lays down a mixture of traditional bluegrass, Irish, African, Scottish, and original tunes. And there's always the occasional Syd Barrett cover.

Of course, he's probably destined to be overlooked in his day and rediscovered by some bearded, eccentric musician or record junkie twenty years from now. White, however, is less analytical about it: "I'm kind of between an old guy and a young guy."

He's the human embodiment of that "I'd Rather Be Fishing" bumper sticker. He's got dirt under his nails and a gracious smile. The lines and creases of his face belong to a man over 50, but the dart of his eye betrays youth. The tattoos on his forearm—a blue heron on his shoulder and a gar (the fish on the cover of his 2002 triumph, *Trash Fish*)—signal something more at work here.

While he has an obvious affinity for the blues, folk, and bluegrass, he doesn't use traditional banjo tunings. His tunings are lower, and as a result, sound haunted. "African slaves living in Arkansas, mixing with Indians—whatever kind of music that was, I would want to explore it," he explains.

Like his bluegrass forefathers, the country wild and nature are recurring themes in his songs, as his cover of Bascom Lamar Lunsford's "I Wish I Was a Mole in the Ground" can attest. White thought he was growing up to be a herpetologist, spurred by his fascination with reptiles, but his day job as a self-employed tree trimmer keeps him in touch with his muse. White built the studio behind his modest South Austin home partially from trees that people paid him to cut down. Inside, wooden banjos, myriad kalimbas, a gourd banjo, cello, accordion, bongos, a turtle shell, various percussion instruments, and his dog, Stella, are splayed around the small room, while a bookshelf hovers over a small bed. The walls are dotted with photos, several of which White took during his African bike ride of 1999.

"It was absolutely wonderful," he says. "I was just gonna go to Zimbabwe and throw my bike on a train from Cape Town. Well, you couldn't take your bicycle on the train. On the map, there looked to be all these dirt roads I could take to Namibia. So I started riding, and I didn't want to stop. I spent a lot of time in wilderness areas where there was nobody. By the time I got to Zimbabwe, I almost wanted to go home. I brought this backpacker's banjo with me so I could learn. Mbiras and kalimbas are everywhere, in the markets, so I would just pick one up and play it, and people would be like, 'Holy shit.'"

Back at the Parlor, this time on a not-so-dreary Thursday night, there are a few more warm bodies, including members of local band Rubble. Again, White's eyes are closed, and his foot taps the floor, matching his dexterous dry-bone picking. He plays a frightening version of "All Along the Watchtower," then a song about native Indians. A song about murder follows. To hear the banjo and fiddle, those mythical instruments that invited the devil and God in equal amounts, with White's voice low and dense like Appalachian fog, is a "holy shit" moment. Then his eyes snap open, suddenly aware again, and he asks the young man behind the counter a very pointed question.

"As usual I don't have a watch. What time is it?" ◄

PETER & THE WOLF

ETERNAL, MARCH 16

The charitable thing to do would be to not review the Peter & the Wolf showcase because any review would have a hard time being charitable. The bottom line is that it just wasn't that musical, which is a little unusual for, you know, a music conference. The local's post-indie, post-folk arrangements sounded like half-finished compositions played to what became half a crowd. If you're going to put an eight-person choir onstage, it's a good idea to use them, although even when they did "coo" they were barely audible. It's not entirely their fault as the sound was less than stellar, but there was just nothing dynamic about the band or the performance. Frontman Red Hunter wasted as much time between songs as he and the band did playing them, and he did about as many tequila shots (five) as the band played songs. Which is fine if you're Yes or entertaining. When your entire set comes off like Stephen Bishop on the stairs in *Animal House* singing "The Riddle Song," you should try to compensate with some personality. **MICHAEL BERTIN**

VOL. 26 NO. 28 ★ MARCH 16, 2007

LI'L CAP'N TRAVIS
TWILIGHT ON SOMETIMES ISLAND

GLURP

Who said no band is an *Island*? Brian Wilson's voices are one inside Li'l Cap'n Travis, the Austin institution's progressive roots and pedal-steel-induced psychedelia flying eight miles high as the '68 Byrds. Now, *Twilight on Sometimes Island* ferries Thom Yorke & Co. onto the roll call, "Get Wise to Yourself" torn from the Radiohead handbook—banging, acidic. Rousing "Sugar Buzz," candy-store hand claps matching clearinghouse riffs, ricochets off instrumental opener "Violeta, Diamond of the Everglades," all nah-nah-nahs and pre-Calexico mariachi trumpet flourish. LCT's fourth platter sequences its sunspots optimally. Christian Braafladt again emerges as the dominant voice, both singer and songwriter. Pedal- and lap-steel master class Gary Newcomb, meanwhile, becomes Capt. Travis himself. His electrolyte mist covers every corner of *Sometimes Island*, "Regatta" especially. Nothing should follow Braafladt's miraculous "Magic of December," minor chords whirling like snowflakes over a white Christmas vocal drift set against some Hawaiian suicide-hotline call before bursting into roaring euphoria. Matt Kinsey's "The Blinding Crash" follows valiantly, and nominal closer cum last prom dance clutcher "My Ship Is Coming In" goes out with the tide. True, no band is an *Island*, but the best ones strand you on the reefs of their siren sound.

RAOUL HERNANDEZ

VOL. 26 NO. 44 ★ JULY 6, 2007

THE OCTOPUS PROJECT
HELLO, AVALANCHE
PEEK-A-BOO

Austin instrumental quartet the Octopus Project has evolutionized electronic textures and made them human. This is so much more than post-post-rock dabbledry; it's warm and inviting, driven and emotional. Opening with the slow chill of xylophone and Yvonne Lambert's multitracked theremin on "Snow Tip Cap Mountain," *Avalanche* blasts familiar with speed trap "Truck," surely a result of Toto Miranda's inexhaustible energy. Unlike the dance party on 2004's *One Ten Hundred Thousand Million,* their third and best LP layers live drums with machines ("Bees Bein' Strugglin'"), studio tracks with demos, and coyness with sampler ("Mmaj"). The merger of digital and analog lives in outdoor looped recording "Upmann," and Yvonne Lambert's theremin prowess is spotlighted on "I Saw the Bright Shinies." Not until the darkness of "Ghost Moves" does Oct Proj leap to the next rung, as Josh Lambert's guitar shrieks and Miranda's drums explode, the party becoming harsh reality. Closing with lullaby "Queen," the only non-instrumental track on the album, the Octopus Project finds a confidence and musicianship that existed before but now shines bright, unafraid of preconception or assumption. Now it's real. **DARCIE STEVENS**

VOL. 27 NO. 5 ★ OCTOBER 5, 2007

Fun Fun Fun Fest Preview
The Stage Names

VOL. 27 NO. 9 ★ NOVEMBER 2, 2007

DOUG FREEMAN

IN WRITING *The Stage Names*, Okkervil River's fourth release for Jagjaguwar, Will Sheff sought seclusion amid the maddening din. In a tiny New York City fourth-floor walk-up apartment, the album emerged as Sheff sat by his open window, staring beyond the fire escape into the human dramas unfolding below.

"It has to do with a kind of background texture that I want," says Sheff outside of Spider House. "*Black Sheep Boy* is more rural, a more natural and organic feeling album. *The Stage Names* is a little bit more gritty and urban feeling in my mind. I picture crumpled up trash in the corners of these songs. It's not sanitary, not tranquil."

Okkervil River is rarely tranquil. Sheff's songwriting has continually mined the dark recesses of both a cultural and personal subconscious, exploring twisted, often violent ambitions through characters treated with novelistic sophistication. *The Stage Names* is no different, exposing a postmodern disillusion that weaves allusions to the tortured lives and suicides of porn star Shannon Wilsey and poet John Berryman among the album's numerous narratives.

"I feel like, within the space of the song, I'm trying to give [the characters] an opportunity to explain themselves," explains Sheff. "Maybe that's enough rope to hang themselves, but I'm not going to be the one doing the hanging. I'm not even going to be the one tying the noose. I'm just letting them say their piece."

Despite the familiarly unsettling portraits, *The Stage Names* remains Okkervil's most polished album, more melodic and pop-driven, with Sheff's unbridled howl largely subdued. The vocal shift is partly the product of the frontman's wounded voice, which interrupted recording in February, the singer ordered by doctors not to speak for almost a month.

"I was so terrified by that experience that when I got my voice back, I was so excited that there was a real amount of joy and love and enthusiasm that went into the vocal performance," says Sheff. "But my voice is just going to change as I sing more. I embrace that. I think it's like an old house that has more charm as it weathers. I fully intend to have a more fucked-up voice when I'm older. I just hope that it's pleasantly fucked up." ←

Off the Record

VOL. 27 NO. 38 ★ MAY 23, 2008

AUSTIN POWELL

WINGED LIFE

Jonathan Meiburg of Shearwater is a noted expert on the Striated Caracara, a rare bird of prey native to the Falkland Islands. Last year, the local songwriter, who also holds a doctorate in ornithology, joined scientists surveying the bird in its natural habitat, following up a study he helped conduct a decade ago. "It was interesting to see how these places had changed," says Meiburg, who officially parted ways with Okkervil River last week. "It was like getting to go back in time and understand it in a different context. It was magical." Whereas 2006's *Palo Santo* culled the femme fatale spirit of Nico for inspiration, Shearwater's exquisite Matador Records debut, *Rook*, explores Meiburg's studies through ornate flights of fancy. "When you're out there, it feels like you're getting this glimpse into the old world that's passing away," Meiburg explains.

"There's an aesthetic loss too, an entire realm of beauty and meaning that most people didn't know was there to begin with. The record is partly an attempt to deal with that, to rail against it, and make peace with it." ←

Terrible Beauty
The Ballad of Sam Baker

VOL. 27 NO. 11 ★ NOVEMBER 16, 2007

DOUG FREEMAN

THE TRAIN RIDE FROM Cuzco to the majestic ruins of Machu Picchu covers seventy miles as the tracks wind northwest through the mountains of Peru. June mornings cast an intensely brilliant sunlight into the ancient city, blinding the broken layers of history competing uncomfortably within the legendary Inca capital.

At 32, Sam Baker is athletic and adventurous. His brown hair is cut short, his body lean and muscular. He's spent the last four years guiding white-water rafting trips down the Rio Grande, and he's come to Peru with three friends to ice-climb and trek the Andes. Unlike most of the country in the 1980s, scarred by guerilla warfare at the hands of the Maoist revolutionaries, the Shining Path, Cuzco is a heavily secured haven, and the four explore the city casually.

The train is nearly full for its 8:30 am departure, and Baker crams into the next-to-last car, finding a seat beside a 19-year-old German boy sitting opposite his parents. He gives no heed to the red backpack lying innocuously on the luggage rack above his head. As they wait to depart, he carries on the idle, awkward chatter of tourists with the family. The explosion silences everything.

"I thought that I had a heart attack, and I thought the Germans hadn't seen and that I was just going to die right there beside them without them even aware," says Baker in a calm, distant reflection. "That's what I thought at first. Then pretty quickly I knew that they were dead and dying."

The time bomb was crudely made, its force driving up through the roof of the train rather than out. Even so, the steel bars of the luggage rack became a rain of shrapnel, killing seven people and injuring nearly forty. A station worker hauled Baker from the debris and sent him to the hospital in a cab.

"I woke up on the table, and I knew it was bad and went back out," Baker remembers. "When I woke up the next day, I was reasonably alert, though I wouldn't say I was in the world. I couldn't hear, my hands were bandaged, my legs were bandaged, and I couldn't move. My eyes worked, and I could breathe, so I was alert. But it was internal alertness, almost on a cellular level, where I knew I was dying, and I was aware of my own death."

In the squalid hospital, gangrene set into the wounds in his legs, where a femoral artery had been severed, and the subdural hematoma from a concussion slowly hemorrhaged in his brain. Baker shifted in and out of consciousness through a morphine haze, reality lost somewhere between fevered dreams and an intense awareness of his broken body. Five days passed before a U.S. military jet could evacuate American survivors from Lima. The plane was scheduled to stop in Panama to relieve the pilots, Baker barely clinging to life.

"A little girl that was there went into a coma, and on the evac out, she arrested," says Baker, relating what he was told later by friends. "They manually kept her alive, so she could see her mother and get her last rites. Because of her, we got to San Antonio just in time for me to get treatment, and had we landed in Panama, I wouldn't have made it. I was dying of everything. I was on the very tail end of this earthly life."

The portraits that slowly develop merge Townes Van Zandt's vivid poetry with John Prine's storytelling, infused with a persistent, if continually frustrated, hope.

Baker pauses and squints his eyes, his thoughts somewhere distant.

"You know, it's funny how that works," he says slowly. "It's all connected in some way that I cannot figure out."

SWEETLY UNDONE

Today is the first day that Sam Baker has heard clearly in more than twenty years, since the explosion in 1986 crippled his eardrums. The new hearing aid is inconspicuous, technology finally progressing enough to convince Baker to wear one. He leans forward in a confidential manner.

"It's my first time really hearing much, and you know what, there's a whole lot I don't need to listen to," he laughs. "I didn't realize there's just so much noise coming at you. Everywhere I've been today has some sort of sound back-screen, commercials everywhere. I didn't realize there's so much sound. And I don't know if I need to hear that. My world goes just fine without it."

Outside Flightpath Coffee House, Baker sits with his back against the wall, his right side directed across the table. His left eardrum is completely shattered, leaving only the constant ringing of tinnitus in his head. With the crooked fingers of his left hand, he draws back the tattered hole in the knee of his jeans, revealing scars crudely healed.

His gray hair is tied into a loose ponytail, and his broad shoulders match his gregarious personality. Baker recalls the events in Peru with a candid, if hesitant, narration. Frequently pausing, he carefully seeks words to relate the experience. It's a search that for the past eight years he's attempted to articulate in his songwriting.

"It's an immensely powerful place that comes to me, and the need to describe it, but I haven't been able to find the words to convey that emotional state, that whole sort of place," he says. Instead, he retreats into metaphors, grasping at analogies in hope of brushing against a peripheral understanding.

"The boundary between living and dying can be a very sharp eddy line or very gauzy," he offers. "With most of my writing right now, I think I'm somewhere in this place where the currents are a little softer, where I think it's a little safer to talk about or describe them."

Baker's songs linger in the same soft wash between waking and dreaming, life and death. Details emerge and recede, ungraspable except within the worn narratives of his characters. Half-remembered histories and fragments of familiar songs rise to the surface, only to subside in the wake of reality.

There's a rough elegance to Baker's work. His voice is coarse, songs more spoken than sung, halting melodies that gesture toward the proper tone yet refract from it elusively. The unpolished imperfection underscores the tenacity and rugged hope of Baker's vision, a world filled with beauty and wonder amid the weary, unextraordinary struggle of life.

MERCY

The characters populating Baker's songs are often the frayed but defiant descendants of inherited hardship, toiling against legacy and the mundaneness of simply plodding forward. The portraits that slowly develop merge Townes Van Zandt's vivid poetry with

Sam Baker, 2007. Photograph by Todd Wolfson.

John Prine's storytelling, infused with a persistent, if continually frustrated, hope.

"We as people are so complex, and we're conflicted about so many things," says Baker about his songwriting. "At some point, the characters take over and tell me what to write. I don't really control them. What I try to do is get me out of the way and let them live the lives they need to live, even if it doesn't follow how I think it would go. My job is to give them the time and space to do what they need to do and say what they need to say."

Baker moved to Austin in the early 1990s. He taught himself to play guitar left-handed to offset his injury and directed his restless energy inward to songwriting. After his sister Chris Baker-Davies recorded four of his songs for her 2000 album, *Southern Wind*, Baker mustered the confidence to begin playing open-mic nights at the Cactus Cafe. He quickly befriended other local songwriters, and in 2004, Walt Wilkins helped produce his debut, *Mercy*.

The album eventually fell into the hands of local producer/guitarist/singer-songwriter Gurf Morlix, who helped get it played on the BBC and Texas radio. The two became fast friends and last year toured together through Italy. This summer, Baker released *Pretty World*, the album further honing his gift for evoking a simple, devastating beauty.

"Let's not kid ourselves; the world can be a very, very brutal place," Baker acknowledges. "But my sense is that we're all trying to do something that we believe in or that makes things better. I think that for the most part people struggle, but most people, even in hard times, you know what they do? They get up, they make themselves a cup of coffee, and they keep going. They walk out the door, and they go to work, they go to school, whatever they do. It's not dramatic, but I see that as a moment of triumph, of major triumph. Maybe I'm a romantic, but I admire that, and I think that's everywhere.

"In my world, I saw some fairly awful stuff and had to actually accept that that's part of being alive," he says. "I think at some point, being able to accept that gave me the freedom to accept all this other stuff that's triumphant, even if it is just making another cup of coffee. It's immensely powerful, that will to get up and do something even when you don't want to do it. I think it's beautiful beyond words." ◄

WHEN DINOSAURS RULED THE EARTH
NOT NOIICE
CHALK CIRCLE

Not nice or not noise? When Dinosaurs Ruled the Earth's sophomore LP is a tomato-tamato affair. The local seven-piece, featuring members of Awesome Cool Dudes; Oh, Beast!; and the late Tuxedo Killers, subscribes to the power of two—on drums, vocals, and guitar—which informed the hot skate-thrash of 2006 debut LP *Snacks*. While not entirely tamed, WDRTE has found its core heaviness: the doom bass of opener "Toeing the Line," early 1990s grunt of highlight "Sick Legs," distortion blackout on "Hypnotic Locks," and instrumental tornado "Big Fuck Party." Vocalists George Dishner and Jesse Hodges have elbowed into a rhythmic odd couple of scream-talk, which helps focus the album, though they still wander in gibberish for a few songs. Closer "Finally Grunge" plants the Dinos' tongue in cheek, and though it's not the biggest bang of an ending, *Not Noiice* is noise's eventual evolution. **AUDRA SCHROEDER**

VOL. 27 NO. 38 ★ MAY 23, 2008

ALEJANDRO ESCOVEDO
REAL ANIMAL
BACK PORCH/MANHATTAN/EMI

Alejandro Escovedo never just wore his heart on his sleeve. He's laboriously stitched his very soul into his material, beginning with his earliest compositions. As a musician, he nearly self-destructed, rising like a phoenix and reinventing himself amid marriages, suicide, several generations of children, life-threatening disease, and a remarkable gift for songwriting. With a panoply of career-defining albums to his name, *Real Animal* maps that journey without misstep. It doesn't hurt that roots-quaking guitarist and peer Chuck Prophet co-wrote with Escovedo or that production by Tony Visconti (David Bowie, T. Rex, Thin Lizzy) feeds *Animal* a sharper edge ("Smoke"). "We don't want your approval—it's 1978," throws down the opening lines of "Nuns Song" well into the album, a challenge also tossed out on the second track, the brutal "Chelsea Hotel '78." In that, Escovedo revisits New York's famed residence hotel as unwitting lyrical witness to Sid and Nancy's decline, while "Real as an Animal" pounds Iggy Pop's sex-beat and "Chip 'n' Tony" twangs with cowpunk abandon. "Hollywood Hills" posits Springsteen lovers from New Jersey into the neon lure of California next to the elegiac "Swallows of San Juan." And *Real Animal* bleeds, as on "Golden Bear," Escovedo's melancholy conversation with hepatitis C. "Why me?" he sings, throbbing with exquisite pain and no soft solution in reply. Maybe the answer is in the bluesy "People," the singer musing that "we still got time, but never as much as we think." For Escovedo fans that have followed the local star through the Nuns, Rank and File, the True Believers, and Buick MacKane, *Real Animal* bares teeth and soul in rock & roll payback.

MARGARET MOSER

VOL. 27 NO. 42 ★ JUNE 20, 2008

Out of the Mouths of Children The Improbable Return of the Butthole Surfers

VOL. 28 NO. 4 ★ SEPTEMBER 26, 2008

AUSTIN POWELL

"I WISH WE'D TAKEN a vow of silence," bemoans drummer King Coffey at the watercooler inside Beerland. "I regret every word I've ever said. . . . I liked it more when there was a bit of a mystique to the band, before the Internet or cell phones, when we were living on the road and no one really knew who we were or where we were going."

At their peak in the mid- to late 1980s, Austin's Butthole Surfers were the physical embodiment of chaos theory, a flaming hemorrhoid of Texas psych, avant-garde expressionism, and iconoclastic noise ripping through the rectum of contemporary culture. Long before the band sneezed "Pepper," the Surfers' sphincter opened like Pandora's box, blurring the barrier between flippant ingenuity and absolute lunacy. Nothing was sacred.

"We were pure performance art with a musical soundtrack," offers frontman Gibby Haynes, who co-founded the group with guitarist Paul Leary at Trinity University in San Antonio in 1983.

"We were angry and unemployed, and being in a band and on the road was a way of avoiding real life," counters Leary with casual amusement. "We weren't looking to advance our career or make it in music. We were just doing it. The whole thing just seemed like a slow suicide."

After several lawsuits and years of drug abuse, the Buttholes' pulse appeared to finally stop beating in 2001, when the band's eighth studio LP, *Weird Revolution*, failed to live up to its name. Then in June, for the first time in nearly two decades, the longest-lasting lineup of the Butthole Surfers—rounded out by second drummer Teresa Nervosa and bassist Jeff Pinkus—reunited at Asbury Lanes in New Jersey. Perhaps even more improbable than the band's return was its orchestration by the Paul Green School of Rock All Stars, which accompanied and backed the band for a monthlong tour on both sides of the Atlantic.

"I tend to avoid children like the plague most of the time," Leary admits. "I don't want to influence them or fuck up in front of them. It just seems bizarre to have a school of rock—rich parents sending their rich kids to play shows with washed-up, famous musicians. It seems like the death of rock once you start doing something like that."

The shah must be turning over in Lee Harvey's grave.

The first thing we did after we landed in Holland, on the way to our accommodations, was stop off at a coffee shop in the closest small town. The band filed out of the bus, left twenty-six children and fourteen adults aboard, bought weed, and got stoned while they waited. It was totally evil. I can't believe we did it, but it felt right. —Gibby Haynes

Reunion is a four-letter word to Gibby Haynes.

"Hell, man, it's just a rock show," the frontman barks from NYC, where he now resides. "Reunions are for high schools that you don't go to. I've never been to a fucking reunion, and I'm not going to go to this one."

Haynes is legendary for such outbursts. Onstage with the Surfers, the sight of him hoisting a 12-gauge shotgun might as well have been Gabriel's trumpet signaling the apocalypse. His hysterical manifestos and crude humor, amplified by a handheld megaphone, were nothing short of revelatory, simultaneously antagonizing and alluring. Without fail, something would end up on fire.

Yet beneath Haynes' transgressive temperament, there lies a noticeable tinge of regret, along with a sincere streak of optimism for the future. He's the only member of the Surfers who wants to record new material and is more than willing to take the rap for the group's gradual unraveling. "I was too fucked up . . . emotionally, chemically, economically, all of 'em." He pauses before clarifying, "The economic part was that I had too much money."

After releasing his most recent solo album, 2004's *Gibby Haynes & His Problem*, the singer largely faded from the public eye, though he cropped up in documentaries on Roky Erickson, the Flaming Lips, and Daniel Johnston. In the latter, he's reclined in a dentist chair refuting the claim that he gave Johnston the LSD that sparked his first major breakdown.

"You have to have the crazy guy talk about the crazy people," Haynes reasoned to the *Chronicle* last year. "If I was just a little bit crazier, maybe I could have gotten into the 'Whitney Biennial.'"

While most parents probably wouldn't trust their children alone in the same room with Haynes, the Paul Green School of Rock Music, through Ween's Dave Dreiwitz, approached him about showcasing the music of the Butthole Surfers. In February, Haynes led the institution's All Stars on a five-date tour of the East Coast.

"The kids are really sweet," Haynes says. "They had to endure many practices with me where I was like: 'Dude, I don't know the words to this song. I don't even know how this song goes. Why don't you play it on your iPod?'"

Butthole Surfers, 1986. Photograph by Andrew Long.

We wanted to make people uncomfortable and explore something that was new to them, but we really just wanted to entertain ourselves. I remember this one time Gibby took a dump in a Big Gulp and had Paul hold his shit without knowing it.
—Jeff Pinkus

Jeff Pinkus was only 16 the first time he saw the Butthole Surfers at the Metroplex in his hometown of Atlanta in 1984. "I was on blue-gel acid," he smiles in fond recollection over a Jim Beam on the rocks at Creekside Lounge. "It wasn't what I expected at all."

Within a year, he had joined the band's traveling freak show.

"I didn't know any better," shrugs Pinkus. "I left home at 15 and was living in a two-bedroom

apartment with seven people. I had no worldly possessions and was looking for a band to play in that I liked. I showed up in a Germs leather jacket, and we played Blue Cheer and Black Sabbath for a little while, then Paul said, 'You wanna go to Europe?'"

Pinkus sums up the remainder of the 1980s as his missing years. By his own count, he lasted longer than the Surfers' other 16 bassists combined, ending a prolific nine-year stint following the release of the band's John Paul Jones–produced Capitol Records debut, *Independent Worm Saloon*, due to personal and creative differences.

"We all slept at the same place, rode in the same vehicle, went out to the same bars together," summarizes Pinkus, who now lives in Dripping Springs, about ten miles from the shack in Driftwood where the

Surfers recorded their lone album for Rough Trade, 1990's *Pioughd*. "We did everything together. It didn't seem abnormal then. We were more functional than a lot of families."

With his main squeeze Honky, Pinkus has been a staple on South Congress and Red River for more than a decade now, serving up Texas boogie with raunchy, roadhouse flair. He's had myriad other projects along the way, including Daddy Longhead, OTC, Areola 51, and his latest, Pure Luck, a seven-piece hardcore country outfit. He also recently enrolled his son at the Austin branch of the Paul Green School of Rock Music.

"I'd like to have a better ending than we did last time," proffers Pinkus on the reunion. "We're all in a different, better place. It's really nice to be able to get back together without a label hanging over our heads and remember why we liked playing together."

Everybody believed that King and I were brother and sister. I don't even know what I'm supposed to tell you right now. We very well may be. There used to be a consensus. —Teresa Nervosa

No one from the Butthole Surfers remembers exactly when Teresa Nervosa left the band, only that it happened sometime in 1989, while touring behind *Hairway to Steven*.

"On the surface, she was such a delicate, frail-looking girl, but underneath, she was so tough to be able to spend that amount of time on the road over the years in those kinds of conditions with us and a dog," Leary recalls. "When she wasn't there, I just felt like she needed a break, like we all did at some point."

Nervosa, born Teresa Taylor, originally joined the Surfers in 1983, after letting the band practice in the warehouse she rented in Downtown Austin for $40 a month. Standing at their drum kits, she and Coffey were two gods of thunder, hammering seismic beats that pressed the Surfers' live shows into the realm of spirit-possession ceremonies.

"Our shows were pretty wicked at that time," recalls Nervosa, who infamously appeared as "Pap-smear Pusher" in local filmmaker Richard Linklater's indie watershed *Slacker*. "We had the penis reconstruction video, the strobe lights, the fire, the naked dancer. Everything was getting really out of control. I didn't always think it was the most positive first LSD experience for someone to have. People were coming away scarred."

By the time of her departure, Nervosa not only needed a break, she was breaking.

"I didn't want to leave the band, but I really wasn't well. I was flipping out, drinking too much and all that," she confides. "I had developed a really big fear of flying. I always thought the plane was going to crash. I couldn't figure out what was wrong with me. I started taking Prozac and trying to get better, trying to find someone who could help me."

As her band ascended to major label status, Nervosa dealt with its side effects. She suffered from strobe-light-induced seizures and underwent brain surgery in 1993 after being diagnosed with an aneurysm. Only recently did Nervosa, who still resides in Austin, begin regaining a sense of normalcy, returning to the stage in May with Coffey's experimental-psych wrecking crew Rubble.

"I'm on medication, and I'm still a little afraid of flying, but I can get on the plane like other people," she says. "I've been doing a lot better and picking back up and feeling pretty good. The timing couldn't have been any better for them to have called me up and asked me to do this."

At Lollapalooza, Siouxsie [Sioux] came up onstage and started wrestling on the ground with Gibby over the shotgun. I look down, and that shotgun is pointed right at me. That thing may have been shooting blanks, but had it gone off, it would have killed me. —Paul Leary

Acid flashback: the Butthole Surfers' Paul Leary and Gibby Haynes at Stubb's, 2008. Photograph by John Anderson.

It was in what Paul Leary describes as "a weak moment" that the guitarist agreed to reunite with the Butthole Surfers.

"We've had a lot of offers over the years to play places like Taiwan and South Africa," says Leary in his living room in Central Austin. "I just couldn't bring myself to do it."

Not even Leary's incinerating guitar work could keep the Surfers' final album, 2001's *Weird Revolution* (Hollywood/Surfdog), from leaving a bad taste in just about everyone's mouth. Envisioned three years earlier as the follow-up to the band's commercial breakthrough, 1996's *Electriclarryland*, the album was scrapped and subsequently shrouded in legal entanglements with Capitol. Adding to the frustration at the time was an acrimonious split from manager Tom Bunch and a heated lawsuit with Touch & Go Records

over the ownership of the band's first four LPs, which, by association, also left Coffey without a distributor for his beloved indie label, Trance Syndicate.

"It was a really brutal, painful experience, like the band was an albatross around our necks," Leary says. "I've never listened to the last record. I hated it before it even came out. Then when we went on tour to support it in the wake of 9/11, people weren't in the mood for mayhem and belching explosions, and neither was I. . . .

"The road just got to be such a grind. I prefer being here in my house with my wife. I have a life here, and I really like working in the studio where I can be in control of everything that goes on."

Leary certainly hasn't had any trouble finding work. Having honed his craft through his work with the Surfers, not to mention the Bad Livers and Meat

Puppets, Leary became one of the most sought-after names in modern music after producing Sublime's eponymous third album, which has bankrolled more than 10 million copies to date. He's since worked with everyone from Daniel Johnston and Weezer to U2 and Nelly Furtado and is now mixing a batch of unreleased recordings by the Toadies.

"It's been nice to be able to enjoy playing music again, especially seeing Gibby at his best," Leary concedes. "I still don't want to make a habit of doing too many of these shows."

The whole band got scabies once, and we had to hold Kathleen down and get her medicated. She had decided she didn't want to kill the scabies because they were her friends. —Paul Leary

One at a time, the students from the Paul Green School of Rock All Stars cautiously join the Surfers onstage for their first show together, breathing in the hallucinatory gas emitted by classics such as "Cowboy Bob" and "Cherub," pulled from the black hole that is the band's 1984 debut LP, *Psychic . . . Powerless . . . Another Man's Sac*. The contrast with the group's early acid-happenings could not be any more apparent.

Haynes no longer loads up the shotgun. Nervosa and Coffey both take a seat behind their respective drum kits and refrain from turning their cymbals into torches, while Pinkus now straps on the Flying V bass

he mastered with Honky. Longtime associate Kathleen (aka "Ta-Da the Shit Lady") shows up to entertain the audience of proud parents and fans with some interpretive dancing but manages to remain fully clothed.

"Everything the Butthole Surfers have ever done has been pretty bizarre," acknowledges Leary. "From that point of view, this seems to fit right in, and it probably wouldn't have happened any other way."

From day one, the Butthole Surfers captured adolescence as reflected through the looking glass, their music a shameless celebration of impulsive tomfoolery and hormonal urges.

"I would say we're one of the most childlike things in rock & roll history," Haynes adds. "Childish, juvenile, intelligent. You know kids say the darnedest things."

Every student gathers onstage for the closing number, "The Shah Sleeps in Lee Harvey's Grave," the first song Haynes ever played for Leary at Trinity. The bloodcurdling opening line sends the night spiraling into complete, cathartic chaos: *There's a time to fuck and a time to pray, but the shah sleeps in Lee Harvey's grave!*"

Kids are crawling all over the stage, torturing instruments and bashing on any object that will make noise. Some just stand in place with their hands over their ears and scream. It's as if, for the first time, the Butthole Surfers' bastardized vision is fully realized.

THE FLATLANDERS
HILLS AND VALLEYS
NEW WEST

Technically speaking, the Flatlanders' millennial reboot, 2002's *Now Again*, constitutes Jimmie Dale Gilmore, Joe Ely, and Butch Hancock's sophomore slump. After all, the three musketeers' original sessions from 1971 and 1972, bronzed for posterity decades later by Rounder Records' *More a Legend Than a Band*, produced West Texas mysticism more a secret handshake than a music legend, yet still a Lone Star singer-songwriter standard. In primary vocalist Gilmore's tremulous croon—sharing the spotlight with the musical saw and buttressed by the compositional wit and wisdom of Hancock and Ely's firestarter command—blew the state's "South Wind of Summer," put into song for *Now Again*. Its 2004 follow-up, *Wheels of Fortune*, proved too much too soon, the album's spokes falling off after two years of touring that followed thirty years of occasional Flatlanders reunions. The culmination of the three amigos' lifelong collaboration—vocally, musically, ideologically, sequentially—*Hills and Valleys* crowns the group's decade. Manned by fellow Lubbock émigré and steel-string sage Lloyd Maines, *Hills and Valleys* rides a line the Southern Pacific Railroad would envy. Writing together where previously each songsmith mostly submitted his own material, Gilmore/Ely/Hancock's first six salvos here are their best run yet, opener "Homeland Refugee" a modern Woody Guthrie standard, rollicking follower "Borderless Love" basically another, and "After the Storm" in the third spot reiterating why Gilmore was the act's original singer. No. 6 slot, "Just About Time," perfects the Flatlanders' campfire bump and grind, while Gilmore's son Colin lands the album's shooting star, "The Way We Are." Master craftsmen Rob Gjersoe (guitar), Glenn Fukunaga (bass), Rafael Gayol (drums), and Joel Guzman (accordion), not to mention original Flatlander Steve Wesson, whose saw on "Cry for

Freedom" lends the Gilmore/Ely/Hancock lament an almost West African quality, hum at cricket frequencies. Closer "There's Never Been" catalogs nature's larger truths. Count the Flatlanders on that roll call. **RAOUL HERNANDEZ**

VOL. 28 NO. 33 ★ APRIL 17, 2009

SXSW Picks to Click Black Joe Lewis & the Honeybears

VOL. 27 NO. 26 ★ FEBRUARY 29, 2008

THOMAS FAWCETT

BLACK JOE LEWIS ladles out all grit, no gravy. He spits lyrics in short bursts of aggression like bricks at glass windows. While his father's favorite singer was R&B god Donny Hathaway, the closest Lewis has come to a sweet soul ballad is the profanity-laced "Bitch, I Love You." The 26-year-old Austin native was less enamored of shucking oysters in the local food service industry.

"I was tired of eating shit every night," barks Lewis. "Zach was like, 'I can throw together a band if you want to try it one more time.'"

That would be Zach Ernst, 21, guitarist for Black Joe Lewis' new eight-piece lineup, the Honeybears. Borrowing some Dap-Kings retro R&B, Ernst rounded up the Honeybears after booking Lewis to open Little Richard's performance on the UT campus. A year later, the group cut an eponymous EP of funky originals and relatively obscure covers by the likes of Howlin' Wolf and Don Covay.

"There's no pretense about what Joe does," Ernst says. "It reminds me of Hound Dog Taylor and Wilson Pickett. To think that someone was doing that so well and so off the radar in Austin was just totally beyond me."

Thankfully, Black Joe Lewis & the Honeybears are no longer casting pearls before swine. At the group's first show at the Beauty Bar, Lewis turned the head of Britt Daniel, an encounter that led to the Honeybears opening Spoon's West Coast tour last summer. Spoon drummer Jim Eno is helping the young soul-shouter cook up a batch of new tracks, including the horn-driven R&B explosion "Gunpowder," which features blazing horns from Grupo Fantasma.

"My dream is to be on the level of James Brown," Lewis says. "I want to be the black Elvis." ◂

SARAH JAROSZ
SONG UP IN HER HEAD
SUGAR HILL

For Wimberley's Sarah Jarosz, *Song Up in Her Head* is the calling card of triple-threat stardom: a voice of maturity at 17, an instrumentalist of precision, and a songwriter of uncommon wisdom in the mold of Dolly Parton by way of Lucinda Williams. Since she's dazzled audiences on the bluegrass and folk circuit since she was 12, Jarosz's brilliant debut is neither fluke nor surprise. Jarosz is at the bruise-tender age of innocence, illustrated by the plaintive query of a lover in "Tell Me True." "Do you think of me the way I think of you?" she pleads with caution in her beautifully sculpted voice and knowledge beyond her years. She draws exquisite emotion from "Broussard's Lament" and weaves alluring tales in "Can't Hide," "Long Journey," "Little Song," and, without words, "Mansinneed-of." Jarosz also exercises impeccable taste in covers, tackling the Decemberists' "Shankill Butchers" and turning Tom Waits' "Come On Up to the House" into country gospel. Under Jarosz's and Gary Paczosa's production, and with help from fellow teens Samson Grisman and Alex Hargreaves, this thirteen-song oeuvre shouts from the mountaintops that Sarah Jarosz has arrived. **MARGARET MOSER**

VOL. 28 NO. 41 ★ JUNE 12, 2009

ROSIE FLORES & THE PINE VALLEY COSMONAUTS
GIRL OF THE CENTURY
BLOODSHOT

Rosie Flores is a classic country woman: Texas-born and doe-eyed, big-voiced and familiar with the barroom stage. Her 1987 self-titled debut on Warner Bros. should have elbowed out a spot in Nashville's scene, but country music careers come and go with the tides, and Flores rolled with it. So there's everything to be said about her latest, twenty years later, being perhaps the best of her forty-year career. The heartbreak and hard living and fast times in between, the ones obligatory for good country songs, crystallize on *Girl of the Century*, her twelfth studio album and Bloodshot debut. She's backed by Jon Langford–led trio the Pine Valley Cosmonauts, an inspired pairing that makes the gun-toting blues of opener "Chauffeur," Broken Spoke honky-tonk of "This Little Girl's Gone Rockin'," and rockabilly of "I Ain't Got You" more than just genres Flores knows well. Her voice is still a thing of wonder; on slow-jam "Dark Enough at Midnight," she turns up the heat under her Patsy Cline come-hither, and "Little Bells," one of two duets with Langford, fares better than the novelty he said/she said shtick of "Who's Gonna Take Your Garbage Out?" Closer "Girl of the Century" is all Rosie, the heaving, lump-in-your-throat finale any classic country woman needs in her back pocket when the spotlight's bathing her. **AUDRA SCHROEDER**

VOL. 29 NO. 8 ★ OCTOBER 23, 2009

VARIOUS ARTISTS
CASUAL VICTIM PILE: AUSTIN 2010
MATADOR

Austin 2010: Sounds both apocalyptic and Olympic, doesn't it? Our city's in an awkward place, on the long walk between skyward progress and preserving the past. Perhaps sensing a quake before it happens, Matador Records co-owner and local dweller Gerard Cosloy knows there's no better time than the present. *Casual Victim Pile*, as he stresses in the liner notes, isn't meant to be a definitive cultural document, but rather the findings of many archaeological digs along Red River over the last couple years. Entering the thunderdome are seventeen locals and a couple Denton groups of the Beerland variety, heavy on decades of punk-drunk love. You hear ghosts of Matador (and Homestead) records past here, like Tre Orsi's Dinosaur Jr.–ish "The Engineer," Follow That Bird!'s tightly wound "The Ghosts That Wake You," or straight-up Sonic Youth paean "Hoboken Snow," by Kingdom of Suicide Lovers. New Matador roster boys Harlem reprise "Beautiful & Very Smart" from last year's *Free Drugs*, and Dikes of Holland's "Little City Girl" demands a full-length album from them this year. Then there's the three-minutes-or-less contingent: the blackout flail of the Stuffies' "No One's Gonna Miss You" and Wild America's "Drink It Dry" are pure Austin, while the No No No Hopes' "Nobody's Fool" and Teeners' (R.I.P.) "Nazis on Film" could be Raul's-era rollers. There's not a dud in the *Pile*. **AUDRA SCHROEDER**

VOL. 29 NO. 21 ★ JANUARY 22, 2010

This Is My Life LZ Love's Message

VOL. 29 NO. 40 ★ JUNE 4, 2010

MARGARET MOSER

LZ LOVE'S GAZE LIFTS, and her light brown eyes shine. Her face displays the high, sculpted cheekbones of her mother's family—black, French, Native American. Her skin bears a coppery sheen within its deep bronze tone, sunlight filtering through the blinds and casting a glow accentuating the curve of her shoulder and the swell of her breasts. In her slender fingers rests a copy of her new CD, *Mysterious*.

This is standard music business 101: An artist has a new album coming out and wants to promote it. There are stories to be told about making it, recording it, writing it, plus the inspirations, the sessions, the production. Generally these are intertwined with the artist's or the band's story—they all have one, in varying degrees of significance and interest.

Love's story is different. She moved to Austin some seven years ago from San Francisco and found a roots niche in local gospel brunches with her gutbucket blues. Possessing a voice that immediately put her in the highest rank of vocalists in town, she's coming out about her real musical love, dance music. And LZ Love has something else to share.

She was born a man.

LOVE AND HAPPINESS

In the natural course of songwriting, artists reveal their stories. In LZ Love's new CD, *Mysterious*, there's no mystery. She tells her story without shame or artifice, and the chapters are her song titles:

"Mysterious." "This Is My Life." "Water Under the Bridge." But this isn't the music Austin's known LZ Love for as she's eked out her local niche singing soul-stirring blues and blues-saturated gospel.

"In Austin, the music was country and blues," she nods. "And I knew I wasn't a country singer, but I knew I could bring a Southern vibe to blues and country-oriented stuff. That's why I wrote songs like 'Higher Ground' with more slide guitar. It worked for me, because I got accepted on a lot of shows—Stephen Marley, the Neville Brothers.

"But I was doing a lot of different things to survive, to fit in: gospel brunches at Stubb's, Threadgill's, Maria's. They were good, but I felt I was sticking to a genre from my past. I've been singing gospel since I was five. It's a no-brainer for me to sing from that place. It's where I sing from anyway. Yet by spreading myself in all these directions, my audience was confused as to when it was important to see me perform.

"And I didn't need a guitar strapped on me like everyone else in Austin. That's not how I perform; I write my songs on keyboard. I needed to pull back and reevaluate, so I did one last show at the Saxon, and afterward Matt Smith from the Monstas came up to me and said, 'I want to produce your next record.'"

Smith's offer to produce came at the right time for LZ Love. "He said: 'If I work with you, you're going to have to write from a very deep place. You got a story, a message.' And I do—being transsexual, moving from California to Austin, trying to fit into a different scene, being a woman of color.

"People say they don't, but some still judge people by pedigree here. Some here still want someone white playing guitar. This might be part of the South, but this is the 21st century. We're in a whole new world.

"That's why I was inspired to write 'New Life.' Things that used to fit in the cubes don't anymore. Things that once fit in a circle don't anymore. Obama. Times are different."

Times were quite different indeed for young Arnold Elzy. Born in Chicago and relocated to the Bay Area at an early age, he found pleasure singing gospel in church, but other, decidedly feminine interests occupied his little-boy world. Though he was 16 before he told his mother, "I am different," the evidence showed early. LZ Love points to a school photo of 8-year-old Arnold, beaming brightly at the camera.

"I'm wearing hair grease for lip gloss. Look at this one: a pink jumpsuit. I'm 13.

"I was the fashionista in my family," she laughs. "My sisters were wearing my clothes, little things I was buying. I'd find them, and they'd be stretched out. I was wearing their things, too."

The early 1980s in San Francisco were a glorious, glittery time to hoist freak flags if you were gay, maybe-gay, bi, or drag. The previous decade, with its tidal wave of post-Stonewall gay culture, even took its siren call mainstream. That thumping bass drum defined a genre that fostered modern dance music, DJs, 12-inch singles, industrial music, and New Wave. Disco was DIY music that spoke an international language, a most progressive, culturally connected, and accessible sound. And disco represented musical subcultures: black, Latino, female, gay.

Where, then, was there a better place to be walking a gender tightrope in high heels than San Francisco, always a town for misfits and rebels? Neo-theatrical groups such as the Cockettes used the port city as a staging ground for outrageous performances, bedecked in makeup, vintage dresses, feathers, glitter, and whatever geegaws they wore that sparkled.

From the Cockettes emerged Sylvester James, but he only used one name. Handsome as a man, more attractive in drag, he could also sing both in an elastic tenor and a strong falsetto. Sylvester was unflappable, unstoppable, and for a time, on the blitz track to unique success that included opening for the Rolling Stones, a role in Bette Midler's *The Rose*, and high-charting disco hits that defined their era. More than Gloria Gaynor, Thelma Houston, and Donna Summer, Sylvester literally stood head and shoulders above the other disco queens.

"Long and strange" hardly begins to describe the journey from Arnold Elzy to LZ Love, one that's spanned the globe, from Castro Street in San Francisco to performing with show bands in Japan.

"Sylvester would walk in as a beautiful gay man with his drag and start painting his face, transforming before your eyes," remembers Love. "And when Miss Thing was finished, she was a radiant, outrageous, gorgeous black goddess. At Winterland, Sylvester would wear wings and fly to the stage. Watching Sylvester gave me the tools as a young teenager to put myself together.

"I got my first break with Sylvester when I was 16 years old. I was already experimenting with my androgyny, but Sylvester was one of the world's greatest drag queens ever, and I got to learn from the source. RuPaul, I love you, but Sylvester was the queen. And I love Lady Gaga doing disco, but Sylvester started all that."

TURN ON YOUR LOVE LIGHT

In the wake of flagging success, Sylvester revamped his band, dropping two female singers with powerful voices, and asked Elzy to join his act. The deposed vocalists—Martha Wash and Izora Rhodes—shortly found fame as the Weather Girls singing "It's Raining

Men." Without the cushion of big voices, the teenager declined to join up with the flamboyant Sylvester, who died of complications from AIDS in 1988.

Love describes her life afterward as "living in the middle," trying life as a woman and pursuing her singing career. Transsexual? Transgender?

"Same thing," she explains. "Transsexual is a person who feels they were born in the wrong body. I felt that way as a kid, like my school photo when I was 8 and wearing hair grease on my lips for lip gloss. The way my sisters acted, that's how I felt. I felt like I should be over there, a feeling of being misplaced. Your feelings inside aren't the same as your outer image. In my case, it was how I looked and how I felt, because I've always been androgynous.

"My female hormones have always been more dominant.

"I've had all the surgery I'm comfortable with. That's how I discuss what's inside my g-string. People that know anything else about me are those I have shared my bed with. And that's not many. . . .

"I didn't have long-term relationships until I became transsexual. Even though I was young, living in the middle, in that other life, when I really started living full time, that's when companions came in my life: men that cared about me, men that I lived with, men who took me home to their families. Because I'm so passable, which I am grateful for, it made it easy for them to take me there and not explain.

"Many people in Austin don't know I am transsexual. Anyone who ever approached me or heard rumors, I always told them, but I wanted to talk about it, because I felt people needed to know me for me and my music. My music is just as important as my gender."

I'LL ALWAYS LOVE MY MAMA

There's a joke that behind every gay man is a woman, and for LZ Love, that woman was her mother, Florida. Florida raised six children without their father around

and still found time to offer much-needed support when Arnold was called "punk" or "faggot" by some of his sisters.

"When I told my mother it was time for me to start living full time, she took me in her room with her beautiful dresser and jewelry and perfumes and all that. She said: 'Here's all my stuff. You're welcome to use anything I have.'"

In 1994, LZ Love rushed home from Europe. Her single "See the Light" rocked at No. 3 on the dance charts in England, but "my beautiful mother with her platinum blonde hair—Cajun, Native American, African-American, Southern—from Monroe, Louisiana," had fallen ill.

The family banded together to look after Florida, paying her insurance and other living expenses when all her state earnings went to the care facility. Love was with Florida in her last days, her mother's death opening a new chapter in her life.

"I want to tell parents, 'Love your children for who they are so they can love themselves for that.' My mother always knew who I was," acknowledges Love. "I came to her at the age of 16 and said: 'I feel I'm different. I don't know if I'm gay or what, but I am different.'

"She said: 'You've always been different, but honey, there's nothing wrong with being different. Whatever you do, be the best.' Before my father passed, he knew I was different, and he said, 'Whatever you do, hold your head up.'

"And that's why when kids get support from their parents, it's so powerful. You know you are loved by the people that brought you here, and it makes your life so much easier."

LOVE MAKES THE WORLD GO 'ROUND

"Long and strange" hardly begins to describe the journey from Arnold Elzy to LZ Love, one that's spanned the globe, from Castro Street in San Francisco to performing with show bands in Japan, at discos in London, and yes, at taco joints in Austin.

LZ Love might have chosen to not play this card of hers in Austin. She could have followed the path of many a fine jazz vocalist here in town, but Love is a participant. She wanted to be part of the scene and not just a black or transgender or female jazz voice.

"I don't have to live in shame no more. That's part of the lyric in 'This Is My Life.' I know I got the right to live my life. It's got nothing to do with gender. I took Matt's advice to mean 'cover as many bases as possible' and get inside who you really are. And that's what it did for me. I wrote 'This Is My Life' about empowering yourself with who you are.

"I took that year break to focus on this music and direction. I feel it's done me justice in coming to terms with writing music that totally represents me and that I feel passionate about. This is one record that will do that for me."

Inside her cozy South Austin apartment, photographs of the faces shaping Love's life look down from the wall. They're a telling and varied grouping: Phyllis Hyman, Billie Holiday, James Brown, Josephine Baker, Andy Warhol, Stevie Ray Vaughan ("I connect and channel his spirit."), Mahalia Jackson, Minnie Riperton, Michael Jackson, Koko Taylor. There's her mother, Florida, and a photograph of an older man. LZ Love pauses, staring at it.

"This is my father. I'm just now able to put this picture up, because I struggled with where I felt he contributed to me and my sisters. He didn't contribute a lot, but he was my father, and I love him. The times I had with him and the words he said matched with the things my mother told me. I felt I wasn't going to be blessed until I was able to love them both."

Love turns her body so the photos surround her like a halo of souls.

"In San Francisco, I worked closer with the gay community, doing performances and gay pride. Here, I am involved. I go to Rain, Oilcan Harry's. I go to see friends perform, to have drinks, hang out, but I'm part of the music community. It adopted me. The musicians love me for who I am, my talent.

"I don't have to go through gay channels or gay doors to be who I am. My music makes me that." ◂

INDEX

Page numbers in **boldface** indicate photos.